FINE WINE
EDITIONS

THE FINEST WINES OF

GERMANY

A Regional Guide to the Best Producers and Their Wines

STEPHAN REINHARDT

Foreword by Hugh Johnson | Photography by Jon Wyand

UNIVERSITY OF CALIFORNIA PRESS
Berkeley | Los Angeles

University of California Press,
one of the most distinguished university presses in the United States,
enriches lives around the world by advancing scholarship
in the humanities, social sciences, and natural sciences.
Its activities are supported by the UC Press Foundation and by
philanthropic contributions from individuals and institutions.
For more information, visit www.ucpress.edu

First published in
North America by
University of California Press
Berkeley and Los Angeles, California

Fine Wine Editions

Publisher Sara Morley
General Editor Neil Beckett
Editor David Williams
Subeditor David Tombesi-Walton
Editorial Assistant Nastasia Simon

Maps Tom Coulson,
Encompass Graphics, Hove, UK
Indexer Ann Marangos
Americanizer Christine Heilman
Production Nikki Ingram

Library of Congress Control Number : 2012937741

ISBN 978-0-520-27322-1 (paper : alk. paper)

Manufactured in China

10 9 8 7 6 5 4 3 2 1
18 17 16 15 14 13 12

Contents

Foreword

by Hugh Johnson

Fine wines detach themselves from the rest not by their pretensions but by their conversation—the conversation, that is, that they provoke and stimulate, even, I sometimes think, by joining in themselves.

Is this too surreal a thought? Don't you exchange ideas with a truly original, authentic, coherent wine? You are just putting the decanter down for the second time. You have admired its color, remarked on a note of new oak now in decline and a ripe blackcurrant smell growing by the minute, when a tang of iodine interrupts you, the voice of the sea as clear as if you had just parked your car on the beach and opened the door. Picture the Gironde, the wine is saying. You know the slope with its pale stones and its long gray view. I am Latour. Keep me on your tongue and I will explain everything: my grapes, the sun I missed in August, and the baking September days up to harvest. Is my strength draining away? Then I am old, but all the more eloquent; you see my weak points, but my character is clearer than ever.

He who has ears to hear, let him hear. Most of the world's wines are like French cartoons, *sans paroles*. Fine wines are thoroughbreds with form and mettle, even on their off days or when they are outrun. If a seemingly disproportionate number of words and, naturally, money are lavished on them, it is because they set the pace. What do you aspire to without a model? And far from being futile, aspiration has given us, and continues to give us, more thoroughbreds, more conversation, and more seductive voices to beguile us.

Just 20 or 30 years ago, the wine world was a plain with isolated peaks. It had crevasses, not to mention abysses, too, but we did our best to avoid them. The collision of continents thrust up new mountain ranges, while erosion turned barren new rock into fertile soil. Do I need to mention the clambering explorers, the pioneers who planted at high altitudes with aspirations that seemed presumptuous at the time? If they started by making wine with little to say, those who persevered found a new grammar and a new vocabulary, to add its voice to conversations that will soon, it seems, be worldwide.

Even among the most established there is continual change, as their language produces its own literature, and its literature new masterpieces. Far from being regions where everything has been discovered and every decision taken, the classic regions of the wine world are where the finest tuning takes place—where it is financially rewarding to go to the greatest efforts and explore in the greatest depth every elusive nuance that soils and techniques can offer.

The stories of most of the great wine regions have been ones of steady, if sometimes intermittent, progress. Germany is different. From being the acknowledged source of the world's greatest white wines, Germany's crystal spring was suddenly fouled. It was an act of astonishing self-harm by a government in thrall to demotic ideas. The whole historic system of discrimination by which the best vineyards were distinguished, centuries in the making, was officially condemned as "elitist." Quality as a concept was abolished and replaced by degrees Oechsle—in other words, sugar content. Picture the Côte d'Or with no distinction between village wines, premiers crus, and grands crus.

For almost three decades, starting in 1972, the German norm was so sweet and insipid that its greatest former fans avoided it. Of course, there were exceptions: proud independents who made their ancestral wine with due self-respect, but their life was hard. They and their successors are the subject of this book. Forget the past, Stephan Reinhardt tells us; we start again, with the same materials—Riesling and Pinot Noir and a vast variety of soils in a cool climate. But we start with fresh ideas, with new definitions of quality, making wine for a new market. I still have 1971 Auslesen in my cellar—at 40 years old, my most precious white wines. This is the place to find their successors.

Preface

by Stephan Reinhardt

This book highlights the quality and variety of German wines, as well as the art of handcrafting them. No matter how steep their vineyards or how capricious the grapes and the weather, the 70 wine producers profiled here —as well as the others who receive honorable mention—practice their craft with dedication, knowledge, passion, and pride in their heritage.

With a culture stretching back to the Romans and the early Middle Ages, German wine has been celebrated for centuries. By the fin de siècle, Rieslings from the Rhine, Mosel, and Saar were among the most sought-after and expensive wines in the world. Now, more than 100 years later, Germany's top producers are ushering in another "golden age" of German wine. They are doing so primarily with Riesling but also increasingly with Spätburgunder (Pinot Noir), which gives world-class wines and has become the second driving force of the rapid evolution during the first decade of the 21st century. Both varieties dominate this book, but great Silvaners (Sylvaners), Weissburgunders (Pinot Blancs), and Grauburgunders (Pinot Gris) also find a place.

Although there is still "a gulf between expert and popular opinion" about German wines, as Stephen Brook wrote in *The Wines of Germany* (2003), the gap has been narrowing. The VDP— an ambitious association of some 200 of the country's leading producers—is bypassing the anti-elitist wine law of 1971, which bases wine quality on sugar levels rather than origin, grape varieties, yields, or vinification techniques, and which perpetuates the "sweet and cheap" image of German wine abroad. Recognizing that in such a cool wine country as Germany, all aspects of terroir have an exceptionally large impact on the originality, personality, and quality of the wine, the VDP has been leading a countermovement and offering a way back "from sugar to terroir." The association developed its private vineyard classification—and

categories such as Grosses/Erstes Gewächs—to market its wines. The grand cru concept has encouraged ever-higher standards in viticulture and winemaking, and the wines themselves have become better and better.

A book on the finest wines of Germany inevitably has to be highly selective, since there are currently some 24,000 German wine producers. My selection of the 70 presented in the central part of this book is necessarily subjective and should not be taken as an attempt to identify Germany's top 70. I have chosen consistent producers whose personalities, philosophies, and authentic handcrafted wines give an accurate impression of the exciting German wine scene today. Most of the featured names are well known, but I also opted to profile some less well-known producers who are giving unrecognized sites a voice, rather than more familiar producers whose wines from famous sites inspire me less.

For the same reason, I could not include here all of the 13 German wine regions. Although some very good wines are also produced in Saale-Unstrut, Hessische Bergstrasse, and Mittelrhein, I could not find a producer whose wines are consistently inspiring enough to merit a profile.

I have revisited all the estates portrayed in this book at least once between August 2010 and January 2012, so all the tasting notes are up to date, including those on the more mature wines; astonishing longevity is one of the most impressive qualities of German Riesling.

German wines, for all their complexity and diversity, share a distinct—indeed, unique—style, which is about far more than just fruit. Fine German wine is not only deliciously drinkable; it is a thing of beauty that can fill its drinkers with wonder. So, get your glasses and open your heart and mind, while I try to uncork some magic bottles on our quest to discover the finest wines of Germany—"the wines most worth talking about."

The Definition of Cool

German wine, particularly Riesling, is sui generis. It is produced in the coolest and most northerly of the classic European wine countries—a country where grapes ripen slowly, with an extended growing season lasting right through to the end of November, and where even the smallest climatic or geographic variations can have a substantial impact on wine style.

So much more than fruit

"I had never tasted a wine with so much flavor that wasn't 'fruity,'" is how Terry Theise, writing in his delightful book *Reading Between the Wines* (2010), remembers his first bottle of Riesling. "It tasted like mineral water with wine instead of water." When you consider what followed from those first sips—Theise became one of the world's greatest Riesling aficionados, a passionate wine writer, and an acclaimed importer of boutique wines from cool-climate regions such as Germany, Austria, and Champagne—you can see just how transformative German Riesling can be. It's a wine that not only has the capacity to provoke "rejoicing and wonder," as Hugh Johnson so tellingly puts it, but one that can, without exaggeration, change people's lives.

Stuart Pigott is another whose life was radically altered after his first encounter with Riesling. The eminent Berlin-based British wine writer, Riesling lover, and talent scout switched jobs (and home) after "a philanthrope" offered him a mouthful of the Kloster Eberbach 1971 Steinberger Riesling Spätlese in London's Tate Gallery, where Pigott was working as a waiter, in 1981. The flavor of the wine reminded Pigott of water running over rocks, and set his mind spinning through geological strata into unknown spheres and the long-lasting, thrilling sensation of pins and needles in the mouth.

Pins and needles, rocks and minerals, rather than pineapples or passion fruit, or even the sense of wine—Riesling seems to be a strange variety indeed. Thanks to its versatility and the manifold styles it produces—infinitely variable, from dry to noble sweet—Riesling is not an easy variety to pigeonhole in the manner of Chardonnay, Sauvignon Blanc, or Cabernet Sauvignon. *Riesling ist Riesling ist Unsinn* ("Riesling is Riesling is nonsense"), as they used to say in Germany. Because of that long ripening period, Riesling is something of a chameleon. "Riesling, like Pinot Noir, seems to adapt with its own particular style to its own microclimate," writes winemaker Owen Bird in *Rheingold: The German Wine Renaissance* (2005). In fact, the variety maintains its unique multifaceted character on a wide variety of soils and can be grown in a surprisingly large climatic range without losing its refined linear wine style. Although its aromatic profile can alter substantially due to the origin or viticultural and winemaking techniques, fine German Riesling is always excitingly subtle, fruity, elegant, racy, refined, multilayered, and a great pleasure to drink.

Innocence and experience

Sadly, however, it is not always easy to deduce whether a bottle contains a fine German Riesling from its label alone. My own first Riesling—sampled when I was still an adolescent in the early 1980s—was a bone-dry and painfully sour example from the Nahe. According to the antiquated label, it was *für Diabetiker geeignet* ("suitable for diabetics"), so it was obviously healthy, but it was more medicinal than pleasurable. "It's good quality," my father said, and since he was convinced that only the dry, sour, and thin tasted good, he would buy cases of this idiosyncratic wine every year and ordered only *trocken* in a restaurant to match his *Zwiebelrostbraten* or beef stroganoff. To my father, *trocken* was a seal of quality and more important than the wine's origin, variety, or color. When it came to red wine, he ordered *trocken* as well; and

Right: The cool, slate soils of Scharzhofberg (Mosel), whose wines often suggest liquid rocks and minerals rather than fruit

when he was asked to specify, he would reply: "Ideally, a dry French Vin de Pays." Mostly, he was poured a generic Bordeaux or Côtes du Rhône— both of which were generally green and rustic, too.

It's not surprising, then, that my first experiences with wine had the effect of driving me away from this strange stimulant for several years. It was only thanks to a fantastically aromatic, crisp, white 1990 Bergerac Sec (€4) that I resumed my relationship with wine, as a student in Munich, with wines from France and Italy. And it was only in the mid-1990s that I returned to German Riesling.

Why am I telling you all this? Because I want to persuade you that, no matter what your initial impressions may be, no matter how different it may be from other wines, German wine really is worth sticking with—that you can, like me, come to love it. All the more so today, when German wine has improved immeasurably from the nadir of the early 1980s. Those were the decades when German wine (which at the time was as much about Müller-Thurgau, Kerner, and a variety of strange crossings such as Ortega, Huxelrebe, Siegerrebe, and Domina as about Riesling) had lost much of its former reputation, not just abroad but increasingly in the domestic market, too. Yields were much too high, and neither residual sugar nor *Süssreserve* could improve what were lifeless wines. The high prices that German wines had once commanded had sunk to an all-time low, and producers' motivation to enhance wine quality was even lower.

The turn from sweet to *trocken* in the 1980s was a change of style, not quality, and the wines remained weak. My father, for example, was a loyal German, who started his career as an electrical engineer in the 1950s during the *Wirtschaftswunderjahren* ("years of the German economic miracle"), who loved cheap and sweet German wines and Sekt but then, suddenly, had to switch to *trocken* for health reasons. Many other Germans, however, were not so loyal and switched to French, Italian, or, later, New

World wines, which were cheap and dry but tasted much better than most German wines.

It was Hugh Johnson and his undaunted love of the finest German Rieslings that helped me get over my old trauma in the mid-1990s. Today, with the experience of innumerable Rieslings tasted from a span of more than 100 years, not even the finest Champagne can give me what a fine Riesling Kabinett, Spätlese, or Auslese can, no matter how old: a light heart and a serene feeling, if not a Faustian longing for "the moment": *Verweile doch! Du bist so schön!* ("Ah, linger on, thou art so fair!") Unlike all other wines, German Riesling with 7–9% ABV and some delicious residual sugar does not send me to bed after a bottle. Rather, it wakes me up and is more likely to send me to the cellar for another bottle. The next morning might come around a little earlier than expected, but I can usually welcome it without a vitamin C tablet.

This is one of the miracles of German wine, perfectly epitomized in the finest Rieslings, which can unite contradictory characteristics such as lightness and complexity, length and grace, subtlety and intensity, richness and purity, power and elegance, steeliness and sweetness, ripeness and freshness, and seriousness and serenity. Really fine Rieslings are always crystalline, delicate, and beautifully balanced, providing not only fruit but a stimulating sensation of minerality or salinity.

The reasons for this unique and paradoxical ideal are many, and they include aspects of chemistry, climate, geography, and soil, as well as viticulture, winemaking, and particular German drinking traditions. It is certainly not niggardliness when neither Dr. Manfred Prüm nor Egon Müller will open another bottle of Riesling before the one they have served (always a mature one) is emptied; it is, rather, an expression of German drinking culture, where wine is not only appreciated with food but also as afternoon tea, apéritif, or digestif, especially in the Mosel Valley and the Rheingau.

The Prüm/Müller ritual is also a dramatic demonstration of two of Riesling's most impressive qualities: salubriousness and longevity. Served blind, I frequently have the impression that their wines are two, three, or even more decades younger than they really are.

The rebirth of cool

My personal journey with German wine—from chronic aversion to full-fledged love—is not at all uncommon. Recent years have seen German wine's fortunes improve dramatically, not only in Germany, but all over the world. Take, for example, Germany's performance at the world's fine-wine auctions. A century or so ago, Rieslings from the Rhine and the Mosel were among the world's most sought-after wines, with prices to match. In 1923, one *Fuder* (1,000-liter barrel) of the legendary 1921 Maximin Grünhauser Herrenberg Trockenbeerenauslese from the Ruwer was auctioned for a world-record price of 100,000 goldmarks ($3.3 million in today's money) and purchased by the Waldorf-Astoria hotel in New York. By the 1960s, however, German wine quality and its image had sunk to such a low that it barely registered on the fine-wine map.

Things began to change in the early 1990s, when Riesling in particular started to improve dramatically, and the best wines (some of them *trocken* or dry-tasting) began to attract high praise from prominent wine critics such as Jancis Robinson MW, Michel Bettane, and David Schildknecht. German Rieslings today are mostly dry, and some of them—mostly Grosses Gewächs wines from leading members of the Verband Deutscher Prädikatsweingüter (VDP)—are sold for high prices such as €40–80 ($50–100) per bottle. Keller's 2009 G-Max Riesling, bottled in magnums (1.5 liters), was auctioned for €4,000 ($5,200) per bottle in September 2010.

Right: Egon Müller's Scharzhofberger exemplifies German Riesling's astonishing ability to improve over decades

Just as impressive, if not more so, is the performance of Germany's unique, low-alcohol, naturally sweet wines. These wines have remained inimitably subtle, precise, and balanced, and they can still be of stupendous quality, with noble sweet wines from world-class producers such as Egon Müller-Scharzhof, JJ Prüm, Markus Molitor, or Robert Weil fetching auction prices of up to €6,000 ($7,700) per 75cl bottle.

Export booms

Further evidence of the so-called Riesling renaissance can be found in recent export figures. In the United States, Germany's most important export market, sales are particularly positive, with an increase of 21 percent in both value and volume during 2010. Sales are also strong in Scandinavia: Germany is the market leader, with a 33 percent share of white-wine sales in Norway, and its whites are the second most popular in Sweden and third in Finland. Sales are also rising in China (up more than 60 percent in 2010), Canada (+15 percent), Russia (+11 percent), Japan (+5 percent), and Switzerland (+29 percent). Increasingly positive media attention, as well as growing recognition of the high quality of German wines among wine professionals worldwide, suggests that quality wine exports will further increase in coming years.

German Spätburgunder

It's not only German Riesling that is in vogue, however: German Spätburgunder (Pinot Noir) is cool, too. This is not as surprising as it might seem: as well as being the world's largest producer of Riesling (55,848 acres [22,601ha] or 62.5 percent of the total worldwide), Germany is the third-largest Pinot Noir producer behind France and the US, with 14.3 percent of the world's total of almost 195,000 acres (79,000ha). In 2011, German Spätburgunder performed spectacularly in a blind tasting in London organized by Tim Atkin MW and Hamish Anderson. The duo handpicked 20 high-

end Pinot Noirs from all over the world (including three premiers crus from Burgundy), pitting them against 19 top Spätburgunders. The result: no fewer than seven German wines made it into the top ten. "The phrase 'world-class' is overused. But these Pinots were just that," said Atkin. Burgundy lover Jancis Robinson MW was only slightly less enthusiastic, saying that she was "in no doubt that Germany is now making some truly fine Pinot Noir that can be compared with some of the best middle-ranking red Burgundy". Even if her wish for a blind comparison of Germany's finest with Burgundy's finest remains unfulfilled, the interest generated by the tasting was a testament to the ambition and class of Germany's finest Pinots today.

Dancing bears

Even more interesting than scores, victories, and improving export figures, however, is the distinctive style of German wine, and the challenge it poses to traditional conceptions of Germany. *Zartestes Deutschland* ("tenderest Germany") is what Swiss writer Thom Held titled an article on German Riesling some years ago. Held was intrigued that the characteristics of German Riesling (which he called "dancing bears") are diametrically opposed to the clichés about Germany and the Germans. "Germany is powerful, imposing, resolute," he wrote. When it comes to Riesling, however, the cliché evaporates: *Zartestes Deutschland* is "inexplicably filigreed and delicate, like no other [wine] in the world." Indeed, the Swiss, traditionally big consumers of high-end Bordeaux and Barolo, have emerged as lovers of German Riesling.

But then, even French Riesling producers now cross the Rhine to stock up on the lightness, finesse, and purity they rarely achieve in Alsace— a reversal of the traffic from a generation ago, when many German Riesling producers sought to unlock the secret of Alsatian icon wines such as Trimbach's Clos Ste Hune. Those German

producers also sailed up the Danube until they reached the Wachau, where Smaragd Rieslings from top producers such as Prager, Pichler, Knoll, or Hirtzberger were so highly appreciated in the 1990s. They were curious people, eager to learn about other methods of working the vineyards, reducing yields, and understanding that doing less in the cellars can be more. Then they sailed back into the Rhine, Neckar, Nahe, or Mosel and discovered their regions were not just beautiful and rich in tradition but also quite cool. German wines weren't new. But they chimed with the desire for more authenticity, purity, freshness, and lower alcohol—and the Anything But Chardonnay movement taking root in the US. Germany's 2001 vintage was praised as an exceptional year for Riesling by Pierre-Antoine Rovani in Robert Parker's *Wine Advocate*; this report, and its reception, was seen in Germany as the start of the Riesling renaissance elsewhere.

Generation Riesling

Indeed, the increasing popularity of German Riesling in the world of fine wine started almost a decade ago but was accompanied by an accumulation of top-class Rieslings bottled by an increasing number of ambitious wine producers. Many of them were under 30 years old but willing to rock the world with authentic Rieslings. "Riesling performs best in our cooler climate, where it produces characteristics that cannot be copied anywhere in the world," they say. They also know that their success is based on the work of avant-garde producers such as Helmut Dönnhoff, Bernhard Breuer (Georg Breuer), Bernd Philippi (Koehler-Ruprecht), Bürklin-Wolf, Fritz and Agnes Hasselbach (Gunderloch), Robert Weil, and Heymann-Löwenstein, who had already managed to develop dry top-quality Rieslings that reflect their individual origins and match perfectly with food.

For today's ambitious producers, cultivating wine is all about personal satisfaction, cultural and historical obligation, and conservation strategies. And while Riesling is the most prominent, it is not the only variety that fits with their worldview. The past decade has also seen the rise of a new love for German classics: Silvaner (though the plantings have been decreasing dramatically for years) and Grauburgunder (Pinot Gris), but also Weissburgunder (Pinot Blanc) and Spätburgunder, are the stars of the new, dynamic Germany. And while the stars of the 1970s and 1980s, such as the crossings Müller-Thurgau or Kerner, may be declining in the vineyards, they have never tasted better than today. Creating young, fresh, well-defined but refined aromatic white wines with moderate alcohol, Müller-Thurgau represents the new, younger Germany of today and has become a new German classic.

Not everything in Germany is so classically styled, however. You can find Sauvignon Blanc, red-wine blends with indigenous and international grapes, blancs de noirs... But it's hard to find a producer who believes the revival of the German classics is nothing more than a fad. "Provided that the wines are created with passion and meticulous craftsmanship, they will remain classics, like the wines from Bordeaux or Burgundy," says Philipp Wittman, one of the top producers in Rheinhessen.

When it comes to wine style, in other words, it's the natural quality potential of a given region, rather than the demands of international markets, that is the most important defining characteristic. To underline the distinctive character of Riesling (or any other noble variety), as well as the unique cultural landscape and heritage, the origin can be defined down to small parcels of a single vineyard. Origin, producer, vintage—this terroir-determining triad is expressed on many front labels today, while the less important (and confusing) compulsory legal statements are given on the back label.

The German wine industry's journey back from Oechsle (the density of grape must) to terroir culminated in the vineyard classification described in Chapter 3. It's a journey that has been undertaken through meticulous vineyard work based on organic principles, as well as noninterventionist winemaking, as discussed in Chapter 4. Today's dry top wines from Germany can be of outstanding quality, with hitherto unknown depths of concentration and power. Some wines went too far, however, and for the past five years there has been a new trend back to lighter, less concentrated and extracted, but more enjoyable wines. Some Riesling producers have also become more tolerant of residual sugar, since this helps to minimize alcohol and to get the balance right.

Marketing Riesling

The marketing of Riesling is a tough business, says editor Filip Verheyden in the issue of *Tong* magazine devoted to German Riesling, "because it means finding easy marketing tools to promote the idea of complexity." But just how tough is it really? Martin Tesch, a wine producer in the Nahe region, keeps his marketing short and simple and almost wordless. He produces almost nothing but dry Rieslings, and his five single-vineyard wines are capsuled with different colors and labeled with different images—thus, you are not forced to read the label to find your favorite wine; it's easy. Tesch became the first German wine producer to win the Red Dot Design Award for best visual communication. A couple of years later, he published a book with no text, just a series of black-and-white photographs of people enjoying wine: *Riesling People Vol. 1.* A second volume followed in 2011, comprising a CD with spoken wine descriptions by sommeliers, thoughts on the relationship between unplugged music and unplugged Riesling by music and wine journalists, and a couple of songs, including "Riesling is Cool, F*ck Chardonnay."

Other producers have taken a more complex route. Mosel producers such as Reinhard Heymann-Löwenstein and Clemens Busch divided their traditional *Einzellagen* into several sub-appellations according to the different colors of slate. So, what would once have been marketed as Winninger Uhlen is now bottled as parcel-specific Blaufüsser Lay, Laubach, and Roth Lay, while Pündericher Marienlay became Fahrlay, Falkenlay, and Rothenpfad.

Tesch's clear, direct communication, and his correspondingly dry and unsophisticated wine style, helped Riesling and the German wine scene to attract drinkers, young and old, who had never been interested in wine before. Today, you can find German wine in bars and clubs where previously there was nothing but beer and whiskey. It's even poured at rock festivals, and rock and punk bands have started to dedicate songs to German Riesling.

Berlin, Germany's vine-free capital, has become the main capital of German wine. The Quadriga restaurant of the noble hotel Brandenburger Hof has an exclusively German wine list, and there are numerous specialty wine shops with a huge range of German wines—which was not the case even ten years ago. Nearly every weekend, there is a presentation of German wines or a party devoted to German Riesling. Berlin's Rutz Wine Bar is a hot spot for German wine, as is the Chinese restaurant Hot Spot, where mature German Rieslings, mostly from the Mosel, are offered in combination with traditional Chinese dishes. The VDP presents the wines of more than 100 producers on two days in September in Berlin's national museum of art, the Gemäldegalerie, framed by masterpieces of older Western painting. Berlin is also the place to find the icon wines of Saxony and Saale-Unstrut. These wines are so rare, in fact, that it is harder to get them on the spot or in Dresden than in Berlin. Today, so many roads lead to Riesling and German wine that there seems to be no way back.

From Sugar to Terroir

Happily, there are good and easily available accounts of German wine history, including Hugh Johnson's *Story of Wine*. Because we are concentrating here on the culture of fine wine, I highlight the events and trends that had the greatest influence on the art of winemaking in Germany today—and resulted in the bewildering diversity of styles and terroirs that it is still struggling to reconcile.

The beginning: 35,000 thirsty legionnaires

Viniculture in Germany started with the Romans crossing the Alps. The expanding empire settled the areas left of the Rhine, founding *Augusta Treverorum* (Trier, 16 BC), *Colonia Agrippinensis* (Cologne, AD 50), and other cities. But it soon had a serious problem: how to satisfy the 35,000 legionnaires' daily thirst for wine. Local viticulture appeared the most practical solution. Especially along the Rhine and the Mosel, the steep slopes and slate soils seemed well suited to viticulture in such a northerly region. But in the late 1st century, Emperor Domitian prohibited the extension of viticulture into the provinces north of the Alps to protect domestic exports. Only after Emperor Probus repealed the edict in AD 280 was viticulture successfully introduced in Germany.

The viticultural landscapes of the Rhine, Mosel, Ahr, Neckar, and Main survived Germanic raids, the collapse of the Roman Empire, and the upheavals of the migration period in the 5th century. Even Germanic tribes adopted viticulture between the 3rd and 5th centuries. The Franks developed viticulture on the right bank of the Rhine, where the Benedictine abbey of Fulda later became one of the largest wine producers for centuries to come.

Charlemagne, monks, and the eternal thirst

Under Charlemagne (748–814), viticulture became an economic mainstay of the Frankish Empire between the Pyrenees and the Carpathians. The farsighted king of the Franks and emperor of the Romans paved the way for the spread of viticulture. He regulated not only viticulture and wine sales but winemaking, too. Some of his edicts are still evident in European Union legislation today.

For the rest of the Middle Ages, the most important impetus for the art of fine winemaking came from monks. The Benedictines improved viticulture and winemaking throughout Europe, where wine became a basic foodstuff, as well as acquiring a philosophical and religious dimension. The Cistercians made Germany one of the largest

wine regions in Europe, and because they produced more than they could drink, they sold the surplus. Thanks to the Rhine, Cologne became the most important wine market of the Hanseatic League, through which Rheinwein was sold across northern Europe. Wine became the drink of the German people, the *Volksgetränk*, until the 17th century.

The downfall of viticulture

The 14th to 17th centuries were nevertheless a difficult period for viticulture. Natural disasters—including terrible weather, crop failure, and starvation—caused death and destruction even before the Black Death arrived, around 1348, and went on to kill between one- and two-thirds of Europe's population. Major religious, social, and economic upheavals followed. One bright spot was the foundation of the Juliusspital in 1579 by Julius Echter von Mespelbrunn, prince-bishop of Würzburg and duke of Franken. He was a leading figure in the Counter-Reformation, and a merciless persecutor, but the Julius-Echter-Berg in Iphofen is one of the most famous grands crus in Franken today, regularly producing some of the finest Rieslings and Silvaners in Germany (*see pp.66–7*).

During the Little Ice Age, from the second half of the 16th century, the limits of viticulture shrank southward. The ripening period for wine grapes was too short, resulting in tart, thin wines. Even the wines grown in protected sites of the Mosel and the Rhine were unpalatable for many years.

By around 1600, there were still at least 740,000 acres (300,000ha) under vine in Germany, three times as much as today. But the Thirty Years' War (1618–48) and the Nine Years' War (1688–97) destroyed landscapes, as well as lives, setting Germany back decades. Viticulture dwindled further, and it disappeared completely from Bavaria and north, east, and central Germany.

New dawn: the discovery of Riesling

In the 18th century, viticulture was reestablished in the regions along the Rhine and its tributaries, though wine was no longer the *Volksgetränk* and became an exclusive privilege of the rich. The clerical and lay aristocracy again dominated viticulture, with Trier, Koblenz, Mainz, Worms, Speyer, Mannheim, Würzburg, Bamberg, and Dresden as its strongholds. Wine was important not only as *Messwein* and a valuable export but

Below: An old stone carving at Weingut Juliusspital in Würzburg (1579) testifies to the ancient origins of German viticulture

Above: A statue at Schloss Johannisberg commemorating the first Spätlese vintage, of overripe or rotten grapes, in 1775

also as an integral element of Baroque court culture. Lords wanted the quality of their wine to be outstanding and introduced strict measures to ensure that it was. Most importantly, vines were pushed back up the hillsides, where they had to struggle in the poor and stony soils, and flat, fertile land was turned over to food crops.

The Cistercians of Kloster Eberbach (Rheingau) had discovered as early as the 15th century that Riesling was the variety ideally suited to the steep slopes and Germany's long, slow growing season. This late-ripening variety was particularly hardy and able to withstand the vagaries of the climate better than any other. It was, therefore, cultivated increasingly all along the Rhine and the Mosel and near Worms from the end of the 16th century. In 1672, the Abbot of St. Clara in Mainz decreed that the existing (mainly red) varieties in the Rheingau be replaced with "Rissling." A century later, the south-facing Schloss Johannisberger was planted with more than 5 million Riesling vines. Kloster Eberbach

continued to back Riesling and, in 1760, protected the vines by walling in the Steinberg vineyard like the Burgundian Clos de Vougeot.

The Rheingau became synonymous with Riesling, but the grape was widely planted all across Germany in the 17th and 18th centuries. It was less dominant only in Würzburg, where Silvaner achieved equally good or better results; Markgräflerland, where Gutedel (Chasselas) ruled; and Baden, where Blauer Spätburgunder (Pinot Noir) became the first classified variety in Germany. Because Riesling found a home, and its own distinct expression, in different regions, it become the primordial cell of the German diversity and individuality that eventually led to 30,000 recognized vineyards by 1971.

The attempt to distinguish the quality of wines by village or, occasionally, by vineyard did not begin until the late 18th century. And already there was an alternative way of classifying the wines: selection.

16

Creating diversity: Spätlese, Auslese, and Eiswein
The late ripening of noble varieties such as Riesling during the cool month of October, in combination with the cool and humid cellar conditions, meant that the naturally sweet musts were not always completely converted into alcohol, so there was some residual sugar in the wine. Some wines tasted lush and lovely the following spring or summer, with unusual but welcome sweetness. Sweet and smooth was sexy in those days; the sexiest came into the Cabinet cellar and, from 1825, were known as Cabinet wines (what we would call "reserve" today).

"Leaving harvest until October must have meant harvesting grapes affected with *Botrytis cinerea*," winemaker Owen Bird deduces in his *Rheingold* book. And indeed, wines were produced exclusively from overripe and rotten grapes in Rheingau by the middle of the 18th century. But it was Spätlese—a late-harvested wine of the finest quality, often with residual sugar due to the fully ripe grapes, with or without rot—that led to further refinements. The first Spätlese vintage is generally reckoned to have been 1775, when grapes were picked late at Schloss Johannisberg. Despite the rotten grapes (noble or not), the resulting wine was apparently so extraordinary that Spätlese was quickly recognized as a legitimate style.

The 19th century brought further refinements. Separating not only rotten from healthy grapes, but picking single rotten or even noble rotten grapes from bunches, gave rise to categories akin to today's Auslese, Beerenauslese, and Trockenbeerenauslese. From 1820, Schloss Johannisberg identified the different styles by differently colored wax seals. The signature of the cellar master on the labels guaranteed authenticity of origin from 1830. In 1858, a new category was added: Eiswein, produced from frozen grapes. The Johannisberger style categories became the prototype of the German Wine Law more than 120 years later.

Zollverein: competition and improvement
Tariffs and taxes greatly improved wine quality in the 17th and 18th centuries, but even more in the 19th century, after the *Deutscher Zollverein* (German Customs Union) equalized taxes from 1834, allowing the best wines to move freely within this union. This increased competition among the wine regions, and better wines received higher prices. The rivalry between the Rheingau, Rheinhessen, Pfalz, and (from the second half of the 19th century) Mosel led to exceptionally fine wines. By the mid-19th century, German wine was the favored white wine at the royal courts of Europe; until the late 1920s, German Riesling was world-famous and as expensive as the best Champagne or Bordeaux.

Celebrating diversity: 19th-century classifications
It was in the second half of the 19th century that vineyard sites became relevant. Consumers clearly associated certain wine characteristics and qualities with the named sites, even though most of the wines were sold under the name of a village or wine region. Only the names of long-established vineyards—those as famous as Steinberger (Rheingau), Kirchenstück (Pfalz), Scharz(hof)berg (Saar), or Steinwein (Würzburg)—appeared on labels. Even then, the sites were not precisely defined until 1909.

Through taxation records, an effective rating of the terroirs was made, and so the first vineyard classifications were created. The first maps based on a vineyard's potential earnings were charted in the Rheingau in 1867; then came the Weinbau-Karte Mosel and Saar (1868, district Trier), Mosel district Koblenz (1898), Nahe (1900), and Rhine between Bingerbrück and Bonn, including the Ahr (1902, 1904). All these historic maps, as well as the Mittelhaardt (Pfalz) classification of 1998 (based on appraisals of soils and classification drafts of 1828), played an important role for the work-in-progress vineyard classification of the VDP.

Naturreiner Wein: the beginning of the VDP

From the second half of the 19th century, the finest Mosel, Pfalz, and Rheingau wines were sold at auction and often fetched extraordinary prices. The more estates produced auction-worthy wines, the greater the competition, and the greater the quest for quality. Quality then meant *Naturwein* (natural wine): wine grown in a particular vineyard that was not chaptalized, fortified, or sweetened, nor blended with other wines. Today, German wine ideology is still based on the supposition that wine quality is defined primarily by the fermentation of natural grape sugar. *Naturwein* was the shibboleth against *Kunstwein* (artificial wine) and led, in 1910, to the foundation of the *Verband Deutscher Naturweinversteigerer* (Association of Auctioneers of Natural Wine), the forerunner of the VDP. The idea was to unite the best wine estates of Germany, whose sites were able to produce natural wines of exceptional quality every year.

Initially, chaptalization was banned. According to Prince Michael zu Salm-Salm, VDP president from 1990 to 2007, the VDP lost its raison d'être after World War II, when sweet wine came into fashion, chaptalization was allowed in the VDP, and the 1971 Wine Law eliminated many traditional site names. The VDP, therefore, decided to produce quality wine and *Qualitätswein mit Prädikat*, which became the new term for unchaptalized wines.

The annihilation of elites: German Wine Law

In Germany, every wine producer has the same opportunity to produce the highest legally recognized quality and to state this on the label—regardless of where the wine is grown, which grape varieties are used, or how it is produced. "Top German wines are not born as such merely because they were grown in certain sites or bottled by prominent producers," the website of the Deutsches Weininstitut (DWI; German Wine Institute) proudly proclaims. "Neither names nor vineyards have the

Above: The proud logo of the VDP, the association of some 200 of Germany's best estates, is also found on labels

exclusive privilege of producing premium wines. Only the proven quality in the glass matters."

The 5th German Wine Law, effective from 1971, divides German wines into four, and then nine further, quality categories (*see pp.21–24*) according primarily to the potential alcohol level of the must. Thus, the sugar level of the grapes when picked is the key legal quality criterion (the higher, the better); origin, yields, varieties, and viticultural and winemaking techniques are of no relevance.

Although all quality wine candidates undergo chemical testing and a sensorial blind tasting, 98 percent of total wine production is classified as *Qualitätswein* or, even better, *Prädikatswein*. This is exactly what the German Wine Law of 1971 was meant to do: highlight the exceptional quality of German wines by comparison with those from other countries and, thus, to ensure its sales. Additionally, the *Deutsches Weingesetz* was intended to shore up unprofitable wine regions.

As a result, quality became arbitrary. It was reduced to the absence of technical flaws and leniently recognized. Wines have a geographical indication, but there is no official relationship between origin and quality. Protected designations of origin do not exist—indeed, they are of no relevance whatsoever under German Wine Law.

The *Deutsches Weingesetz* is the negation of origin, individuality, and competition. In 1971, the 30,000 previously recognized single vineyards were reduced to the roughly 2,700 *Einzellagen* and 1,300 *Grosslagen* used today. Historical sites were eliminated and saddled with lesser sites to form huge *Grosslagen*, while other, lesser sites became part of absurdly enlarged former top *Einzellagen*. Due to *Grosslagen* whose impressive names sound like elite *Einzellagen* but are actually the exact opposite, and due to the fact that almost all German wines are classified as *Qualitätswein*, there is no chance for consumers to deduce real wine quality from the label. Amazingly, this chaotic situation—which many regard as tantamount to legalized fraud—was, and still is, intended by the German authorities, in that it corresponds to the constitutional and democratic principles of egalitarianism. The *Weingesetz* guarantees equality of opportunity—for Riesling hand-picked on the steep slope of a historically validated vineyard, as well as for Huxelrebe machine-harvested in a potato field; but it excludes consumers. It may be politically correct, but it is a disaster for wine lovers

From Oechsle to terroir: the VDP classification

Since the mid-1980s, some leading members of the VDP have been striving to counter the negative impact of what Owen Bird has accurately dubbed the 1971 *"wurst law."* They had three aims: to restore the best German vineyards to their rightful reputation; to improve the quality and to restore the reputation of great dry German wines; and to redefine the traditional predicate system for wines with natural residual sugar. The most important component of the quality definition became terroir: "Only a vine that grows in harmony with its vineyard can yield grapes for truly great, distinctive wines that perceptibly reflect their soil and climate," claims Steffen Christmann, the current VDP president.

In 1993, the VDP first considered its own classifications. Parallel to developments within the VDP, the Charta wine estates—an independent association in the Rheingau, including some VDP members—were already working on their own classification, which became law in Hessen in 1999 but did not apply in any other region or state. The term Erstes Gewächs is still a regional term exclusive to Rheingau.

The VDP finally agreed on its own classification in 2001. The result was the three-tier model described on p.25, though it will be changed into a Burgundian four-tier model from 2012. With the introduction of Grosse and Erste Lage, and Grosses Gewächs for the highest-quality dry wines, the German wine-producing elite has reestablished the reputation of German wine—especially thanks to Riesling, which benefits from the wide variety of soils and topographic conditions in Germany. Since 2006, sweet Mosel wines have also been labeled as crus (Erste Lage, or Grosse Lage in future) whereas previously the VDP classification was not primarily a vineyard classification, but rather an attempt to establish a prestige class of dry German wine: Grosses Gewächs. This has since become a prominent category in the Mosel as well, because although it is still best known for its unrivaled charming, light, and floral wines, more and more producers are trying to be all things to all people by offering all kinds of wines from top sites.

The German authorities are now trying to introduce another paradigm, based on the supposition that the smaller the origin of a wine, the higher the anticipated quality. The time has indeed come to end the specious, vinous *Sonderweg*.

Understanding German Wine

Understanding German wine is no easy matter—for consumers, professionals, or, indeed, for the producers themselves. Nor is explaining an issue as complex as Goethe's *Faust* in six pages. But both are possible and well worth the effort. What you do not learn here, you do not have to know to appreciate German wine. And even if you read no more of this chapter, you will generally fare very well if you remember these three very simple rules for buying fine German wine. It should be: Riesling (from a top site or not); bottled by a top producer; offered by one of the growing number of German wine fanatics running wine stores from Singapore to San Francisco.

Dry, medium, or sweet?

This question applies only to the grape varieties and wine styles that combine high acidity with high ripeness levels—such as Riesling. It it not relevant for fine German Silvaner, Weissburgunder, Grauburgunder, or red wine. Most of the wines produced in Germany actually taste dry, and this is now the case even for Riesling. In export markets, German Riesling is rarely dry, but the natural sweetness of *Prädikatsweine* is well balanced by its acidity and its mineral or saline piquancy. Due to their residual sugar, Kabinett and Spätlese wines often taste sapid rather than sweet and are delightfully low in alcohol.

According to EU labeling rules, the following terms may be used to indicate how a wine tastes.

- *Trocken* (dry): up to 4g/l RS, but if balanced with suitable acidity, then up to 9g/l; formula: TA must be less than 2g/l below RS
- *Halbtrocken* (medium-dry): 9g/l RS to 12g/l RS, but if balanced with suitable acidity, then up to 18g/l; formula: TA must be less than 10g/l below RS
- *Lieblich* (medium): 18g/l RS to 45g/l RS
- *Süss* (sweet): more than 45g/l RS.

Since August 2009 a tolerance of 1g/l RS is allowed.

Asking for analytical data without contextualizing it is a German passion. But even contextualized figures do not really help us anticipate the wine's taste. The desire to know RS, TA, and ABV figures is caused by the fact that only *trocken* is regularly used on German wine labels. Since *lieblich* and *süss* wines are perceived by many consumers as being of lower quality than dry wines, neither term is much used. *Halbtrocken* is also rarely used, and an increasing number of producers prefer the unofficial but accepted term *feinherb* (literally "fine-dry"), which describes an analytically medium-dry, or analytically medium yet rather dry-tasting, wine.

As we know—by experience and thanks to Emile Peynaud's classic *The Taste of Wine*—it is not only sugar levels that influence a wine's taste. How sweet a wine tastes is also controlled by other factors—above all, by its acidity and alcohol levels. A sweet wine from the Mosel or the Rheingau can taste dry due to its high acidity or when aged for a decade or more. By contrast, a dry wine can taste sweet if the alcohol level is high. Any wine with more than 45g/l RS would be considered sweet. And yet many of the great sweet wines—BA, TBA, icewines, Sauternes—have residual-sugar levels far higher than this but are beautifully balanced by their acidity. Many of Germany's finest and most acclaimed wines—Kabinett and Spätlese Rieslings from the Mosel, Nahe, or Rheingau—have residual sugar due to an arrested fermentation. Yet residual sugar, acidity, low alcohol, and high dry extract in thrilling balance make these wines delicious, digestible, and long-lived. Not only with Riesling, wine quality is more a question of balance and complexity than of high numbers.

So, if a German wine is labeled *trocken*, then it tastes really dry. In case no sweetness level is indicated, the wine is probably not dry, and it may contain sugar that was either not fermented or was added as *Süssreserve* (unfermented must). If you

Above: Checking with a refractometer to measure grape-sugar levels, which are of crucial importance for a wine's legal status

prefer natural sweetness, look for a *Prädikatswein* or what was traditionally called a quality wine with predicate (*QmP*). But remember: predicate wines can taste dry, medium-dry, medium, or sweet. So if a Kabinett, Spätlese, or Auslese is dry, it is indicated as Kabinett, Spätlese, or Auslese *trocken*. If only the predicate is given, the wine does not taste really dry but can be anything from medium-dry to sweet. If the alcohol level is closer to 11 or 12%, then the wine is analytically medium-dry but can still taste quite dry; if it is lower than 11% ABV, it will probably taste fruitier or sweeter. Almost anything is possible. But if the wine is good, any sugar will be balanced by acidity, minerality, and body—a joy to drink.

German quality levels: all theory

As we saw in the previous chapter, there is almost nothing but quality wine in Germany—which means flawless wine and not much else. Nevertheless, there are two different basic quality wine categories, and two higher, as below.

Deutscher Wein

This new category replaced Tafelwein or Table Wine in August 2009. Made from German grapes from approved areas and grape varieties, this appellation-free wine may indicate the grape variety and the vintage. The quality requirements are lower than for quality and predicate wines.

Landwein

German country wine is one of the wines with a geographical indication. It should be (and mostly is) an uncomplicated wine typical of its region, but some more complex wines are downgraded higher-quality wines labeled as, say, Badischer or Sächsischer Landwein. A Landwein is always dry or medium-dry and produced in one of the 26 specified Landwein areas.

Qualitätswein bestimmter Anbaugebiete (QbA)

Sourced only from one of the 13 specified wine regions. The grapes need to be at least 51–72° Oechsle, the wine at least 7% ABV. Chaptalization is allowed. Most German wines (57–75 percent) are *Qualitätswein* but range from Liebfrauenmilch-like wines to extremely fine Grosses Gewächs wines from VDP members.

Prädikatswein (formerly *Qualitätswein mit Prädikat, QmP*)

Ranging from Kabinett to Trockenbeerenauslese, *Prädikatsweine* or quality wines with predicate (or distinction) are from grapes with higher sugar levels when picked. Chaptalization is prohibited. The minimum must weights vary with the grape variety and the region. There are six *Prädikate*, which were intended as a quality hierarchy but can also be regarded as a stylistic range. They are:

Kabinett Grapes must be at least 67–82° Oechsle; the final wine, at least 7% ABV. Unfortunately, there is no defined maximum alcohol level for Kabinett, so what should be a light, delicate, enjoyable wine is often a downgraded Spätlese or even Auslese, with 13% ABV or more. Kabinett wines are offered from dry to sweet. They taste crisp when young, but fine Riesling from the Mosel, Nahe, or Rheingau can be surprisingly complex after ten or even 20 years.

Spätlese Must be at least 76–90° Oechsle and at least 7% ABV. Only fully ripe late-harvested grapes are allowed. A classic German Riesling Spätlese is fruity and supple, medium or sweet, with just 8–10% ABV. It tastes alluring one and two years after bottling, then again ten years after harvest. If the balance and concentration are right, it can age for more than two decades. Because the fruit fades over time, mineral flavors dominate the taste of a mature Spätlese, which often seems much drier than it really is. Today, though, there are also many dry and medium-dry Spätlese wines of top quality that have higher alcohol levels.

Auslese Must be at least 83–100° Oechsle and at least 7% ABV. Only fully ripe or botrytized grapes may be used. Although there are also dry, medium-dry, and medium Auslesen from healthy or lightly botrytized grapes, the classic Auslese is sweet and intense but also light, piquant, and precise. Many of the finest are still digestible at table, while the dessert-wine or meditation category starts with the higher predicates. Before 1971, three kinds of Auslese were defined: fine, finer, and finest, the last with the greatest concentration and finesse. Because this distinction is no longer allowed, producers use stars (*, **, or ***) or gold capsules and long gold capsules to mark their own classification. Many Auslesen are downgraded BAs. After Riesling, excellent Auslesen can also come from Silvaner, Rieslaner, Scheurebe, Muskateller, and Traminer.

Beerenauslese (BA) Must be at least 110–128° Oechsle and at least 5.5% ABV, from botrytized or at least overmature grapes. A noble sweet wine of high concentration and intense flavor. Sometimes dry wines come from BA-worthy grapes and must weights but are downgraded to Auslese or QbA. The best BAs are from the same varieties as for Auslese.

Trockenbeerenauslese (TBA) Must be at least 150° Oechsle and at least 5.5% ABV, from largely shriveled botrytized grapes (or, exceptionally, from shriveled overmature grapes). A TBA can be one of the finest and lightest sweet wines in the world. In 2003 and 2011, TBAs with more than 300° Oechsle were produced. A great TBA is an ethereal, immortal wine. Even low-acid vintages such as 1959 taste brilliant today, and 1921 produced some of the finest wines in German history (not only TBAs). Another great botrytis vintage, reputedly still wonderful today, is 1893, but I have not yet had the pleasure.

Eiswein Must be at least 110–128° Oechsle and at least 5.5% ABV, from grapes that were frozen when picked and pressed (which normally requires temperatures of 19°F [−7°C] or below). Sometimes an icewine is picked in the new year but has to be bottled under the vintage of the growing season. Riesling is by far the best icewine variety; it can give astonishingly precise wines, with penetrating acidity.

Above: The completely shriveled, botrytized grapes that will be used to create exceptional TBA at Weingut Markus Molitor

What about origin?

The 13 wine regions, most introduced in later chapters, are divided into *Bereiche* (districts), which are in turn divided into *Grosslagen*, which are composed of *Einzellagen* (individual vineyards). The indication of a site rarely gives any useful information regarding the character or quality of the wine (which should be "typical"). So far, the *Lage* (vineyard site) is not a protected designation of origin. A site can be an *Einzellage* (ranging from at least 12 acres [5ha] to more than 500 acres [200ha]) or a *Grosslage*, a huge collective site embracing several *Einzellagen* and totaling more than 2,500 acres (1,000ha). To know which might be best, you have to acquire experience, or turn to the press or trade, or take a look at the capsule: if there is a stylized eagle logo, the wine was produced by a member of the VDP, so you can be sure the quality is very good, if not excellent. Certainly, there are great wines from non-VDP members, but identifying them is far harder.

VDP Erste and Grosse Lagen and Gewächse

As explained in the previous chapter, the VDP and other wine growers' associations have established quality pyramids linking wine quality with origin and flavor profiles rather than with grape-sugar levels. Until the spring of 2012, Germany's most prominent pyramid, based on the VDP vineyard classification, was a three-tier model.

1. **Basic level:** *Gutswein* Estate-bottled wine of upper quality and with regional character.
2. **Second level:** *Ortswein* Village wine from classified sites, or bedrock wine (such as "Quarzit") with distinctive character and of superior quality.
3. **Top level:** **VDP Erste Lage** Wine from the best classified vineyards. Erste Lage wines, with or without *Prädikat*, are off-dry up to noble sweet; Erste Gewächse (in the Rheingau) or VDP Grosse Gewächse (in all other regions) are dry. For each region, the permitted grape varieties are specified. While Mosel produces only Riesling wines from VDP Erste Lage sites, Württemberg allows more varieties: Riesling, Chardonnay, and Pinot Gris for white wines; Pinot Noir and Lemberger for reds. In Franken, there is Silvaner instead of Lemberger, but all the other varieties above also qualify.

The above model, however, was quite undifferentiated in its middle tier; and the terms VDP Erste Lage, Erstes Gewächs, and VDP Grosses Gewächs caused considerable confusion. So, as of this writing, it was due to be broadened into a clearer, more Burgundian-style four-tier model in 2012, introducing VDP Erste Lage for VDP Erste Lage wines (premiers crus), without *Prädikat* for dry wines and with *Prädikat* for off-dry wines; and VDP Grosse Lage for VDP Grosses Gewächs (grand cru), again without *Prädikat* for dry wines and with *Prädikat* for off-dry wines.

1. **Basic level:** *Gutswein* Estate-bottled quality wine or *Prädikatswein trocken* and off-dry.
2. **Second level:** *Ortswein* Dry quality wine or *Prädikatswein* off-dry reflecting village character.
3. **Third level:** **VDP Erste Lage** (optional) Premier cru wine from classified sites. In the old model, Erste Lage was the highest level; here it is the second highest, but the former Erste Lage sites are not downgraded and are instead named Grosse Lage (not to be confused with *Grosslage*!). The new Erste Lage category will include all or most of the VDP-classified sites of the former second tier. In April 2012 it was still unclear how wines from VDP Erste Lage sites will be identified, since the term Erstes Gewächs has been a Rheingau exclusivity so far. When the Rheingau legally renames Erstes Gewächs as Grosses Gewächs, the worst-case scenario would be that the term Grosses Gewächs could be used only in the Rheingau.
4. **Top level:** **VDP Grosse Lage** Grand cru wine from the best classified sites. These vineyards were previously called Erste Lage; only the name is changing. Dry wines from Grosse Lage sites are called VDP Grosses Gewächs; off-dry or sweet wines are marketed as VDP Grosse Lage, with or without *Prädikat*. In April 2012 it was still unclear what will happen to the former Erstes Gewächs wines from Rheingau VDP members. Evidence suggests that these top wines will be marketed as VDP Grosse Lage Riesling or Spätburgunder *trocken*, whereas the Erste Lage wines will go into the market as VDP Erste Lage Riesling (or Spätburgunder) *trocken*. Visit www.vdp.de/en/classification for the conclusion to this saga.

Producers will not be forced to use all four levels, even in regions that adopt them. While the VDP retains Kabinett *trocken*, recognizing the German tradition of light wine, and while it will remain an important category in the Rheingau, Spätlese *trocken* and Auslese *trocken* ought to be integrated into the village, premier, or grand cru levels.

It will take time for the new four-tier model to become reality. However, it shows that the German elite is able and willing to unravel the Gordian knot tied by the 1971 German Wine Law.

The Lay of the Land

Germany is not, like Bordeaux, Burgundy, or Rioja, a wine region; it is a wine-producing country. At the 50th parallel, Germany is one of the most northerly wine countries in the world. It is primarily the warm Gulf Stream and its moderating influence on western Europe's climate that enables grapes to ripen this far north.

Germany extends from the North and Baltic seas down to Lake Constance and the Alps. There are 13 wine regions in Germany, and all face climatic and weather challenges that are unknown in more southerly regions. During vegetation, there is much less sunshine in Germany than in more southerly wine regions. Average temperatures are lower; frost threatens the vines in May and November; and does any wine country have more rain than Germany? Most precipitation occurs over the summer, and rainfall generally declines during the fall. But rot is always on a German wine grower's mind—and often on his grapes, if he does not protect them.

In short, Germany is at the climatic limits for viticulture, but that is often where the best wines are made. Some 24,000 fearless wine warriors are ready to fight in the battlefields of the *Einzellagen* and *Grosslagen*, totaling 252,000 acres (102,000ha).

The moderately warm summers, favorable amounts of precipitation during vegetation, and the long ripening period in Germany allow the grapes to develop their fruit intensity and to retain acidity, the hallmark of German white wine. The quality and size of each vintage depends largely on the weather—so in Germany, vintage really matters.

Macroclimates and mesoclimates in Germany are probably the most varied of all the world's vineyards. According to *The Oxford Companion to Wine*, "mesoclimatic variations within an *Einzellage* can result in simultaneous pickings of the same variety which exhibit significant differences in potential alcohol and flavor."

Research at Geisenheim has shown that "the average alcohol content of wine of the same vineyard can vary from one vintage to another by over 6 percent. The degree of latitude, topographical features such as a favorable exposition to the sun, shelter from frequent cold winds or damaging frosts, and the altitude are some of the factors that dramatically influence the quality of its viticulture."

The most favorable locations for viticulture in Germany are the south- or southwest-facing slopes of protected valleys—for example, along the Rhine and its tributaries, or in the valleys of the Elbe, Saale, and Unstrut rivers. The exposure to sunlight is more intense on slopes than on flat sites, and slopes with a southerly exposure also profit from longer periods of sunshine, so the vines can bring the grapes to full ripeness. On occasion, the river amplifies the effect by reflecting sunlight on to the vineyard. The other effect is the temperature regulation during the night, so that the risk of spring and fall frost is minimized, and the prospects for noble rot in fall are increased. The heating effect is reinforced due to the rocky or stony soils, which store the heat by day and radiate it at night. Since the poor soils are on the steep slopes of a mountain range (which also protects from rain and wind) rather than at the bottom, water supply can be quite good, thanks to subterranean mountain springs.

Soils

Grapes in Germany are cultivated in a wide variety of not only climates but also soil types, even within regions, villages, or vineyards. It is these geological, as well as climatic, factors that are responsible for the differences among the various vineyard sites. Thanks to this great diversity of soil types, there is no homogenized style of German wine; rather, there is a wide range of quite distinctive wines. So, generalizations are difficult, and more detailed discussion is better undertaken in the regional introductions and profiles of later chapters.

Germany

0   100 km

0   100 miles

SWEDEN

DENMARK

Baltic Sea

North Sea

POLAND

Hamburg

Bremen

BERLIN

NETHERLANDS

Dortmund

SAALE-UNSTRUT

Düsseldorf

SAXONY

Cologne

BELGIUM

AHR

MITTEL-RHEIN

MOSEL

RHEINGAU   Frankfurt

FRANKEN

CZECH REPUBLIC

LUX.

RHEIN-HESSEN

NAHE

HESS. BERGSTR.

PFALZ

WÜRTTEMBERG

FRANCE

Stuttgart

BADEN

Munich

AUSTRIA

SWITZERLAND

LIECH.

Above: Sunset on the Mosel, where, despite climate change, the future of resilient Riesling still seems relatively secure

Climate change: goodbye Riesling?

Wine character is shaped by vintage but also by the region and place where it is grown, and this includes a certain climate, soil, and culture. But there are several indications of climate change in viniculture: budburst, flowering, veraison, and harvest occur earlier now. Higher sugar levels and, thus, higher alcohol levels are also often cited as a result of climate change but may equally be due to viticultural and winemaking improvements. Ernst Loosen on the Mosel still produces the classic crisp and light Kabinett style, whereas many of his colleagues sell Kabinett as downgraded Spätlese—and with much more residual sugar than 20 years ago. Another indication, perhaps, is that 2011 was one of the earliest vintages in German history; budburst and flowering were three weeks earlier than normal, as was the case in 2007, too. Another sign is that German vineyards are increasingly red: over 20 years, the area devoted to red varieties has tripled. But this is also due to the fact that German consumers prefer red wine—not only from abroad but also from Germany. Thus, new crossings from Weinsberg—such as Cabernet Dorsa, Cabernet Dorio, Cabernet Mitos, or Acolon—are widely planted now for the creation of new internationally styled red-wine blends with German classics such as Portugieser. Pinot Noir is also increasing slightly and remains a German classic.

What will happen to Riesling, though? By 2050, it is predicted, the variety will ripen 10–14 days earlier in the Rheingau. However, Hans Reiner Schultz, professor of viticulture at Geisenheim, reassures us that climate change does not pose a direct threat to German Riesling and the refined linear wine styles it produces. "High-quality Riesling is not only grown across a much larger climatic range than is commonly believed; it also maintains its unique character on a large variety of soils." Furthermore, viticultural techniques can protect existing styles but also "substantially alter the aromatic profile" of Riesling to "create new wine styles."

On a more cautionary note, however, Stephen Skelton MW warns that, as temperatures rise, pests and diseases associated with warmer regions will move northward and force growers to adapt their growing and spraying techniques.

Finest grape varieties

In Germany, a total of almost 140 grape varieties are cultivated, of which about 100 are for white wine and 35 for red wine or rosé production. However, fewer than 30 are important, and when it comes to fine wine, the figure is even smaller.

White grape varieties

Riesling This is Germany's number-one variety for quality and quantity, accounting for 22.1 percent of the total area under vine. Almost two out of three Riesling vines worldwide are cultivated in Germany. Due to remarkable quality improvements during the past 20 years, German Riesling has become part of "Brand Germany," like Goethe, Schiller, Bauhaus, Beckenbauer, Volkswagen, Porsche, and German beer. No other white wine is so versatile, providing so many different wine styles of the highest quality. It can be light, delicate, and subtle but also powerful and rich. Riesling has the ability to be great as dry wine, medium-dry, sweet, and noble sweet. It is amazing with 7% ABV, appetizing with 11%, and still promising with 13%. Riesling is tremendously fruity and has plenty of natural acidity even in late fall, in combination with concentrated sugar levels. Riesling begs for sweetness or extract or both. As long as the balance of sugar, acidity, fruit flavors, and alcohol is right, nothing can happen to a good Riesling. The balance of sugar and acidity in finest Beerenauslesen or Trockenbeerenauslesen or electrifying Eisweins remains in balance eternally. Its robust and terroir-specific nature makes it taste impressive from marl, stunning from limestone, and fascinating from slate. No other variety has a greater ability to age; no other variety remains so fresh, so subtle, so fruity, so distinctive, and so complex after decades or even a century or more. The 1911 Kiedrich Berg Auslese from Robert Weil today? Unforgettable. The 1921 Berncasteler Doctor Trockenbeerenauslese? Thank you, God. History has taught us, though, that even dry Riesling does not need high alcohol levels to taste impressive with age, as long as the site and the grapes were good. Please note: Schwarzriesling (literally "Black Riesling") has nothing to do with Riesling but is the German term for Pinot Meunier.

Silvaner This variety, a centuries-old cross of Traminer and the largely unknown Österreichisch Weiss, is sui generis. More often than not, texture characterizes Silvaner better than its bouquet does. It gives elegant, subtle, well-balanced, and digestible wine that appears in different, mostly dry styles but also as an incomparable noble sweet wine. Silvaner offers a brilliant reflection of its origin and is just as richly varied. Rheinhessen is the largest Silvaner-producing region in Germany (and the world) with 6,099 acres (2,468ha). In Franken, Silvaner is deeply embedded in the regional wine culture and, with 3,289 acres (1,331 ha), is the image-building *Leitsorte* there. Franken is the only German wine region allowed to produce Grosses Gewächs wines from Silvaner. Due to Silvaner's elegant but gentle acidity and soft style, it matches perfectly with food.

Weisser Burgunder (Pinot Blanc) This is the rising star in German vineyards today and is cultivated in every region, even in the Mosel, Saar, and Nahe. Its share of the total is only 4 percent (4,106ha [10,146 acres]), but it was just 1 percent in 1990. Baden is the most important region, especially the Kaiserstuhl, home to some of the best Pinot Blancs of Germany, many of them marketed as Grosses Gewächs. This is also the case in the Pfalz, Franken, Saale-Unstrut, and Sachsen. Racier than Pinot Gris, Pinot Blanc bridges Burgundian Chardonnay with German Riesling, if you will. It is a perfect food wine and available in different styles: as creamy barrel-fermented wine, as well as in a more fresh, lean, and reductive stainless-steel style without malo.

Grauer Burgunder (Pinot Gris) This mutation of Pinot Noir has been cultivated since the Middle Ages in Germany. It is one of the most prominent varieties in southern Germany—in Baden, the Rheinhessen, and the Pfalz, but also in Franken, Sachsen, and Hessische Bergstrasse. Although it is a white grape, the berries, when fully ripe, have reddish cheeks, so the wine is often deep-colored. The quality and stylistic range is wide, but the finest wines are rich, full-bodied, and intense, especially when sourced from old, low-yielding vines. The Kaiserstuhl produces excellent dry wines today that are classified as Grosses Gewächs. Especially in cooler years such as 2010 and 2008, a Grauburgunder grand cru can be of exceptional quality, whereas in warmer years, the wines tend to be too broad and heavy. Like Spätburgunder, Grauburgunder needs acidity to balance its weight and concentration. The finest wines are often barrel-fermented.

Müller-Thurgau Early-ripening Müller-Thurgau is a top cool-climate variety and, thus, Germany's second most important grape. If the yields are kept low and the soils are not too rich, it performs deliciously as a light and subtle fruity white wine, with some mineral complexity when grown in continental climates and especially on limestone soils, as in Franken, Saale-Unstrut, and Sachsen, where Müller can taste like the little brother of Riesling.

Gelber Muskateller A late-ripening relative of Muscat à Petit Grains, which is one of the oldest and most aromatic, but also most refined, grape varieties. Nevertheless, it is extremely rare (512 acres [207ha]), due to its requirement for top sites and susceptibility to *coulure*. It gives lean, aromatic, and racy wines. Delicious as sweet Spätlese or Auslese wine (Pfalz) and as Kabinett-styled wine, with or without residual sugar. Some of my very favorites have just one gram of RS per liter, and I cannot think of a better wine for the first days of spring.

Gewürztraminer (Traminer) Grown on only 2,145 acres (868ha), Traminer performs best on loess soils in the Pfalz, Baden, and Sachsen, where it can give world-class Eiswein, as well as strong and

serious, and expensive, white table wine. Dry wines are always rich and powerful and super-aromatic (spicy, dog roses) but also fine and balanced by an elegant acidity. In the late 16th century, women were warned not to drink too much of this heady stuff.

Rieslaner This late-ripening crossing of Silvaner and Riesling has been dubbed "the Riesling-Viagra" by Terry Theise. It is extremely rare (213 acres [86ha]) but often compared with Riesling (a mystery to me) when grown in a warm top site. It is very aromatic but lacks the complexity and finesse of Riesling. It became famous at Müller-Catoir (Pfalz), where exceptional TBAs are produced, as at Schmitt's Kinder in Franken.

Scheurebe One of the new crossings (Georg Scheu, 1916: Silvaner x Riesling) that survived and thrived in all categories—from bone-dry to noble sweet. It is a late-ripening, aromatic variety with a characteristic pink grapefruit and cassis aroma (as well as the occasional whiff of cat pee). It has been less popular since Sauvignon Blanc started to take off but can give excellent dry wines and noble sweet wines.

Red grape varieties

Spätburgunder (Pinot Noir) In case you are sick of drinking cool-climate white wines and cannot afford the finest red wines of Burgundy anymore, German Spätburgunder (Pinot Noir) is the latest rage, though the variety has already been planted in Germany (in the Rheingau) for more than 700 years. Wine professionals in the press and trade are currently debating whether Germany's most important red grape variety (11.1 percent of the total area under vine, and 14.3 percent of the worldwide total) produces wines that can compete with the finest Pinots of the Côte d'Or. Even the most critical and demanding commentators, such as Jancis Robinson MW, now score some German Pinots as high as finest premiers crus from the Côte d'Or.

As an equally interesting and worthwhile exercise, I recommend comparing a German Pinot Noir made from Dijon clones or cuttings from top producers of the Côte d'Or with, say, an old-vine Spätburgunder from Baden. I think you will agree that it is almost as though you were tasting two completely different varieties. The French German is charming and elegant (some even dignify it with the title of "red Riesling"), whereas a genuine Kaiserstühler can be distinctive, rich, and powerful, almost fiery or short: self-assured, copying nothing, but expressing a distinctive German twist on Pinot Noir. The wines are less refined, perhaps, but lush, robust, and firmly structured. And since the producers care not only for ripeness but also for freshness and have reduced the proportion of new oak (or started to use better barrels), the wines have become much finer and fruitier than they were a decade ago. In Germany, Pinot Noir gives impressive results even on Devon slate—in the Ahr, Mosel, and Rheingau. Limestone is the basic soil of the best wines from the Pfalz and from Baden, whereas in Franken, Pinot Noir gives the finest results on the red sandstone soils. Top wines such as Grosse Gewächse start their real life no sooner than six to ten years after harvest. If you prefer a younger Spätburgunder, there is nothing better than a really good blanc de noirs, which has become very fashionable in Germany over the past few years.

Frühburgunder Blauer Frühburgunder or Pinot Madeleine, better known in France as Pinot Noir Précoce, is believed to be a natural mutation of Pinot Noir. With veraison in August, it ripens roughly two weeks earlier than its big brother (*früh* is German for "early," while *spät* means "late"). The grapes are smaller than those of Pinot Noir, and the skin is thicker. Due to vulnerability to *coulure* and to small yields, Frühburgunder became rare after World War II and was almost extinct in the 1960s. In the 1970s, the research center at Geisenheim started to breed clones, and today Frühburgunder is cultivated with growing passion and success. It now occupies 640 acres [260ha] of vineyard, most of all in the Ahr Valley, where it is cultivated on weathered soils of Devon slate, and in the western, warmer part of Franken, around the villages of Miltenberg and Bürgstadt on red sandstone. The wines are characterized by an intense ruby-red color, elegance, and a charming fruity character that is often black-currant-dominated. The grapes need to be picked exactly at the right time to prevent *surmaturité*, to preserve a clear definition and the *Spiel* between fruit, freshness, and alcohol. The finest results are obtained with must weights below 92–94 Oechsle. Frühburgunder is normally vinified like Pinot Noir but mostly without stems. It is quite charming soon after bottling, but the top wines can age for more than ten years.

Lemberger The very successful career of Austrian Blaufränkisch or Hungarian Kékfrankos has not yet been repeated by its German twin Lemberger, though it is classified for Grosses Gewächs production in Württemberg, where 4,048 acres (1,638ha) of the German total of 4,369 acres (1,768ha) are planted. The variety, which is sensitive to late frost and *coulure*, requires the best sites and a long vegetative period. All this is available and supplied in Württemberg, where it settled after 1840, yet Rainer Wachtstetter, one of the top Lemberger producers in Germany, complains there are no high-quality clones available in Württemberg and that he has to cut off more than 50 percent of the crop to achieve good quality. The finest Lembergers are dark and robust wines, with a pronounced acidity and striking tannins when young, but round, velvety, and intense with two or three years of bottle age. As with other varieties, it is the old vines (30 years or more), carefully grown in top sites, that give the best wines.

Perfect Grapes and Purest Wines

What God has joined together, let no man put asunder. To separate viticulture and winemaking would not occur to a good German vintner, who has to be everything at once: grape grower, leaf-plucker, grape picker, cheerleader, crusher, cellar master, taster, critic, bottler, marketer, seller, artist, entertainer, philosopher, visionary, wife or husband, mother or father, son or daughter... On most of the estates in this book, there is neither an agronomist (normally the father's job) nor an enologist (usually the son's or, increasingly, the daughter's job). Most German vintners, especially of the younger generation, are trained in both viticulture and winemaking. They are also influenced by family and local tradition, intuition and vision, peers and trends, and hard-won experience. Passion (often allied to a certain masochistic tendency) is their driving force, and a spellbinding wine is their highest reward.

Several viticultural and winemaking techniques were invented in Germany. But when you talk with good German vintners about the technical aspects of making of fine wine, the first thing you hear is that they are not "winemakers" at all, but "interpreters," "mediators," or "wine watchers." And indeed, when you see their cellars, you realize that the essential work has already been done when the grapes get here. Rather than a tour of the cellar, you are swept off for a tour of the vineyards, culminating at the highest point of the steepest slope with an out-of-breath proclamation: "This is where our wine is born, the land we work, the soil our vines grow in, the sun that ripens our grapes. It is this very special origin, through the grape variety and the vintage, that we want to express in our wines. So we aim for healthy, ripe grapes that we select and translate into a wine that we are proud of, that I want to carry the name of the vineyard and mine as its interpreter."

Fine, handcrafted German wine is the vintner's silent and subtle rebellion against the negative effects of globalization, and the standardization of taste is fought with something mightier than the sword (or pruning shears): with *Heimat* (habitat), the bedrock of their existence—the place where they live and work, where their wines and visions grow. Born of the place and its culture, their wines have a sensual charisma that goes straight to the heart.

This might all sound rather whimsical where I might be expected to dwell on matters technical. But as Owen Bird observes, "there is no right way to make wine," even if "there are, unfortunately, a lot of wrong ways to go about it." There are no recipes, especially in Germany, which is so varied in its climatic conditions, soil types, grape varieties, and wine styles, that generalizations about viticulture or winemaking are of little value. I discuss a few of the details, where particularly relevant, in the producer profiles, highlighting here only some of the key themes and trends.

Viticulture: location, management, and selection
All grapevines in Germany are grown in rows (downhill, as long as there are no terraces), and most are trained on wires. *Flachbogen*, cane pruning with one or two canes, is the most common training system, but the semi-arched *Halbbogen* is also used. A newer trend is spur-pruning (cordon), which for some growers yields looser bunches and smaller grapes with more intense flavors. The Mosel, though, remains predominantly Roman, persisting with the *Doppelbogen*, or single-pole, at least on the steepest slopes. The vines are trained on a wooden stake, and two canes are bent downward in the shape of a heart. In these exceptionally steep vineyards, nearly everything has to be done by hand, and the workers (or their buckets or machines) are transported by monorail.

Flurbereinigung has rationally reorganized—and rejuvenated—most of the vineyards, but some of the most fascinating sites, especially in the Mosel, remain as they were a century ago and more. While 20–30 years ago, old vines were often considered

Above: The careful hand-harvesting into small buckets at Weingut Friedrich Becker typifies the work of meticulous growers

as inefficient low-croppers and ripped up, they are highly esteemed today for the same reasons, as well as for genetic reasons. Especially along the Mosel and its tributaries, many vines are still ungrafted and up to 100 or more years old, yielding grapes as small as peas but with fabulously intense aromas and flavors. Ambitious producers want to keep them—even if this means more effort and higher costs. The preservation of the viticultural heritage matters more. By auctioning world-class BAs, TBAs, or

Eisweins at high prices, they can afford the luxury.

For new plantings, massal selections from the best older vines are increasingly preferred to clones. They are sourced from neighboring vineyards and other German regions, but also from Austria, Alsace, and Burgundy, to create genetic diversity and yield more complex and thrilling wines. Klaus Peter Keller in Rheinhessen has grafted Pinot Noir from Burgundy onto 60-year-old Silvaner vines to compensate for the lack of old Burgundian vines

in Germany. Pinot clones from Dijon are still in vogue, but even the oldest plantings are only about 20 years old, and a growing number of German producers prefer old or new low-yielding German Spätburgunder clones or selections to young Pinot clones from Burgundy. They would rather have the one-year-old barriques from top Côte d'Or producers, suspecting that they do not receive such fine barrels, even from the same coopers, as their famous French neighbors. Most also want to reduce the proportion of new wood that they use anyway.

The best growers keep yields low—through high-density plantings, low-vigor rootstocks, pruning, natural or induced *coulure*, bunch-halving, or green harvesting. Even more crucial is extending the hang time—not to get higher sugar levels but to achieve more intense flavors. With climate change, harvest dates tend to be earlier than 20 years ago, while ripeness is less of a problem.

Low yields are not always better, however, as growers learned in 2006, when warm temperatures and rain at the beginning of October forced the spread of botrytis, because the grapes were already ripe and thin-skinned: the harvest (and sorting) had to be done in six to eight days rather than six to eight weeks. Today, more vintners prefer not to reduce yields too drastically or too early, waiting to see what will be best. Some of the first Grosses Gewächs wines were deemed too high in alcohol and too concentrated, while sweet wines are much richer and sweeter than 20 years ago, which makes them even more impressive but more difficult to drink or to match with food.

Sensitive canopy management (a technique borrowed from the New World) is another flexible and useful way of achieving the goal of a balanced vine. In high-vigor vineyards, cover crops reduce the amount of water and nutrients to the vine, as do higher planting densities and the pruning of

Left: The most natural form of *pigeage* at Schlossgut Diel reflects the prevalent less-is-more philosophy of top producers

roots. The two latter techniques also give more "minerality" to the wines, many growers argue. More minerality and more individuality, as well as better balance, looser bunches, smaller grapes, lower sugar levels, and higher physiological ripeness, are also among the alleged benefits of organic and biodynamic farming. Since 2004/05, several of the finest wine producers in Germany (as in Austria) have gone organic and/or biodynamic for quality reasons, whereas 20 years ago, it was more a question of *Weltanschauung* or ideology.

To produce great wine in Germany, two things have been crucial for almost 250 years: a top vineyard (*Lage*) planted with high-quality vines, and a late harvest of perfectly selected grapes. Because of the many different wine styles, "perfect" grapes can be almost anything other than unripe or ignobly rotten, or a mix of grapes at different stages.

Until 20 years ago, Kabinett was the wine picked first, while TBA and Eiswein were last. Today, with warmer and wetter fall weather, Kabinett and noble sweet wines are often picked the same day: green and yellow grapes go into the black bucket for Kabinett, the botrytized grapes into the red one. "Today, it is as time-consuming to select crisp grapes for an authentic Kabinett as it was a decade or two ago to gather raisins for the BA," says Ernst Loosen.

"You have to know exactly which type of wine you harvest before you pick," says Markus Molitor, the godfather of selective picking. A classic fruity Spätlese needs ripeness but also balancing acidity so is picked a week or two earlier than the Spätlese *trocken*. The latter is harvested not with higher must weights but with more intense flavors and higher extracts; the acidity is riper and residual sugar unnecessary. The same applies to Auslese but on an even higher level. Many top producers work like jewelers today, endlessly sorting their grapes to reach the highest possible quality in every category.

Botrytis is generally not admitted for lighter dry wines, is tolerated at low levels for Grosses Gewächs wines, and is welcome for noble sweet wines. For Reinhard Löwenstein in the Mosel, botrytis is part of terroir, so he (almost alone) accepts up to 70 percent for his Erste Lage Rieslings.

Picking Pinot Noir and Pinot Madeleine is tricky: there are only two or three ideal days, says Paul Fürst, who aims for fruit that retains freshness. The overall balance (acidity, fruit, and tannins), rather than a blind preoccupation with ripeness, is the hallmark of his or Bernhard Huber's wines. They are grown and vinified like the great wines of Burgundy and have reached the same quality.

Winemaking: less is more

Coming into the cellar, the guiding principle is: "As little as possible; as much as necessary." If ever there was a flirtation with the notion of *Vorsprung durch Technik* ("advancement through technology"), those days are over, and less is more. Wine is grown in the vineyard, while in the cellar the character of the fruit should be retained in the wine. Whether, or for how long, a white wine macerates, depends greatly on the desired style and the vintage. Musts ferment increasingly with indigenous yeasts. Some producers prefer wooden barrels or vats; others, stainless-steel tanks—and some use both. Vintners who want a reductive style prefer a short fermentation, while others are happy for the process (and the malolactic fermentation) to take a year. Equally, long lees contact is standard today for top dry wines, while the sweeter Kabinett, Spätlese, and Auslese wines are racked earlier to preserve the primary fruit and freshness. Most of them ferment in stainless steel, with some high-octane BAs or TBAs in glass demijohns. Dry wines tend to be bottled unfined, and reds unfiltered as well. Acidification or deacidification is practiced very rarely, if at all, by top producers, certainly as far as Riesling is concerned, and many spurned the latter technique even for the spiky 2010 vintage. If you don't like acidity, you'd better not drink German wine.

Saxony and Saale-Unstrut

Saxony (1,140 acres [462ha] in 2008) is the most easterly, as well as northerly, wine region of Germany; Saale-Unstrut (1,693 acres [685ha]) is about 90 miles (150km) farther west. The southern end of Saxony is at roughly the same latitude (51° N) as the northern end of the Mittelrhein where, near the former German capital Bonn, West German viticulture comes to an end. However, along the Elbe River, between the areas of Meissen and Dresden, it's possible to produce top-quality wines—particularly whites but also reds, as Schloss Proschwitz has recently shown. (If you want to travel the impressive Saxon Kulturlandschaft, with its old wine terraces, take the Sächsische Weinstrasse, which guides you over the 34 miles [55km] from Pirna to Diesbar-Seusslitz via Dresden, Radebeul, and Meissen.)

Viticulture, selective hand-harvesting, and modern enology are important reasons for the dramatically improved quality in eastern Germany over the past decade. But it is the continental climate and soils that give the wines their unique character. If the vines survive the extremely hard winter (down to −22°F [−30°C]), the early spring frosts, and/or the cool flowering period, they then benefit from an average of 1,570 hours of sunshine, as well as from the changes from warm days to cool nights, and from sunny to rainy or windy days. Thus, must weights are rarely as high as in western Germany, resulting in a lighter structure.

As long as the berries reach full physiological ripeness, what could have been inadequate elsewhere is actually beneficial here, because the soils are quite complex and can give the wines a pure and mineral character.

The geological formations are manifold, so vineyards in Saxony are characterized by many different soil types. In the Elbe Valley, there is a lot of granite, dating back to the Carboniferous period. There are also layers of sandstone and Pläner (a gravelly marl sediment consisting mainly of minerals such as quartzite, calcium carbonate, clay, and mica), and layers of decomposed soils from the Cretaceous, which can be overlaid by thick layers of loess, clay, and sand.

In the valleys of Saale and Unstrut, there are three distinct layers of soil—the Trias (from which the Triassic period takes its name)—so the vines root in sandstone (from the Early Triassic), limestone (Middle Triassic), or black shale (Late Triassic).

The same applies in Franken, and there are other analogies with that region, too. As in Franken, which has the same continental climate, so in Saxony and Saale-Unstrut many different grape varieties are cultivated, ranging from early-ripening Müller-Thurgau, Bacchus, and Kerner, to Pinot Blanc and Pinot Gris, to Silvaner and Riesling. The wines, however, are quite distinct. Those from the Saale and Unstrut valleys are less rich and powerful than those from Franken but not as light and filigreed as those from Saxony.

Both regions have a long tradition of winemaking. Viticulture in Saxony is at least 850 years old, and in Saale-Unstrut, more than 1,000 years old. In the beginning, wine was made mainly for monks but also for nobles. Viticulture was an important branch of the economy, and it shaped the landscape itself, impressive terraces climbing up the slopes along the Elbe River. The golden age of viticulture was the 16th and early 17th centuries, but it had almost disappeared by the late 19th century due largely, but not only, to phylloxera. After World War II, there were only 150 acres (60ha) of vines left in Saxony. (In 1840, there were 4,040 acres [1,636ha], though viticulture was fading even then.) Replanting started from 1955 onward, but the crushing of single-vineyard grapes did not happen until German reunification in 1990.

Today, more and more good to very good wines are produced in Saxony, most of them white. I profile two producers who have been bottling excellent wines since 2005 or so: Schloss Proschwitz

Above: The view from Schloss Proschwitz toward Meissen, whose soaring towers symbolize the finely pointed style of the wines

from Zadel near Meissen, and Klaus Zimmerling from Dresden-Pillnitz. I would have loved also to include young Friedrich Aust from Radebeul, whose white wines are so direct, pure, refreshing, and salty that I always have to drink an Aust as soon as I can find a bottle. But that's the problem: it's not easy to find Aust's wines unless you are actually in his tasting room. They are much in demand, especially in Dresden and Berlin, but they are not exported. Annual production is microscopically small. And yields in 2009 and 2010 were so low—about 30–50 percent below normal—that Aust had to blend both vintages for some of his wines, just to have a reasonable amount to offer.

Another producer worth looking for is Frédéric Fourrier, a former sommelier from France, whose white wines from Radebeul are very clear and delicious. The wines (and Sekte) from Schloss Wackerbarth are also attractive but focus on fruit and harmony rather than complexity.

As for Saale-Unstrut, the Grosses Gewächs wines from Uwe Lützkendorf in Bad Kösen (Silvaner from the Karsdorf Hohe Gräte) and Bernhard Pawis in Zscheiplitz (Freyburg Edelacker Riesling and Weisser Burgunder)—both members of the VDP and pioneers of their region—are worth exploring. They are always very good and full of character when I taste them a couple of weeks after bottling, but will they become deeper and rounder with bottle age? At least Lützkendorf also offers mature vintages of his top wine, like 1999 and 2001, but unhappily I have not yet had a chance to taste them.

Schloss Proschwitz / Prinz zur Lippe

S chloss Proschwitz is both the oldest and the largest private estate in Saxony, and since the 1990s it has been by far the most dynamic winery in all Germany. The 250-acre (100ha) property in Zadel, near Meissen, is owned by Dr. Georg Prinz zur Lippe-Weissenfeld, whose family is one of the oldest aristocratic families in Germany. His branch of the family has been based in Saxony since the beginning of the 18th century.

From the 12th century until the Reformation, the vineyards of Schloss Proschwitz belonged to the Bishop of Meissen. It has been family-owned since 1770, though it was in the earlier part of the 20th century that the princely Lippe family got in through marriage. In 1945, the family was expropriated without any compensation, incarcerated in various camps and prisons, and later expelled to West Germany. It was in Schweinfurt (Franconia, in former West Germany) that Prinz Georg zur Lippe was born in 1957. He became a Master of Agriculture and received a PhD in economics while working as a freelance consultant. From 1990, he gradually bought back his family's then-bedraggled castle and sterile vineyards.

For the first few years, the wines were aged in the premises of an old fruit-farming cooperative in Reichenbach, then in Castell in Franken. But since 1998, they have been produced in a new, ultra-modern winery in Zadel. In 1996, Schloss Proschwitz became the first Saxon member of the VDP.

Schloss Proschwitz is based 2 miles (3km) north of the center of Meissen and is used as the venue for many cultural events. The wines are produced on the estate in Zadel. There is also a guesthouse, a restaurant, a distillery, a shop, and a tasting room, as well as the administrative offices. Proschwitz currently cultivates 200 acres (80ha) of vines. Another 25 acres (10ha) are not replanted yet, and a further 25 acres are still leased to the Saxon

Right: Dr. Georg Prinz zur Lippe is of noble lineage but had to win back his wine estate through industry and intelligence

Schloss Proschwitz is both the oldest and the largest private estate in Saxony, and since the 1990s it has been by far the most dynamic winery in all of Germany

Staatsweingut Schloss Wackerbarth. The vineyards are on both sides of the Elbe River. On the left bank, south- and southwest-facing, is the 88-acre (35.7ha) single vineyard, Kloster Heilig Kreuz. The 126-acre (50.7ha) right-bank vineyards comprise the monopoly Schloss Proschwitz grand cru. On both sides, the soil is based on red granite, covered by a 10–16ft- (3–5m-) deep layer of loess and sandy loam. This, the southern exposure, and the continental climate, with its warm days and cool nights, make Burgundian varieties such as Pinot Blanc, Pinot Gris, and Pinot Noir "the core competence of Schloss Proschwitz." But other varieties are also planted: Elbling, Riesling, Goldriesling, Scheurebe, Müller-Thurgau, and Traminer for whites; Dornfelder, Dunkelfelder, Regent, and Frühburgunder (Pinot Madeleine) for reds.

Schloss Proschwitz produces high-quality red, white, and sparkling wines, and, more recently, an excellent Port-like fortified red. All of them are very clear, elegant, and sophisticated, with concise acidity and a lingering minerality.

The most complex and elegant wines from Schloss Proschwitz are the Pinots, with their ripe yet precise and spicy fruit and mineral depth. There are two Spätburgunder (Pinot Noirs), one of them classified as Grosses Gewächs since the 2006 vintage, whereas the other, Kloster Heilig Kreuz, was first produced in the 2008 vintage. Both go on the market only after three years. Since 2006, a Schloss Proschwitz Weissburgunder GG has been produced, and the ambition is to market a Grauburgunder GG as well. The GGs are released in Germany from €20—a very fair price by comparison with other Saxon wines.

With the 2010 vintage, the new Weingut zu Weimar Prinz zur Lippe was launched in Weimar (Thuringia). Here, the vines are on Muschelkalk (shell-bearing limestone), and Prinz zur Lippe is striving for red and white Pinots that show even more elegance, finesse, and roundness.

FINEST WINES

(Tasted in June 2011)

Schloss Proschwitz Weissburgunder GG

This wine is regularly of very good to excellent quality. The grapes are destemmed, then crushed, and after some hours of skin contact in the press, the clear must is fermented at cool temperatures and aged mostly in stainless steel and a very small part in barrels. The **2009** is charming, elegant, fruity, and round, but not that complex. The **2008★** is exciting, offering aromatic fresh fruit with subtle floral and spice notes. Concentrated and rich on the palate, with distinctive acidity and a spicy aftertaste, its deeper mineral structure gives it greater potential.

Schloss Proschwitz Spätburgunder GG

This traditionally made wine (18 months in barrique) is on the right road to freshness, elegance, and finesse. The first GG was made in 2006, before which it was marketed as Barrique. The **2004** was a potentially excellent Pinot but a bit overextracted and matured in barriques, which caused somewhat green and harsh tannins. The **2005** was much better and more moderate, at 13% ABV instead of 14%: rich and full-bodied, yet fresh and mineral, if still a little overdone. The **2006** was disappointingly sweet to taste, clumsy and astringent, tasting more like a Pinot from Sicily. But the **2008** (with 10% *saignée*) was delicious. Picked in late October, it has a deep, fresh, pure, and peppery bouquet. On the palate, it is powerful and distinctive, silky and deep, with spicy fruit flavors, tangy tannins, and a long finish. Very good to excellent potential.

Kloster Heilig Kreuz Spätburgunder

The **2008** is clear, intense, and quite sweet, but delicate on the nose, with aromas of red berries, cherries, freshly milled pepper, spices (including cloves) and smoke. Rich and silky, with good concentration and a carpet of dark berries balanced by elegant acidity and fine tannins. A very good Pinot, full of character and with a fine reverberating finish. This first vintage should make us curious enough to taste the subsequent ones.

Weingut Schloss Proschwitz Prinz zur Lippe
Area under vine: 200 acres (80ha)
Average production: 300,000 bottles
Dorfanger 19, 01665 Zadel über Meissen
Tel: +49 352 176 760
www.schloss-proschwitz.de

Weingut Klaus Zimmerling

Klaus Zimmerling, a former mechanical engineer born in Leipzig, began making wine in 1987—"just to offset my home requirements," he says. In May 1990, half a year after the Berlin Wall had been torn down, Zimmerling, then 30 years old, left for Austria to work as "a cook and bottle washer" at Nicolaihof in the Wachau for one year. In 1992, the autodidact founded his own winery, producing his first wines in his laundry room in Wachwitz, about 6 miles (10km) up the Elbe River from Dresden. At that time, his vineyards were also located there. In the mid-1990s, Zimmerling and his wife, the polish sculptor Malgorzata Chodakowska, moved to Pillnitz, 3 miles (5km) upstream, where they were able to purchase a few acres on the terraces of the steep south-facing Königlicher Weinberg (King's Vineyard).

Yields are as low as 20–30hl/ha, bringing forth a range of concentrated, deep, and mineral wines of great purity and elegance. The wines are rare and much sought after

This famous vineyard was mentioned as early as 1721. The soil is decomposed granite and gneiss. Zimmerling has cultivated his 10 acres (4ha) organically since the beginning, though without certification. His vineyards are planted with Riesling (35 percent), Weissburgunder (Pinot Blanc, 20 percent), Grauburgunder (Pinot Gris, 16 percent), Kerner (12 percent), Gewürztraminer (12 percent), and Traminer (5 percent). The yields are as low as 20–30hl/ha, bringing forth a range of concentrated, deep, and mineral wines of great purity and elegance. Selective harvesting in late October or early November is followed by whole-berry crushing and a maceration of up to 12 hours. After being pressed in a small basket press and settled overnight, the must is allowed to start fermenting spontaneously in stainless-steel tanks of varying size. Zimmerling then inoculates the fermenting must with cultured yeasts, but with "only 20–30 percent of the recommended amount," he explains. Fermentation lasts from one week to five months, normally without temperature control. Only if the temperature reaches 72°F (22°C) is the tank cooled with clammy cloth down to 64°F (18°C). After racking, the wine is sulfured for the first time and matures on its fine lees for another four to six weeks before being filtered and bottled. Zimmerling's wines are rarely dry, partly because he thinks that in many years the right balance needs a little residual sugar. But it is the wine that decides what's right: Zimmerling neither cools the fermenting must nor stops the natural process by adding sulfur. If a wine is declared *trocken* (as in 2008 and 2010), it is really dry, with less than 4g of residual sugar.

All of the Zimmerling wines are rare and much sought after. If you can't find them elsewhere, go to Berlin's top wine bars or restaurants and try them. Riesling is number one in terms of both quantity and quality, but Zimmerling is also well known for his Pinots and Traminers, from which outstanding Eisweine can be produced in Saxony. Until the 2008 vintage, all the wines were bottled as Tafelwein, but since 2009 they have been marketed as *Qualitätswein*. In 2010, Zimmerling was accepted as the second Saxon member of the VDP, but so far he has not used any Prädikate. In order to indicate quality levels and styles, he instead uses letters: R for Reserve, A for a kind of Auslese (more an off-dry style), AS for a real Auslese, and BA for a kind of Beerenauslese. Most Zimmerling wines are filled in 50cl bottles (higher predicates in 37.5cl). Since the 2009 vintage, most of the wines (and from 2012 all of them) have been closed with Stelvin—only the BAs and icewines are closed with Vino-Lok (Vino-Seal in the US). All of the wines are labeled with annually changing images of sculptures by Zimmerling's wife Malgorzata, which populate not only the private house but the garden and cellar.

FINEST WINES

(Tasted in May 2011)

2010 Riesling R [V]

The R indicates a quality selection of grapes, from the steepest parcels of the Königlicher Weinberg. It is a golden, wonderfully rich, but firm and mineral Riesling that made me think of a great Meursault. Succulent and concentrated, thanks to perfect botrytis, this Riesling also shows great purity, with a fascinating saltiness and perfect balance.

2010 Riesling BA★

A blend of two different parcels. The botrytis was perfect in both, resulting in outstanding quality. Its high noble raisin aroma is combined with brilliant passion-fruit aromas and a fine aromatic touch of honey. On the palate, it is concentrated and zesty, nobly textured and enlightened by a high noble acid beam. For all its richness, this Riesling shows great mineral purity, a very complex finish, and an extremely long and fine aftertaste. Unforgettable.

2005 Riesling BA★

A clear, very elegant, and powerful bouquet of ripe tropical fruits, peach, apricot, passion fruit, and finest caramel. Spicy and intense on the palate, with noble and pure fruit flavors, which linger for an impressively long time. There are finest spice and noble honey flavors as well, all on a mineral foundation. Perfect balance, elegance, and finesse.

2003 Eiswein vom Traminer

This wine is called Traminer instead of Gewürztraminer to stress that Saxon Traminer is different. Saxons believe that their older vines are descendants of a single Traminer vine in Radebeul. There was no botrytis in the dry and hot 2003 vintage, so the grapes were frozen healthy when picked on January 4, 2004. Superbly clear and stimulating fruit flavors, with delicate spice. Bright on the palate, with fine if heavy sweetness, dancing acidity, caramel notes, and delicious length.

Left: Klaus Zimmerling and his wife Malgorzata Chodakowska, with some of her sculptures that adorn the labels and winery

Weingut Klaus Zimmerling
Area under vine: 10 acres (4ha)
Average production: 16,000–24,000 50cl bottles
Bergweg 27, 01326 Dresden (Pillnitz)
Tel: +49 351 2618 752
www.weingut-zimmerling.de

Franken

When one speaks about the wines of Germany, one speaks about Riesling first—about the wines of the Mosel, Nahe, Rheingau, or Pfalz—whereas the wines of Franken are mentioned quite late, if at all.

This Bavarian wine region is one of the largest in Germany, covering 14,982 acres (6,063ha) of vines between the cities of Aschaffenburg, Schweinfurt, Würzburg, and Bamberg. Franken is not only quite distant from Germany's most famous wine regions but is also isolated, not bordering any other wine region apart from little Taubertal in the south, where offshoots from Franken (225 acres [91ha]), Württemberg (554 acres [224ha]), and Baden (1,646 acres [666ha]) come together to share a total of 2,426 acres (981ha) of vines.

Last but not least, Franken is deeply attached to Silvaner but not well known for Riesling, even though it is home to some of the finest dry Rieslings in Germany. Franken Rieslings are not comparable to the stylistic leaders from the Rhine, Nahe, or Mosel. They are not only bone-dry (with residual sugar levels of 3–6g/l), full-bodied, and powerful, but also earthy rather than fruity, light-footed, and delicate. A real Franken Riesling—like any other authentic *Frankenwein*—does not debauch wine drinkers with attractive fruit flavors, higher residual sugar, elegance, or finesse. It is, instead, a deep, serious, and distinctive wine, with good structure and thrilling minerality, which wine drinkers have to learn to love, preferably with food. The *Bocksbeutel*, Franken's quaint, traditional, and legally protected bottle (allegedly shaped like a ram's testicles), is the proud symbol of the authenticity, originality, and high quality of *Frankenwein* since the 14th century. And yes, it can contain German Riesling as well!

In Franken, though, Riesling does not play an important role in terms of quantity. Its holding is only about 4 percent of the area under vine, because this late-ripening variety needs top sites, warm and sheltered from winds, with shallow rather than deep soils. And this is exactly where Riesling, as well as Silvaner, grows in Franken today—in well-known if not widely famous south-facing sites such as Würzburger Stein, Würzburger Innere Leiste, Randersackerer Pfülben, Escherndorfer Lump, Iphöfer Julius-Echter-Berg, Homburger Kallmuth, and Bürgstadter Centgrafenberg, to name only the very best. Most of the sites are steep, concave, and close to the Main River, benefiting from temperature regulation, as well as from reflected sunlight. The finest grape varieties get ripe here, whereas in the flat and less protected sites, only early-ripening varieties have a chance to develop full physiological maturity—but even then, little or no complexity.

Franken is particular in many respects. The climate is continental, with dry, very hot, but rather short summers, and winters that can be bitterly cold and long. Sunshine averages 1,600–1,800 hours per year, the amount of precipitation is 24–28in (600–700mm), and the average temperature only 47–48°F (8.5–9°C). Franken's wine producers are threatened by frost not only in winter but also in spring. In 1985, they harvested only 10 percent of the normal crop because more than 2 million vines were killed by the extremely low temperatures that winter. On May 4, 2011, many producers lost up to 70 percent of their crop because frost destroyed many of the young buds. Moreover, the late summer and early fall have become both warmer and wetter this century, due to heavy rains. So harvest has to be highly selective and is finished in the third week of October most years.

This special climate largely explains why Franken has as many as 90 legally permitted grape varieties, most of them classic and newer crossings such as early-ripening Müller-Thurgau (30.3 percent of the total), Bacchus (12.2 percent), Kerner, Scheurebe, and Rieslaner; curios such as

Right: A sign in the shape of a *Bocksbeutel*, the proud symbol of Franken wines, identifies one of its most famous villages

Albalonga, Ortega, Perle, and Faberrebe; and reds such as Domina, Regent, Acolon, Zweigelt, and Cabernet Cubin. Roughly a third of the 14,982 acres (6,063ha) of vines in Franken is of top quality and is, therefore, dedicated to classic varieties such as Pinot Noir, Pinot Blanc, Pinot Gris, Silvaner, Traminer, Muskateller, or Riesling. In total, about 80 percent of wines produced in Franken are white and 20 percent red or rosé; 62 percent of the quality wines are dry, 32 percent off-dry, and 6 percent sweet. Yields average between 75hl/ha (2009) and 90hl/ha (2007), with 30–50hl/ha in the very best vineyards.

Silvaner (with 21 percent of the area under vine) is the signature wine of the region, and there are indeed many spectacular Silvaners—full-bodied, ripe, and complex, with great aging potential. In 2008, 350 years after the first Silvaner vines were planted near the village of Castell, I had the chance to join a historic Silvaner tasting, with wines up to 100 years old. Not all of them were noble sweet wines, which can age for decades easily. More impressive was that even dry Kabinett wines can age for up to eight years, whereas Grosses Gewächs wines (or Spätlese *trocken*) from top sites and good vintages can age at least ten years. Last but not least, Silvaner reflects its terroir as well as Riesling or any other grape variety does. You just have to accept that it is a subtle variety and not a relative of Riesling or something similar. It's something quite distinct and unique in the world of fine wine.

There are three *Bereiche* in Franken: Mainviereck (literally, "Main quad"), Maindreieck ("Main triangle"), and Steigerwald. This division is based not only on the course of the Main River but on different soils. These originate in the three epochs of the German Triassic that shaped the *cuestas*, or *côtes*, of the Franconian Schichtstufen landscape around 205 million to 250 million years ago.

The oldest Buntsandstein period formed the red sandstone at the base of Mainviereck, between Homburg and Erlenbach. The soils are sandy and loamy on the top, with more clay deeper down.

Because the climate is more gentle here than in the central part around Würzburg, the vineyards are best suited to red varieties such as Pinot Noir and Pinot Madeleine. Both varieties are able to produce extremely fine and elegant wines from the very best sites of Klingenberg—the very steep and terraced Schlossberg has been cultivated since the 8th century—and Bürgstadt. But Riesling, Silvaner, and Pinot Blanc can also be delicious, with fine, fresh, lightly herbal and fruity flavors and a refined yet racy acidity. In the terraced south-facing part of spectacular Einzellage Homburger Kallmuth, exclusively owned by Fürst Löwenstein and mainly dedicated to Silvaner and Riesling, there is Bundsandstein in the lower part, Muschelkalk in the uncultivated upper part, and a mixture of both in the middle, which makes for very special Silvaners.

Maindreieck—between Schweinfurt, Würzburg, Ochsenfurt, and Gemünden—is the center of viticulture in Franken. It is the driest area of the region, with only 24 in (600mm) of rainfall. Some 70 percent of Franken wines are produced here, on different kinds of Muschelkalk soils that can be quite poor and stony (as in Würzburger Stein) or sandy (as in Frickenhausen) but also quite deep where mixed with loess and clay (as in Escherndorfer Lump). The wines—predominantly whites—have a completely different character from those from Buntsandstein. The aroma is very fruity and smoky, whereas the body is full, the texture rich and supple, the structure complex, the minerality thrilling, and the acidity more gentle and elegant. Silvaner is queen here, but Riesling, Pinot Blanc, Chardonnay, and Traminer can also shine.

Quite far from the Main River, but protected by the mountain range of the Steigerwald, is the third *Bereich*, Steigerwald. It is quite a dry and warm area, because the blacks soils from the Keuper, the youngest of the Triassic period, store the heat during the day and radiate it back to the vines during the night. The wines—mainly whites but also some

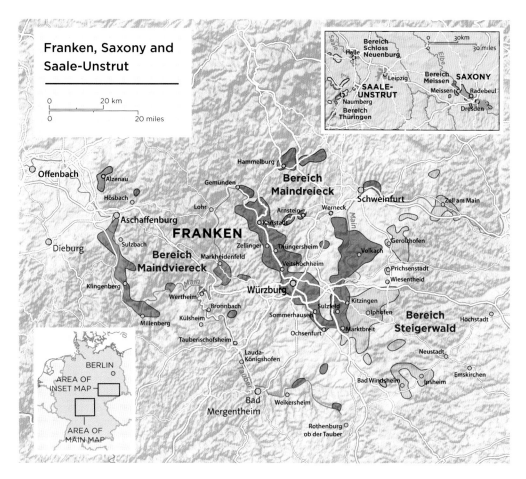

good reds—tend to be reductive (because of the high portion of gypsum in the soils) but are very rich and elegant and have great aging potential. Their bouquets show white rather than yellow fruits, and fascinating herbal aromas as well. Silvaner can be excellent here, as can Riesling, Pinot Gris, Traminer, and Scheurebe. A good Keuper wine combines power with elegance and finesse, whereas a less good one tends to be quite alcoholic.

Between Grosswallstadt and Alzenau, in the far western part of Franken, the soil has a crystalline bedrock, with gneiss, mica schist, and quartzite—ideal for bringing out the elegance and finesse, as well as the piquant but refined fruit flavors, of Riesling.

All in all, one has to say that Franken produces not only excellent Silvaners (especially on shale limestone and Keuper) but also great dry Rieslings and Pinots, especially Pinot Noirs, which can be among the finest in all of Germany. But it is also worth discovering Traminer, Muskateller, Scheurebe, and Rieslaner, which can perform very well as either dry or noble sweet wines.

Weingut Rudolf Fürst

Paul Fürst became responsible for the family business in Bürgstadt after the early death of his father, Rudolf, in 1975. It was a mixed agriculture then, with only 3.7 acres (1.5ha) of vines. But Fürst, still only 20 but trained at Schloss Johannisberg in the Rheingau, decided to focus only on wine and started buying parcels in Centgrafenberg, which has always been planted mainly with Pinot Noir and Riesling. The parcels are handkerchief-sized due to *Realteilung*, the process of buying, swapping, and tweaking the boundaries, in which he has been engaged for more than three decades. Now with 44 acres (18ha), the project is still not finished even today. In 2004, Paul and his wife Monika bought another 3.7 acres in the spectacularly steep and terraced Klingenberger Schlossberg, farther up the Main River, whose Spätburgunders were famous right through to the 19th century.

The Fürst Pinots, already excellent for 15 years, have become even more elegant, being both finer and purer. In all Germany, there are not many that can compete on quality or style

Since 2007, son Sebastian (born in 1980) has also been involved in the family business. He served part of his apprenticeship at Domaine Marc Kreydenweiss in Alsace and learned a lot about Pinot Noir and the finest wines of Burgundy from his friend Olivier Leriche at Domaine de l'Arlot in Nuits-St-George, where Sebastian worked for six months. Since the 2008 vintage, the young father has been responsible for the family's red-wine production, while young grandpa Paul has focused on the white wines. They discuss all the key decisions together, however, and Paul is very happy that his son "has always shown much more interest in meticulous artisanal wine production than in exaggerated modern winemaking and marketing."

With Sebastian vinifying the reds, the Fürst Pinots, which had already been excellent for 15 years or so, have become even more elegant, being both finer and purer. From the 2009 vintage, the Fürsts have presented their finest Pinots ever, with three world-class Grosses Gewächs leading an impressive range: Schlossberg Spätburgunder GG, Centgrafenberg Spätburgunder GG, and Centgrafenberg Hunsrück Spätburgunder GG. As fine as the other wines of the estate are—not only the Centgrafenberg Riesling GG, the barrel-fermented Centgrafenberg Weissburgunder R, and the Volkacher Karthäuser Chardonnay, but also the other Klingenberger and Bürgstadter Pinots—I have to focus here on the three Pinot grands crus. In all of Germany, there are not many Pinots that can compete on quality or style. Last but not least, I should stress that even their Frühburgunder (Pinot Madeleine) is worth at least ten years of bottle age.

Along with all the other Fürst wines, the Spätburgunders are grown in red Buntsandstein, the oldest soils of the Lower German Triassic. The topsoils are loamy, sandy, and well structured, with little stones. This warm and well-draining soil has been ideally suited to the capricious red variety that is Pinot Noir for hundreds of years. The lower layers of clay and decomposed sandstone have a good capacity to store water, so that even in extremely dry and hot vintages such as 2003, there are no problems with drought, at least for older vines.

The climate in the Miltenberg basin, between the Spessart and Odenwald mountain ranges, is mild, though the Schlossberg Pinots in Klingenberg ripen some ten days earlier than those in Centgrafenberg in Bürgstadt. This is mainly because of the 2.5 miles (4km) of dry red sandstone walls per hectare that have, for centuries, terraced the steep Schlossberg vineyard, also reflecting light and warmth to the grapes and vines.

Right: Paul Fürst and his son Sebastian against a wall of the red sandstone whose soils contribute so much to their wines

The Fürsts bought two different parcels in Schlossberg and, in 2005, replanted two-thirds of the area with new Burgundian Pinot clones, whereas the older vines—presumably Freiburg clones—were planted in 1985. Both new clones—Fin and Très Fin—are grafted on rootstock 16149 and yield much less than clones such as 777, 828, 667, 115, or 112, Paul reports. "The maximum is 30hl/ha," whereas the older clones, which the Fürsts started to plant in Centgrafenberg in the early 1990s, can easily yield 80hl/ha if the crop is not reduced. "The Fin and Très Fin Pinots are smaller, as are the berries, which are looser as well and have thicker skins," says Paul.

The planting density in the south-facing Schlossberg is quite high, at 10,000 vines/ha. (It is 5,000–7,500 vines/ha in Centgrafenberg.) All the Schlossberg vines are single-cane pruned 20in (50cm) from the ground (*Flachbogen*), with six to eight buds per cane during the ripening period. (In Centgrafenberg, it is 20in for the Dijon clones and 28in [70cm] for the German clones.) Intense canopy management is practiced throughout the vegetative period on both sites, but shoots are trimmed as late as possible.

Green harvesting is not necessary in Schlossberg, but it is in Centgrafenberg, with its slightly deeper loam and clay soils and higher-yielding clones. In some years, as much as half the fruit has been dropped. This proportion will gradually reduce, though—partly because since 2005, new plantings in the 7.5-acre (3ha) Hunsrück parcel have been with Fin and Très Fin (1.2 acres [0.5ha] so far), and partly because the German clones (mainly the small-berry Ritter 21-90, planted in 1983) are lower-yielding as the vines age.

The Fürsts plow their soil and produce their own compost over a three-year period. Every second row of the vineyard has a cover crop but is mulched several times to protect the soil from

Left: The steep Schlossberg grand cru, where the sandstone terraces help ripen the wines by reflecting heat and light

evaporation and erosion. Depending on the weather conditions, the other row is also allowed to become green toward fall but is mowed if the plants (clover, rapeseed, vetches) get too close to the grapes.

Paul and Sebastian believe that Pinot has to suffer a little bit to give its best and should not be overnourished. Thus, they like the leaves to be lime green rather than dark green in summer, and they prefer them to turn color early in fall. "We get more distinguished and sophisticated wines, with more finesse and purity and less fat, if the vines are given fewer nutrients," Paul explains.

Aiming for healthy and fully ripe, but also firm and freshly structured, berries, and the finest Pinot flavors, the Fürsts never completely deleaf. "We always keep a small canopy to protect the grapes from too intense sunlight, whereas air circulation

Sebastian wants to keep the seeds in the berries as long as possible, preferring the tannins of the stems to those of the seeds. The grands crus are made with a high proportion of whole bunches

is still possible," says Paul, who prefers to pick the Pinot with 93–100° Oechsle. "We definitely tend more toward 95° than 102° Oechsle," adds Sebastian. To get the wines to 13% ABV, the Fürsts have had to chaptalize their musts "three or four times over the past ten years."

The harvest is done manually and selectively. If necessary, the grapes are selected again on a sorting table but are not crushed. Sebastian wants to keep the seeds in the berries as long as possible, preferring the tannins of the stems to those of the seeds. Thus, the three crus, Schlossberg, Centgrafenberg, and Hunsrück, are always made with a high proportion of whole bunches, the rest being very gently destemmed. "The warmer the year and the older the vines, the riper the stems and the more whole berries we use," Sebastian explains. In hot years such as 2003, the portion of stems retained in the Hunsrück was 100 percent; in 2009, at least 90 percent. In normal years, Hunsrück is made with 70–80 percent of stems, Schlossberg with 50–60 percent, and Centgrafenberg with 30–40 percent. "We use the stems not to have more tannins but to have finer tannins," Sebastian says.

The firm, spicy, darkly fruity Hunsrück is from the oldest vines (mostly German clones planted in 1983) and the ripest stems, whereas the fine and elegant Centgrafenberg comes mostly from younger French vines and has a more red-fruit character. In Schlossberg, only the stems of the older German vines are used, whereas the Fin Pinots are destemmed.

I am always amazed by how well the Fürst wines—whether red or white—age, becoming even finer, rounder, and more generous over the years

After a cold maceration of five to seven days in open wooden vats (with the whole bunches on the bottom and the destemmed grapes on top, but only a little bit of carbon dioxide), fermentation starts inside the grapes, using the grape's own enzymes, and then, thanks to warming of the vats overnight, proceeds normally using the yeasts from the skins of the grapes. As soon as the fermentation starts (with temperatures up to 95°F [35°C]), *pigeage* and *remontage* are performed. Fermentation finishes nearly completely after five to seven days, but the young wine is not pressed until shortly before the cap sinks, after another four to six days. Then the vat is drained, the juice separated, the skins basket pressed, and the seeds and yeasts thrown away. Finally, the press juice is added to the free-run juice and settled for 12–24 hours in stainless-steel tanks, before the wine is racked into 100 percent new French barriques (from François Frères, Rousseau, Seguin Moreau, and Damy) for 17–18 months. Malolactic fermentation is preferable in spring but also possible in winter.

Because the wines should be bottled without clarification or filtration (most barrels do not need either), they are racked very carefully through the bungholes rather than the tap holes, so that only about 8 fl oz (25cl) remain with the lees. This part is clarified and blended with the other red wines, which have been produced like the crus, though the grapes have been destemmed completely and the wines mature in barrel (partly new or used, depending on quality) for a shorter period. All of the red wines are bottled unfiltered.

The whites are vinified in a fairly reductive style, the better to preserve their fresh fruit, as well as their acidity and minerality, over several years. Whenever I am at this beautiful estate (the cellar has been completely rebuilt recently), the family offers mature whites and reds from their treasury for dinner. I am always amazed by how well the Fürst wines—whether red or white—age, becoming even finer, rounder, and more generous over the years. But the Fürsts never use a decanter, even for their younger wines. "We prefer to open the bottle and drink the wine promptly. It has to be present from the first moment on," Paul insists. "But it develops in the glass if you don't pour too little..."

FINEST WINES

2009 Schlossberg Spätburgunder GG★ [V]
Fermented with at least 60% of the stems, this fragrant, alluring Pinot Noir from the Klingenberg Buntsandstein terraces is lavish, succulent, and sweet but also very elegant and silken in its texture. The tannin is ripe, mellow, and refined, as is the whole structure of this beautifully balanced feminine Pinot, produced both from older German clones and younger Burgundian clones such as Fin and Très Fin. If you did not know that this persistent, red-berry-redolent, very vibrant Pinot was from Klingenberg, you would imagine it to be a top-flight Volnay or Vosne-Romanée.

2009 Centgrafenberg Spätburgunder GG★

This Pinot is from predominantly traditional Dijon clones planted in the early 1990s. It is picked at least ten days later than the warmer Schlossberg. Fermented with 30% or more of the stems, it is deep and striking on the nose, displaying refined but red-berry aromas. On the palate, it is fresh and firm but also elegant, silky, and succulent, showing plenty of finesse, as well as a ripe yet meaty and spicy tannin structure.

2009 Hunsrück Spätburgunder GG★

The Hunsrück Pinot is from a parcel on the south-facing Centgrafenberg hillside, separately vinified from 2003 onward. Here, the Fürsts cultivate their oldest vines: German Ritter clones that were planted in 1983 and ripen a few days earlier than the neighboring Centgrafenberg parcel. Because there is always good ripeness of the stems, this distinctive grand cru is fermented with up to 100% of the stems (90% in 2009). The Hunsrück is the most powerful and structured wine of the trio. This 2009 is already very deep and spicy on the nose, showing more dark than red fruits. On the palate, it is intriguing: fresh, very firm, and very vibrant, if still a little astringent at this early stage. But there is a silky texture, too, and the potential for it to soften gracefully over 10–15 years or more. If the Schlossberg might remind you of Volnay, this might make you think of Pommard. But beware: it's completely different from either.

Centgrafenberg Frühburgunder R★

Frühburgunder (Pinot Madeleine) is a very rare, earlier-ripening kind of Pinot Noir that may originate from the area around Bürgstadt, where it has been cultivated for a very long time. Paul Fürst was one of the pioneers of this variety, which resembles Pinot Noir as both vine and wine but is more fruity and upfront. "The art of making Frühburgunder is to avoid a jammy wine with too much gloss and opulence, and instead to reflect its terroir," says Paul. The 2009★ is deep, dark, fresh, and wild on the nose, then very intense, powerful, and succulent on the palate. The tannin is fine and as mellow as it is meaty, the acidity refreshing and refined, and the cassis aromas lingering. The 2001★ demonstrates how well Frühburgunder can age. Very elegant on the nose, displaying the finest, freshest dark-fruit aromas like cassis; it shows a silky elegance and finesse on the palate. The texture is supple and sweet, but the wine is still mineral and vibrant.

Above: Perfectly healthy bunches of ripe Pinot Noir, carefully hand-harvested into small cases to protect the fragile skins

Weingut Rudolf Fürst
Area under vine: 48 acres (19.6ha)
Important varieties: 60% Pinot Noir/ Frühburgunder, 15% Riesling, 12.5% Pinot Blanc/Chardonnay, 5% Silvaner
Average production: 120,000 bottles
Best vineyards: *Klingenberg* Schlossberg; *Bürgstadt* Centgrafenberg, Centgrafenberg Hunsrück; *Volkach* Karthäuser
Hohenlindenweg 46,
63927 Bürgstadt am Main
Tel: +49 9371 8642
www.weingut-rudolf-fuerst.de

Weingut Horst Sauer

Horst Sauer is probably the best-known Franconian producer outside Germany. He has won numerous prestigious awards, especially in the UK, and has lived "a life between gumboots and patent-leather shoes," as he puts it. While in Germany Franken is mostly associated with dry wines, Horst Sauer has built his international reputation mainly on noble sweet wines from Escherndorfer Lump, one of the best sites in Franken. In fact, there is no other producer with Sauer's consistency in the noble-wine category. It's equally remarkable that Sauer won all his trophies not only with Riesling but also with Silvaner. No other Silvaner producer in the world of fine wine can match his success.

And yet if you go to Escherndorf and enter the modern, renovated family estate at 14 Bocksbeutel Street, you don't meet a self-important producer. Horst Sauer is a quiet man, contemplative and reflective, a poet and a philosopher. Despite his success, he still feels as though his "life is a dream" and is afraid of waking up from it one day.

Indeed, nearly every year (apart from dry and warm 2003 or 2009), there are times when Sauer wishes he were a wine producer somewhere far away from Franken. The summer and fall of 2010 was one such time: "We had so much rain. Our soils soaked up the water like a sponge, and the grapes got bigger and bigger. We feared they would burst; we feared the flies and botrytis. But in the end, after a nice period between the end of September and the end of October, all our berries were extremely concentrated, and at the beginning of November we picked the most beautiful botrytized berries I have ever seen."

So, finally, Sauer's dream went on, with no rude awakening—though the 2010 vintage was not one for noninterventionist winemakers, in either the vineyards or the cellar. "If you want to produce

Right: Horst Sauer and his daughter Sandra at their modern winery in Escherndorf, source of multi-award-winning wines

world-class wines, you have to have a plan," says Sauer. "But you also have to adapt it to the vintage, especially in Lump, which does not allow you to work schematically."

In 2010, flowering was very late, and July and August were cool and wet. Hence, leaf-plucking in the grape zone was necessary before harvest in order to ensure healthy grapes. But because the concave, steep Lump vineyard (with a gradient as sharp as 75 percent, and 60 percent on average) catches every ray of sun, this should never be done too early: "Otherwise we risk sunburn, or the wine has a smoky aroma, which we don't like," Sauer explains.

Since 2007, when Sandra became responsible for the grands crus, the style has become even finer. The wines have become less overtly powerful and voluptuous

Even so, in 2010, acidity levels were very high and alcohol levels 1% lower than in 2009. Sauer—supported since 2004 by his daughter Sandra, born in 1977—abandoned the option of chemical correction to the acidity levels and decided instead to block the malolactic fermentation of half of the wine before blending it with the other half. "It was very important to get the pH levels, the SO_2 levels, and the temperature levels into the right balance—otherwise things would have gone wrong," Sauer says.

Horst Sauer found his personal style of wine in the 1990s. The 1997 Rieslings and Silvaners from the Lump vineyard were—indeed, still are!—powerful, rich, and succulent, with concentrated tropical-fruit flavors and a supple texture, as well as a mineral and salty structure. They are impressive expressions of the unique Lump terroir. And Sauer's wines—especially the Grosses Gewächs wines—have been in this same style ever since.

Sandra became responsible for the grands crus in 2007, and this style has become even finer since then. The wines have become less overtly powerful, tropical, and voluptuous, but more reductive, elegant, and precise—and thanks to the even more marked acidity, really appetizing.

"The Lump vineyard can give you too much of everything, and the wines can lack grace, lightness, and vibrancy," states Sauer. Indeed, the sunlight in this homogeneous, steep, and warm 81.5-acre (33ha) VDP Grosse Lage close to the Main River, which turns from southeast to southwest, is very intense. In addition, the soil—shell limestone, Lettenkeuper, loess silt—is rich and retains warmth during the night. In some parts, the soil is only 20in (50cm) deep; in others, up to 60in (1.5m).

"After more than 20 years of experience, we know in which parts of the vineyard we have to produce which styles of wine," Sauer says. Down close to the river are the best spots for the noble sweet wines, because the higher humidity levels and mist in fall help promote botrytis. In the hot and steep center of the south-facing slope, where the rocks are covered by soil only 20in (50cm) deep, the Grosses Gewächs wines of Riesling and Silvaner are produced, while in the southeast- and southwest-facing parts, the grapes for the dry Kabinett wines are harvested.

"Until the beginning of this decade, we picked according to the grape variety: Müller and Bacchus first, then Silvaner and Pinot, and finally Riesling. Today, we pick according to wine style." This ranges from light and fresh Kabinett wines, through piquant but succulent Spätlese wines, to the higher Prädikate and all the way up to TBA, plus the two Grosse Gewächse. "Each wine type needs its own exact picking dates," says Sauer. He now picks eight to 14 days earlier than he did ten or 15 years ago. Thus, alcohol levels have come down, today ranging from 11–12% ABV for the Kabinett wines, up to 12.5–13.5% ABV for the Grosse Gewächse.

Leaf-plucking is much less rigorous than it was in the 1990s, and the older high-density plantings (5,000–6,000 vines/ha) of the Grosse Lage parcels cause more shadow than do newer plantations. If the season is not extremely wet, there are no green rows in Sauer's parcels. Instead, bark mulch protects against erosion and evaporation.

The harvest is highly selective and done by hand only. The Grosse Lage are picked three times in years like 2010 but only once in perfect years like 2009. Botrytis is not accepted at all for the Kabinett wines, and the Grosses Gewächs wines are nearly botrytis-free, if possible. Apart from the Pinot Blanc and the Silvaner for Sehnsucht (literally, "Desire"), the grapes are not destemmed, and skin contact (up to 12 hours) is done only with healthy grapes (but never with Riesling).

The musts ferment in stainless-steel tanks with cultured yeasts at temperatures of 54–57°F (12–14°C) for the basic wines, 61°F (16°C) for the Kabinetts, and 64°F (18°C) for the Grosses Gewächs wines, for between four and six weeks, and are then cooled down to 43–46°F (6–8°C) in order to avoid an early addition of SO_2. The Grosses Gewächs wines are on the first lees as long as possible (in 2009, through to July 2010), Kabinett wines until December/January. Some 40–50 percent of the Weissburgunder and the Sehnsucht are fermented in barrels (including the malolactic fermentation) and finally blended with the rest from tank. All the wines are on their fine lees until shortly before bottling.

FINEST WINES

Escherndorfer Lump Silvaner GG (planted in 1958)
2010★ Concentrated grape aromas on the nose; piquant. Salty and vibrant, as well as voluptuous on the palate. Firmly structured, with pronounced acidity balancing the rich, ripe fruit. Great concentration, great potential.
2005★ The dry and hot vintage, with rain in September, produced many powerful wines, but few as great as this. Succulent and supple, with

great concentration, but balanced by a pronounced acidity and its mineral structure; very persistent and appetizing. Intense fruit aromas again on the finish, which is also appetizingly salty.

Escherndorfer Lump Riesling GG (planted in 1972)
2010★ Complex, concentrated, and herbaceous on the nose. Very pure and salty, yet concentrated and intense, and elegant despite the steely acidity.
2005★ Golden yellow. Leafy aromas, as well as honey on the nose. Elegant on the palate, with fine acidity, a touch of spearmint, and a salty finish.

2010 Escherndorfer Lump Silvaner Auslese★
The 2009 Auslese (with no botrytis at all) was already delicious—succulent yet pure and precise. But the 2010 (with botrytis and 10g/l TA) is breathtaking. Very pure and almost salty on the nose, it is not only sweet and concentrated on the palate but also extremely pure, racy, and salty. Yes, it's sweet, but it's even more piquant.

2010 Escherndorfer Lump Silvaner BA★
Golden yellow color. Very fine botrytis and raisin aromas, but also grapefruit. Perfect concentration, piquant and spicy, the noble sweetness balanced by extremely fine acidity. Very precise. Beautiful BA.

2010 Escherndorfer Lump Silvaner TBA★
Again, the 2009 TBA seemed almost perfect in its accomplished ripeness and sexiness. The nose of this 2010 is spicy rather than fruity, and the attack is almost Riesling-like because of the piquant acidity (16g/l TA). Very noble and rich on the palate; perfectly balanced, frisky, and spicy.

2010 Escherndorfer Lump Riesling TBA★
Perfect botrytis aromas that you can't imagine any better or finer. Very piquant, rich, and sweet, like an essence (200° Oechsle, 18g/l TA), precise and salty, with grapefruit on the very long finish.

Weingut Horst Sauer
Area under vine: 42 acres (17ha);
45% Silvaner, 25% Müller-Thurgau, 15% Riesling;
95% dry, 5% noble sweet
Average production: 170,000 bottles
Best vineyard: *Escherndorf* Lump
Bocksbeutel Strasse 14, 97332 Escherndorf
Tel: +49 9381 4364
www.weingut-horst-sauer.de

Zehnthof Luckert

Whenever you look for an authentic *Frankenwein*, you should check out the offerings of brothers Wolfgang and Ulrich ("Uli") Luckert (born in 1961 and 1973 respectively) from the Zehnthof in Sulzfeld am Main. Their wines—mainly white, but there are also some rare and impressive reds—are deep, ripe, rich, and elegant, as well as fresh, mineral, and *fränkisch trocken*, normally containing less than 4g RS per liter. "Franken wines don't need residual sugar to be balanced, thanks to their body and extract," says Uli Luckert.

And Franken wines don't need the *Bocksbeutel* to be authentic. The Luckert brothers prefer the Burgundian bottle shape for the finest wines. Only the Kabinett wines go into the curious bottle of which the Franconians are so proud.

Whenever you look for an authentic Frankenwein, you should check out the offerings of Wolfgang and Ulrich Luckert. Their wines are deep, ripe, rich, and elegant

The earthy, mineral flavor of the Zehnthof wines is typical of the shale limestone soils in this part of the Main Valley. The Luckerts work hard in the vineyards to produce impressive terroir wines. The only barrier to an even higher reputation has been the fact that their Sulzfeld vineyard sites— Cyriakusberg (250 acres [100ha]) and Maustal (150 acres [60ha]), both dominated by co-op grape growers—are far less famous than, say, Würzburger Stein.

On their 40 acres (16ha) of vineyards the Luckerts cultivate an impressive range of varieties: Silvaner (50 percent, including the rare blue-skinned Blauer Silvaner) dominates, but there are also Pinot Blanc and Chardonnay, Riesling and Müller-Thurgau, Gelber Muskateller and Muscat-

Silvaner (Sauvignon Blanc) for whites, and Pinot Noir, Cabernet Sauvignon, Merlot, Frühburgunder (Pinot Madeleine), and Blauer Portugieser for reds. The vines are between 20 and more than 50 years old. In 2004, the Luckerts started to work parts of their vineyards organically, and since 2009 all of their holdings have been certified.

"Our wines should transfer the concentrated and spicy taste of our grapes. Therefore, we don't manipulate the vinification but work a lot in our vineyards in order to produce the best possible grapes: healthy, ripe, and intense," Uli explains.

To him, Silvaner is the most spectacular grape variety: "Although Silvaner does not have an intense aroma or even a special aromatic profile, it expresses its special origin like no other variety."

And sure enough, each of the five Luckert Silvaners displays a distinct character. The explanation can be found in the different soils. In Sulzfeld, the vines are planted on the transition from shale limestone (from the Upper Muschelkalk age) to Keuper (Late Triassic). Whereas the Maustal is dominated by Muschelkalk and delivers complex, deep, smoky, and structured wines, the upper part of the Cyriakusberg has layers of Lettenkeuper 10–23ft (3–7m) thick on top of the limestone; this has an impact on the wines, making them more elegant and sophisticated.

The high quality of the Luckert wines is based on their work in the vineyard. Canopy management (shoot-thinning, leaf removal, summer pruning) is important. In every second row, green manures are used to improve the soil structure and limit vine vigor, whereas in the other rows, straw protects against evaporation.

More unusual for German wine producers is the cordon training of the vines (the spur-pruned system used, for example, in Champagne). "With the cordon, we restrict our yields from the very

Right: Brothers Wolfgang and Ulrich Luckert (*middle* and *right*) with Wolfgang's son Philipp and their wide range of barrels

beginning and harvest smaller grapes with smaller berries and more intense flavors," says Uli—hence, green-harvesting is not necessary. Two to three weeks before harvest, the grapes are exposed completely to the sun. Harvest (with up to four selective pickings also for the whites) starts with Müller-Thurgau in late September and lasts until early November with Riesling.

The grapes are not destemmed and are pressed directly. Sauvignon Blanc, Gelber Muskateller, Silvaner, and Riesling are left on the skins for eight to 15 hours. The musts are transferred into barrels of different sizes (400–5,000 liters, mainly Spessart oak). Fermentation starts spontaneously

For less than €10, the Alte Reben Kabinett is a spectacular Silvaner from Cyriakusberg vines that were planted in 1961: deep, ripe, quite powerful, and complex

and lasts until the end of February or March. The wines are kept on their lees until one month before bottling. *Bâtonnage* is performed for three to four weeks after fermentation has stopped. A week or two later, they are filtered (with *kieselguhr*), and they are bottled a week later. In years like 2010 and 2008, the whites are allowed to go through malolactic fermentation.

FINEST WINES

Silvaner Kabinett Alte Reben [V]
For less than €10, this is a spectacular Silvaner from Cyriakusberg vines that were planted in 1961: deep, ripe, quite powerful, and complex. The **2010** is as intense and succulent as it is pure and salty, and the excellent concentration is firmly structured. The **2009** is very rich and succulent, yet precise, piquant, and mineral. It shows smoky aromas, as well as generous fruit aromas, and with a little bit more residual sugar than usual (5.2g/l), it's quite voluptuous.

Silvaner Gelbkalk
Officially from the Cyriakusberg, the more-than-40-year-old vines root in yellow banks of limestone that mark the border between the Keuper and the Muschelkalk soils. The Luckerts bought this parcel in 2008 and discovered the completely different taste of both the grapes and the resulting wine, which is quite unlike all the others from Sulzfeld: subtle and piquant, full of finesse, salinity, and lingering minerality. The first vintage, **2008**, is delicate and refined on the palate, with intense fruit flavors on the finish, lingering minerality, and a salty aftertaste. The **2009★** is more rich and intense but also smoky, racy, and very mineral; the wine seems to dance over the palate. The **2010** is also very noble and elegant, supple thanks to full malolactic fermentation, but also firm, racy, and salty.

Silvaner ★★★
This top Silvaner grows in the steepest part of the Maustal and is selected from the oldest vines, which were planted in 1962. They provide smaller, succulent berries with very intense flavors. The wine is deep, powerful, rich, and supple, with impressive concentration and a complex structure that needs three or more years to develop. The **2009★** displays almost tropical-fruit flavors, with the finest herbal aromas and a slightly smoky-stony touch. The round and creamy texture is balanced by the delicate play of acidity and an elegant, lingering minerality. Very salty and intense finish. The **2008** is less rich but pure, very delicate, and elegant, and full of finesse. The **2007** is deep, complex, and dense on both nose and palate. Powerful, rich, and supple, this is the vintage for those who prize texture. The **2004★** (still under cork rather than screwcap) is as rich as 2007 but has more acidity and more drive. It's very salty, structured, and vibrant—a really great Silvaner that is only just ready to drink.

Zehnthof Luckert
Area under vine: 40 acres (16ha)
Most important grape varieties: Silvaner, Riesling, Pinot Blanc
Average production: 100,000–120,000 bottles
Kettengasse 3–5, 97320 Sulzfeld a. Main
Tel: +49 932 123 778
www.weingut-zehnthof.de

Weingut Weltner

Paul Weltner, born in 1975 and located in Rödelsee in the Steigerwald area, has produced serious, complex, and elegant wines with great aging potential since he first started out. He took over the winemaker's job from his father Wolfgang in the tricky 2000 vintage, and those first wines still taste pretty good today.

On his 20 acres (8ha), Weltner focuses on Silvaner (60 percent) and Riesling (10 percent) but also cultivates Müller-Thurgau, Scheurebe, Sauvignon Blanc, Pinot Blanc, and Pinot Noir. The vines root in Keuper soils from the Late Triassic. In Rödelsee and Iphofen, these soils have a high gypsum content, so the wines tend to be naturally reductive. Paul underlines this character, offering dynamic and wild but precise, subtle, and long-lived wines, full of minerality and tension.

"We have top sites here, with very interesting and complex soils full of minerals. To reflect this in my wines, I have to work very precisely," Paul says. "I don't want to have overripe grapes, and I don't like the exotic style of wine that can be produced everywhere. I prefer reductive wines that need a couple of years to open up and that are marked by their freshness, lightness, and mineral depth."

Weltner's best wines are produced in Rödelseer Küchenmeister and Iphöfer Julius-Echter-Berg (JEB), both classified as VDP Grosse Lage. Because there are at least three other top producers in the south-facing JEB (Juliusspital, Ruck, and Wirsching), Paul decided to concentrate more on Küchenmeister, where he holds 11 acres (4.6ha) of vines. The southwest-facing foothill of Schwanberg rises from 820 to 1,120ft (250 to 340m) and is protected from cool winds from the east, as well as the north. "Hang-time is a week longer here than in JEB, perhaps resulting in even more sophisticated wines, with herbaceous flavors and a pronounced acidity," Paul says. His Riesling Kabinett wines from the Küchenmeister are best after five or more years, while the Silvaners—whether the lighter Kabinett

Above: The colors of the artisanal sign at the family winery reflect the cool and mineral style of the wines themselves

or the more complex Grosses Gewächs—are excellent after six or more years.

Weltner harvests late but not too late, because he aims for dry wines that are not too high in alcohol and communicate their terroir rather than the character of ripe or slightly overripe berries. For him, 13% ABV should be the maximum, and in 2010 his wines performed extremely well with 12–12.5% ABV, as well as very low levels of residual

sugar. Botrytis is completely excluded every year, and skin contact is normally two to eight hours, depending on the vintage and variety. Fermentation is mostly natural and takes place in stainless-steel tanks at temperatures of 64–68°F (18–20°C) for a period of three weeks. In some years, the late-picked Riesling needs another two weeks, but then stops with a higher level of residual sugar, which is fine (6.4–11.4g/l RS over the past decade, whereas Silvaner ranged from 1.8 to 4.6g/l RS).

Paul Weltner's Sylvaners are unique and provide a new and self-confident Franconian style that is far from Riesling. They are less fruity and opulent than most Silvaners

Paul Weltner's Sylvaners (since 2005, he has used the old-fashioned Sylvaner spelling in order to accentuate the Franconian Sylvaner tradition) are unique and provide a new and self-confident Franconian style that is far from Riesling but even farther from those fruit-bombs that emerged in the late 1990s and are still successful. They are less fruity and opulent than most Silvaners. Instead, they are pure, earthy, spicy, herbaceous, and piquant, built on deep mineral foundations and structured by the elegant acidity and lingering, salty finish.

FINEST WINES

In August 2011, Paul set up a vertical tasting for me, covering his first ten years: it was impressive. Outside the Rheingau, I have very rarely tasted dry Kabinett wines that can age so well. And yes, Weltner's Kabinetts, whether JEB or Küchenmeister, reflect their terroirs very well, while the Grosses Gewächs—always made from the best grapes of the oldest vines with the lowest yields in the best parcels—could be regarded as a reserve version.

Left: Paul Weltner, wise beyond his years, and the originator of a unique style of Franken Silvaner, both mineral and spicy

Iphöfer Julius-Echter-Berg Sylvaner Kabinett trocken [V]
2010★ Ripe and concentrated fruit aromas, very clear and spicy. Succulent, supple, and mineral on the palate, with more fruit intensity than the Küchenmeister. If you want to become a Küchenmeister, you should crest the Echter-Berg first.
2004★ Brilliant and fresh on the nose, earthy and floral, with subtle but quite intense fruit aromas. Light-footed, clear, and elegant on the palate, very salty and appetizing; minerally structured and very long.

Küchenmeister Sylvaner GG
2010★ Very pure, elegant, and complex, with herbal and floral aromas and earthy but delicate fruit flavors. Salty minerality. Good acidity, very nice balance, and persistence. Great potential.
2009 More rich and more tropical than earthy, but also complex and concentrated. The mineral character still shines through. Powerful and long on the palate, again appetizingly salty and elegant. Great potential.
2008 Still closed and nutty, but elegant and herbaceous. Light-bodied but with good length. Still evolving, but worth the wait.
2007 Very intense fruit aromas, mirrored on the palate, which is also elegant, piquant, and mineral. Very attractive at four years old.
2004★ This is a great Sylvaner. Rich on the nose, as on the palate, but very pure, subtle, and salty at the same time—all advanced by a very sophisticated acidity. Still many years to go.
2001★ Nice, evolved maturity. Herbal aromas and flavors. A very delicate sweetness, balsamic and mineral, with a firm but elegant structure and fine straightforward tannins. A classic.
2000 An herbal nose and palate. Concentrated and still vivid, with nice acidity. Delicious with food.

Weingut Weltner
Area under vine: 20 acres (8ha) (60% Silvaner)
Average production: 56,000 bottles
Best vineyards: *Rödelsee* Küchenmeister; *Iphofen* Julius-Echter-Berg
Wiesenbronner Strasse 17,
97348 Rödelsee
Tel: +49 9323 3646
www.weingut-weltner.de

Bürgerspital z. Hl. Geist Würzburg

The Bürgerspital is a charitable trust that houses needy people, founded as early as 1316. Every bottle that its wine estate sells helps promotes the trust, which is deeply linked with the cultural and economic life of Würzburg.

Weingut Bürgerspital is one of the biggest wine estates in Germany and the biggest Riesling producer in Franken. It owns 272 acres (110ha), of which 250 acres (100ha) are currently cultivated, in some of the very best sites in Franken. Würzburger Stein, where the Bürgerspital owns 69 acres (28ha, including the Stein-Harfe), is the most prestigious Lage, but the other Würzburg sites—Innere Leiste, Pfaffenberg, and Abtsleite—are also first-class. Less famous, but no less outstanding in quality terms, are sites in Randersacker, where the Bürgerspital produces some impressive dry Rieslings, especially from Teufelskeller, Pfülben, and Marsberg.

Most of the vineyards are located on the banks of the Main River and face southeast, south, or southwest. And they are steep. Whereas the impressive, large Würzburger Stein (203 acres [82ha]) rises up to 60 percent, the Randersacker Teufelskeller rises up to 100 percent. The vines always root in Muschelkalk soils that can be quite stony but are deeper in the lower parts. Riesling is planted in the hottest spots with the poorest soils, while Silvaner prefers the deeper, more clay soils.

Despite all this potential, the Bürgerspital did not perform as a top producer for many years. But since 2007, when Robert Haller (the former longtime managing director and winemaker of Weingut Fürst Löwenstein) took over, the supertanker has been back on course and making good progress.

For many years, Haller has championed a dry, elegant, reductive style of wine that is driven more by terroir and longevity than upfront fruit character. Haller aims for healthy ripe grapes but not the lowest yields. They are around 50hl/ha in the VDP Grosse Lage sites and average 65–70hl/ha overall. Since the past decade has brought more rain than usual, especially in August and September, Haller has decided to exercise two different viticulture strategies in the parcels dedicated to his finest wines. In one part, he green-harvests in July, to reduce yields to 50hl/ha. But as the grapes ripen more quickly, the condition of the Silvaner in particular is threatened by rain, rot, and botrytis in late summer and early fall (as in 2000 and 2006). "But if I am forced to harvest too early, even the best grapes don't have Grosses Gewächs quality," Haller explains. Therefore, in the other part of his top vineyards, he keeps yields to 60–70hl/ha until the beginning of fall. Then he harvests the greenish-yellow grapes for the Kabinett in a first pass; the more yellow ones for the Spätlese in a second pass; and the remaining grapes up to three weeks later.

In the hot south-facing Hagemann parcel of Stein (2.5 acres [1ha]), the 7,500 Riesling vines planted in 1967 don't yield more than 25–30hl/ha. "Reducing yields is much more important with Silvaner, because the variety is so vigorous and there are no better clones. So, it's not easy to produce a rich and complex Silvaner if you don't have top vineyard sites and old vines," Haller admits.

His best Silvaner vineyard is the 5-acre (2ha) Lindlein parcel, planted in the mid-1980s, from which the Grosses Gewächs is produced. It is in the south-facing, concave, eastern part of the Stein, which rises gently from right behind the city of Würzburg. The climate is conducive here, but Haller discovered that the vertical shoot positioning of the vines did not bring the grapes to full physiological ripeness every year. So he has retrained 1.85 acres (0.75ha) with a trellising system. "I can manage the canopy more accurately now and keep the grapes healthy for a longer time. Last but not least, they become really ripe," Haller says. In the near future, he will extend the new trellising system to the remaining part of the vineyard.

The *Prädikatswein* and Grosses Gewächs wines are handpicked, while the high-volume wines are

Above: A stained-glass window, including Franken's famous ram symbol, reflects the Bürgerspital's medieval origins

Franken's most famous vineyard. The Grosses Gewächs wines, however, are deeper and finer, with the potential to age for ten or more years.

FINEST WINES

Würzburger Stein Hagemann Riesling GG

2010★ Perhaps the best vintage so far, but a tiny production of 900 bottles, because only the seedless virgin fruits with 96–98° Oechsle were selected for this cru. The grapes were destemmed and macerated for about 18 hours because of the high acidity levels. The resulting must fermented spontaneously in a 1,200-liter barrel (*Stückfass*) but was then racked into stainless steel until March. Subtle and elegant on the nose: the purest fruit aromas and flint. On the palate, very elegant, pure, and refined, but also complex and mineral. Very intense and persistent, though this Riesling has the finesse and weight of a bird on the wing. Salty aftertaste.

2009★ Fruity aromas, with an exotic touch of ginger and nuts; really ripe yet subtle. Rich and concentrated on the palate, well structured, very mineral and spicy, with a fine and delicate acidity. Very complex and long on the finish. Impressive.

Würzburger Stein Silvaner GG

2010★ A subtle nose, with fine and elegant ripe fruit flavors, herbs, and a touch of caramel. Light, delicate, and very elegant on the palate, with fine acidity, nice mineral flavors, and a quite long, salty finish. A delicious, digestible Grosses Gewächs, with only 12.5% ABV.

2009 Elegant on the nose, ripe and spicy—a typical Stein Silvaner but quite powerful. Round and refined on the palate, but more mineral than succulent. Slightly bitter on the finish—perhaps because of the higher-than-normal alcohol (13.5% ABV).

Bürgerspital z. Hl. Geist Würzburg
Area under vine: 250 acres (100ha)
Most important grape varieties: Riesling (30%), Silvaner (27%), Müller-Thurgau (10%)
Average production: 850,000–900,000 bottles
Best vineyards: *Würzburg* Stein, Stein-Harfe
Theaterstrasse 19,
97070 Würzburg
Tel: +49 931 350 34 41
www.buergerspital.de/weingut

machine-harvested. Whereas many Kabinett and several Spätlese wines are fermented in stainless-steel tanks, the best Spätlese and Grosses Gewächs wines (three in 2010) are mostly fermented in large wooden barrels—spontaneously when possible. All Silvaners from Würzburger Stein are also fermented in barrels (of different sizes, up to 5,000 liters). After being racked and lightly sulfured, the wines are kept on their fine lees in stainless-steel tanks or wooden casks until spring, before being filtered and bottled under screwcap (Long-Cap).

The Bürgerspital's cash cows are the clean, fresh, Kabinett wines. From Würzburger Stein, there are 60,000–70,000 bottles each of Silvaner and Riesling, and every *Bocksbeutel* is worthy of

Juliusspital Würzburg

The Juliusspital is the largest wine estate in Franken and the second-largest in all of Germany. All the more remarkable, then, that the institution—which was founded by Julius Echter von Mespelbrunn in 1579 and is managed by Horst Kolesch today—is also one of the best producers of the region and probably the best-known representative of *Frankenwein* in the world of fine wine. Of the 1.2 million *Bocksbeutel* per year, there is not a single weak wine. So it is no wonder that you can find "Juspi" wines on five continents.

There are several reasons for this great success. Horst Kolesch, managing director since 1986, is a very ambitious man who strives not only for the highest possible wine quality but for recognition

Of the 1.2 million Bocksbeutel per year, there is not a single weak wine. So it's no wonder you can find "Juspi" wines on five continents. The wines always sell out soon after release

as well. "There is no reason for us not to produce the best wine, and there is no gold medal that we don't want to win," he once told me. And indeed, the awards that the Juliusspital wines have received over the past 20 years are staggering. The wines—most of them Silvaner (there is no bigger Silvaner producer in the world), always made from ripe and healthy grapes—always sell out very soon after they have been released. This is a great success for the foundation, but it is also a pity, in the sense that the top wines could age for decades but often don't have the chance.

The Juliusspital not only has holdings in some of the top vineyards in Franken (about 20 all together) but also has some of the very best parcels within these sites. So, if you want to taste Franken wines from the Buntsandstein soils in the west,

then compare them to those from the Muschelkalk soils around Würzburg or the Keuper wines from the Steigerwald, you don't have to look any further: enter the estate's shop or Vinothek Weineck Julius Echter in Würzburg, and you have excellent examples of all three.

The wines—90 percent white, most fermented in stainless-steel tanks and made by cellar master Benedikt Then until the 2010 vintage (he retired after 47 years in 2011)—are very modern and easy to drink but not lacking complexity when it comes to the single-vineyard wines. These are partly fermented in large wooden casks, very intense in color and fruit, and almost tropical on the nose. On the palate, they are round and supple but also piquant and salty, like many Smaragd wines from the Wachau (Austria).

Each *Einzellagenwein* has its own specific character. The Rieslings and Silvaners from the Stein, for example, are always fine and elegant, slightly smoky on the nose, racy and salty on the palate. The Lump Rieslings and Silvaners are rich, succulent, and salty as well, whereas the Julius-Echter-Berg is rich and powerful, yet vibrant and herbaceous. In recent years, I have always favored the wines from Iphofen to those from Würzburg, because they were rounder and deeper.

I would not call the Juspi wines intellectual (as the top wines of the Bürgerspital can be), but neither would I rate them as typical blind-tasting wines (even if I always score them quite highly). Because they have to be sold quickly and in large volumes, they are not allowed to be shy or very sophisticated. They have to be attractive from the very first moment and, of course, of very good if not excellent quality, too. In 2010, however, when even the finest wines of Germany acquired a racy if not searing acidity, I found some of the basic varietal wines slightly too soft. Obviously deacidification took away not only acidity but vintage character as well. The Grosses Gewächs wines have been outstanding, though. The noble sweet wines—especially the Beerenauslesen and Trockenbeerenauslesen—can be very good as well, pairing their rich and concentrated fruit with grip, piquant minerality, and pronounced acidity. Since 2008, the wines have become a little bit more reductive and fresh. With Nicolas Frauer now responsible for making the Juspi wines, only time will tell if this trend is going to continue.

FINEST WINES

While the Kabinett wines are made for drinking soon, the Grosses Gewächs wines from Riesling and Silvaner can easily age for ten or more years, and the noble sweet wines are best after a couple of decades. Because nobody cares very much, nobody knows what is lost when a top Juspi wine is drunk too soon. I am happy to have had the chance to taste mature Juliusspitäler in several tastings. But because there is no chance to buy or drink mature wines, even in the spital's own Weinstube in Würzburg, I comment only on the most impressive wine I have had so far.

2010 Würzburger Stein Silvaner Kabinett trocken [V]
Ripe apples and pears on the nose, very elegant and spicy. Very succulent, but also racy on the palate; straight, as always, but more rich and Spätlese-like than usual.

2010 Iphöfer Julius-Echter-Berg Silvaner Kabinett trocken★ [V]
Brilliant nose, with herbal aromas. Succulent, round, and supple on the palate, lifted by a vibrant and piquant acidity.

Würzburger Stein Riesling GG
The **2010** is very elegant and refined on the nose. Full-bodied, dense, and firmly structured on the palate. Nice salinity and piquancy, with great finesse. The **2009** is firm and nicely reductive on the palate, very mineral but also succulent, with nice grip, clear fruit expression, and a salty finish. A good mix of power and elegance. Very good potential.

2010 Julius-Echter-Berg Silvaner GG★
Herbal aromas and ripe fruit flavors. Supple

and elegant on the palate, this JEB has brilliant fruit, lifted by a refined acidity and fundamental minerality. Well balanced, thanks to less than 13% ABV. (The 2009 is much richer, with 14% ABV.) On the nose, this cru is very clear, fresh, and subtle, displaying the finest herbal aromas and white-fruit flavors. On the palate, it is very intense, powerful, rich, and almost viscous. The acidity is refined, and the potential should be great.

1967 Rödelseer Küchenmeister Silvaner TBA★
(200° Oechsle, 12g/l TA; tasted in May 2008)
Amber color, with a greenish glimmer. Clear and malty on the nose. A delicate structure in the mouth, with a lot of elegance and finesse. An intense and malty texture, sweet but even more piquant. Very well balanced by a refined acidity and spicy minerality. Great noblesse. Should be served with game.

Weingut Juliusspital Würzburg
Area under vine: 425 acres (172ha)
Most important grape varieties: Silvaner (43%), Riesling (22%), Müller-Thurgau (17%)
Average production: 1.2 million bottles
Best vineyards: *Würzburg* Stein,
Innere Leiste; *Randersacker* Pfülben;
Escherndorf Lump; *Volkach* Karthäuser;
Iphofen Julius-Echter-Berg;
Rödelsee Küchenmeister
Klinikstrasse 1, 97070 Würzburg
Tel: +49 931 393 1400
www.juliusspital.de/weingut

Weingut Johann Ruck

Hans "Hansi" Ruck, born in 1971 and owner of the long-established Weingut Johann Ruck in the center of Iphofen since July 2009, is a rather tight-lipped wine producer. If you want to learn something about his work and the wines he has produced since the 2000 vintage, you have to pull nearly every second sentence out of his mouth. If you don't have the time or nerves to do so (and if Hansi's entertaining father Hans is not available), it is more useful to taste Ruck's excellent Rieslings, Silvaners, Traminers, or Scheurebes. In fact, most of them are also quite withdrawn, but at least they are pure, straight, resolute, and profound reflections of their origins—and the winemaker's mystical mind.

Iphöfer wines—predominantly white—are mostly cultivated on the south-facing slopes of the Schwanberg, a foothill of the Steigerwald. The small, dark, schisty clay plates of Keuper store water (quite important in an area with only 22in [550mm] of annual rainfall), as well as heat, providing a long growing period. Hence, wines from Iphofen can be quite rich and powerful, going beyond 14% ABV.

"High alcohol levels can be a problem here," says Ruck. Because, for him (and his clients), wine should always be pleasant to drink, Ruck wants to produce wines with, at most, 12.5–13% ABV. Thus, he picks up to ten days earlier than his father did ten years ago, as long as the grapes, with average yields of 55hl/ha, are ripe. With different viticultural techniques—low-yielding clones and rootstocks, planting density of 5,000–7,000 vines/ha, green manures, canopy management, green harvesting—he tries to arrest the sugar ripeness of the grapes, as well as to reach earlier physiological ripeness.

Ruck, assisted by his father in the vineyards, cultivates 30.5 acres (12.3ha) of vines and 12 different varieties, producing up to 25 wines a year, 80 percent of them dry. Silvaner dominates the Iphöfer and Rödelseer vineyards, then come Riesling, Müller-Thurgau, and Bacchus. Ruck's finest wines are made of Silvaner and Riesling, old-vine Pinot

Gris, Sauvignon Blanc, Traminer, and Scheurebe. (Estheria is one of the finest Scheus I know.)

The warm and south-facing Iphöfer Julius-Echter-Berg is the best site in the Ruck portfolio. The family owns 7 acres (2.8ha) here, with 4.7 acres (1.9ha) of Riesling and Silvaner classified as Grosse Lage, each yielding 45–50hl/ha.

The parcel for the Silvaner Grosses Gewächs is at the bottom of the Echter-Berg, where the decomposed clay is quite deep. The vines were planted in 1987, but the vigorous clone is very labor-intensive. "It can easily yield 200hl/ha," Ruck confesses. Canopy management is crucial here, and in some years the bunches have to be halved.

The neighboring Riesling parcel is also classified as Grosse Lage, but there is another, slightly larger parcel above, in the steeper part of the Echter-Berg, that was planted in 1986. The soil is poorer here, and because Riesling is less vigorous than Silvaner, these parcels are less work.

The hand-picked grapes are not destemmed, are slightly crushed and, after a short maceration (Riesling up to four hours, Silvaner up to 12), gently pressed. After settling, the must of the Grosses Gewächs wines has been fermented in 1,200-liter barrels of Iphöfer oak since the 2004 vintage (in stainless steel till then), mostly now with the help of cultured yeasts. After the fermentation has finished, some 20–25 days later, the wine is racked and sulfured for the first time and stays on its fine lees until May. After *kieselguhr* filtration, the Silvaner is fined with bentonite; the Riesling, only if necessary. Some four weeks later, both wines are filtered and bottled (under screwcap since 2004), the Silvaner containing at most 2–3g/l RS; Riesling, 4–5g/l.

A vertical tasting in summer 2010 conclusively proved the longevity of the Ruck wines. Since the excellent 2007s, they have become even purer and more refined, if less powerful. Although they are rarely big or superficially smooth, Ruck wines are always profound and a great pleasure to drink.

Above: Three generations of the Ruck family, with grandfather Hans and father "Hansi," at the entrance to their historic cellar

FINEST WINES

Iphöfer Julius-Echter-Berg Riesling GG

1990 Golden yellow. A mature nose, sweet and herbaceous. Nice chamomile and caramel flavors. Elegant and mineral, still with vibrant acidity and good length. Impressive.

2007★ Herbal and stony aromas, plus the brilliant, fresh fruit flavors of great Riesling. Firm and salty on the minerally palate; very good concentration of fruit and acidity; great complexity and length.

2010 Fresh and aromatic fruit aromas of good intensity. Succulent and thrillingly mineral on the palate, very elegant and complex, with brisk acidity and a salty aftertaste. Appetizing and persistent.

Iphöfer Julius-Echter-Berg Silvaner GG

2003 One of the rare really good 2003s, because it is less alcoholic, if sweeter, than usual (12g/l RS). Ripe, almost tropical- and cooked-fruit flavors, yet also cool and precise, nutty and piquant. Supple and voluptuous, yet well structured and salty, with surprising vibrancy for the vintage.

2004★ Intense yellow, with green highlights. Very deep and complex on the herbaceous nose. Piquant and succulent on the palate; very salty, pure, and appetizing. Really complex.

2005 Very fresh and precise white-fruit aromas. Full-bodied and succulent, yet very mineral, with fresh acidity and a salty finish. Still young.

2009 Refined and complex on the nose, with delicious herbal flavors. Pure, light, and elegant; very mineral, almost ascetic; yet complex, dense, salty, and very long.

Weingut Johann Ruck
Area under vine: 30.5 acres (12.3ha)
Most important grape varieties: Silvaner (39%), Riesling (15%), Müller-Thurgau (11%)
Average production: 70,000 bottles
Best vineyard: *Iphofen* Julius-Echter-Berg
Marktplatz 9, 97346 Iphofen
Tel: +49 9323 800 880
www.ruckwein.de

Weingut Rainer Sauer

The history of the Rainer Sauer family estate in Escherndorf dates back to 1979, but 1995 was a far more important year in terms of the outstanding quality that Rainer, Helga, and their son Daniel Sauer produce today. At that time, a Sauer wine from 1994 received a top score at a national wine competition but was flavorless and moldy only a few months later. "We were ashamed and bought back every single bottle we could find," Rainer remembers. "Then we decided to harvest radically selectively, to reject botrytis, and to work much harder in the vineyards in order to receive nothing but ripe and healthy grapes."

A late—but not too late—manual harvest, with two or three selective pickings per parcel and no botrytis at all, then a very gentle vinification: this explains why the bright, green-gleaming wines of Rainer Sauer are so clean and aromatic, with absolutely nothing disturbing the magical, yet always subtle, fruit and terroir expression of his beautifully balanced and elegant wines.

Currently, the Sauer family cultivates 30 acres (12ha) of vines in the Escherndorfer Lump grand cru (10 acres [4ha]) and the Escherndorfer Fürstenberg (20 acres [8ha]). Almost two-thirds of the area is dedicated to Silvaner. "For me, Silvaner is the iconic grape of Franken," affirms Sauer. "A really dry Silvaner, with less than 5g/l of residual sugar, is what I regard as a typical *Frankenwein* and what lends our region its distinctive profile."

Sauer aims, and is well known, for rich, elegant, intense, and complex terroir-driven wines with a great potential to age. His most impressive wines are the Silvaners from the Escherndorfer Lump. Sauer starts to harvest his Silvaners in the first week of October, picking all the grapes for the basic estate wine, the Kabinett, and the more generic Spätlese wines. In any case, the must weight is normally around 85–90° Oechsle. The Sauers don't care too much about analysis and sugar levels, putting more trust in their experience and tasting ability. "Even if the sugar levels do not rise further, the intensity of the grapes' flavors increases the longer they hang on the vines," Sauer has learned. So, for his top Spätlese wines, such as the L, he waits as long as possible—"but not too long. We pick when the grapes have a deep-yellow, almost golden color. I don't want them overripe, because Silvaner with only moderate acidity risks becoming too broad." Today, Sauer harvests at least two weeks earlier than he did ten years ago, and his top wines are normally picked around the middle of October.

In the cellar, Sauer works as gently as possible in order to preserve the fruit flavors he has been cultivating assiduously for several months in the vineyards. "The more you have to intervene, the earlier the wine reveals the original flaws," he says.

The grapes are partly destemmed and partly slightly crushed, and there is skin contact (with some stems) for six to 12 hours. After natural settling, the must is fermented in stainless steel for three to six weeks—about one-third spontaneously, the rest inoculated with cultured yeasts. After the wines have been racked, they are sulfured and kept on their fine lees until the end of February (for the Kabinett), the end of March (for the Spätlese), or the end of May (for the Spätlese L). They are then lightly filtered before being bottled under screwcap.

Sauer's wines are always perfectly balanced and enjoyable from the very beginning, because the acidity levels are less high than at Horst Sauer. (There are several Sauers in Escherndorf, though they all insist that they are not related.) With Rainer's son Daniel assuming more and more responsibility, the estate is moving farther toward organic viticulture and innovative winemaking experiments: Vom Muschelkalk (fermented spontaneously), Freiraum, and Ab Ovo (a great, refined, and vibrant Silvaner fermented in an egg-shaped concrete tank of 900 liters) are three experimental wines that Daniel already has under his belt.

FINEST WINES

Escherndorfer Lump Silvaner Kabinett trocken [V]

While very few producers in Burgundy would ever declassify a grand cru if they were not forced to do so, this excellent Silvaner is a good example of what the German tradition of selective pickings can give: a light, harmonious, elegant wine that still reflects its terroir in a pure, lively, and salty—albeit slightly less complex and persistent—manner. Sauer's Lump Kabinett comes from younger, 15-year-old vines in the upper part of the grand cru. The ripe and succulent apricot and pear fruit of the **2009★**, however, is as typical of Lump as its elegance, finesse, and saltiness. Last but not least, the Kabinett is drier than the L Grand Cru. The **2010** is more piquant and racy than the 2009 but, again, very pure and full of joy and finesse.

Escherndorfer Lump Silvaner Spätlese trocken L

The letter L represents the German words *Leidenschaft* (passion) and *Lust* (desire), but also *Leid* (suffering, because there is no top quality without suffering, as many German wine producers say, knowing that the most beautiful outlook is on the brink) and *Lump* (this being the quintessence of the vineyard). The wine comes from the very best parcels in the concave center of this steep grand cru along the Main River. The wine is always very intense, powerful, rich, and supple, and ideally it should be left for a few years, though it also tastes very impressive on release. To me, however, the L can occasionally be too much of a good thing, being slightly too opulent for my taste, while lacking the freshness and finesse of the Kabinett or the purity of the Ab Ovo.
1999 The first vintage. Refined and spicy to smell. Very dense and rich, yet fresh and mineral thanks to the bright acidity and salty finish. Still excellent.
2005★ Rich and viscous, but balanced by a refined acidity and piquant minerality. Very intense, succulent, and persistent.
2009 Concentrated, opulent aromas of very ripe fruits, with a smoky touch, too, though less from the chalky soil than from the sun in this warm vintage. A generous mouthful of wine, concentrated, rich, and round, but also beautifully pure and salty.
2010 An unusually high acidity level of 7.1g/l, balanced by a residual-sugar level of 3.8g/l. Refined tropical-fruit aromas. Creamy and elegant, quite powerful and complex, with a lingering minerality and salty aftertaste.

Escherndorfer Lump Silvaner trocken Ab Ovo

This pure, refined, lively, and mineral Silvaner from the Lump vineyard is one of Daniel Sauer's successful experiments and was first produced in the 2008 vintage. It ferments spontaneously in a single concrete tank of 900 liters that is shaped like an egg and reflects Daniel's passion for "natural" and biodynamic wines. As producers in Alsace, Chablis, the Loire, and the Jura have demonstrated, concrete eggs can work very well for white wines. "Unlike oak," Daniel explains, "concrete is a neutral, tasteless material. Nevertheless, like oak, it affords microoxygenation because of the extremely fine porosity." Because the yeasts multiply more rapidly in concrete than in stainless steel when the fermentation starts, Daniel believes that the wine develops more finesse and also, perhaps, more authenticity. He also expects better aging potential from concrete, thanks to the better polymerization and stabilization during the maturation process. "But all this, only time will tell," he admits philosophically. The inaugural **2008** is firmly structured, straight, and vibrant, the finish lingering and salty. The **2009★** is elegant and complex, very pure and subtle in its fruit and terroir expression, with a lovely salty finish.

Weingut Rainer Sauer

Area under vine: 30 acres (12ha)
Important grape varieties: Silvaner (62%), Müller-Thurgau (22%), Riesling (7%)
Average production: 90,000–95,000 bottles
Best vineyard: *Escherndorf* Lump
Bocksbeutelgasse 15, 97332 Escherndorf
Tel: +49 9381 2527
www.weingut-rainer-sauer.de

Weingut Schmitt's Kinder

Viticulture in Randersacker dates back more than 1,200 years. Weingut Schmitt's Kinder ("Schmitt's Children") is one of the most traditional family estates in Franken. The family has cultivated grapes for more than 300 years, Karl and Martin being the ninth and tenth generations.

Both men are proud Franconians, as you taste in their grippy and powerful wines. They are quite distinctive, electrified by the Muschelkalk soils of Randersacker. Here, the limestone is so hard that it was used to build the Berlin Olympic stadium for the 1936 games. The calcareous marl soils are quite deep, and there is a good water supply, resulting in rich, structured, and persistent wines, with exciting acidity and longevity.

The Schmitts cultivate 35 acres (14ha) of vines, most in the best sites of Randersacker. The steep, south- and southwest-facing sites along the Main River are planted mostly with Silvaner (30 percent) and Riesling (14 percent). The microclimate is ideal, thanks to the exposure, gradient, and proximity to the river. Where the hillsides turn more to the east into the cooler tributaries, the early-ripening Müller-Thurgau and Bacchus are cultivated. Since 2004, the Schmitts have offered an elegant, fragrant, fruit-driven Spätburgunder GG, with remarkable freshness and finesse. Pinot Blanc, Scheurebe, and Rieslaner round out the range. Most of the wines are dry, but there are also noble sweet wines of extraordinary quality.

The Schmitts work fastidiously in the vineyards, aiming for healthy soils (plowing, green cover in every second row), well-balanced vines, and slow ripening. They pick rather late, but to keep the acidity fresh and the alcohol level below 14%, they favor 95–96° Oechsle rather than 100°—"rich in flavor yet not in alcohol," as Karl defines the goal. Low RS levels also matter: "We want to reflect our special terroirs in our wines. Therefore, we want them *fränkisch trocken* [below 5g/l RS], because too much residual sugar smudges the expression of terroir."

Harvest is manual, and there are several selective pickings per parcel, all of them separately vinified. Now that Martin is responsible for the vinification, botrytis is less tolerated in the dry wines than it was some years ago. The wines are, thus, less baroque but more precise, pure, and elegant. They ferment in stainless steel at 64–68°F (18–20°C) and are kept on their fine lees only until January or February. The best wines are normally bottled in April or May.

FINEST WINES

There are three Grosses Gewächs wines each year: Silvaner and Riesling from Pfülben and, since 2004, the Spätburgunder from Sonnenstuhl. All are very good if not excellent. I often prefer the piquant and salty Pfülben Riesling from the higher, cooler Weinberg Mendelssohn parcel to the Pfülben GG from the steep but lower part close to the river, which can be extremely rich. Nor is the Marsberg Riesling Spielberg from the stony, steep (70%), southwest-exposed top parcel of the site necessarily a lesser wine, though it is always pure, delicate, and firm.

Randersacker Pfülben Riesling trocken Weinberg Mendelssohn [V]
The **2009★** is darker, richer, and more powerful and persistent than all the other Mendelssohns I have tasted. The acidity is crisp; the finish, long and salty.

Randersacker Marsberg Riesling trocken Spielberg
The **2009** (labeled as Spätlese trocken) is very pure and racy, with white-peach aromas and marked minerality and salinity on the finish. The **2008** is also pure yet firm, mineral, and racy. The **2007** is herbal on the nose, smooth yet mineral on the palate. The more baroque **2006** was influenced by botrytis so tastes full and supple but is still well balanced.

Weingut Schmitt's Kinder
Area under vine: 35 acres (14ha)
Most important varieties: Silvaner (30%), Riesling (14%), Müller-Thurgau (14%), Pinot Noir (8%)
Average production: 100,000–120000 bottles
Best vineyards: *Randersacker* Pfülben, Marsberg, Sonnenstuhl
Am Sonnenstuhl 45, 97236 Randersacker
Tel: +49 931 705 91 97
www.schmitts-kinder.de

Weingut Hans Wirsching

This is not only one of the largest private wine producers in Franken but also one of the most traditional. The family history of the estate in Iphofen dates back to the year 1528 and is represented today by Dr. Heinrich Wirsching.

Currently Wirsching cultivates 200 acres (80ha) of vines on the southern side of the Steigerwald, most in the best vineyards of Iphofen, such as the VDP Grosse Lagen Julius-Echter-Berg, Kronsberg, and Kalb. Wirsching cultivates a range of varieties. Silvaner is queen (40 percent), Riesling king (22 percent), and Scheurebe court jester (7 percent). Pinot Blanc and Pinot Noir, as well as specialties such as Rieslaner, Gewürztraminer, Bacchus, and Müller-Thurgau, complete the royal suite.

The grands crus, especially from the Julius-Echter-Berg, are excellent and can age for 20 years or more. The noble sweet wines are also world-class

Wirsching is a proud Franconian producer, symbolized by the half a million *Bocksbeutel* he releases each year. About 80 percent of the Wirsching wines are white, and all of them are distinctive *Frankenweine*—even if purists could argue that only the dry Spätlese wines from the S series are typically Franconian in being *fränkisch trocken* (lower than 5g/l RS). By contrast, the rich and powerful GG wines from Riesling and Silvaner contain a little more residual sugar. The reason is that "with our grands crus, we have to compete on the international market, where dry wines used to be sweeter than a traditional wine from Franken. Thus, we aim for more fruit and roundness in our Grosses Gewächs wines," managing director Uwe Mattheus explains.

The grands crus, especially from the Julius-Echter-Berg, are excellent and can age for 20 years or more. But many of the other wines are also well worth tasting—especially the S-class wines, but also the Kabinett wines, which form the most important category for the estate in terms of quantity. The noble sweet wines can be of world-class quality but are very rare, since the humidity is generally too low.

FINEST WINES

2010 Iphöfer Kronsberg Scheurebe Spätlese trocken S ★

Wirsching's S-class Scheu is an icon wine, at least in top restaurants. It's an amazing, brilliant, fresh, and refined white, with subtle aromas of grapefruit and nettles on the nose. Due to its purity and mineral character, it seems to be weightless on the palate but is very elegant and persistent.

2010 Julius-Echter-Berg Silvaner GG ★

From old vines rooting in clayey gypsum Keuper soils, yielding 35hl/ha, this has been one of the most complex Silvaners in the world for many years, always rich, elegant, and persistent. The 2010 is remarkably subtle on the nose, displaying typical herbal aromas and a fine concentration of fruit. It is dense and supple but also salty and very well balanced by its fresh acidity and minerality. Great aging potential.

2010 Iphöfer Julius-Echter-Berg Grauer Burgunder TBA ★

This breathtakingly clear, precise, and elegant TBA was made from grapes with a sugar level of 190° Oechsle and 19g/l TA. It was bottled with 260g/l RS and 7% ABV and can compete even with the finest Riesling TBAs from Rhine and Mosel. Quite tropical-fruit flavors like pineapple and green figs; terrific acidity and finesse. Whenever this wine leaves the Wirsching winery, you should try not to be too far away, or somehow try to secure some.

Weingut Hans Wirsching
Area under vine: 200 acres (80ha)
Important grape varieties: Silvaner (40%), Riesling (22%), Scheurebe (7%)
Average production: 520,000 bottles
Best vineyards: *Iphofen* Julius-Echter-Berg, Kronsberg
Ludwig Strasse 16, 97346 Iphofen
Tel: +49 932 387 330
www.wirsching.de

Württemberg

In Germany, Württemberg is affectionately known as the Ländle, a diminutive of "land" in the Swabian dialect. It actually seems quite fitting, not only for the picturesque landscape but for the admirably modest Swabian people, who underplay almost everything—even themselves and their homeland.

They actually have much to be proud of. The region and former state, with its capital in Stuttgart, is economically extremely successful, and because Württemberg is not rich in natural resources (besides wine, of course), the people have always had to be very creative, innovative, and industrious. Porsche, Daimler/Mercedes-Benz, and Bosch are from Württemberg—to name only three of the hundreds of well-known brands based here. It is one of the most advanced areas for industry and high-tech not only in Germany but in all of Europe. Consequently, the cities and villages have long since conquered the hilly landscape (rendering it rather less picturesque than it was in its pristine state).

Politically, the Württemberger are less conservative than generally thought. In 2011, Germany's first Green prime minister, Winfried Kretschmann, was inaugurated in Stuttgart, which is also the city that mobilized the whole state of Baden-Württemberg to protest (unsuccessfully in the end) against Stuttgart 21, a very expensive urban-development and transportation project, with much of the new infrastructure being underground.

Then there is the University of Tübingen, one of the oldest universities in Germany; the Staatsgalerie Stuttgart, one of the most popular museums in the country; the Staatstheater Stuttgart, which shelters one of the most innovative theaters, opera houses, and ballets in Germany... So there is really no need for the Württemberger to be modest or for anybody else to be condescending.

This applies equally to the growing elite of private wine producers, who are also far more innovative than is normally supposed. Thanks to some brave pioneers, it was one of the first regions in Germany where (from the mid-1980s) wines were aged in barriques. It was also here that international grape varieties such as Chardonnay, Cabernet, and Merlot were planted—even before they were legally sanctioned. The replanting of Sauvignon Blanc may have followed the worldwide trend, though the variety was already very common as Muskat-Sylvaner in the Remstal in the 19th and early 20th centuries (before the Nazis denaturalized it as *undeutsch*). Varietal wines have been familiar in Württemberg since World War II; and red and white blends, often barrique-fermented, since the early 1990s. These wines mostly blend local varieties such as Lemberger with international superstars such as Cabernet, Merlot, or Syrah. Since the mid-1990s, the new red crossings from Weinsberg—such as Cabernet Cubin, Cabernet Dorsa, Cabernet Dorio, Cabernet Mito, and Acolon—have been added to blends to lend color, body, and smoothness.

Indeed, Württemberg is a red-wine region but does not have any image. Of the total 28,222 acres (11,421ha) of vines, between Reutlingen in the south and Bad Mergentheim in the north, 71.3 percent are planted with red varieties. Trollinger (Schiava in Italy) occupies almost 20.8 percent and is the most important red wine, even though it looks rather like a rosé and often tastes like a sweet nothing. Curiously, the high-yielding pride of Württemberg is cultivated in the best sites but, even here, does not give much more than an enjoyable red wine for lunch. Schwarzriesling (Pinot Meunier), the second most important red variety in Württemberg, with 14.5 percent of the total, is also unconvincing as a red wine. Much more interesting is Lemberger (Blaufränkisch), which occupies 14.3 percent and may have been brought to Württemberg in the 19th century by Graf Neipperg in Schweigern. Although the available clones are too productive,

Right: The vineyards above Stuttgart suggest the extent to which cities and villages have encroached on the landscape

Above: Württemberg is mainly a red-wine region, as reflected by the rows of red-stained barriques at Weingut Dautel

many producers bottle very good, if not excellent, reds due to rigorous yield reductions. Several Lembergers are classified as Grosses Gewächs by the VDP, even if they rarely have the class of the finest Blaufränkisch from Burgenland in Austria.

The other red variety to qualify for Grosses Gewächs status is Spätburgunder (7.7 percent), which has performed very well in Württemberg for several years. Some opinion leaders in Germany rated Rainer Schnaitmann's rich and intense 2009 Fellbach Lämmler Spätburgunder GG as highly as any other German Pinot Noir. Schnaitmann, who bottled his first vintage in 1997, is the most prominent and rapidly rising newcomer of the past decade. His wines, both red and white, are quite modern—dense, fruit-driven, and powerful— but also elegant, and they perform very well in blind tastings. Personally, I wish they were a little fresher, purer, and less satin-smooth. The 2010 whites were the best, leanest, and purest I have had so far from Schnaitmann, but I am not sure if this was due to the cool vintage or to a new, less flattering wine style. Purely for reasons of space,

there is no profile of him here, but he is certainly one of the finest wine producers in Württemberg, and among the brightest rising stars in Germany.

Riesling, which holds 18.2 percent of the total area under vine, is the second most important grape variety (and most important white variety) in Württemberg, and the third to qualify for Grosses Gewächs status. While more than ten years ago, most of the Rieslings were too broad, round, and soft to attract Riesling fans outside the region, they have become much better recently. The finest are dry, pure, lean, mineral, and vibrant, and they can compete with the finest dry Rieslings of Germany today. The variety performs very well on the poorer sandstone soils and on limestone but tends to be quite rich and powerful on the deeper Gipskeuper soils. Graf Neipperg, Jochen Beurer, Rainer Schnaitmann, Jürgen Ellwanger, Gerhard Aldinger, and Jürgen Zipf are top producers. The 2010 Grosses Gewächs Rieslings were outstanding, and even more impressive than many of the Erstes Gewächs Rieslings from the Rheingau.

Vines in Württemberg are cultivated along the Neckar River and its tributaries, such as Rems, Enz, Kocher, Jagst, and Tauber, but also by Lake Constance (*see map, p.89*). There are six districts, though the heart of the region is the Württemberg Unterland district, between Ludwigsburg and Heilbronn. East and southeast of Stuttgart is the Remstal/Stuttgart district, which is now perhaps the most dynamic area of the whole region. This is due mainly to the vicinity to the capital of Stuttgart and the density of independent wine producers striving for the highest quality. The amicable competition here has led to many really good wines over the past 20 years, but quality has reached new and impressive heights since the 2007 vintage.

The landscape of Württemberg is a *cuesta* with many table mountains, so the soils are highly diverse. The different Keuper strata alternate calcareous marl with (often lime-free) sandstone in rapid succession, like a cake with chocolate and cream layers. (The yellow Schilfsandstein was used as building material in former times and transported not only to Stuttgart, Frankfurt, and Düsseldorf but also Berlin and even Amsterdam.) When producers in Württemberg speak of their Keuper soils, they mean loamy-clay marls. They are mineral-rich, warm, and mostly well aerated. Depending on the composition and thickness, they can be either quite stony and poor, or deep and rich. The oft-mentioned Gipskeuper is a deeper clay soil with a high gypsum content, but there are also some limestone areas.

The climate in Württemberg is mild, with 1,685 hours of sunshine, an average temperature of 51°F (10.6°C), and rainfall of 28in (724mm) in the Neckar Valley near Stuttgart. In Weinsberg, farther north, the sun shines 1,638 hours, temperature averages 49°F (9.6°C), and rainfall 30in (758mm).

Viticulture began in the 8th century, and there are many impressively steep slopes along the Neckar, often terraced, which give a special mesoclimate. The potential of the different terroirs is very high, but due to *Flurbereinigung* in the 1970s and '80s, old vines are rare, and much of what has been planted since was neither well adapted to the site nor selected for quality. This is because Württemberg is dominated by the 50 cooperatives (Weingärtner) that produce 80 percent of the wine, of mediocre quality. Württembergers drink some 10.5 gallons (40 liters) of wine per person per year—much more than consumers outside the region. But most of them do not care about high-quality wines. (Again, the modesty of the Swabians!) They work hard and like their wine quaffable, sweet, and smooth. In 2010, of the 999,000hl of wine produced, almost 43 percent was off-dry, one-third was sweet, and less than a quarter was dry. 937,000hl were marketed as *Qualitätswein*, so *Prädikatswein* does not play an important role in Württemberg.

Another interesting fact is that of the 260 *Einzellagen* in Württemberg, very few are mentioned on the labels of top producers. They prefer fantasy names instead and have developed their own classification system, mostly with up to four stars. The co-ops have ruined the reputation of the *Einzellagen* names with mediocre wines, but since Württemberg has widely accepted the VDP concept of Grosses Gewächs, 26 sites were classified by 2011, and these are mentioned on labels.

Because even Württemberg's consumers have begun to buy wines from other domestic and international wine regions, for the sake of quality, the co-ops have great difficulty selling their wines. Prices have dropped dramatically, and many leisure-time grape growers have sold their parcels or will soon do so. Because of these structural changes, the importance of the co-ops is slowly diminishing, while there are talented young producers striving for high-quality wines. The more of them who take over the abandoned parcels in top sites, the better.

Although Württemberg had shed its lethargy by the mid-1990s, its glory days for wine are still ahead. What it still lacks is a clever communication and marketing strategy to publicize the excellence of its wines. With Trollinger and the co-ops still dominating Württemberg's lackluster image, it should perhaps be something self-deprecating. Some years ago, the state of Baden-Württemberg created the slogan *Wir können alles. Ausser Hochdeutsch* ("We can do everything. Apart from High German"), which was a great success and has become a popular phrase throughout Germany. Maybe the Württembergers should communicate something like *Trollinger war gestern. Heute erzeugen wir Klassiker* ("Trollinger was yesterday. Today we produce classics"): Riesling. Spätburgunder. Lemberger. But let's end here with Wallenstein by Friedrich Schiller, born in Marbach south of Stuttgart: *Des Menschen Wille, das ist sein Glück* ("Man's will, that is his luck"). In this sense: Good luck, Swabia!

Weingut Dautel

rnst Dautel—who bottled his first wines in 1978, though his family has been involved in viticulture since 1510—is one of the pioneers of the German wine revolution that started almost 30 years ago. Putting quality first, he was always breaking traditions, bottling wines such as Württemberg had never seen and then did not want to be without. Ernst Dautel was one of the first wine producers in Germany to use barriques (in the mid-1980s) and to plant international varieties like Chardonnay, Cabernet, and Merlot, though this was not officially permitted in 1988. He was also one of the first winemakers in single-variety Germany to create a blend (Kreation, 1990). Today, Weingut Dautel is one of the finest addresses in Württemberg, and no matter which wine from the extended range you taste (60 percent red, 40 percent white), it is always very good or better.

Currently, the family cultivates numerous parcels, adding up to 30 acres (12ha) of vines, of which 30 percent are Riesling, 20 percent each Pinot Noir and Lemberger, 15 percent Pinot Blanc, and another 15 percent is a mix of different varieties such Zweigelt, Merlot, Cabernet, and Trollinger.

Two *Einzellagen* are cultivated in a particularly eco-friendly way. Sonnenberg in Bönnigheim is characterized by deep, nutrient-rich Keuper soils (colored marl, Gipskeuper, and Schilfsandstein), which produce full-bodied, powerful wines with very good aging potential. Besigheimer Wurmberg, a few miles southwest, is a steep, terraced, very warm slope close to the Enz River, where limestone soils bear salty wines of elegance and grace.

As a recent tasting of some 20 wines showed, there is a remarkable shift toward elegance, freshness, and purity since the 2008 vintage. I do not wish to take anything away from Ernst Dautel, but I suspect it is the energy and spirit of his son Christian that have taken the wines to an

Right: The father-and-son team of Ernst and Christian Dautel, mavericks who helped revolutionize the German wine scene

Putting quality first, Ernst Dautel was always breaking traditions, bottling wines such as Württemberg had never seen and then did not want to be without. Weingut Dautel is one of the finest addresses in Württemberg

even higher level. Christian was born in 1985, and after graduating from Geisenheim and working stints in Austria, Oregon, Australia, South Africa, and Burgundy (with Comte Lafon), he was fully integrated into the family business in early 2010. He is an intelligent, enthusiastic, and open-minded wine freak, who has been lending inspiration at home from 2008.

Although Christian obviously benefited from all his experiences abroad, the biggest influence on his ideas was Burgundy, as he readily admits. "The purity, freshness, and longevity of the finest wines of Burgundy really astonished me. I drank 50-year-old wines, and they were still vibrant and complex." Wherever he was, he was always comparing the wines he tasted abroad with his own family's wines. "So I recognized what we have to work on, and I learned that we have to focus completely on our strengths, which are all about fruit, finesse, and elegance."

As a consequence, he focuses on Spätburgunder and Lemberger, as well as on Chardonnay and Weissburgunder. He picks earlier than in the past, with must weights around 92–95 Oechsle. The premium S-class red wines of the estate, as well as the Riesling Grosses Gewächs, were fermented spontaneously in barrels in 2010, and in 2011 the Chardonnay S and the Weissburgunder S were, too. New barrels from Damy were bought but with a lighter toasting than before. Christian does not clarify the musts as much as his father did, and for him, "Lemberger has to be vinified more like a Pinot Noir than a Cabernet Sauvignon," mainly with less extraction. The 2010 Chardonnay, Weissburgunder, and Grauburgunder are less powerful, rich, and sweet than previously, now tending toward purity, salinity, and freshness. I am quite sure that the next 30 years at Weingut Dautel will be no less exciting than the first three decades.

Left: Neat rows of barriques, which Ernst Dautel was among the first in Germany to introduce from the mid-1980s onward

FINEST WINES

2010 Besigheimer Wurmberg Riesling ✳✳✳ [V]
Pure and reductive on the nose. Light, racy, and salty on the palate, very pure and thrilling, with good concentration and subtle fruit flavors. Delicious.

2010 Chardonnay S
From Gipskeuper soils. Fermented in new 600-liter and used 400-liter barrels. Quite Burgundian on the nose, very clear and slightly sweet: honeydew melon. Rich, sweet, and smooth on the palate due to *bâtonnage* but also mineral, fresh, and with great finesse. Quite powerful yet thrilling.

2010 Weissburgunder S
From 300-liter oak barrels and with malolactic fermentation. Refined fruit flavors on the nose, very clear. Elegant, pure, and succulent on the palate, very fresh and salty. Less powerful than the Chardonnay but very drinkable.

2009 Lemberger S
Pure and refined floral and fruit aromas of cherries, dark berries, and licorice. Silky, with ripe, sweet fruit flavors, refined tannins, and a well-balancing acidity. Very fine, harmonious, and appetizing.

2009 Bönninheimer Sonnenberg Spätburgunder GG
The first Grosses Gewächs made. Deep, cool, and slightly smoky on the nose, pure and fresh, with floral aromas and red-berry flavors. Silky, fresh, and precise on the palate, very elegant, fruity, and juicy, with grip and a delicious kick on the finish. Very delicate.

2001 Kreation Rot ✳✳✳✳
This blend of Lemberger, Merlot, and Cabernet had two years in French barriques. A deliciously mature bouquet, with floral aromas, dried fruits, cherries, plum skin, and black tea. Fresh, round, and silky on the palate, still with power and a touch of sweetness. Refined and vibrant, with a salty finish.

Weingut Dautel
Area under vine: 30 acres (12ha)
Average production: 90,000 bottles
Best vineyards: *Bönnigheim* Sonnenberg; *Besigheim* Wurmberg
Lauerweg 55, 74357 Bönnigheim
Tel: +49 7143 870 326
www.weingut-dautel.de

Weingut Beurer

lthough Württemberg is mainly a red-wine region, there are some very good and excellent white-wine producers as well. Some of the finest whites come from the Remstal, east of Stuttgart, and Jochen Beurer (born in 1973) is my favorite producer here. The immediacy, purity, and race of his very authentic wines—80 percent white, 50 percent Riesling—are unique. The Rieslings in particular are uncompromising downhill wines (Jochen was Europe's BMX champion in 1992, if this helps you understand what I mean), so elegance is not their strongest suit, nor are they easy-drinking. Although they are light- to medium-bodied, they are very intense, and you have to decant them for a while or, even better, have a mature Riesling with at least four years of bottle age instead. Maturation is rather slow, since Beurer uses screwcaps, though the firmly structured 1999 Stettener Pulvermächer Riesling Spätlese *trocken* was still dense, youthful, and long when Jochen served it from magnum 12 years after the harvest.

The immediacy, purity, and race of Jochen Beurer's very authentic wines are unique. The Rieslings in particular are uncompromising downhill wines

Beurer's family estate is located in Kernen-Stetten, a small village in a windy side valley of the Rems River. The Keuper soils are very diverse, with marl and different sandstones (Stubensandstein, Kieselsandstein) in the upper parts and Gipskeuper and Schilfsandstein in the middle and lower parts. The slopes form an amphitheater, with the village of Stetten as the backdrop. Vineyards climb from 900 up to 1,350ft (280m–410m) and are protected by forest on the top of the slopes. The partly terraced slopes are quite steep and range from east to west.

As a result, the grapes take full advantage of the sheltered site, as well as the cooler and longer vegetative and ripening period.

After his training and first practical winemaking experiences at Elisabetta Foradori's estate in Trentino (Italy), Jochen Beurer returned home in 1997 and started producing and bottling his own wines—in a garage and from only 8.5 acres (3.5ha) of vines. The family previously ran a mixed agriculture and sold grapes to a local co-op for many years. Today, Jochen Beurer cultivates many different parcels, totaling 25 acres (10ha) of vines. For quality reasons, Jochen went organic from the very beginning but was Ecovin-certified only in 2011. Since 2007, he has been biodynamic, cultivating his vineyards along Demeter guidelines. "The biodynamic approach helps detect the real profile of our vineyards. With every year, it gets sharper," Jochen enthuses.

Beurer's goal is to mirror the character of both the vineyard and the vintage in his wines, as well as to develop a distinctive "Beurer Riesling" style. His vines are quite old (planted in 1963, 1968, and 1975), and new plantings are massal selections. He aims for deep roots and vines that can help themselves. With every row green-covered by different herbs, flowers, and cereal/grass mixtures, there is flowering throughout the vegetative period, and the life in the soils has been revitalized.

Beurer hand-harvests late and in two or three passes to get healthy and physiologically ripe grapes. He is not concerned about sugar levels and does not fear higher alcohol levels, "because it is the ripeness that is crucial."

Beurer is "organic" in the winery, too. The grapes are destemmed but not crushed. After eight or nine hours, the whole berries are pressed pneumatically "but with enough pressure to get structure and intensity." Beurer uses no additives; nor does he fine the must. Fermentations with indigenous yeasts take place in stainless-steel vats and wooden barrels of different sizes and can take up to ten months due to the naturally cool cellar temperatures. The wines are kept on their lees until August and are filtered and bottled in September.

Among many other wines and Schnapps, there are three interesting and one excellent, if not great, Riesling every year. "Interesting" because Jochen bottles three Rieslings from three different soils, which also give the names to the wines. The Stettener Häder Riesling *trocken* Gipskeuper is from a lower southeast site, which is shaded during the afternoon and has soils with high proportions of gypsum, limestone, and mudstone. It is a light, transparent, and lively wine with a juicy texture and appetizing spiciness. The next two Rieslings are from the Stettener Pulvermächer, classified as Grosse Lage by the VDP (to which Beurer does not belong). The Riesling *trocken* Schilfsandstein is from a rather windy west-southwest-facing Pulvermächer parcel at 1,000ft (310m) in altitude. The Keuper soil is completely free of active lime, so the pH is quite low and the wine correspondingly racy. This Riesling is fuller and more serious compared to the Gipskeuper, showing ripe stone-fruit aromas on the nose, and elegance, succulence, and salinity on the palate. The Kieselsandstein and Junges Schwaben Rieslings, though, are discussed more fully below.

FINEST WINES

(Tasted in December 2011)
2008 Stettener Pulvermächer Riesling Kieselsandstein [V]
From a south-southwest parcel at an altitude of 1,250ft (380m) with very stony, mineral soils. Fermented in barrels and stainless steel, this is a medium-bodied Riesling with delicate herbal, stony, and white-fruit flavors. Full, dense, and racy on the palate, but also pure and piquant. Firmly structured and quite expressive. I prefer the purity of the '08 to the power and richness of the '09, though this is noble as well as very succulent. Both wines should be stored for at least five or six years.

Riesling trocken Junges Schwaben
Grown on marl and sandstone Keuper soils at 1,250ft (380m) high on the Pulvermächer cru, this late-harvested, golden-yellow wine, from yields of 35hl/ha, is fermented in a large wooden barrel and combines richness with elegance and a cool and lingering minerality. It is released only two years after harvest. Junges Schwaben ("Young Swabia") refers to the group of five (formerly) young Württemberg wine producers founded in 2001 to promote the quality and diversity of their region. Each member's best wine is labeled Junges Schwaben.

2007★ Subtle and fresh on the nose (12.5% ABV), with thyme and other herbal and spicy flavors, as well as ripe fruits. Very precise and backed by the delicious and fresh aroma from the Kieselsandstein soil that lends finesse. Very elegant, mineral, and straight on the palate, perfectly balanced. This is a classic Riesling, with a lingering minerality. Very long and fine.

2005★ Almost orange in color. Ultra-ripe but also mineral on the nose. The fruit is almost South Italian, but the cool and fresh minerality and precision are quite German. On the palate, the wine is complex, balanced, and elegant, and the lingering salinity is amazing. There is finesse and *Spiel* on the palate, which allows the monster to fly, so you don't feel the alcohol of 13.5% ABV. Theoretically, wines with enormous rich extracts and almost overripe fruit flavors are broad and burly. But wines from a cooler climate and the right soils care nothing for theory—they just want to be drunk!

2004★ Very interesting on the nose, with tobacco, almond, marzipan, and green aromas (salad leaves and sorrel). Just ripe but very pure, as on the palate: firmly structured, really straight, tight, and grippy. There is a delicious residual sweetness, too, though, which rounds the wine off and makes it delicious to drink now. Very salty on the lingering finish; this gives great pleasure to drink now, but I am sure it will remain forever young.

Weingut und Spezialitätenbrennerei Beurer
Area under vine: 25 acres (10ha)
Average production: 70,000 bottles
Best vineyard: *Stetten* Pulvermächer
Lange Strasse 67,
71394 Kernen-Stetten im Remstal
Tel: +49 715 142 190
www.weingut-beurer.de

Weingut Wachtstetter

Like Jochen Beurer, Rainer Wachtstetter is a member of the Junges Schwaben ("Young Swabia") quintet, founded in 2001 to demonstrate that Württemberg does not have to be mediocre and can produce much better wines if only they are made in a more authentic and traditional way. Rainer Wachtstetter, who is based in Pfaffenhofen in Zabergäu, southwest of Heilbronn, has made his mark with spotlessly clean, elegant, and extremely well-balanced red wines, especially Lemberger. For several years, his Junges Schwaben Lemberger has been one of the finest red wines of Württemberg. In 2009, Wachtstetter produced his first Hohenberg Lemberger Grosses Gewächs, which I have yet to taste. Because it was very difficult to get fully ripe tannins in 2010, he will not release the wine from this tricky year.

Rainer Wachtstetter has made his mark with spotlessly clean, elegant, and extremely well-balanced red wines. His Lemberger is one of the finest red wines of Württemberg

Wachtstetter became a member of the VDP in 2009, an important milestone in the history of the estate, which had been a mixed-agriculture estate with a typical Swabian restaurant for three generations until 1985. Since Rainer took over responsibilities for the wine in the same year, however, the estate has developed enormously. He slowly extended the area under vine from 3.7 acres (1.5ha) to 40 acres (16ha) today. Some 75 percent of the total area is planted with red varieties—mainly Lemberger (35 percent), Trollinger (15 percent), and Pinot Noir (10 percent), but also with rarities such as Cabernet Franc, Merlot, and Syrah. Riesling accounts for 20 percent of the total, and the Riesling Anna from grand cru Hohenberg is really worth discovering.

Thanks to Heuchelberg and Stromberg, two mountains rising up to 1,300ft (400m), Zabergäu is a well-protected area with almost no wind, a very warm mesoclimate, and only 20–24in (500–600mm) of rain. It has always been a red-wine area, and Lemberger, which was imported from Hungary more than 100 years ago, plays the leading role here, whereas elsewhere in Württemberg the star is Trollinger. With a gradient of 30–60 percent, the vineyards are quite steep, rising from 750 to 950ft (230m–290m). Soils are quite sandy and stony in the upper parts where based on Schilfsandstein (the castle of Stuttgart was built from this yellow, rather soft sandstone), whereas the lower Gipskeuper parts are deeper. Because the humus layers in the upper sandstone parts are only 16–20in (40–50cm) deep and the rocks beneath are fractured, water supply is poor. Wachtstetter, therefore, has to irrigate his best and steepest parcels if it is too dry. Due to *Flurbereinigung* between the late 1960s and the early 1980s, 40–45 percent of the vines are no older than 15 years. Wachtstetter's finest wines, though, are produced from parcels planted in 1979 (Lemberger Junges Schwaben), 1990 (Hohenberg Lemberger GG), or even between 1971 and 1973 (Riesling Anna).

Rainer's main focus is on Lemberger, which he loves to transform into ripe, igneous, and expressive red wines. Unfortunately, there are no high-quality clones in Württemberg, so to reduce the high yields and to get intense and aromatic wines, 50 percent or more of the crop has to be cut off—by halving the bunches (which is also done for the basic wines), removing the shoulders (for the top wines), or even taking off whole bunches. Because dropping this much fruit would not really make sense, in 1995 Rainer planted 500 cuttings from a very old Blaufränkisch vineyard in Burgenland (Austria), from which he has already grafted 1,000 plants. There are another 48 Lemberger vines from cuttings of an old mixed vineyard near Heidelberg, which is another source for a special Wachtstetter type of Lemberger from massal selections.

Normally in the second half of October, the late-ripening varieties such as Riesling and Lemberger are picked by hand, in three passes, of which the last selection, toward the end of the month, gives the finest wines. At the winery, the grapes are directly covered by dry ice, for reduction and cooling. The Lemberger is mostly destemmed but not crushed, before being placed into stainless-steel vats with a maximum of 10 percent of whole bunches in very ripe years. After five to eight days of cold maceration, fermentation starts, and the maceration lasts five to seven weeks. After pressing and settling, the must is transferred by gravity into barriques, which are made of Swabian and German oak by Mercurey and François Frères. For the Junges Schwaben Lemberger, 50 percent are new, while the Grosses Gewächs sees 75 percent new oak. Malolactic fermentation occurs in the spring, and after 15–20 months the unmoved wine is racked and bottled without fining or filtration. The grand cru goes on to the market two years after the harvest; the Junges Schwaben, after 26 months.

FINEST WINES

(Tasted in December 2011)
2010 Riesling trocken Anna [V]
From 40-year-old vines that grow in pure Schilfsandstein soils at 1,000ft (300m) in altitude, this potential cru from the Hohenberg is a medium-bodied, rather than full-bodied, wine of great elegance and length. Fermented with natural yeasts—partly in barrels (with malolactic fermentation), partly in stainless-steel tanks—it has a succulent texture, with ripe acidity and salty minerality, which extends the lingering and scintillating finish. If you look for elegance rather than scale among the Riesling crus of Württemberg, this is one you should not miss.

2007 Lemberger trocken Ernst Combé
Burgundian color; brighter than the 2008. A fruity nose with red cherries and spices such as cloves and pepper; nice freshness, with delicate sweet flavors. Well balanced on the palate; sweet, fruity, and round, but very elegant, because the acidity and tannins are fully integrated. Good concentration and length; still a little bit smoky on the finish but also sweet. Very enjoyable now.

2009 Lemberger trocken Junges Schwaben ★
This wine comes from an old vineyard in Pfaffenhofen Mühlberg. The parcel is very steep, at a gradient of 60%, and faces south-southeast. Due to the stony and sandy parts of the upper Schilfsandstein, the colored marl soil of the lower Gipskeuper is not too heavy but full of minerals, and the roots penetrate it easily. The old vines (planted in 1979) give smaller grapes of good concentration and structure, which Rainer transforms into a full, ripe, and complex wine of excellent intensity, spiciness, and length. Dark cherry color. Ripe, sweet, and noble on the nose, with pure red- and dark-cherry aromas, as well as blackberry, and earthy notes from the warm sandstone terroir. Very well balanced. On the palate, dense and intense, elegant and pure, with excellent concentration, a certain roundness due to the ripe and velvety tannins, and a long and succulent finish. Delicious, and well worth keeping back until 2015 or so, if you can resist it till then.

Weingut Wachtstetter
Area under vine: 40 acres (16ha)
Average production: 110,000 bottles
Best vineyard: *Pfaffenberg* Hohenberg
Michelbacher Strasse 8, 74397 Pfaffenhofen
Tel: +49 704 646 329
www.wachtstetter.de

Baden

Because Baden, in the far southwest of Germany, is more than just the Kaiserstuhl, Breisgau, and Spätburgunder, a typical Baden wine—like Pinot Noir or Chardonnay in Burgundy, or Riesling in the Mosel—does not exist. A broad range of distinctive wines is produced over the 250 miles (400km) between the Markgräflerland near Basel and the picturesque Taubertal in the north (which is not so tiny that it cannot be shared by three German wine regions: Franken, Württemberg, and Baden). We could easily finish this book with wines from Baden, so I can highlight only the most interesting facts and most fascinating wines from one of the most beautiful and diverse wine regions of Germany, which also has some of the best restaurants in the country.

Baden starts at Lake Constance and stretches across the Upper Rhine lowlands, the Badische Bergstrasse and the Kraichgau, northward to Tauberfranken. It includes nine different districts, 16 *Grosslagen*, and 306 *Einzellagen*, making it the third-largest German wine region. In 2010, it had a total of 39,134 acres (15,837ha) of vines, of which 56.4 percent are white and 43.6 percent red. Pinot Noir is the most important variety, accounting for 36.3 percent, but the five next important varieties are white: Müller-Thurgau (16.8 percent), Pinot Gris (11), Pinot Blanc (7.8), Riesling (7.2), and Gutedel (7).

While Pinot Noir is planted almost everywhere in Baden, Gutedel (Chasselas) is mainly cultivated in the Markgräflerland, close to the Swiss border. This subtle, early-ripening variety is badly underrated in Germany, though the Swiss appreciate it not only as Fendant to match their cheese fondue, but also as the key variety of the Dézaley Grand Cru. A century ago, the rather sweet Markgräfler, based on Gutedel, was well regarded and, as documents prove, was even more expensive than Château Mouton Rothschild or Schloss Johannisberger. Hanspeter Ziereisen in Efringen-Kirchen is raising awareness of this old variety with stunningly complex wines

from limestone soils that are barrel-fermented dry. The Markgräflerland between Freiburg and Basel cultivates 7,734 acres (3,130ha) of vines. The soils are highly diverse, but loess and loess-loam is nearly everywhere, and limestone quite common, too. Vineyards are planted at altitudes of 700–1,500ft (210–470m), mainly with Gutedel (34 percent) and Spätburgunder (30 percent). Fritz Wassmer and Martin Wassmer are two producers to watch, as is Weingut Schneider in Weil am Rhein.

Some 250 miles (400km) farther north, in Wertheim-Reicholzheim (Taubertal), Konrad Schlör bottles an excellent Schwarzriesling (Pinot Meunier), a barrel-fermented red wine with the soul of Pinot Noir. The pure and refined 2004 Reicholzheimer First Schwarzriesling *trocken* is still excellent. Schlör is also one of the best Müller-Thurgau producers in Baden, if not all of Germany. His Müller is always discreet yet swinging. This is partly because the 1,580-acre (640ha) Tauberfranken district, between Wertheim and Rothenburg, is significantly cooler than, say, the Kaiserstuhl or Breisgau. The soils are also different, the vines being mostly on Muschelkalk soils, ideally suited to both Müller and Schwarzriesling. No wonder these are by far the most important grape varieties of the district, which does not conform to the Baden cliché *von der Sonne verwöhnt* ("spoiled by sunshine").

The next district is the Badische Bergstrasse, which goes from Laudenbach north of Weinheim via Heidelberg down to Wiesloch. With 965 acres (390ha) of vines, this is the smallest district of Baden. You could size it up, though, if you added Germany's smallest wine region, which is Hessische Bergstrasse, between Sebastian Vettel's hometown of Heppenheim and Seeheim-Jugenheim, south of Darmstadt. This 1,077-acre (436ha) region continues the Badische Bergstrasse northward, and indeed there is no difference between the two areas apart from political ones: the northern Bergstrasse belongs to the state of Hessen; Badische, to the state of Baden-Württemberg. Most of the vineyards face west, and the vines—Pinot Noir, Müller-Thurgau, and Riesling—grow in loess or granite north of the Neckar River, and in pure or loess-covered Muschelkalk or Buntsandstein south of the river. Although the name Bergstrasse suggests the wines might be cool, lean, and mineral mountain wines, the opposite is the case. The climate, as well as the soils, are warm and bear full-bodied wines with intense fruit flavors. Some of the finest wines of the district are bottled by Thomas Seeger in Leimen, close to Heidelberg. Most of his wines come from limestone soils, and his finest Spätburgunder, Lemberger, Grauburgunder, Weissburgunder, and Riesling can be great. The Spätburgunder (the more Rs that are added, the more intense the wine) is concentrated, grippy, powerful, and rich.

South of Bergstrasse is Kraichgau, where the soils are different, since loess covers the Buntsandstein completely here. The oblong-shaped district between the cities of Wiesloch, Sinsheim, Pforzheim, and Karlsruhe is in the basin between Odenwald and the Black Forest, so it is rather flat, rolling country. Some 2,953 acres (1,195ha) of vines are cultivated here, mainly on loess, but there are also Keuper and Muschelkalk soils. The favorite varieties are fairly typical of the Baden cliché: Pinot Noir, Riesling, Müller-Thurgau, Pinot Gris, Pinot Blanc, and Schwarzriesling account for 83 percent. Hummel and Klumpp are good producers, as are Heitlinger and Burg Ravensburg, which merged in 2009 as Weingut Heitlinger.

The Ortenau—which stretches 37 miles (60km) from Baden-Baden, in the northeast, down to Berghaupten, near Offenburg, in the southwest—is a very interesting region: the vines in the northern part (6,720 acres [2,720ha] on the steep slopes of Hochschwarzwald) grow in weathered granite. Pinot Noir (47 percent) and Riesling (25 percent) dominate the vineyards and produce some really elegant and complex wines. The aromatic, intense

Above: The barrels of one Baden's leading producers, Huber, proudly proclaim the name of the region as well as his own

Rieslings from Durbach can have cool flavors and vibrant minerality while being rich and persistent. Two of the finest are Andreas Laible's Plauelrain Riesling GG and Durbacher Plauelrain Riesling Spätlese *trocken* Achat. Schloss Neuweier in Baden-Baden also produces fine Rieslings from famous sites—Mauerberg and Schlossberg—which were both cultivated as early as the 12th century. Jacob Duijn in Bühl is an excellent Spätburgunder producer and perhaps the only one in the district. The Dutchman cultivates 16 acres (6.5ha) of Pinot Noir, and has been biodynamic for a few years. His Spätburgunders are unfined and unfiltered and are rich and powerful, but not without finesse.

The charming Breisgau (3,950 acres [1,600ha]) starts a little south of Offenburg and goes straight down 37 miles (60km) to Freiburg. The vineyards are at altitudes of 600–1,500ft (180–450m) and produce some of Baden's finest wines. Pinot Noir (43 percent) dominates, but Pinot Gris, Pinot Blanc, and Müller-Thurgau (I wonder why) are also important. In the northern part, there is mainly loess and loess-loam on the west side and sandstone on the east, though here there is also Muschelkalk, Jurassic limestone, and conglomerates. The last third of the district, the southern part, is based on gneiss. Here—in Glottertal, for example—Pinot Noir is vinified as Weissherbst, a fresh, delicate, and elegant rosé, which is absolutely delicious from a producer like Salwey. The finest Spätburgunders are grown on weathered shale limestone and taste almost Burgundian, especially from Bernhard Huber. New, very promising producers of Spätburgunder are Shelter in Kenzingen and the garage winery Enderle & Moll in Münchweier. Sven Enderle and Florian Moll cultivate just 4.4 acres (1.8ha) of old vines, but their handcrafted, archaic, and wild Spätburgunder Muschelkalk (2009) and Spätburgunder Buntsandstein (2007) are quite extraordinary. Nor should you pass up the aromatic, pure wines from the Wöhrle family at Weingut der Stadt Lahr.

The Kaiserstuhl district (10,292 acres [4,165ha]) is of course dominated by the Kaiserstuhl, a Mittelgebirge stretching northeast from the city of Breisach. The primeval volcano rises from the Rhine basin to a height of 1,830ft (557m). Its slopes bear vines from 600 to 1,300ft (190m–400m) and expose them mercilessly to the sun. It is here, in the warmest part of Germany, that the Baden cliché becomes a reality. The sun shines 1,739 hours per year, so Pinot Noir (39 percent) is in the advance guard. I do not see much sense in burning Müller-Thurgau here, but the grape still accounts for 20 percent of the area under vine. The same area is occupied by Pinot Gris, which makes more sense, as does the 10 percent taken by Pinot Blanc. Silvaner still holds 2 percent (most of it in Ihringen) but had as much as 70 percent many decades ago. The soil is based on volcanic stone but is mostly covered by loess, as the characteristic loess terraces demonstrate. Pure volcanic sites are rare, Achkarrer Schlossberg and Oberrotweiler Kirchberg being the most famous. In Oberrotweil, Eichberg and Henkenberg are predominantly volcanic; in Ihringen, Winklerberg is. The most typical wines of the Kaiserstuhl are Grauburgunder from volcanic soils and Spätburgunder. The latter has a distinctive character: the fruit is ample yet clear, and the delicately textured palate has a refreshing minerality, as well as firm tannins. Kaiserstühler Grauburgunder is rich and complex, very powerful but also refined, elegant, and mineral, finishing with a lingering salinity. I profile three producers here but could easily have included others, such as Weingut Knab in Endingen or Holger Koch in Bickensohl, who is organic. The latter is the man to watch, since his Pinots (Blanc, Gris, and Noir) are very pure, refined, delicate, and elegant.

The Tuniberg district (2,620 acres [1,060ha]) is west and southwest of Freiburg. The vines (again mainly Pinot Noir, at 57 percent, Müller-Thurgau, Pinot Blanc, and Pinot Gris) grow in loess on a plateau some 1,000ft (300m) high. I have not tasted a memorable wine from here so far.

The last district is Bodensee (1,435 acres [580ha]), where mainly Pinot Noir and Müller-Thurgau are cultivated in a Mediterranean climate. Müller can be very delicate and elegant here (as well as on the Swiss side of the lake in the Thurgau district), while Pinot Noir tends to be filigreed and light, especially when vinified as Weissherbst. Schloss Salem and Aufricht are the best producers.

Baden is so diverse, with its nine quite different districts, that it is impossible to profile as a whole. What does a Taubertäler producer near Wertheim care about what is happening near Basel in the Markgräflerland, which is a four-hour drive away? On the other hand, wine lovers the world over should get to know and love this region. You should probably start in Breisgau or the Kaiserstuhl. Avoid the cooperatives that dominate Baden (and Württemberg), and instead have a fiery Pinot Noir from Bercher or a Pinot Gris from Fritz Keller, discovering in the process that exceptional wines from these varieties need not taste like those from the Côte d'Or, Alsace, or Oregon.

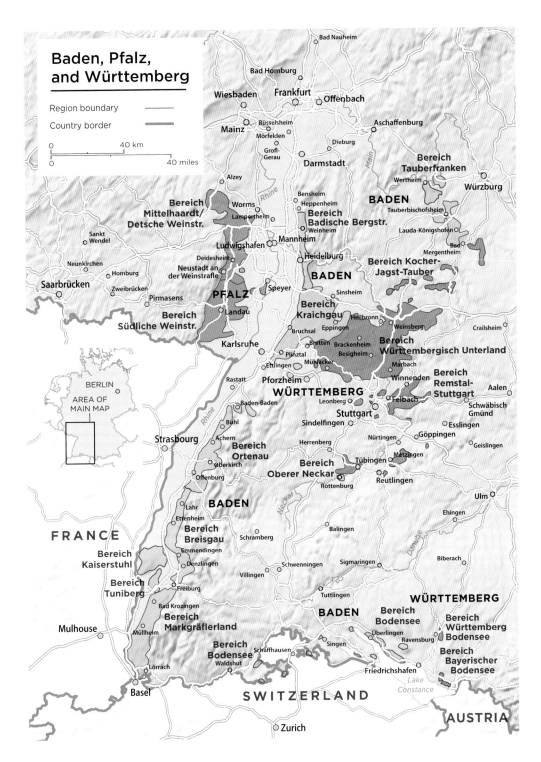

Baden, Pfalz, and Württemberg

Region boundary
Country border

40 km
40 miles

Bad Nauheim

Bad Homburg

Wiesbaden · Frankfurt · Offenbach · Aschaffenburg

Mainz · Rüsselsheim · Dieburg

Mörfelden

Großl-Gerau · Darmstadt

Bereich Tauberfranken

Alzey · Wertheim · Würzburg

Bensheim · **BADEN**

Bereich Mittelhaardt/ Detsche Weinstr. · Worms · Heppenheim · Tauberbischofsheim

Lampertheim · **Bereich Badische Bergstr.** · Lauda-Königshofen

Sankt Wendel · Weinheim · Bad Mergentheim

Neunkirchen · Deidesheim · Ludwigshafen · Mannheim

Homburg · Neustadt an der Weinstraße · Heidelburg · **Bereich Kocher-Jagst-Tauber**

Saarbrücken · Zweibrücken · Speyer · **BADEN**

Pirmasens · **PFALZ** · Sinsheim

Bereich Südliche Weinstr. · Landau · **Bereich Kraichgau** · Heilbronn · Weinsberg · Crailsheim

Bruchsal · Eppingen

Karlsruhe · Bretten · Brackenheim · **Bereich Württembergisch Unterland**

Plinztal · Besigheim

Ettlingen · Mühlacker · Marbach

Rastatt · Pforzheim · Winnenden · **Bereich Remstal-Stuttgart** · Aalen

WÜRTTEMBERG · Leonberg · Felbach

Baden-Baden · Schwäbisch Gmünd

Bühl · Sindelfingen · **Stuttgart** · Esslingen

Strasbourg · Achern · Herrenberg · Nürtingen · Göppingen · Geislingen

Bereich Ortenau · Metzingen

Oberkirch · Tübingen

Offenburg · **Bereich Oberer Neckar** · Reutlingen · Ulm

Rottenburg

BADEN · Ehingen

Lahr

Ettenheim · Balingen

Bereich Breisgau · Schramberg

FRANCE · Emmendingen

Bereich Kaiserstuhl · Denzlingen · Schwenningen · Sigmaringen · Biberach

Villingen

Bereich Tuniberg · Freiburg · Tuttlingen · **WÜRTTEMBERG**

Bad Krozingen · **BADEN** · **Bereich Bodensee**

Mulhouse · **Bereich Markgräflerland** · Überlingen · Ravensburg · **Bereich Württemberg Bodensee**

Müllheim · Singen

Bereich Bodensee · Schaffhausen · **Bereich Bayerischer Bodensee**

Lörrach · Waldshut · Friedrichshafen · Lake Constance

Basel · S W I T Z E R L A N D · AUSTRIA

Zurich

BERLIN
AREA OF MAIN MAP

8 9

Weingut Bernhard Huber

Bernhard Huber is one of the most important wine producers in Germany of the past 20 years. His Spätburgunder, especially the four grands crus, are world-class and often mistaken for their own wines by famous Burgundy producers. No less impressive is the pure yet highly complex Hecklinger Schlossberg Chardonnay, from one of the most spectacular sites of Breisgau. Huber's Pinots (the Pinot Blanc and Pinot Gris are equally extraordinary) combine concentration, ripeness, and complexity with elegance, freshness, and purity in a way that is unrivaled in Germany.

There are two main reasons to excuse those who confuse Huber's Spätburgunder with top Burgundy. The soils of Malterdingen, Hecklingen, and a few other villages, says Huber, are the same as those of the Côte d'Or: weathered shale limestone (Muschelkalk). Maybe this was why Cistercian monks from Burgundy brought Pinot Noir to Malterdingen more than 700 years ago. This and the climatic influence of the Belfort Gap have let Huber concentrate on Pinot varieties since his beginnings 25 years ago.

Even more Burgundian than the history and soil are Huber's Pinot Noir vines, whether clones or massal selections. The finest Pinot vines now, though, in Huber's opinion, are the clones from the Frank nursery in nearby Kenzingen. "Small berries, loose bunches, very aromatic—I never saw anything as fine in Burgundy," Huber raves over the clones of Rainer Frank.

The freshness, elegance, and finesse of Huber's Spätburgunder also owe much to when the grapes are harvested (all by hand, of course). Huber picks when the berries are ripe, yet not overripe. "I like them just ripe," he explains, preferring to pick a day too early than a day too late. "Sugar levels are certainly relevant, but I want to have a vibrant acidity as well." Must weights are between 95 and 98° Oechsle, but since 0.5% ABV is lost during the fermentation,

Right: The brilliant but modest Bernhard Huber, with his wife Barbara and son Julian, at their Malterdingen winery

Huber's Pinots (the Pinot Blanc and Pinot Gris are equally extraordinary) combine concentration, ripeness, and complexity with elegance, freshness, and purity in a way that is unrivaled in Germany.

Huber chaptalizes by up to 0.8% ABV to reach 13.3% or (at most) 13.5%.

In the end, it is the blend of many different parameters that gives Huber's Spätburgunder their immense complexity and finesse: the mineral limestone soils; old vines and the mixture of old and new top-quality clones from Burgundy and Germany; low-yielding yet well-adapted rootstocks; high-density plantings; reduced yields (green harvesting); 900 working hours per hectare in the vineyards; precise picking dates for each parcel; gentle processing ("We handle the grapes as if they were glass balls," says Huber); and maturation in carefully selected French barriques—to say nothing of heart, intuition, understanding, and so on.

Huber, who started his own wine production in 1987 with 2 acres (5ha) of vines, an old basket press, and three oak barrels from 110 to 330 liters in a rented cellar, has now attained the summit. He cultivates 66 acres (27ha) of vines, of which 65 percent are Pinot Noir, 10 percent Chardonnay, 10 percent Pinot Blanc, and 7 percent Pinot Gris. I can hardly imagine how the wines can get any better. Maintaining this level of quality is probably even more difficult than reaching it. But Bernhard Huber is rooted in the soil, and if anybody can stay on this pinnacle, it is he.

Since 2004, he has offered as many as seven Spätburgunders, including Huber Spätburgunder, from the youngest vines, which yield 65hl/ha; the excellent Malterdinger (village), 50–55hl/ha from 12- to 20-year-old vines; Alte Reben (premier cru) from 20- to 40-year-old vines, with yields at 37hl/ ha. This is an impressive blend of the second wines from the four grands crus that I introduce below.

One further recommendation first: if ever you get the chance to taste Huber's delicate Gelber Muskateller Kabinett, which can be dry or off-dry depending on the vintage, taste it, quaff it, love it. This is the wine in which Breisgau is kissed by the Mosel and brings tears to your eyes.

FINEST WINES

(Tasted in May and September 2011)
After a cold maceration of five to six days, with *pigeage* three times a day and a final *remontage* via gravity, the 2009 wines were fermented for 22–25 days in wooden vats, with uncrushed grapes and up to 70 percent of whole bunches, at temperatures up to 90°F (32°C). Post-fermentation maceration lasts only one day, to preserve the fruit. After pressing and settling, the cloudy wines were aged in 100% new French barriques (mainly from Rousseau, François Frères, and Taransaud) until malolactic fermentation was finished (which lasted until May/June 2011 for the 2009s). Shortly before the next harvest, they were racked—with plenty of the lees, to avoid harsh tannins—into one- or two-year-old barriques, depending on the character of each wine. After another couple of months, the wines were bottled unfined and unfiltered. "Spätburgunder has to dance on both nose and palate," Huber declares. So let's rock!

Bienenberg Spätburgunder GG
Since 1971, Bienenberg has been the largest site of Malterdingen, extending over some 370 acres (150ha). Nevertheless, with 37 acres (15ha) of vines here, it is Huber's most important vineyard, even more so since 26 acres (10.45ha) are classified for Grosses Gewächs production. Pinot Noir accounts for 60 percent and is planted in the southeastern part, whereas Chardonnay, Pinot Gris, and Pinot Blanc are in the southwestern part. Bienenberg does not look very spectacular, since the gradient, rising from 750 to 1,000ft (230m–310m) is rather soft. The oldest Pinot Noir vines, though, were planted in the 1950s, in the weathered shale limestone that is very similar to that in Burgundy's Côte de Nuits. Younger plantings were with Burgundy clones and at a density of up to 10,000 vines/ha. Yields average 30hl/ha. The wine has firm tannins and benefits from being decanted if you prefer to drink it young.
2008 A bright garnet, with a blue shimmer. Amazingly fresh and precise on the nose, this is a delicate Burgundian-style Pinot, with ripe red-berry, cherry, violet, and white-pepper aromas. Very silky and fresh on the palate, almost dancing, refined and elegant. Alluringly sweet but carried aloft by a fascinating, delicate, and mineral acidity that runs through the wine.

Sommerhalde Spätburgunder GG

This 5.3-acre (2.15ha) grand cru parcel in Brombach is located on the eastern border of Breisgau. The southeast-facing vineyard benefits from cooler night temperatures, since it is framed by forest to the north and east. The slope rises from 780 to 1,000ft (240–300m), with an inclination of 20–50%, and is planted mainly with Pinot Noir (80 percent), since the variety never has problems with botrytis here. The vines were planted between the mid-1960s and the early 2000s, with a density of 4,500–9,000 vines/ha. Some 40 percent are clones from Burgundy, 12 percent from Freiburg, "and the rest is too old, so nobody knows," admits Huber. They grow in ferrous marl soils with massive veins of Muschelkalk (shale limestone), and yields are restricted to 30hl/ha. The wine has an intense fruit and a mineral structure, so it can be enjoyed young.

2009★ Dark ruby color. Deep, ripe, and supple on the nose, with mellow fruit aromas. Full and dense on the palate, powerful and voluptuous, but also firmly structured. Vibrant acidity, grippy tannins; very elegant, persistent, and round. It's a pleasure to drink it young—as long as there are also enough bottles for aging.

Schlossberg Spätburgunder GG

This is the most spectacular Breisgau grand cru. The 15-acre (6ha) slice of the 125-acre (50ha) Schlossberg in Hecklingen is very steep, with a gradient of 72–96%, and faces south/southwest. The site has been under vine since at least 1492, and because the stony soil, with yellow Muschelkalk (shale limestone), is similar to that of the Côte de Beaune, as Huber reports, it is planted with both Pinot Noir (80 percent) and Chardonnay (20 percent). The vines were planted between 1975 and 2004, but most of them are from the early/mid-1990s, when Huber started to plant French clones. The planting density is remarkably high, with 6,250–13,000 vines/ha, whereas the yields are low, averaging only 28hl/ha. Due to the dramatic incline and exposure, sunlight intensity is very high, which lends the wine a deep, supple, and warm character. It is, nevertheless, tightly structured and very intense and mineral; to many of my colleagues, this is the most noble of Huber's grand cru Pinots. But I have been trying to rank Bernhard's grands crus for many years, without any conclusive results, and am happy to persevere. Cheers!

2008★ Fascinating herbal and smoky terroir characters, with oaky coffee and chocolate aromas, quite exotic, yet still quite closed initially. After a while, very deep and intense yet refined raspberry aromas emerge. I came back to this wine 20 hours later, and then the perfumed bouquet was luxurious but extremely fine and spicy. A mouthful of finest Pinot, very intense and supple, amazingly sweet and infinitely juicy. Rich, round, and silky, with extremely fine tannins and a warm, lingering finish. Very young but clearly of exceptional quality.

Wildenstein Spätburgunder Reserve

A parcel in the huge Malterdinger Bienenberg, the Wildenstein is not (yet) a Grosses Gewächs, though it is certainly worthy of grand cru status. The terraced Willistein parcel (Wildenstein was the medieval name) is close to the winery and, as Huber reports, was already being cultivated 700 years ago by Cistercian monks from Burgundy. The vines grow in a reddish, partly very rocky soil. Because the planting density is quite high (at 5,000–10,000 vines/ha), the roots go deep, supplying micronutrients and minerals to the vines. The resulting wine is always expressive: deep and extremely persistent, but also refined and delicate. The aging potential is immense.

2008★ Purity, elegance, and finesse—this is what great Pinot is all about. Luminous garnet. Fascinating, delicate flavors of red berries, very elegant and harmonious, deep and slightly smoky. Brilliant and refined on the palate, very mineral and firm, still slightly astringent but straightforward. The texture, though, is very refined and silky, the structure filigreed, and the freshness amazing. This wine does dance on the palate, and the pirouette lasts and lasts. Great potential.

2005★ Quite dark garnet. Highly refined Pinot flavors, almost floral, very delicate and alluring, with mineral spiciness. On the palate, this is one of the most refined German Pinots I can remember. Very intense, sweet, and long, but also ethereal, flowing, and silky. Delicate acidity. Thrilling wine.

Weingut Bernhard Huber

Area under vine: 66 acres (27ha)
Average production: 170,000 bottles
Best vineyards: *Brombach* Sommerhalde; *Hecklingen* Schlossberg; *Malterdingen* Bienenberg, Wildenstein
Heimbacher Weg 19, 79364 Malterdingen
Tel: +49 7644 1200
www.weingut-huber.de

Franz Keller / Schwarzer Adler

F ritz Keller is not only a charismatic and well-known vintner in Vogtsburg-Oberbergen on Kaiserstuhl. He is also a successful hotelier and restaurateur (the Schwarzer Adler restaurant has had a Michelin star since 1969), an enthusiastic wine merchant (finest Bordeaux and Burgundy), and first chairman of SC Freiburg—a club that belongs to the German Bundesliga. Above all, Fritz Keller is a very generous host. For my last visit, he prepared 50 wines to taste, despite my having asked for only ten. We tasted and discussed them all, even though it grew late and there was Champions League football on TV.

The 153-acre (62ha) wine estate, run by Fritz Keller as the fourth generation since 1990, has been well known for really dry wines of first-class quality for a long time. Pinot Gris (36 percent), Pinot Noir (26 percent), and Pinot Blanc (17 percent) dominate the vineyards in Achkarren, Oberrotweil, Oberbergen, Schelingen, Bischoffingen, and Jechtingen. But the first wine you are served in the Schwarzer Adler, or the more indigenous Rebstock, restaurant is always the concentrated yet fresh and lighthearted Silvaner Bassgeige from almost 40-year-old vines. "I like the crisp finish of this wine—and this is what all my wines should have, even the finest," Keller says.

Indeed, his dry and elegant wines, produced in a reductive style, are always animating, especially with food. Keller calls them "Bauhaus wines: pure, clear, and functional. Wines of high quality but without gimmicky pretension. Not luxury products for a few, but attractive wines for everybody, to match with food." Since he started to produce typical Baden wines for a German discounter under the brand Franz Keller Edition, he has received some harsh criticism from the more snobbish section of the German wine scene—even though the wines are quite good and really quaffable.

Right: Fritz Keller, the fourth generation at his family estate, is a man of many parts but manages to produce superb wines

This family wine estate, run by Fritz Keller as the fourth generation
since 1990, has been well known for really dry wines
of first-class quality for a long time

Even if you prefer full, intense, rich wines, you will probably still enjoy the crispness and verve of Keller's white and red Selection wines. "Especially over recent years, we have reduced the alcohol levels but have raised the extracts and so extended the aging potential of our wines," Keller explains. He reduced the height of the canopy to extend the vegetative period, benefits from cooler conditions at altitudes up to 1,245ft (380m), and picks fully ripe and healthy grapes with must weights of "not more than 98° Oechsle," so chaptalization is not necessary. "Our clones and massal selections would never reach more than 100° Oechsle anyway," he insists. The oldest Pinot Noir vines are about 50 years old, and French Pinot clones are used only for new plantations. "To be honest," Keller admits, "I really prefer the German clones from Freiburg to the clones from Dijon, once the vines are 30 or 35 years old, because the grapes ripen later. The same is true of massal selections."

Although the estate produces mainly Burgundian varieties, the finest wines are made more on a Bordeaux model. Single-vineyard wines are offered only in the mid-price segment, while the top wines are blends from different sites.

About one-third of all the wines produced by Keller are from the Oberbergener Bassgeige. This is a huge site between Oberrotweil and Schelingen that is exposed mostly to the south, southwest, and west. The loess layers are partly mixed with basalt and volcanic stones, so the wines counter their overall fruity character with a fine and refreshing minerality, even in warmer years.

The south-facing Oberbergener Pulverbuck, where Keller's Mâconnais-like Pinot Blanc originates, reaches from the top like a tongue into the Bassgeige, lending the late-harvested wine ripe fruit flavors, as well as pronounced acidity and lingering minerality.

Achkarrer Schlossberg is one of the best sites of the district: very steep, south-facing, and with rocky volcanic soils that force the Pinot vines deep.

The top wines of Weingut Franz Keller, however, are to be found in the Selection ranges Franz Anton, S, and A. Whether you call the A-class wines grands crus or not does not really matter— they are produced only in outstanding vintages of extraordinary quality and are even richer and more complex than the impressive premiers crus of the S class. The wines in either category, though, come from more than one site. As the fine yet less complex wines of the Franz Anton range are blends of the lowest and highest parcels of several sites, to play with the different harvest times, so the S- and A-class wines blend careful selections from different vineyards. Whereas wines of the S class are made from vines growing in mixed soils, where the dominating volcanic rocks are covered by layers of loess, the A-class wines are sourced from small parcels with pure volcanic and basalt soils, with massive seams of limestone running through them. This soil type is probably unique in Europe, and it lends the wine a distinctive minerality and structure. The marriage of grapes from different altitudes and ripening times gives the A-class wines an additional complexity.

The fresh varietal white wines are destemmed and directly pressed, then they ferment and age in stainless-steel tanks, whereas the more complex wines age in large traditional oak barrels. The whites of the S and the A class are fermented in stainless steel but aged in small barrels of 225 liters and 350 liters for four to eight months. The red wines age in French barriques for 12–14 months. The aging is done in the Bergkeller, a spectacular tunnel system Keller constructed in the loess soils. The temperature here is a constant 54°F (12°C). Some 2,400 bottles of the finest wines in the world, mainly from Bordeaux and Burgundy, are also stored here. This is the stock for one of the most attractive restaurant wine lists in Europe.

In spring 2011, Keller started to construct a new winery that should be finished in 2013.

FINEST WINES

(Tasted in November 2011)

2010 Oberbergener Bassgeige Grauburgunder Vum Steinriesen [V]
The tall green Rhine wine bottle signals that this is a fresh, pure, straightforward Pinot Gris that has nothing in common with either the old-fashioned Ruländer wines of the past or the mostly overblown Grauburgunders of today. Sourced from small terraces with weathered volcanic rocks and layers of loess, it was fermented in traditional oak barrels and did not go through malolactic fermentation. Very clear and punchy on the nose, as on the palate, with white-fruit aromas, racy acidity, and salty minerality. Cleanses everything and should be served with poached fish.

2010 Achkarrer Schlossberg Grauburgunder [V]
This is an excellent Pinot Gris from one of the best sites of the district. Facing south, this is a very steep and rocky volcanic slope with 40-year-old vines. Brilliant on the nose, this lean and reductive wine is dense, tight, salty, and vibrant—volcanic, indeed—and quite persistent, too.

Grauburgunder A
2010 Discreet on the nose. Very clear, pure, and salty on the palate; straightforward, with grip and a long aftertaste. Full-bodied and complex. Needs two or three years to develop.
2007 Bright, ripe, and concentrated fruit flavors. Full-bodied, dense, sweet, and complex in the mouth; very salty and Burgundian. Long finish.

Chardonnay A
2010 Very pure and refined on the nose, as in the mouth. Succulent and complex, extremely salty, with just a touch of new oak (100 percent new barriques); very thrilling and long. Great wine.
2009 Dense, juicy, and with the acidity to lift the mighty body of this ripe, complex yet elegant wine.
2007 Analytically bone-dry, this brilliant, pure, and elegant wine tastes quite sweet due to the rich extract, as well as the new oak. Very salty finish.

Spätburgunder S
2008 Clear, fresh, and floral on the nose. Thrilling and tightly woven on the palate, silky and cool, very pure and straight. The tannins are still a little rough, but this helps you enjoy this Bauhaus wine rather than idolizing it.

2007★ Very alluring in its generous sweet bouquet. Silky and pure, very chalky and firm, but animating thanks to its freshness and purity. Just great.

Spätburgunder A
The grapes are mainly sourced from the Eichberg cru in Oberrotweil, but also from the Kirchberg cru, from certain parcels in Jechtingen and the Achkarren Schlossberg cru.
2009 Deep, ripe, and complex flavors of cherries and tobacco. Full, round, and velvety on the palate, rich and quite powerful, but well structured with grippy tannins and very good length. Think of a Baden-Pommard, but do not touch it before 2014.
2008 Spicy and floral aromas, even lime. Firm and still very young on the palate; very fresh, pure, and silky, immediate and persistent. There is more finesse in the 2008 than in the 2009, though the latter will probably age longer.
2007★ A dense yet refined and floral bouquet. Rich, concentrated, and succulent on the palate, with the finest tannins and sophisticated acidity. Power meets finesse. Great potential; great wine.
2005★ Intense, ripe, and mature on the nose, with aromas of sweet cherries and plums; slightly smoky, but there are also nice floral aromas. Very noble and charming in the mouth, this impressive wine is supple, sweet, and smooth but lifted by its very elegant acidity and refined tannins. Floral aromas on the long finish. Really great wine that is perfect to drink now or over the next five years.

Weingut Franz Keller / Schwarzer Adler
Area under vine: 153 acres (62ha)
Average production: 450,000 bottles
Badbergstrasse 23,
79235 Vogtsburg-Oberbergen
Tel: +49 766 293 300
www.franz-keller.de

Weingut Dr. Heger

Weingut Dr. Heger in Ihringen was founded in 1935 when Dr. Max Heger, a practicing physician, became a part-time vintner as well. He bought parcels of vines in Ihringer Winklerberg and Achkarrer Schlossberg, both spectacular *Einzellagen* on the southwestern slopes of Kaiserstuhl. Both sites are terraced and south-facing and, due to the heat-storing stone walls and soils of weathered volcanic rocks, benefit from a very special microclimate even in cooler years. Wine quality, it is reported, was already exceptional 75 years ago, when about 70 percent of the sites were planted with Silvaner, but bottles were scarce. Luckily, the wines can still be exceptional today, though there is only a little Silvaner left.

Joachim Heger started making wine in 1982 and, together with his wife Silvia, took over the estate ten years later from his father Wolfgang (Mimus). Since then, he has focused on Spätburgunder, Grauburgunder, Weissburgunder, and Riesling. Of each variety, there are two grands crus: Winklerberg GG and Schlossberg GG. Although both sites are extremely warm (the summer of 2010 was the 17th in a row with above-average temperatures) and the wines are accordingly full-bodied and rich, they do not lack elegance and finesse. The volcanic soils are very mineral, and so are the wines: very salty and complex, but also elegant.

Heger aims for elegant, refined, and persistent wines of mineral depth and vibrant acidity. So his team works very precisely in the vineyards, which have always been the base for the high quality at Dr. Heger. To work out the needs of the crus and of parcels within them, Heger engaged French soil biologist Claude Bourguignon as a consultant for "terroir issues" such as sustainable soil cultivation, vine management, and organic fertilizer.

Indeed, something has changed at Dr. Heger. Although it had been one of the most highly

Right: Joachim Heger, who, despite the already high reputation of his wines, has had the vision to take them higher still

Although Dr. Heger had been one of the most highly regarded estates in Germany ever since the 1990s, the wines have never been finer or more subtle than they have been since the 2008 vintage

Above: The south-facing Winklerberg is a warm site, but the mineral-rich volcanic soils seem to contribute complexity and elegance

regarded estates in Germany ever since the 1990s (especially for its Winklerberg Spätburgunder), the wines have never been finer or more subtle than they have been since the 2008 vintage. They are less broad and weighty, fresher, and more precise and mineral—and much more fun to drink.

The whole-bunch-pressed whites have always been made in a reductive style. They are less powerful today because the crus are fermented and aged in traditional oak barrels rather than stainless steel. The gentle oxygenation adds complexity and finesse to their natural richness.

Really stunning, though, is the change in the 2009 Spätburgunder wines, which were bottled unfiltered for the first time and are drier, fresher, purer, and more delicate, filigreed, and silky than ever.

Yields are still kept low (through bunch-thinning and green harvesting) but are not as "idiotic" (in Heger's own words) as some years ago. "Well meant is not always well done," he concedes. The Pinots are also picked much earlier today, especially in the hot spots. For Heger, "100° Oechsle is the maximum, and more and more I prefer must weights in the low 90s. If there is not enough alcohol, we chaptalize but keep the freshness." In 2010, the old Häusleboden parcel was picked twice in ten days, and the wine will be a blend of both batches.

Heger also bought new open vats (wood and stainless steel) to ferment each parcel separately. For a couple of years, he has used 20–35 percent of the stems, too. Maceration time is now 17–24 days (including a cold maceration)—much shorter than the four to six weeks previously. Extraction is more gentle, too, since *pigeage* is done by hand and only once or twice a day. Heger uses more new barriques today, but with a much lighter toast.

Really stunning is the change in the 2009 Spätburgunder wines, which were bottled unfiltered and are drier, fresher, purer, and more delicate, filigreed, and silky than ever

The finest wines are classified in-house with three stars. All the Grosses Gewächs wines shine, but so, too, do the Silvaner, produced from both crus, and the Muskateller (which I have still to taste). About 95 percent of production is fermented dry, though 17 noble sweet wines were offered in the 2011/12 price list, including a 2001 Schlossberg Riesling Spätlese, a 2004 Winklerberg Ruländer BA, and a 2008 Winklerberg Muskateller Eiswein.

In 1986, Weinhaus Heger was established to meet the demand for Heger wines. Under this label, fresh and fruity wines are offered, produced mostly from the grapes of contract growers.

FINEST WINES

2010 Winklerberg Gras im Ofen Weissburgunder GG ★

This wine was produced in 2010 for the first time to highlight the special character of this very stony south-/southwest-facing parcel, which was always part of the Winklerberg GG but considered too interesting to be hidden in a parcel blend. It is a very firm, pure, and salty Pinot Blanc, with a racy acidity and an almost astringent minerality. This is an impressively complex wine and will be a great wine two or three years from the harvest.

2010 Winklerberg Grauburgunder GG ★

At least since the 2008 vintage, this has been one of my favorite Pinot Gris. Grown on weathered volcanic rocks, this deep, elegant, and refined grand cru is pure and spicy on the nose, and rich and complex on the palate, where clear and intense fruit flavors are carried by a thrilling minerality and brisk acidity to a persistent finish. Honed and salty. Terrific.

2009 Winklerberg Häusleboden Spätburgunder *** ★

This is the first vintage from a higher parcel planted in 1956 and cultivated organically. Fermented with 20–35 percent stems. Deep and meaty on the nose, very pure and intense. Velvety, sweet, and full on the palate, dense but also transparent, fresh and firm, finishing with a refreshing kick and red-berry aromas. Very concentrated and impressive.

2009 Schlossberg Spätburgunder GG

Dark color. Smoky toast aromas of blackberries and dark cherries. Supple, ripe, concentrated, but very refined and silky. Very fine tannins, succulent and fresh, quite firm; some thrilling edges. Persistent.

2005 Winklerberg Spätburgunder ***

Sweet, warm, and floral on the nose, with dried fruits, plums, and raisins. Very juicy and velvety on the palate, tobacco and violet flavors; generous, yet refined and silky due to the acidity and ripe tannins. Cassis on the finish. Delicious now.

Weingut Dr. Heger

Area under vine: 50 acres (20ha)
Average production: 120,000 bottles
Bachenstrasse 19/21, 79241 Ihringen/Kaiserstuhl
Tel: +49 7868 205
www.heger-weine.de

Weingut Ziereisen

Hanspeter Ziereisen, whose estate is located in Efringen-Kirchen in the very south of Germany and just a ten-minute drive from Basel (Switzerland), was already producing very fine Spätburgunder in the 1990s. German critics, though, found them too light and asked for more power and extraction. Although he kept on picking rather early to preserve freshness, he chaptalized his Pinots in 2000 and kept doing so for several years. He got higher scores but was not really lucky with the results. "The wines were quite rich and had up to 14% ABV, but I wondered if this was really necessary—especially since the wines of the 1990s taste better today than the younger ones," he says. So, in 2007 Hanspeter decided not to chaptalize any more and to accept Pinots with 12 or 12.5% ABV (as in 2008 and 2009). "The grapes are fully ripe when we pick them, so what's wrong with fermenting the must without any additives?" he asks rhetorically.

Ziereisen, whose family also grows and sells potatoes, vegetables, fruits, and wonderful wood-fired bread, owns 37 acres (15ha) of vines, of which 50 percent is Pinot Noir and 20 percent Gutedel (Chasselas), the rest Pinot Gris, Pinot Blanc, Chardonnay, and Syrah. All his vines are planted in the south-facing Ölberg *Einzellage* and grow in Jurassic limestone at altitudes from 900 up to 1,300ft (270m–400m). The site is quite steep and was never *flurbereinigt*. Thus, it is divided into many small parcels with diverse soil compositions and vines up to 50 years old. While the more fruit-driven *Sortenweine* are marketed under the names of the varieties, the *Parzellenweine* (the crus) are labeled with the name of the parcel whose character Hanspeter wants to express. The Jaspis wines are selections from the very best barrels.

The climate in Efringen-Kirchen is "Burgundian," Hanspeter says, due to the Belfort Gap. The Markgräflerland is protected by the Black Forest to the east and by the Vosges to the west. The wind comes from the south, by way of the Rhône-Rhine Canal, so there are very rarely problems with botrytis. "In former times, the Markgräflerland was much more renowned than the Kaiserstuhl," Ziereisen notes. "Even the early-ripening Gutedel was a noble wine and was served on the *Graf Zeppelin* in the early 20th century." The Gutedel had a higher price than the Mouton Rothschild or the Schloss Johannisberger.

By keeping his Steingrüble Gutedel on its lees for 11 months in traditional oak barrels and bottling it unfined and unfiltered, Ziereisen is trying to recreate this glorious tradition. He even has a 2007 Gutedel in a large barrel, aging it like a *vin jaune* without sulfur and planning to keep it under *flor* for about ten years.

In 2003, Ziereisen bottled his first unfiltered white wine, and since 2004 he has fermented all his wines spontaneously in oak, bottling all his crus unfiltered. As a result, though, some of the wines struggled to receive official recognition (the AP number). So, Ziereisen decided to renounce the *Qualitätswein* category and started marketing his wines as Tafelwein (until 2010) or Landwein. Pure understatement, but the resignation allows him to do what he thinks best for his wines: aging in oak barrels from a Franconian cooper, long *élevage* on lees for up to 30 months for the white crus and up to five years for the red crus.

In the vineyards, Ziereisen aims for balance and slow growth, so he has not used any fertilizers since 2005, allows vegetation between the rows, arrests flowering to get looser bunches and smaller grapes, and halves the biggest bunches. Everything is done by hand, not only because the sites are steep, but also because the newer plantings are remarkably dense, averaging 10,000 vines/ha. Ziereisen planted French clones of Pinot Noir in 2000, but on discovering that they tend to rot, he uprooted them. He prefers German and Swiss clones, so he planted several different low-yielding clones and massal selections.

Harvest starts when the grapes taste fully ripe, which normally happens at 94–95° Oechsle. The first variety picked is Pinot Noir, and only then follow Pinot Gris, Chardonnay, Pinot Blanc, Gutedel, and finally Syrah. The whites are whole-bunch basket-pressed, normally for up to 12 hours, but for up to 24 hours when the quality is extraordinary. After settling and cooling down to 41° F (5°C), the must is transferred into barrels of 300–7,000 liters and kept without sulfur throughout *élevage*.

The Pinot Noir is handpicked selectively in the vineyard and again at a sorting table. The grapes are destemmed, cold-macerated for five to 14 days, and kept on the skins for six or more weeks. There is some *pigeage* but much less extraction than before 2007. Ziereisen also experiments with whole bunches and foot-treading. The Syrah is done similarly, but never in contact with the stems. After being basket-pressed, the must is transferred into small barrels, of which only 20–30 percent are new for the Spätburgunder and 50 percent for the Syrah.

FINEST WINES

(Tasted in November 2011)
2010 Gutedel Steingrüble [V]
This Gutedel from 25-year-old vines, fermented spontaneously in large wooden casks, was kept on lees for 11 months. I do not know of any other Gutedel that has such a long *élevage*. Very clear silex aromas and yellow stone-fruit flavors, almost like Riesling. Reductive and lean in style. Pure, salty, and racy, yet elegant, persistent, and really thrilling.

2008 Spätburgunder Rhini
A delicate, fragrant Spätburgunder from a protected parcel in a dell with limestone soils covered by ferrous layers of loam and silty to sandy clay. After six weeks of maceration, the wine is kept for 18 months in 30 percent new and 70 percent used barriques. Only 12.5% ABV. Floral, slightly leafy, and just ripe in its fruit flavors, red rather than black. Silky and remarkably fresh, chalky, dense, and firm, showing more bones than flesh at the moment. Very complex, though, and with great aging potential.

2008 Jaspis Pinot Noir Alte Reben ★
This is a selection of the best barrels from the oldest Pinot Noir vines planted in the 1950s and '60s. Bright garnet. Alluringly sweet on the nose. Rich and supple on the palate, powerful and sweet, with intense ripe-fruit flavors, but this complex wine is also fresh and tightly structured. Great aging potential. I would not drink it before 2018, but enjoy the great 1997 and 1999 Rhini till then.

2009 Jaspis Syrah ★
Until I was poured this garnet-ruby wine from nine-year-old vines, Ziereisen's Gestad was my favorite Syrah from Germany. Both wines come from an extremely steep parcel where there is almost no topsoil but pure limestone. Planting density is up to 14,000 vines/ha. This barrel selection is amazing. After seven weeks of maceration, it was aged for 20 months in half new and half used barriques. Fascinating spicy flavors of dark fruits, pepper, and sandalwood. Rich, full, and concentrated, with drive, precision, and length. Very succulent, thanks to the delicious acidity and ripe, silky tannins.

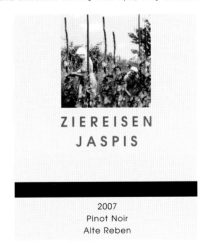

ZIEREISEN
JASPIS

2007
Pinot Noir
Alte Reben

Weingut Ziereisen
Area under vine: 37 acres (15ha)
Average production: 100,000 bottles
Markgrafenstrasse 17,
79558 Efringen-Kirchen
Tel: +49 7628 2848
www.ziereisen.de

Bercher

The history of the Swiss Bercher family dates back to 1457, but it has been settled in Burkheim for more than 300 years. Pinot Noir (40 percent) rules the vineyards of 62 acres (25ha), which are located in Burkheim, Sasbach, Jechtingen, Königsschaffenhausen, and Leiselheim. Pinot Gris is the second most important variety (23 percent), then Pinot Blanc (17), Riesling (8), Chardonnay (7), and other varieties. More than 90 percent of production is dry.

Martin (who cares for the vines) and Arne (winemaking), the tenth generation of the Bercher family, are responsible for the wine production today. The cousins aim for "authentic wines with character and soul—wines that reflect the distinctive characteristics of their origins, the different soils and microclimates," Arne says.

The finest and most complex wines are the Grosses Gewächs wines from Burkheim, especially from Feuerberg. Bercher's best parcels for Pinot Blanc and Pinot Gris (vines average 16–17 years) are located in the upper third of the south-facing, terraced slope, at up to 800ft (240m) in altitude. The soil is almost loess-free and quite stony; thus, the wines are characterized by pure, weathered, volcanic rocks that lend a fascinating freshness and saltiness to the wines. The two cousins have worked better and better during recent years. Since the soils are less chalky, the wines attack the mouth without any buffers. Because the dark soil stores the heat of the day and gives it back to the vines at night, this is a special climate that guarantees full ripeness even in cool years such as 2010.

The Pinot Noir parcel of the Feuerberg, with 20- to 25-year-old vines, also faces south. Since there are no terraces, there is an inclination that gives additional sunlight. The Berchers prefer an authentic Kaiserstühler Spätburgunder to the more aromatic and fresher French style, so only German clones are planted. The color of their Spätburgunders is bright garnet rather than ruby,

and the aromas are warm without being overripe, tending toward bright red fruits and sour cherry rather than dark berries or sweet cherries. On the palate, a Spätburgunder from the purest soils of the Feuerberg is always powerful and fiery. Grapes are picked when they are fully ripe, and the Berchers do not fear must weights of 100–104° Oechsle. Indeed, the wines have the tension to balance volumes of 13.5–14% ABV. Because they are bone-dry, firmly structured, and very complex, they need a couple of years in bottle to become more elegant.

FINEST WINES

2010 Feuerberg Grauer Burgunder GG
This wine was fermented and matured for nine months in barriques, one-third of which were new. Brilliant and delicate on the nose (which is still unusual for Pinot Gris from Baden, especially from Kaiserstuhl), beautifully pure and mineral, really volcanic. Clear, elegant, and refined on the palate, due to its remarkable purity; very salty and intense, with concentrated fruit and impressive length and complexity. Good grip; great wine.

2009 Feuerberg Spätburgunder GG
This energetic Pinot is, together with the 2007, the most impressive red I have tasted from this estate, though I find it still slightly overoaked. Smoky-toasty on the nose, with intense fruit flavors of ripe dark cherries and berries; spicy, too. Supple, concentrated, and intense on the palate, very powerful and deep, and with pronounced (and still astringent) tannins, which lend a firm structure and promising future to this rich yet elegant wine. Should be enjoyed with peppered wild boar or venison, but not before 2014, when the tannins will be rounder and the wood more fully integrated.

Weingut Bercher
Area under vine: 62 acres (25ha)
Average production: 180,000 bottles
Best vineyards: *Burkheim* Feuerberg, Schlossberg
Mittelstadt 13,
79235 Vogtsburg-Burkheim
Tel: +49 7662 212
www.weingutbercher.de

Salwey

It was a huge inheritance Konrad Salwey had to accept after the tragic death of his father Wolf-Dietrich in early 2011. Although he had been fully involved in the family business in Oberrotweil for more than seven years, it is different to vinify the crop of almost 125 acres (50ha) of vines without the advice of an experienced father. Happily, however, Konrad has a clear idea of what he wants and can follow his ideas without any compromises now, which is exactly what the uncaged bird is doing. His latest wines—wild, fresh, pure, and unpretentious—hint at how hard he must have fought with his beloved dad over styles and techniques.

Konrad Salwey has a clear idea of what he wants and can follow his ideas without any compromises now. His latest wines are wild, fresh, pure, and unpretentious

Spätburgunder and Grauburgunder are the main focus at Salwey, since these varieties each occupy 40 percent of the total area under vine. The finest wines come from the three Oberrotweil crus, Kirchberg, Eichberg, and Henkenberg. In the Kirchberg, Salwey has 13.5 acres (5.5ha) planted with Pinot Gris, Pinot Blanc, and Pinot Noir, which have grown in this rocky volcanic soil since the 1970s and '80s, giving discreet wines with a distinctive personality and lingering salinity. The Spätburgunder and Grauburgunder from the Eichberg is more supple and velvety due to the volcanic tufa soil, whereas the Weissburgunder and Grauburgunder from the Henkenberg can be quite mineral. Newer plantations are mainly from massal selections rather than clones, and there are no French Pinot clones because they ripen too early.

Konrad aims for expressive yet elegant, authentic, and enjoyable wines with around 13% ABV. Even with his reds he wants to accent the fruit rather than the body, while the white Pinots should not only be fruity but also mirror the mineral volcanic soils. So he picks earlier, at 92–97 Oechsle, yet chaptalizes only in certain vintages. Fermentations have been spontaneous since 2004 but less cool than under Konrad's father, and he uses larger barrels—from 300 to 1,700 liters—for aging, to minimize wood flavors. Extraction for the reds is very gentle. The wines benefit from the cooler climate, by comparison to Winklerberg, and have higher acidity. After cold maceration, the must is fermented for 15–25 days in stainless steel, in ripe vintages like 2003 or 2009 with 100 percent of the stems. The crus age in mostly new barriques from Taransaud and Rousseau for 12 months. They are bottled unfined and unfiltered and can age for ten or more years.

FINEST WINES

2010 Kirchberg Weissburgunder GG
Because there were very low yields in 2010, Konrad bottled only 370 magnums of this wine. Fermented and aged in oak barrels (30 percent new), it is very fresh and pure on the nose, with floral aromas. The palate is very delicate and refined, the salinity appetizing, and the finish long and complex.

2010 Kirchberg Spätburgunder Rappen★
The grapes were picked at the bottom of the Kirchberg cru, where the weathered volcanic soil is deeper and more loamy than in the top parcel used for the Grosses Gewächs. Although it was a cooler and wetter vintage, this wine was fermented with all the stems (*Rappen*), which lends it a certain wildness. Concentrated dark-berry aromas on the nose, with cloves and forest-floor flavors. Firm and vibrant on the palate; silky but with drive, freshness, and grip—Konrad's style. Very alluring.

Weingut Salwey
Area under vine: 121 acres (49ha)
Average production: 350,000 bottles
Hauptstrasse 2,
79235 Oberrotweil
Tel: +49 7662 384
www.salwey.de

Pfalz

You can read it, hear it, see it—you can even feel it—when you enter this wine region in Germany's far southwest: the Pfalz is a paradise. This has, admittedly, been written for much more than 200 years. But this is, after all, a crucial trait of paradise: it lasts.

There are 1,800 or more sunshine hours a year; an annual average temperature of 50°F (10°C), with about 40 summer days of at least 77°F (25°C); usually well-distributed rainfall of 20–28in (500–700mm); and due to the Palatinate Forest, which holds back wind and rain, a sheltered location in the Upper Rhine Graben. There is virtually nothing that does not grow between the Rhine and Haardt, between the villages of Schweigen in the south and Bockenheim in the north: almonds, lemons, and peaches; oleander, kiwis, and figs; corn, potatoes, and cabbages—and vines, large and small, with plump golden or deep dark grapes.

For viticulture, too, the Pfalz remains a paradise—albeit an overexploited and threatened one. The second-largest German wine region after Rheinhessen, it cultivates 57,934 acres (23,445ha) of vines, and yields have averaged 100hl/ha over the past ten years. For roughly 50 years, most of the crop has been harvested by machine in the flat and sandy Rhine Valley, which is no more promising than the fact that—*Zum Wohl!*—every third bottle of German wine comes from the Pfalz. In 2010, 45.56 percent of the quality wines were dry, 24.2 percent were off-dry, and 30.24 percent were sweet (and many of them cheap as well). Most of these wines are technically correct but lack character. The best wines come from the east-facing hills and slopes of the Haardt Mountains, which continue as the Vosges to the north. Riesling (23.6 percent of the total vineyard area), Pinot Blanc (4.1 percent), Pinot Gris (4.7 percent), Pinot Noir (6.8 percent), Chardonnay, Gewürztraminer, Muscat (à Petit Grain), Rieslaner, and Scheurebe can all be of very good or great quality.

Due to the special climate and the great diversity of soils, there is virtually no important variety that is not cultivated in the Pfalz. Apart from Müller-Thurgau, Kerner, and other early-ripening varieties that do not like too much sun, I cannot name many grape varieties that are out of place here. The varieties mentioned—supplemented by Auxerrois, Silvaner, and St. Laurent—bear the best, while Dornfelder (13.3 percent), Müller-Thurgau (9.7 percent), and Blauer Portugieser (8.7 percent), which together occupy nearly one-third of the total vineyard area, provide most of the wines produced. Sauvignon Blanc is still booming, and red wines from Syrah, Cabernet Sauvignon, Cabernet Franc, Merlot, and Tempranillo can be excellent.

In 2010, 61.7 percent of the area under vine was devoted to white varieties and 38.3 percent to red, which is even more interesting when you compare these figures to those from 1979, when white occupied almost 91 percent and red just 9 percent. The German trend toward red wine, since the late 1990s, is mirrored in the Pfalz and has led to many modern, dark red wines—often blends, with intense fruit flavors and full bodies. In terms of area, Dornfelder is the superstar among the reds, covering 7,690 acres (3,112ha). Even Blauer Portugieser is making a comeback, with 5,046 acres (2,042ha) so far. Many Pfalz red wines are off-dry, while many others can be massive and oaky. The finest, though, are dry, subtle, fresh, and elegant. Pinot Noir is performing very well on limestone but also on Buntsandstein soils, while St. Laurent can be excellent, especially in the northern Pfalz where this Pinot relative is grown on calcareous soils. Just to complete the offering, new crossings from Weinsberg are being planted—such as Cabernet Mirto, Cabernet Cubin, Cabernet Dorsa, and Acolon—mostly for color and smoothness in blends and the rare Port-styled wines.

Right: The eponymous church and name stone at Kirchenstück in Forst, reputed to be Germany's most expensive vineyard

There are also excellent traditional-method sparkling wines (with the second fermentation in the bottle), often offered as vintage Sekt. The finest are made from the Burgundian varieties but also from Riesling. Wilhelmshof and Ökonomierat Rebholz (both in Siebeldingen), Anders & Mugler (Ruppertsberg), and Reichsrat von Buhl (Deidesheim) are among the finest producers.

Over the past decade, the heart of the Pfalz has suffered drought, hail, and heavy rain during the growing season. Recent vintages were therefore very labor-intensive and yields relatively low for conscientious producers. To avoid bad botrytis or unripe grapes damaged by hail, strict selections in the vineyards, as well as increasingly on sorting tables, had to be done. Many wines, even from well-known producers and top sites, did not convince me. They lacked vitality, tasting like wines that were manicured to taste faultless. On the other hand, I was really impressed by wines from producers who converted to organic or biodynamic farming some years ago. The aim of producing authentic wines from ripe and healthy grapes has resulted in pure and vibrant wines of balance, elegance, and finesse. Organic culture does not protect vines from hail. But chemical corrections or higher residual-sugar levels to mask wine faults are not part of the philosophy of producers who strive for authentic wines that reflect their origin as well as the vintage. In Bürklin-Wolf, Christmann, Rebholz, and Dr. Wehrheim, the organic movement has leading producers here.

Twenty years ago, Pfalz fine wine meant wine from Mittelhaardt, especially refined Riesling from the weathered Buntsandstein soils of the villages of Forst, Wachenheim, and Deidesheim, which have been world-famous for more than 100 years. Today, though, Pfalz means not only the Mittelhaardt district, from Bockenheim down to Neustadt an der Weinstrasse, but also the Südliche Weinstrasse, from Neustadt to Schweigen, on the border with France (see map, p.89). Soils are very diverse in the picturesque southern Pfalz, but the finest wines—from Riesling and Burgundian varieties—are grown on soils based on limestone, Muschelkalk, Buntsandstein, and the Rotliegendes. Delicious aromatic white wines are also produced from Gewürztraminer, Gelber Muskateller, Rieslaner, and Scheurebe. These varieties grow predominantly on deeper loess or Keuper soils and are often bottled as sweet wines. The Spätlesen and Auslesen can be of world-class quality, since they always have elegance and finesse—even the Gewürztraminers.

The quality revolution of the southern Pfalz—which long produced bulk wines and had no image other than cheap and sweet—was initiated 25 years ago by six wine-producing friends: Hansjörg Rebholz (Ökonomierat Rebholz), Karl-Heinz Wehrheim (Dr. Wehrheim), Friedrich Becker, Thomas Siegrist (Leinsweiler), and the brothers Rainer and Gunter Kessler (Weingut Münzberg in Landau-Godramstein). I cannot profile all of them here, unfortunately, though the Chardonnay, Weissburgunder, and Spätburgunder of Weingut Münzberg, as well as the Riesling Sonnenberg GG from Siegrist, are of excellent quality and longevity.

The success of the group motivated other, younger producers to explore their terroirs and produce high-quality wines as well. The Südpfalz Connexion is one very promising result, and the wines of Gies-Düppel and Peter Siener (Birkweiler), Boris Kranz and Sven Leiner (both Ilbesheim), and Klaus Scheu (Schweigen-Rechtenbach) are well worth discovering. So, too, is the Gräfenhauser Edelburgunder—a fine Pinot Noir from a higher vineyard brought back to life by the Connexion from the 2004 vintage. The history of this wine dates back to 1355. In 1822 it was one of the costliest Pfalz wines, and in 1929 it was served on the Hapag-Lloyd liners *Europa* and *Bremen* en route to the US.

Other wines you should try come from Tina Pfaffmann (Frankweiler), Theo Minges (Flemlingen), and Müller-Catoir (Haardt). The

latter was a driver for quality under winemaker Hans-Günther Schwarz for almost 40 years. Today the wines (mostly Riesling) are very clean, elegant, and racy, but they do not really touch me any more. Because I was one hour late for an extensive scheduled tasting in August 2010 and unable to reach anybody at the estate to announce my delay, Philipp David Catoir was not willing to welcome me and sent me away. I was, therefore, unable to verify my reservations before I had to finish the research for this book.

The northern Pfalz, where most of the vines in good sites grow in limestone or marl soils, always had the potential to produce fine wine, though top producers were rare until 20 years ago. Even then, however, Koehler-Ruprecht's unique Kallstadter Saumagen Rieslings (Spätlese *trocken* R [Reserve] or Auslese *trocken*) had become iconic Pfalz wines and some of the finest Rieslings on earth. The estate's Burgundian-styled Pinot Noirs, Grauburgunder, and Chardonnay also became famous, though they remain very rare today. Pfeffingen (Weingut Fuhrmann-Eymael in Bad Dürkheim-Pfeffingen) and Karl Schaefer (Bad Dürkheim), too, were

already excellent producers 20–25 years ago, and Knipser, in the formerly unknown Laumersheim in the far north of the region, became recognized for dry Rieslings and red wines (Spätburgunder, St. Laurent, Cabernet Sauvignon, and Syrah). Philipp Kuhn (Laumersheim), Weingut Schumacher (Herxheim am Berg, where the Spätburgunders are mightily impressive), Rings (Freinsheim), Karl Pfaffmann (Walsheim), and Weingut Odinstal (far above Wachenheim), to name only a few, are all producers that could have made it into this book if there had been more space.

The hardest decisions, however, were over two well-known estates in Deidesheim: Reichsrat von Buhl and Bassermann-Jordan. Both producers own parcels in the best sites of the Mittelhaardt, and their wines can be of world-class quality, while others can be rather disappointing. Von Buhl will be under new day-to-day management from 2013, and instead of Bassermann-Jordan I have decided to profile Weingut von Winning (formerly Dr. Deinhard), since this estate has produced thrilling wines since 2008 and is an upcoming superstar on the German wine scene.

Weingut Friedrich Becker

For many years, Weingut Friedrich Becker, in the far south of the Pfalz, has been one of the top producers of Spätburgunder in Germany. The top wines—Spätburgunder Reserve and Pinot Noir, both "special selections"—regularly receive the highest scores in the German wine press. From the 2001 to the 2009 vintages, one or the other was awarded Best Spätburgunder by the Gault Millau *German Wine Guide* no fewer than eight times. However, both wines are very rare and expensive and not really representative.

Since I was not willing to write about wines that are almost virtual in this book, I asked to taste the two Grosses Gewächs Spätburgunders, St. Paul and Kammerberg. Curiously, both wines rank in-house a step below the awarded rarities, though with 3,000–4,000 bottles of each, are more representative. Becker Jr.—Friedrich Wilhelm or Kleiner Fritz—poured me the 2009, 2008, 2007, and 2005 vintages of the Grosses Gewächs wines, as well as the 2004 Pinot Noir, and I was really impressed by the quality. For many years, I have to admit, I found Becker's Pinots slightly overextracted, whereas their aromatic bouquet was always fresh and perfumed like a fine Burgundy. Today, however, both grands crus qualify as great Spätburgunders. "We have changed a lot since 2007 in the vineyards and during vinification," Becker Jr. told me. He is the seventh generation of the family, and he took over the vinification of all the wines in 2005, while his father Friedrich, Grosser Fritz, looks after the vines.

Before we get into more detail, though, let us see exactly where we are. The family estate is located in Schweigen, close to the French border. Most of the family's vines are actually cultivated in France (Alsace), though the area between Schweigen and Wissembourg is subject to German wine law. In 1971, the many different *Einzellagen* were grouped into one huge 600-acre (240ha) site—the Schweigener

Right: Friedrich Becker with his son Friedrich Wilhelm, the sixth and seventh generations to run the famous family estate

Sonnenberg. This was once a famous 25-acre (10ha) cru, but today the name means almost nothing, because the soils, expositions, and cultivated grape varieties are so diverse.

The best wines are grown on limestone and marl soils. Therefore, Friedrich Becker Sr., a pioneer of high-quality wines in the southern Pfalz, started planting mainly Burgundian varieties from 1966 onward—especially Pinot Noir, which, after a glorious past, became a rarity after World War II due to low yields. In 1973, when Becker took over the estate from his father, he stopped selling grapes to the cooperative and started bottling and selling his own wines. As an aficionado of the wines of Burgundy, he was one of the first wine producers in

As an aficionado of the wines of Burgundy, Becker was one of the first wine producers in Germany to use barriques for his Pinots as well as for Chardonnay

Germany who, around 1990, used barriques for his Pinots, as well as for previously "forbidden" grape varieties such as Chardonnay, Cabernet Sauvignon, and Merlot. "We knew we had the same climate and nearly the same soils as our colleagues in Burgundy, though when we started producing wines, we did not know how to transfer the gifts of nature into fine wine," Becker Sr. told me. Today, his Spätburgunder challenges the finest wines of Burgundy.

Since the 2007 vintage, the Beckers have picked their physiologically ripe Pinots with only 92–98° Oechsle, rather than 100 or more. "An alcohol level of 13% is enough for Pinot Noir," Fritz Jr says. "I have learned that with Pinot it is much more important to have good acidity than high sugar levels." In 2008, he reports, acidity was 6g/l; and even in 2009, 5.9g/l. So the Beckers reduced the

leaf canopy, intensified canopy management, and green-covered the rows to boost the competition with the vines.

In the winery, the Beckers have increased the number of wooden vats from two to seven, so since 2008 they have extended the maceration time to three weeks, whereas it was only 10–18 days before. There is no cold maceration, and the temperature during fermentation (which lasts 10–14 days) is allowed to rise to 36°C (97°F) early on, for a better extraction of color and tannins. There were some experiments with stems, but Fritz Jr. is not convinced so far, so all the grapes are destemmed before going into the fermenters. When the seeds and tannins are ripe, the pressing is less gentle than previously. "We press until the cake is dry," Fritz Jr. announces proudly. After settling in stainless steel, the uncleared must is transferred to barriques. For quality reasons, the Beckers prefer barrels from Burgundy, so they buy one-year-old barriques from top Burgundian producers, including Domaine de la Romanée-Conti. "Our French colleagues get the very best barrels, and since we would never get the same quality, we prefer to buy top-quality used barrels rather than 'less top-quality' new barrels." Consequently, the use of new oak (mainly François Frères and Taransaud) is less extensive today, and even a rich and powerful vintage such as 2009 is aged in "only" 80 percent new wood. The aging lasts 12–18 months, depending on how the wines taste. Since 2007, there has been no fining before bottling, so the unfiltered wines are less brilliantly bright today.

Although Pinot Noir is the most prestigious variety the Beckers cultivate, there are other wines of excellent quality as well. From the 46 acres (18.5ha) under vine, 65 percent are Pinot varieties (including Chardonnay), 22 percent Riesling, and the rest Silvaner, Muskateller, Gewürztraminer, Dornfelder, Portugieser, Cabernet Sauvignon, and Merlot. With Becker Jr. doing the vinifications (helped by the family's long-standing and well-known red-wine consultant Stefan Dorst), the white wines have also attained greater spiciness, elegance, and finesse. Most of the Rieslings (light, delicate, and racy) are grown on loess and sandstone soils, whereas the pure and salty Sonnenberg Grosses Gewächs is from poor limestone soils. The vines were planted in the mid-1960s in a relatively windy plot and give a surprisingly light and elegant wine of good expression. Cabernet and Merlot are planted in deeper clay and loam soils and give a full-bodied, intense, and powerful blend.

FINEST WINES

(Tasted November 2011 from 50cl samples)
St. Paul Spätburgunder GG
This "French" vineyard was already cultivated in the 14th century by the Cistercian monks of Wissembourg, but for the past century, except for this small plot (from which the one to four barriques of Pinot Noir is sourced), nothing but fruit trees have been cultivated here. Becker bought the quite steep and south-facing parcel, with its rocky limestone soils, at the beginning of the 21st century, uprooted the trees, and planted a mixture of Pinot clones from Dijon and the German Marienfelder clone. The first vintage was 2004. The wine is very fruity, yet pure, straight, and always fresh, showing great elegance and silken finesse. It goes on the market two years after harvest.

2009 Brilliant garnet. Cool, fresh, and spicy redberry and cherry aromas on the nose; very pure. Nice purity and refreshing acidity on the palate, too. Silky, very elegant, yet straight, and with clear fruit expression. The wine is full and dense and structured by a delicate acidity, as well as ripe and refined tannins. Really appetizing.

2008 More ruby-colored. Very clear and deep on the nose, with dark and spicy fruit aromas. Dense, succulent, and silky, but firmly structured by fresh and grippy tannins and a lively acidity. A distinctive character, with good concentration and power.

2007★ A very long hang time after a rather cool summer. Dark garnet. Finest fruit and floral aromas, very pure and intense, quite generous and sweet on the nose. Full, concentrated, and ripe on the rich palate; this is a mouthful of wine with a very long aftertaste of fruit and floral aromas. The refreshing kick on the back palate forces you to drink more and more. Delicious.

Kammerberg Spätburgunder GG
The Kammerberg is a steep and south-facing former *Einzellage* close to Wissembourg that was recovered by Becker in 1966/67. The old vines—a clonal mix but with many fewer French clones—grow in deep marl lime soils and give a rich, intense, and powerful but also fine, elegant, and fresh Spätburgunder. The proportion of new oak is therefore higher than for the St. Paul, but one-year-old barriques from Domaine de la Romanée-Conti are also used. Since the 2009 vintage, the wine has been released only three years after harvest.

2009 A deep and serious bouquet, with pure and concentrated aromas of cherries and roses. Rich, meaty, and full-bodied on the palate, with firm tannins due to the thicker clay topsoil. This wine is more concentrated, sweet, chocolaty, and powerful than the more transparent, aromatic, and Burgundian St. Paul. Excellent aging potential.

2008 Very ripe yet refined fruit aromas of dark and pickled cherries. Luscious and silky on the palate, this is a very rich and powerful Burgunder of great complexity and length; it is perfectly structured by an animating acidity and firm tannins. It verges on overripeness but stays just on the right side. Great wine.

2007★ An alluring bouquet with brilliant fruit and floral aromas. Rich, round, and intense on the silky palate, this is a very sappy yet firmly structured, refined, and chalky Pinot of great elegance and finesse. Thrilling.

2005★ Deep, pure, and silky on the nose, with aromas of pepper and raw meat. Elegant and silky, but also distinctive and powerful on the palate, this is a world-class Pinot of excellent concentration and complexity, which is excellently structured by firm and grippy tannins. It has impressive length, with leather aromas on the finish. Should be even better after being decanted.

Weingut Friedrich Becker
Area under vine: 46 acres (18.5ha)
Average production: 100,000 bottles
Best vineyard: Schweigen Sonnenberg
(including the Kammerberg and St. Paul parcels)
Hauptstrasse 29, 76889 Schweigen
Tel: +49 634 2290
www.friedrichbecker.de

Weingut A Christmann

The history of Weingut A Christmann in Gimmeldingen/Mittelhaardt dates back to 1845, though it was Steffen Christmann who put the 47-acre (19ha) family estate on the list of the very finest wine producers of the Pfalz over the past ten years. Christmann, a qualified lawyer and trained viticulturist who became president of the VDP in 2007, is one of the most prominent advocates and driving forces of German vineyard classification and the Grosses Gewächs concept. He imported the idea of the hierarchy of origins into a clearly structured wine program similar to that in Burgundy for his own wines: the fruity and tangy

For years, Steffen Christmann has offered one of the finest and most distinctive wine ranges in Germany. Now the wines are even more transparent, vibrant, and digestible

basic estate wines—Riesling, Pinot Blanc, Pinot Gris, Pinot Noir, and St. Laurent—are topped by the distinguished village wines from Königsbach and Ruppertsberg (Riesling), Gimmeldingen (Riesling, Pinot Blanc, Pinot Gris, and Gewürztraminer), and again by the fine premiers crus from classified sites such as Deidesheimer Paradiesgarten (Riesling), Gimmeldingener Bienengarten (Riesling, Pinot Blanc), and Königsbacher Ölberg (Riesling, Pinot Noir). At the top are five expressive Grosses Gewächs wines from the very best sites: Reiterpfad in Ruppertsberg (Riesling), Langenmorgen in Deidesheim (Riesling), Mandelgarten in Gimmeldingen (Riesling), and Idig in Königsbach (Riesling and Pinot Noir).

The crus reflect two types of soils: most of the Christmann wines come from weathered Buntsandstein soils from the Triassic, while the Königsbacher vines grow in limestone soils of the Tertiary. The latter give very mineral and complex wines with buffered acidity and a silky texture, whereas the wines from sandstone are fruit-driven and racy, showing a lot of elegance and finesse.

Back in the 1990s, Christmann was quite content to produce spotlessly fruit-driven wines but then realized he could not do them any better, only differently—more complex and terroir-driven. Since then—Christmann identifies 2000 as the turning point—his holy grail has been "to exploit the true character of the vineyards and to reflect them in distinctive wines." So he changed to organic farming and then, in 2004, to biodynamic viticulture. At the same time, he abandoned the use of enological additives, the better to express the natural vineyard character. He also introduced oak barrels to his cellar, so since the 2004 vintage his grands crus have been partly fermented and matured in traditional *Halbstück*, *Stück*, and *Doppelstück* barrels (600–2,400 liters), as well as stainless-steel tanks. For the past couple of years, the best wines have fermented spontaneously, though Christmann is not dogmatic when it comes to yeasts. He is also quite relaxed about malolactic fermentation: "In some years, malo occurs; in other years, it does not. You don't taste it anyway."

Christmann strives for harmony, nobility, and vibrancy in his wines, believing that the key lies in the vineyards. Thus, he looks for vital soils and balanced growth of deep-rooting vines, which average 20 years of age. The planting density ranges from a traditional 5,000 vines/ha to a more modern 8,000 vines/ha, and in normal years every second row has green cover. Every four or five years, the shallow roots are cut to force the roots deeper into the soil. To boost the natural resistance of the vines, biodynamic preparations and "teas" are sprayed on them. Christmann reports that with the biodynamic approach, the vegetative growth of the plants finishes earlier, so that the grapes achieve

Right: The cheery and dynamic Steffen Christmann, who heads the VDP, as well as his own revitalized family estate

Above: A suitably bibulous coat of arms in Idig, now a Christmann monopoly and renowned since the 14th century

35–40 people picks late, selectively, and by hand only, starting in September and finishing if possible no earlier than late October or early November. Only ripe and healthy grapes are acceptable, with a maximum of 5 percent of botrytis if it cannot be avoided. To get wines as precise as possible, there is a second selection on a sorting table at the crush house, which is quite rare in Germany.

After being lightly destemmed and macerated for between three and 18 hours, the grapes are pressed and the fermentation runs until Christmas. While the grands crus and the Pinots ferment partly or wholly in oak, the other wines ferment in stainless-steel tanks. Temperatures are allowed to rise up to 73°F (23°C) for the whites. The wines are sulfured for the first time only after fermentation; and after another two to six months, they are lightly filtered and bottled with residual-sugar levels of less than 5–6g/l. Predicate wines such as the 2009 Idig Riesling Eiswein or the noble 2010 Idig and Reiterpfad Riesling Auslese are rarely produced.

For years, Steffen Christmann has offered one of the finest and most distinctive wine ranges in Germany. But I find the wines even more transparent, vibrant, and digestible since he changed to organic viticulture and more natural winemaking. Christmann's *Gutsweine* are very good for everyday consumption and to entertain friends. The village wines are already impressively distinctive, and the premiers crus even more so: I like the steel-fermented Königsbacher Ölberg Riesling best because of its complexity, elegance, and salty length. Since 2007, the Königsbacher Riesling SC has been produced as the second wine of the Idig GG. It is made from younger vines (less than 20 years) and the parts Christmann did not deem good enough for the grand cru. Fermented in stainless-steel and traditional barrels, with must weights of up to 97° Oechsle, this is a quite complex and persistent wine that intimates the merits of Idig but costs much less.

full ripeness without excessive sugar levels. Indeed, the grands crus rarely exceed 13% ABV, and for a couple of years they have been considerably lower. This is also the result of the leaf wall being not only thinned out but lower than previously.

Yields are kept low, averaging about 38hl/ha for the grands crus. Christmann's harvest team of

FINEST WINES

Reiterpfad Riesling GG
This flattish, southeast-facing, 190-acre (77ha) site is characterized by its almost Mediterranean climate and calcareous sand, sandy loam, and weathered sandstone. Christmann owns 2.2 acres (0.9ha) here, and his wine shows brilliant apricot and peach flavors but is less rich than many other wines from this site. Instead, it is—as the **2010** demonstrates—very pure and elegant, almost weightless, with a piquant minerality. Equally excellent is the brilliantly precise **2009**, which is elegant, racy, and backed by its salty minerality.

Langenmorgen Riesling GG
First mentioned in 1491, Langenmorgen is a long, southeast-facing terrace with the typical weathered Buntsandstein soils of the Mittelhaardt. The calcareous loess-loam layers lend depth and fullness to the intense fruit flavors of this rich cru. The **2010** is creamily textured but also thrilling in its mineral salinity and piquant raciness. The **2009** is very deep, spicy, and elegant—a thrilling Riesling that is less rich but fascinatingly pure and refined. Because Christmann owns just 0.44 acre (0.18ha) here, his Langenmorgen is extremely rare.

Mandelgarten Riesling GG
Mandelgarten is part of Meerspinne and is surely the best vineyard of Gimmeldingen. The monks of Wissembourg (in Alsace) had noted its exceptional quality by 1456. The south-facing Mandelgarten is in the Gimmeldingen Valley and benefits from cooler night temperatures. The soil is dominated by sandstone boulders and loess, but there is a massive limestone bank that can be reached by the oldest vines. The **2010** matches cool flint-stone and herbal aromas with yellow stone fruits, while the wine is very complex on the palate, marked by its kittenish yet racy acidity. The **2009** is quite cool and typically Riesling, despite the warm vintage. On the palate, it is succulent, elegant, and piquant in its mineral flavors, while the acidity is ripe and less racy than in 2010. Good length.

Idig Riesling GG
Remarkably elegant, supple, complex, and persistent, the mineral and silky Idig Riesling GG is the most impressive Christmann wine each year. It comes from a steep, south-facing 10-acre (4ha) site in Königsbach, mentioned as early as 1346. Protected by Rolandsberg to the west, the rounded site benefits from its warm climate and high physiological ripeness. Idig was mostly owned by Reichsrat von Buhl during the 19th and 20th centuries, but the Christmann family has had parcels here since 1937, rented the complete site in 1992, bought it in 2005, and developed what has become a signature wine of the modern Pfalz. The Riesling vines are 20 years old on average and grow in calcareous marl soils. Yields have been kept between 16.7hl/ha (1999) and 48.5hl/ha (2007) over the past 15 years (3,200–13,900 bottles), harvest dates varying from mid-October to early November. It can age for 20 years, and three wines of the past decade were exceptional:

2010★ Spicy on the nose, and supple, elegant, and amazingly forward on the palate. Very concentrated and impressively structured by its delicate acidity and distinctive minerality, it develops great length and complexity and will easily age ten years.

2009★ Rich in body and fruit flavors but also very elegant and almost weightless. Very persistent on the complex finish, with great aging potential.

2004★ Ripe, rich, and concentrated yet delicate on the nose. On the palate, it pairs its sweet maturity, excellent concentration, and complexity with remarkable vibrancy and persistent salinity.

1990 This golden wine (tasted in 2009) showed a delicate fruit maturity matched by chamomile, caramel, and honey aromas. On the palate, it was very pure, refined, elegant, long, and mineral.

Idig Spätburgunder GG
From 40-year-old vines, yielding 35hl/ha, this is one of the finest German Spätburgunders. The grapes are destemmed, and after fermentation the wine is transferred into small barrels, where it ages for almost two years. The **2008** is very delicate and transparent on the nose, with cherry and tobacco aromas. Silky, subtly concentrated, and firmly structured, this Pinot has freshness, elegance, finesse, and persistence. The **2007** is deep, ripe, and intense on the nose, and rich on the palate, where the sweet fruit carpet is well structured by fine, ripe tannins and lifted to good, spicy length.

Weingut A Christmann
Area under vine: 47 acres (19ha)
Average production: 130,000 bottles
Peter-Koch-Strasse 43, 67435 Gimmeldingen
Tel: +49 6321 660 39
www.weingut-christmann.de

Weingut Koehler-Ruprecht

Hugh Johnson once said that the top wines were those that inspired the wish to buy not only the wine but the whole estate. Even so, you can imagine how fascinated American investors must have been by the wines by Weingut Koehler-Ruprecht in Kallstadt when they bought the revered family estate in 2009. Moreover, the Americans not only bought the estate: to preserve the beloved wine style, they also bound in the former owner, Bernd Philippi, as the CEO and winemaker for another couple of years. Since then, Philippi—whose grandfather Ernst Koehler established the estate around 1920, but who has remained childless himself—has continued to do what he did for so many years, but as a rich man now. He has many other projects, too: Quinta Carvalhosa in the Douro

In the space of 30 years, Bernd Philippi
made Kallstädter Saumagen
one of the most famous and treasured
dry Rieslings of Germany

Valley in Portugal, which he co-owns with the Breuer (Rheingau) and Näkel (Ahr) families, but also the Mont du Toit Estate in South Africa and new consulting projects in China.

In the space of 30 years, Philippi made Kallstädter Saumagen one of the most famous and treasured dry Rieslings of Germany. So what is the Saumagen myth all about?

The site, in the shape of a pig's stomach (*Saumagen* in German), is a 100-acre (40ha) south-/southeast-facing site on the western outskirts of Kallstadt. Due to its contours, it is protected to the west and north from cold air, though it is relatively high at 400–500ft (120–150m). As a result, the grapes ripen a bit slower and later than in other vineyards of the village. Saumagen was a limestone quarry in Roman times. The friable and chalky marl and

loess-loam soil is still riddled with millions of small limestones, which warm up and make the grapes ripe and the wine rich. But however charismatic, powerful, and substantial Philippi's mostly dry Saumagen Rieslings are, they remain moderate in alcohol, rarely exceeding 12.5%.

According to Philippi, there is no secret behind his magic Saumagen or any of the other wines he produces. "I just make the wines as my grandfather did in the 1920s," he says. "No irrigation, no fertilizers, no herbicides, no chaptalization; up to five selective pickings by hand of nothing but perfect grapes, spontaneous fermentation, and aging in traditional oval *Halbstücks*, *Stücks*, and *Doppelstücks* of 600, 1,200, and 2,400 liters—that's it."

Indeed, all his vineyards are farmed sustainably. Spraying operations, particularly against fungal diseases, are rare. Philippi neither green harvests nor halves bunches. Instead, each vineyard is picked up to five times with different maturity levels. The higher the predicate, the more concentrated the wine, and the longer it takes to reach the market. The Spätlese *trocken* R is released after four years, the Auslese *trocken* R after six. The additional term R stands for special selections. These are rare wines of exquisite quality and aging potential.

Philippi produces more than Saumagen Rieslings, however. Koehler-Ruprecht owns 26 acres (10.5ha) of vines. About 50 percent of the total is planted with Riesling, another 20 percent with Pinot Blanc, Pinot Gris, and Chardonnay, 20 percent with Pinot Noir, and the remaining 10 percent with Gewürztraminer and Scheurebe.

The white grapes are crushed and macerated for 12–24 hours. The juice is separated by centrifuge and fermented spontaneously in traditional oval-shaped oak or chestnut barrels, the capacity ranging from 300 to 2,400 liters. The fermentation temperature is not controlled but

Right: Bernd Philippi (seated) at the family winery he sold to American investors in 2009, with winemaker Dominik Sona

Above: Although now owned by American investors, the name of the winery and the family crest proudly remain

never rises above 64°F (18°C) due to the clarity of the must and the small size of the barrels. After three or four weeks of fermentation, the wines are racked into different barrels, where sweet wines remain until April or May, dry wines until September. All the wines are only lightly filtered.

The Pinot Noir vinification is also traditional. The grapes are destemmed and cold-soaked for two days, then fermented in stainless-steel tanks (700–4,000 liters) with the addition of cultured yeasts for two to three weeks. After pressing and settling, they age for several months or years in French oak barriques. The proportion of new wood varies according to the wine quality, ranging from 20 percent for the rather simple Philippi, up to 100 percent for the more concentrated Philippi R. All of the Pinot Noirs are filtered only through a strainer before being bottled.

For the international reputation of the winery, however, it is the Kallstadter Saumagen Rieslings that have pride of place. The Saumagen Riesling Auslese *trocken* is a rich and powerful but, above all, idiosyncratic Riesling that can easily be picked out among hundreds of the finest Rieslings. The wine combines its baroque opulence with a Gothic strength and structure. The wine is always complex but also vibrant, elegant, full of finesse and impressively persistent. It should be given at least 15 years but is at its best after 20.

Because Bernd Philippi, who turned 60 in 2011, is obliged to spend only 60 days per year at Koehler-Ruprecht, he installed Dominik Sona, a young viticulturist and enologist, as his locum and successor. Since Sona was a great Philippi and Saumagen fan before he was hired from Ernst Loosen's Weingut JL Wolf in Wachenheim (Pfalz), he swore never to alter the style of the Koehler-Ruprecht wines. Indeed, since 2009 I have not noticed even the slightest change. Is that only because of Philippi's contracted 60 days? As for the wines themselves, time will tell.

FINEST WINES

(Tasted in August 2010 and February and November 2011, from an ISO tasting glass, which Philippi prefers to fancier, larger stemware.)

Kallstadter Saumagen Riesling Spätlese trocken R

This is made from small and seedless golden berries picked earlier than the amber berries used for the Auslesen. The **2008★** is complex on the spicy nose, pairing salty and nutty aromas. On the palate, there is the inimitable mix of succulence, purity, silkiness, elegance, and salinity, which is so effortless and irresistible that you would never think of spitting out the wine. Powerful but not weighty, as usual, this is a very persistent wine with the potential to age gracefully for at least 10–15 years. As I write this, I pour myself a glass of the **2001★**, which, a decade after harvest, is sheer perfection: very delicate and elegant, almost light-footed on the palate, mature but still vibrant, really salty and sappy, with fruit that is absolutely delicious now but far from fading.

Kallstadter Saumagen Riesling Auslese trocken R

The Auslese R is made from seedless bunches that are not much bigger than pears but golden amber when picked. The wine is released no sooner than six years after harvest and can age for 20 or more. It was produced in 1990, 1996, 1997, 1998, 2001, 2004, 2005, 2007, 2008, and 2009.

2009★ This is silky and amazingly brilliant on the palate, its complexity, purity, and salinity reminding me of a great white Burgundy from the Côte d'Or. Dense and succulent, with the noble acidity and salty minerality perfectly integrated into its full body, this is an impressive Riesling of great elegance, finesse, length, and longevity.

2008★ Quite an intense color, whereas the wine is normally rather pale when young. Concentrated yet pure on the nose, with wet stone and lime. Pure, expressive, and powerful on the palate, like a Puligny from Anne-Claude Leflaive; incredibly succulent, though firmly structured, bone-dry, and highly complex. Available 2014 at the earliest.

2004 This is very distinctive on the nose, with herbal scents but also notes of tar, licorice, iron, and rust. Succulent, spicy, and well concentrated on the palate, very elegant and persistent, with herbal aromas returning on the long and salty finish. At around seven years of age, this is only now starting to show the first signs of maturity.

Kallstadter Saumagen Riesling Auslese trocken RR

Philippi has twice produced an Auslese RR and calls it the Rolls-Royce of his wines. It is even more rare than the R and dramatically expressive, with "a spellbinding beauty and resonance, leaving the drinker with a sense of wonder," to borrow Andrew Jefford's evocative description of wines worthy of the highest score in *The World of Fine Wine*.

2009★ This was already bottled when I tasted it nearly one year after the harvest, when it was very reductive still. It will go on to the market no earlier than 2015, but I am already very much looking forward to it, since its youthful promise touched my soul as soon as I swallowed it. (You better not ask for a spittoon at Koehler-Ruprecht...) A thrillingly mineral tang on the palate, almost like iodine, mighty and rich but also pure and piquant; still completely closed but very persistent. A legend in the making.

2007★ This is of the same quality and with the same spellbinding beauty as the 2009. Very complex and fresh on the nose. On the palate, this is a dramatic wine, very compact and incisively mineral, with great length and, again, leaving me with a sense of wonder. It will be released in 2014.

Koehler-Ruprecht
Area under vine: 26 acres (10.5ha)
Average production: 75,000 bottles
Best vineyard: *Kallstadt* Saumagen
Weinstrasse 84,
67169 Kallstadt an der Weinstrasse
Tel: +49 6322 1829
www.koehler-ruprecht.com

Weingut Ökonomierat Rebholz

In November 2011, Hansjörg Rebholz's 2010 Kastanienbusch Riesling Grosses Gewächs left me with a sense of wonder—and a question everyone has to answer for oneself: can a dry Riesling with 11.8% ABV be full and intense enough to be called grand cru? I had rarely had a lighter Grosses Gewächs than this. On the other hand, it was one of the most authentic, fine, and precise German Rieslings I had come across for a long time. The nose and palate were so ethereal, pure, light, and refined as to remind me of engravings by the German Renaissance artist Albrecht Dürer.

"If a great wine combines power with elegance and finesse," I asked Rebholz, "do you think your rather prim 2010 Kastanienbusch will be accepted by fine-wine consumers as a great wine?"

"I hope so," he replied, "because I think it is a great wine. We struggled for ripeness that year, but we finally picked healthy grapes of perfect physiological ripeness. Must weights were not that high, but I like to have a light wine that lacks neither concentration nor complexity. I believe this is indeed a fine wine and needs neither more richness nor more power."

I agreed but admitted that I still thought most wine lovers would prefer a grand cru more reminiscent of a Michelangelo or Rubens than an engraving by Dürer.

"I also like this wine," said Port and Douro producer Dirk van der Niepoort, who was sitting next to me. He has been a great lover and connoisseur of German Riesling for many years and tries to capture the grace, elegance, and finesse of the finest Mosel wines in his Douro and Minho wines.

Like Niepoort in Portugal, Rebholz also strives for elegance and precision in his wines, which should have "an almost fragile structure," he believes. As a producer from the Pfalz, which is generally known for full-bodied wines with intense

Right: Hansjörg Rebholz, with examples of the different soil types from which he produces a range of authentic wines

The Rebholz family has created a typical Rebholz wine style, which is always an uncompromising "natural" reflection of the vintage. Its clients are connoisseurs and used to the radical consequences of nature's caprices

fruit flavors, the striving for fragility is rather unusual. On the other hand, it fits the tradition of this historic estate in Siebeldingen and its development under Rebholz over the past 20 years.

Although the history of the Rebholz family dates back to the early 16th century, viticulture has been the focus here for only three generations. Grandfather Eduard and father Hans Rebholz were pioneers of dry quality in the Südliche Weinstrasse (Southern Wine Road) district, which was stigmatized as the Süssliche Weinstrasse (Sweetish Wine Road) for four decades after World War II because of the huge volume of cheap and sweet wines produced in this rural southern part of the Pfalz. Over 70 years now, the Rebholz family has created a typical Rebholz wine style, which is always an uncompromising "natural" reflection of the vintage. This means that the wines are neither chaptalized nor deacidified. Therefore, the same wine can have 11.8 % ABV one year and 13.5% ABV the next. Not many consumers would accept this variability, but Rebholz's clients are connoisseurs and are used to the radical consequences of nature's caprices.

Since the end of the 1980s, Hansjörg Rebholz has perfected his father's style, pairing precise fruit aromas and flavors with a purity that lets the sense of place express itself. "My goal is to reflect every characteristic of a variety, an origin, and a vintage in the most perfect way possible," Rebholz explains. This is abundantly clear in his radical 2010 wines. While many colleagues chaptalized, deacidified, or put their wines through malolactic fermentation to soften their high acidity, Rebholz did nothing but pick late and highly selectively, bottling bone-dry wines with 10g/l of acidity.

The basis for the quality of the Rebholz wines is the soil and the complex geological structure of the Queichtal, where the vines grow on loess, loam, clay, Rotliegend, sandstone, limestone, or Keuper. Three Rebholz generations have sought out the best locations for all the different varieties the family cultivates today. In the villages of Siebeldingen, Birkweiler, and Albersweiler, the family cultivates 50 acres (20.5ha) of vines, 40 percent dedicated to Riesling, 50 percent to the different Pinot varieties (including Chardonnay). Since 2005, the vineyards have been managed organically, "to produce even more striking and more natural wines."

The grapes are harvested selectively by hand in multiple passes, with the grands crus picked last: "We always go to the limit with our picking dates but get fully ripe, intense, and 100 percent healthy grapes in the end." They are destemmed, macerated for 24 hours, and gently pressed, before the must is fermented in stainless-steel tanks or barrels (Chardonnay and Pinot Noir). The large new presshouse at the back of the historic estate allows each harvest batch to be processed individually and stored in suitably sized tanks, so that the origins can be kept separate until the final blending or bottling.

The Rebholz program reflects the typical southern Palatinate mix of varieties. Although the estate is internationally renowned for its Rieslings, it also produces one of Germany's finest Gelber Muskatellers and Gewürztraminers. These wines can be dry, late-harvest, or noble sweet, depending on the vintage. Moreover, the black-labeled vintage Sekt Pi No R (from Pinot grapes) is one of the finest sparkling wines produced in Germany. The elegant, vibrant Chardonnay R is superb, too.

Hansjörg is very proud of his Spätburgunders, of which the Im Sonnenschein is classified Grosses Gewächs. It comes on the market only five years after harvest. Although this rich and persistent wine is very good and always fresh, it never fascinated me quite as much as the whites, especially the Weissburgunder Im Sonnenschin GG and the Rieslings. There are three Grosses Gewächs and three bedrock Rieslings from different soils, as well as the basic NatURsprung (the word play combining *Natur* [nature] and *Ursprung* [origin]).

FINEST WINES

Kastanienbusch Riesling GG

The Kastanienbusch Riesling Grosses Gewächs is Rebholz's signature wine. He holds 7.6 acres (3.08ha) in this 30–40 percent steep, south-facing cru, which rises from 800 up to 1,050ft (240m–320m). It is the highest grand cru in the Pfalz and benefits from permanent air circulation, as well as a prolonged vegetative period. Rebholz's vines average 20 years and grow in the ferrous conglomerate soil of the Rotliegend, an extremely stony mixture of granite, slate, and melaphyre. The "Keschdebusch" performs brilliantly in normal and wet years, thanks to the good drainage, but can have problems with drought in extremely dry years. Rebholz has therefore occasionally irrigated his vines since 2003, but only if really necessary. "It's nothing more than life insurance," he says. The most important thing was to build up a humus layer for better water-storage capacity. Since 2006, every row has been green-covered by clover to protect from erosion and to attract beneficial organisms.

Harvest is always late but, due to climate change and organic farming, has tended to be earlier for the past couple of years. Until 2002, the grapes were picked in the first two weeks of November, but in 2003 and 2005–11 they were picked around mid-October, with yields averaging 30hl/ha. The handpicked grapes are destemmed, crushed, and kept on the skins for 24 hours before being pressed. The must is fermented in stainless-steel tanks for a period of up to eight weeks, and the wine is kept on its lees until March or April, before being racked with Kieselgur filtration. The wine is bottled unfined between April and June.

Rebholz's Kastanienbusch is a wonderfully spicy, herbal, flinty Riesling with delicate fruit aromas and amazing finesse on the palate. It is always elegant and filigreed, but also dense and persistent, with the potential to age gracefully for up to 20 years. The following vintages were my favorites in two vertical tastings, the first in September 2009 and the second in November 2011.

2010★ (Harvested 27/28 October; yield 18.6hl/ha) Not the biggest but next to 2004 the most fascinating vintage I have tasted from this cru. My mind's eye saw the rocky reddish Rotliegend soil when I sniffed the bouquet, which offered subtle, slaty volcanic and herbal aromas. On the palate, the late, just-ripe Riesling from the problematic 2010 vintage was amazingly pure, refined, and transparent, offering no flesh but lots of salty minerals, which gave way to a long and complex finish. No Michelangelo fresco, indeed, but an incredibly fine Dürer engraving. A rather intellectual wine.

2008 (25 October/4 November; 30.1hl/ha) Subtle white-fruit and herbal aromas on the nose. Full and dense on the palate, this a juicy-mineral and complex Riesling of great elegance and finesse. Very typical.

2007 (13/14 October; 49.2hl/ha) Very clear and delicate on the nose, with white-fruit, nut, and herbal aromas, very elegant and full. Quite rich and creamy on the palate, this warm and sunny vintage has led to a rich and succulent Kastanienbusch, with subtle acidity and lingering minerality. Elegant and still not weighty.

2004★ (15/17 November; 35.2hl/ha) Very pure and clear on the nose, with green herbal aromas. Very fine and delicate on the palate, with a light, filigreed, almost fragile structure and a refined acidity; amazingly salty, round, and succulent, but always fine, subtle, and precise, with a lot of finesse and *Spiel*. Great.

2001 (12 November; 23.6hl/ha) Almost golden. Nice mature aromas of chamomile, honey, ripe nectarines, and apricot tart. Ripe, sappy, and very elegant on the palate, with a vital acidity and salty minerality, nice herbal flavors, red slate and oriental spice, and mint and caramel on the finish. Excellent.

1990 The first vintage after the former terraces were taken away. This wine is mainly from the parcel in which the grand cru is grown today. I tasted it from a 50cl bottle. Dried fruits, caramel, and a nice sweetness on the nose. Vibrant on the palate, very mineral, still in an excellent condition. Light and complex, despite the young vines.

Weingut Ökonomierat Rebholz
Area under vine: 50 acres (20.5ha)
Average production: 130,000 bottles
Weinstrasse 54, 76833 Siebeldingen
Tel: +49 6345 3439
www.oekonomierat-rebholz.de

Weingut von Winning

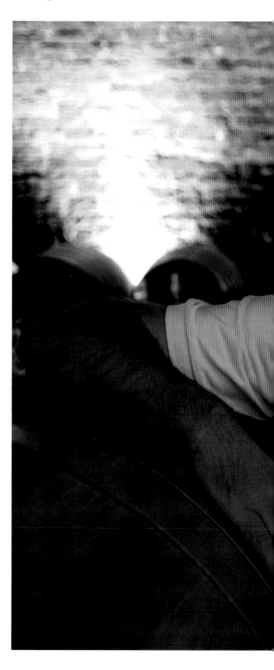

The grape robbers came in the middle of the night, with an 8-ton harvesting machine that apparently could be neither seen nor heard. It was from about 3 o'clock in the morning on September 23, 2011 that Stephan Attmann, winemaking CEO of Weingut von Winning in Deidesheim, lost 2.5 tons of his finest Pinot Noir grapes from the Herrgottsacker vineyard. "It was as if somebody in the Louvre had scratched out the eyes of the *Mona Lisa*," Attmann lamented. While he calculated the financial loss at €100,000, the police estimated it at only €12,000, on the assumption that grapes are grapes are grapes.

Because this all-grapes-are-equal thinking is still very prominent among the many down-home vintners in the Pfalz, a wine freak such as Stephan Attmann is often regarded as a busybody who knows how to play the PR machine. And indeed, since the first vintages he bottled for von Winning (2008, 2009, and 2010), Attmann has become the producer everybody is talking about—not only in the Pfalz but throughout Germany. The reason, though, is the outstanding quality of his wines. It was with good reason that several wine guides named him Newcomer of the Year in 2011.

It is Achim Niederberger, however, who made the rocket launch of von Winning possible. Niederberger is not the scion of an indigenous wine family but an entrepreneur from Neustadt/Weinstrasse who made his fortune in advertising. Since 2000, he has been buying up some of the most important and traditional wine estates in the Pfalz—in Deidesheim, Reichsrat von Buhl, Bassermann-Jordan, Biffar, and Dr. Deinhard. To rejuvenate the latter after decades of missed opportunities, Niederberger hired Stephan Attmann, who was dealt great winemaking talent, in fall 2007. One of the first things the duo did was to rename the estate from Dr. Deinhard to Weingut von Winning

Right: The talented Stephan Attmann, amid the oak barrels from which he crafts controversial but thrilling Rieslings

Stephan Attmann has become the producer everybody is talking about——not only in Pfalz but throughout Germany. The reason is the outstanding quality of his wines. Several wine guides named him Newcomer of the Year in 2011

in 2008. Leopold von Winning was son-in-law of Dr. Andreas Deinhard, son of the estate's founder, Friedrich Deinhard. Under the direction of Leopold von Winning (1907–17), the estate had its golden era and became one of the founders of the Verband der Naturweinversteigerer, forerunner of the VDP. With the purchase of Dr. Deinhard/von Winning, von Buhl, and Basserman-Jordan, Achim Niederberger reunited the three estates that arose from the division of the celebrated Jordan'sches Weingut in 1849. The three estates, though, remain three different brands and companies, with different teams and wine styles.

The potential of Weingut von Winning is exceptional. Of the 100 acres (40ha) of vines, 80 percent is dedicated to Riesling, and 25 acres (10ha) are classified for the production of Grosses Gewächs. In Deidesheim, the Grosse Lagen are Kalkofen, Kieselberg, Langenmorgen, Grainhübel, and Paradiesgarten; in Forst, Pechstein, Jesuitengarten, Kirchenstück, and Ungeheuer; in Ruppertsberg, Reiterpfad and Spiess. While the Grosses Gewächs wines (only Riesling so far) are mostly fermented and aged in barrels, the other *Lagenweine* and the varietal wines are fermented in stainless steel. The name Dr. Deinhard still exists as a range of well-balanced and elegant wines with a mouthful of ripe fruit and a refined acidity. By contrast, the von Winning range, with its eye-catching Jugendstil label (gold/white for the Deidesheim and Ruppertsberg wines; black/gold for the wines from Forst), comprises ambitious and sophisticated wines that reflect terroir rather than variety. Most of them are Riesling, but there is also Pinot Blanc, Pinot Noir, and Sauvignon Blanc. Yields are kept low, and the meticulous selection of completely healthy grapes is conducted in the vineyards. After slight crushing and a longer maceration period, the untreated musts are fermented spontaneously in wooden barrels of different sizes from Burgundian barrels (300 liters)

up to *Doppelstück* (2,400 liters). The wines are kept on their lees until August and bottled without fining but with Kieselgur filtration. "We want our wines as natural as possible, so we aim for unfiltered Rieslings in the future," Attmann says.

The investment in the well-equipped cellar but also in the vineyards has been enormous. Attmann has increased eightfold the harvest team, and during harvest there are up to five passes per site to select the best grapes. Botrytis is not acceptable, because Attmann believes this would cloud the terroir character he focuses on with his wines. To get small grapes with rich extract and good acidity levels, new plantings are extremely dense, with up to 9,000 vines/ha, while the canopy is generally kept low (at 3ft 7in [1.1m]). Between the vines are planted dozens of expensive herbs and rye, to structure and aerate the soils and to keep them vital. Herbicides and chemical fertilizers are not applied; nor does Attmann spray copper.

Attmann loves wild, aromatic wines that offer much more than just fruit: depth, complexity, persistence, and a thrilling minerality. Since he worked in Burgundy (at Domaine Jayer-Jilles), the finest wines from the Côte d'Or, as well as from Bordeaux, represent the level he wants to reach with von Winning. He knows both regions very well, since he traveled and tasted extensively before becoming a winemaker.

Attmann has received some harsh criticism for his love-me-or-leave-me wines in Germany. Some critics do not tolerate Riesling fermented in newer barrels, and accuse Attmann of copying the wines of Burgundy and Pessac-Léognan rather than following the classic style of the Mittelhaardt. I do not have any problems with young wines with a touch of oak, even it is unusual for German Riesling. As long as the material is good and the wine is complex and not masked by the wood, I do not see the problem. It is a question of style rather than quality. Attmann believes that Riesling gains complexity with wood and has bought some (new) barrels of exceptional quality every year, since there were no barrels at Dr. Deinhard previously. The new oak touch is not sweet; the wines are neither smoky nor buttery, nor do they have wood tannins. They are pure, mineral, racy, persistent, and rather on the slim side. In normal years, such as 2009, most of the grands crus are part fermented in oak (50–70 percent) and part fermented in stainless steel. Since quantities were quite low in 2010, some wines saw only wood, which they easily withstand, due to their exceptional quality.

The portfolio of the spicy and characterful von Winning wines is so comprehensive that it is impossible to describe all of them. Even wider is the Dr. Deinhard range, with typical wines from the Mittelhaardt, which grow in Buntsandstein soils and are characterized by their racy elegance, finesse, and brilliant fruit flavors. The grands crus, though, are the most complex wines, and I highlight below those wines that have impressed me most in the first three years of von Winning. Since I find 2010 the best vintage here so far, I describe only this 2010 quartet.

FINEST WINES

(Tasted in November 2011)
2010 Kalkofen GG
Although Bassermann-Jordan also produces a very good Kalkofen, I never had this Deidesheim cru on my list of the finest wines of the Pfalz until von Winning's first Kalkofen in 2008. The "lime kiln" of the name is a 12-acre (5ha) site with lime marl soil. The 2010 is superb, showing brilliant citrus aromas combined with chalk, yeast, and nuts on the complex nose. On the palate, the wine is rich and round, with a seductively smooth texture, yet is full of elegance and finesse as well, and the salty minerality extends the finish that is again flanked by fresh flavors of lime. Impressive.

2010 Kieselberg GG
Deidesheim Kieselberg is a 38.5-acre (15.5ha) south-facing site at 500–525ft (150–160m) in altitude. The soil is quite complex, with loamy sand on the top, rubble, sandstone, and weathered sandstone below. Von Winning has 1.2 acres (0.5ha) here, and the GG is very delicate: pure and refined on the nose, with fresh green aromas of lime and gooseberries initially, but then ripe apples and apricots mixed with flinty aromas. On the palate, this is a typical Buntsandstein Riesling: very elegant, pure, and racy, with finest Riesling flavors and a lot of *Spiel*, finesse, and grace. Salty finish. Delicious.

2010 Pechstein GG ★
This is from the 42-acre (17ha) cru in Forst, with a high proportion of basalt and clay in the dominant sandy loam and weathered Buntsandstein soils. I love the elegance and purity of this Pechstein, which is often quite a rich and powerful wine. I have never detected the high basalt content of the soil more clearly than in this vintage. Herbs and flint, if not volcanic ash, on the nose, with discreet fruit aromas—though Pechstein is always very backward. Dense and very mineral on the palate, bone-dry, pure, and racy; firmly structured, yet elegant and persistent. 100 percent oak, but I do not smell it at all. Only 12% ABV. Great wine, for connoisseurs only.

2010 Kirchenstück GG ★
Kirchenstück is only 9.1 acres (3.7ha) and, since 1828, has vied to be the most expensive vineyard in Germany. The site is like a *clos*, surrounded by a small sandstone wall that makes the mesoclimate even warmer. The soil is deep (therefore warm) and very complex, a mix of basalt, sandstone, limestone, and clay. The wines (all Riesling) are always very concentrated, complex, and rich, yet also noble, elegant, and refined, while their aging potential is huge. Attmann's 2010 is very clear and pure on the nose, showing subtle Riesling scents and finest flinty notes. On the palate, it is dense and powerful, yet pure and refined, very long and thrillingly complex, defined by its salty acidity. Although still in its infancy, it is clear that this is a great wine and one that I would not touch until at least 2016.

> **Weingut von Winning**
> Area under vine: 96 acres (39ha)
> Average production: 300,000 bottles
> Weinstrasse 10,
> 67146 Deidesheim an der Weinstrasse
> Tel: +49 6326 221
> www.von-winning.de

Weingut Dr. Bürklin-Wolf

This estate in Wachenheim is one of the largest and most important private wine producers in Germany, offering some of the greatest and most persistent dry Rieslings on Planet Wine. The 272-acre (110ha) estate is run by Bettina Bürklin-von Guradze, whose family tradition dates back to 1597. For quality reasons, only 200 acres (81ha) are cultivated, the rest rented out. About 80 percent of the total area (farmed biodynamically since 2005) is dedicated to Riesling, most of which has been fermented dry since 1990.

The vineyards are located in the villages of Forst, Wachenheim, Deidesheim, and Ruppertsberg, and have been classified in-house since the early 1990s, when Bürklin-Wolf was one of the pioneers of the Grosses Gewächs idea. Since 1994, 30 percent of Bürklin wines have been classified premier or grand cru. The classification is based on a tax map from 1828, but also on geology and mesoclimate, in-depth tastings, and the recognition that "not every site is predestined to produce great wine. If it were not the terroir that expresses itself in the wine in an unmistakable way, we would not have classified crus," Bürklin-von Guradze insists. Consequently, in the crus, nothing else is picked but crus. On the front label, the grape variety is not mentioned, because Riesling is regarded as "nothing more than the tool with which to express the *climat.*"

Today, there are eight grand cru wines (signed as GC), seven premiers crus (PC), two village Rieslings (the grapes for the Wachenheimer and Ruppertsberger are sourced from unclassified sites only), and the Estate Riesling *trocken.*

Early in the morning, the grapes for the crus are hand-picked into small boxes with must weights of 95°–98° Oechsle. If any botrytis is fine, up to 20 percent is accepted. After the crop is cooled down to 35.5°–37.5°F (2–3°C), the grapes are whole-bunch pressed. "I believe in whole-bunch pressing because it keeps the acidity, and we get wines with great aging potential," Fritz Knorr told me. He is the fourth Knorr cellar master in a row at Bürklin-Wolf. While the estate and two village Rieslings are fermented and aged in stainless steel, the crus are treated to traditional oak barrels. For the past few years, they have fermented spontaneously for up to six months at temperatures of 59–64°F (15–18°C). The first racking is after three or more months. The premiers crus are bottled in May; the grands crus, July.

Since the 2005 vintage, I have found the wines even more delicate, transparent, and vibrant. Bürklin-von Guradze and Knorr agree, adding that they find the crus more distinctive, too. Both believe that this is due to the biodynamic farming. The crus are always full-bodied and complex but also very elegant, and their aging potential is amazing. This is one of the very few German wine estates where you can buy mature wines of top quality for very reasonable prices. The Forst grands crus from Jesuitengarten and Kirchenstück are quite expensive, granted, but the price is not that much higher after the bottles have spent several years under perfect conditions in the estate's cellars.

FINEST WINES

(Tasted in October 2010 and November 2011)
2005 Wachenheimer Rechbächel PC
This is from a 4-acre (1.6ha) monopole with vines planted in 1971. Weathered Buntsandstein soils with very good water-storage capacity. A brilliant yellow-green color. Noble bouquet with clear fruit and herbal aromas. This full-bodied, powerful, and complex premier cru has ripe fruit and an opulent texture but is balanced by its racy acidity and salty minerality. A very thrilling wine that is only now starting to open up.

Pechstein GC
The Pechstein from Bürklin-Wolf is one of the classics of German wine culture. It's not easy to understand its finesse and thrilling complexity when this smoky, herbal, pure, and persistent wine is tasted young. My experience is that you should

Right: Bettina Bürklin-von Guradze, who is brilliantly maintaining a proud family tradition dating back centuries

Above: A plaque marks the date of the Bürklin-Wolf cellar, in the basalt that also contributes so much to some of the wines

not touch it for eight years, otherwise you will not experience its full potential, which is all about elegance, purity, race, and lingering salinity. Bürklin holds 4.2 acres (1.7ha) in this 42-acre (17ha) cru, where the vines grow in dark, stony basalt soils.

2002★ A bottle I had in November 2011 was slightly reductive on the nose but dense, succulent, and very persistent on the palate, which ended with dried yellow-fruit flavors. One year earlier, I tasted the same wine in Priorat (Spain), where it was absolutely breathtaking. Very concentrated and precise on the nose, with yellow stone fruits and a delicious maturity. Complex and dense (as always), this bottle was extremely elegant, refined, and almost piquant—fresh, linear, and mineral. Beautiful aromas of dried apricots and peaches on the long, lingering finish.

Kirchenstück GC

Bettina Bürklin-von Guradze refers to this as "the Montrachet from the Pfalz." In fact, there is no Riesling of similar weight and complexity with comparable elegance and finesse. The finish of this liquid monument is almost infinite, as is, perhaps, its longevity. However, great vintages such as **2008** or **2002** need almost ten years over which to reveal their true potential. This cru, which is supposed to be the most expensive vineyard in Germany, is just 9.1 acres (3.7ha) and the 1985-replanted share of Bürklin-Wolf is 1.3 acres (0.54ha). The wine is, therefore, not only very rare but also quite expensive (€80). It is, however, worth every cent.

2008★ After a few more years, this could be the legitimate successor of the unforgettable 2002. Although picked quite early (on October 11), this wine is beautifully clear and pure, noble and refined, and, due to the absence of botrytis, like a liquid photograph of the basalt terroir. Very pure, mineral, and salty on the palate, but also extremely young and undeveloped. Very vibrant and zesty, with flavors of lime and green grapes. Not yet as mighty as a typical Kirchenstück, but the length and complexity are hugely promising.

2002★ One of the most beautiful Kirchenstücks I have tasted. This is a unique wine: very deep, rich, and ripe on the nose, with finest herb and caramel scents. Opulent and fleshy on the palate, this has tremendous intensity and power, substance and persistence. Due to its concise minerality and refined acidity, it is always alluring, combining power with elegance and finesse almost perfectly.

Weingut Dr. Bürklin-Wolf
Area under vine: 200 acres (81ha)
Average production: 500,000 bottles
Best vineyards: *Forst* Kirchenstück, Jesuitengarten, Pechstein, Ungeheuer; *Deidesheim* Hohenmorgen, Kalkofen; *Ruppertsberg* Gaisböhl (monopole), Reiterpfad
Weinstrasse 65,
67157 Wachenheim an der Weinstrasse
Tel: +49 632 295 330
www.buerklin-wolf.de

Weingut Knipser

This is one of my favorite wine estates in the Pfalz, and not only because of its distinctive wines. Everything is a little bit crazy here, and unforeseen things are always happening. The first thing you get is not a handshake but a glass, here called a "tool." Your tasting may be guided by four Knipsers: brothers Werner and Volker, Werner's daughter Sabine, and Volker's son Stephan. All of them are trained wine experts, though they do not always hold the same opinion. This leads to vigorous discussions, to which private clients also contribute in the new tasting room. Thus, a wine tasting with the Knipsers (they call it *Frühschoppen*—"morning pint") is always an event.

The first wine you are served, even before you take your seat, is the Kapellenberg Riesling Kabinett *trocken* (bone-dry), which is light but focused, quite intense, really racy, and impossible to spit. It is grown on sandy soils and lets you forget that, in Germany, Knipser is mainly known for red wines, since it started to plant Cabernet Sauvignon in 1991.

The estate is in Laumersheim, an unspectacular village in the northern Pfalz, close to the border with Rheinhessen. The area is quite flat, but the partly rich, partly poor soils are calcareous enough to produce great and powerful wines of whichever color or variety. Is there any serious grape that is not cultivated by Knipser? Bacchus, I suppose.

I could recommend cheaper everyday wines or rarities such as the Gelber Orléans, but this would be unfair. "If you write about the Saumagen and Idig Rieslings in your book, you can't recommend only the Kapellenberg," Volker Knipser said to me as he set up verticals of the Saumagen Riesling GG and Kirschgarten Spätburgunder GG. He also wanted to show me several vintages of the Cuvée X, one of the finest Bordeaux blends in Germany; the Syrah, really great in 2003 and 2007; and, not to be forgotten, the other Riesling and Spätburgunder grands crus the family produces. "Last but not least, we have some Riesling Réserves on which we want your opinion."

This is the only problem at Knipser: it is impossible to explain the whole wine range in a few sentences. There are several basic wines, mid-range wines, and grands crus, but there are also wines above the grands crus, and others above those. Many wines sell out shortly after the price list is sent out, but then comes another list with mature wines and others you have never even heard of. The good thing is that, from 140 acres (57ha) of vines, there is always something good available.

FINEST WINES

Steinbuckel Riesling GG

Since 2009, the south-facing Steinbuckel has been a new *Einzellage* of Laumersheim. From 1971 to 2008, it was a parcel in the Mandelberg Grosse Lage, but the Knipsers always used the Steinbuckel name for their Riesling Grosses Gewächs. It is grown on limestone, which is covered by rather thin layers of loess and loam and thus characterized by its firm structure, thrilling minerality, and drinkability. For the past few years, the grapes have been picked slightly earlier, and with a maximum of 95° Oechsle, to keep the ABV at 12.5%. Residual sugar has been close to zero for several years, to accentuate the structure of the wine, which is fermented partly in stainless steel and partly in *Halbstück* barrels of 600 liters. Annual production: 7,500 bottles.

2008 This was fermented mainly in stainless steel and is very subtle and elegant on the nose. On the palate, it is light yet dense and intense, and balanced by a refined acidity and lingering salinity.

2007 This shows fine white-fruit and herbal aromas on the nose, whereas on the palate the wine is very elegant and refined but also firmly structured, scintillating, and long.

Halbstück Réserve Riesling trocken

To me, this is the real grand cru of the estate, even though the grapes come from two different sites: Laumersheim Steinbuckel and Grosskarlbach Burgweg (both limestone). The Réserve is produced only in great vintages such as 2004 or 2009, while the standard Halbstück was produced in 1999, 2001, 2003, and 2008. It is a selection of the very best 600-liter barrels (*Halbstücks*) in which the wine was fermented. The Réserve is kept on its lees for one year and released several years later.

2009★ Brilliant, fresh, and pure limestone and finest Riesling aromas. Very firm and fresh on the palate, very clear and pure, with not a gram of residual sugar but a racy acidity, great complexity, and scintillating minerality. Great wine.

2004★ A selection of the four best barrels. Intense yellow. Very concentrated and complex fruit aromas, with herbs and spice. Racy, full, and intense, with only 12% ABV; very elegant and balanced but also persistent and succulent—a world-class Riesling.

Kirschgarten Spätburgunder GG

This is from the southern part of Kirschgarten, where the pure limestone is covered by thin layers of loess, loam, and sand. Since 2008, the Knipsers have harvested a little earlier and with lower sugar levels. Fermentation takes place in open wooden fermenters, and the extraction is more cautious than before. The aging in barriques is also shorter now, taking 12–18 months rather than two years.

2009 The family believes this is the best Pinot Noir vintage in Knipser history. The proportion of Burgundian clones (Fin and Très Fin) is more than 50 percent, though the plants are only 5–8 years old. Until the 2007 vintage, this cru was from German clones planted in 1989. Almost 100 percent new oak. Very intense on the nose, with smoky ripe- and dark-cherry aromas. Silky and succulent on the palate, full and firm, with good acidity and still granular tannins. Very good potential. 13% ABV.

2004 Ripe cherries and fascinating Pinot aromas on the nose, refined and intense. Concentrated and pure on the palate, quite austere and direct, with good freshness. Good aging potential, though most of the bottles might already be consigned to history and memory today.

2003 New oak, 100%, but with little or no toasting. The grapes were picked at the beginning of September. Cherry and floral aromas; no overripeness. Full, elegant, and silky on the palate; warm, gentle, and sweet, with excellent concentration and length.

Left: The challenging and welcoming Knipser family: Werner (*right*) and daughter Sabine (*center*), Volker and son Stephan

Weingut Knipser

Area under vine: 140 acres (57ha)
Average production: 380,000 bottles
Johannishof, Haupstrasse 47,
67229 Laumersheim
Tel: +49 6238 742
www.weingut-knipser.de

Dr. Wehrheim

Should you be interested in one of the finest Pinot Blancs of Germany, Karl-Heinz Wehrheim's Mandelberg Weissburgunder Grosses Gewächs is the wine to track down. This grand cru from Birkweiler in the southern Pfalz is an impressive wine, matching depth, power, and richness with a brilliant and elegant texture, vibrancy, and length. What I find especially interesting is that this is a 100 percent stainless-steel Pinot Blanc that does not go through the process of malolactic fermentation. While many of the top German Pinot Blancs are fermented and aged in barriques, with lees-stirring for more Burgundian richness and roundness, Wehrheim prefers a more German style of Weissburgunder: direct, firm, and pure, but also defined by its intense yet subtle fruit and noble elegance. This, in combination with the silky texture, gives the Mandelberg not only a distinctive and thrillingly mineral personality but also great longevity.

Weingut Dr. Wehrheim was established in 1920 by Karl Wehrheim and succeeded by his son Heinz, who brought the doctor's degree into the name. For decades now, Weingut Dr. Wehrheim has represented uncompromisingly pure, uncorrected, and unchaptalized dry wines of the highest quality. They always represent both their place of origin and their vintage and could, thus, be quite light and searing before climate change. When third-generation Karl-Heinz Wehrheim, the agricultural engineer who has run the estate since 1992, poured me a 1987 Riesling Kabinett *trocken* a few years ago, I really loved it—not as a great wine but as an authentic *Gaumenputzer* ("mouth-scourer") that, even after all those years, cleansed the mouth as a basic 2008 Silvaner *trocken* might do today.

It is a tradition that from 42 acres (17ha) of vines, Karl-Heinz Wehrheim produces almost nothing but dry wines from classic grape varieties—above all Riesling (40 percent) and Pinot Blanc (25), but also Pinot Noir (12), Silvaner (10), and St. Laurent (5).

There is a Riesling Auslese from the 2007 vintage, and another from 2011, but that's it as far as the sweet wines are concerned.

The wine program is well structured. Fruity varietal wines form the base of the quality pyramid, above which are characterful terroir-driven wines such as the Rieslings vom Rotliegenden and vom Buntsandstein or the Pinot Blanc vom Muschelkalk. At the top of the pyramid are the Grosses Gewächs Rieslings and Pinots (Blanc and Noir).

Wehrheim's vineyards are all located in a side valley of Birkweiler, rising from 500 to 1,000ft (150m–320) and benefiting from cool breezes from the Pfälzer Wald. Since the end of *Flurbereinigung* in the middle of the 1970s, the vines have averaged only 25 years, though the oldest are more than 35 years old.

To express the particular terroir in his wines, Wehrheim focuses on the soil first, and finally aims for a long hang time after which to pick fully ripe and healthy grapes. Since 2006, the family has been running the vineyards organically, and since 2007 there have been biodynamic experiments as well. "We want to enhance the natural expression and salubriousness of our wines, but we also want to pass healthy vineyards on to our children," Karl-Heinz explains. His son Franz has already been employed as his assistant since 2010. Yields are kept low, at 50hl/ha on average (15–40hl/ha for the grands crus), by pruning, halving bunches (Pinot Noir only), and green harvesting. Harvest is rather late, which means October or sometimes even November. Picking is by hand and selective. Most vineyards are picked three times, and botrytis—already very rare because of the high altitude, windy exposure, and late veraison—is accepted only to a very small extent and only if the grapes affected are ripe.

All the grapes, including Pinot Noir, are destemmed. The juice of the whites is kept on the skins for five to 15 hours before the pressed and settled must is fermented with cultured yeasts in stainless steel or barriques (Chardonnay only) at temperatures of 61–68°F (16–20°C) for Riesling or 64–72°F (18–22°C) for Pinot Blanc. The wines are kept on their lees until bottling in April (for the basic wines) or August (for the grands crus). The Spätburgunder GG is fermented in a stainless-steel vat but aged in barriques from Palatinate oak, of which roughly 60 percent are new.

Most of Wehrheim's parcels are located in the Kastanienbusch grand cru, which is a geologically complex and climatically unique basin site from which you can overlook the Rhine lowlands, the Odenwald, and the Black Forest. Wehrheim produces three Grosses Gewächs wines here. The subtle, refined, and spicy Kastanienbusch Riesling GG is (like Rebholz's Kastanienbusch) grown on ferrous and stony soils, the Rotliegendes, whereas the elegant, fruity, and racy Kastanienbusch Köppel Riesling GG comes from Buntsandstein soils of a south-/southeast-facing parcel rising from 750 to 850ft (230m–260m). It is the purest Riesling Wehrheim picks. For all practical purposes, botrytis does not occur, because the parcel is windy and, thus, late-ripening. These are also good conditions for Pinot Noir, so below the Riesling parcel the Kastanienbusch Spätburgunder GG is cultivated. This is a delicate, fresh, and firmly structured Pinot, with dark-cherry aromas and a spiciness that needs some years to settle down; it is of excellent quality and longevity.

The most impressive wine of the estate, however, is the Mandelberg Weissburgunder GG, from vines that were planted around 1985. Grown in a northeast-facing site, on deep clay and marl soils based on shale limestone, this is a rich and elegant Burgundian wine with an authoritative German accent. It tastes best after five or six years but can easily age gracefully for ten or more. The alcohol level is always around 14%, but since the 2010 vintage, which had 13.5% ABV, I think the wine is even better with less.

FINEST WINES

(Tasted in December 2011)

Mandelberg Weisser Burgunder GG

2010★ A brilliant pale to straw yellow color. Amazingly fresh and subtle fruit aromas of apples, pears, and limes, very pure—just grapes and a touch of *sur lie*, but no cosmetic winemaking. Very clear and elegant on the attack; pure, intense, and racy; round without being too opulent; immediate, persistent, and still very young.

2005★ This wine is in top form six years after the harvest. Intense and complex on the chalky nose, mineral, and with ripe yet fresh and subtle fruit aromas and *sur lie* scents. Full-bodied, clear, and elegant on the palate, but also concentrated, rich, and spicy, well balanced by its ripe acidity and underlying salinity. Very good length, with herbal (thyme) notes on the finish.

Kastanienbusch Spätburgunder GG

2009 Intense fruit aromas of ripe dark cherries and berries, but there is also freshness and spiciness. Silky-textured, full, and intense; more meaty than the 2008 but also fresh and vibrant, with good length. Excellent aging potential.

2008 Clear cassis aromas. Fresh, pure, and silky on the palate, this is a cool, elegant, and linear German Pinot, which is amazingly vital and should age well for at least four or five years.

Dr. Wehrheim
Area under vine: 42 acres (17ha)
Average production: 100,000 bottles
Best vineyards: *Birkweiler* Mandelberg, Kastanienbusch
Weinstrasse 8, 76831 Birkweiler
Tel: +49 6345 3542
www.weingut-wehrheim.de

Rheinhessen

Rheinhessen, at the northern border of the Upper Rhine Valley, is the largest wine region in Germany. Of 136 villages, 133 are connected to viticulture, as are more than 3,200 businesses, of which 1,770 bottle and market their own wine (2007). This region between the cities of Worms, Mainz, Bingen, and Alzey has 65,540 acres (26,523ha) of vines, so 20 percent of the total area is dedicated to Bacchus, the god of wine.

The natural conditions are almost perfect, so the Romans cultivated vines here; and during the Middle Ages, the Church held the vineyards now identified as VDP Grosse Lagen. In 1402, the first Riesling (Rüssling) was mentioned in a document in Worms. The region on the left bank of the Rhine is surrounded by the Mittelgebirge of Nordpfälzer Bergland, Hunsrück, Taunus, and Odenwald, so it benefits from the protected climate of a basin. As part of the Upper Rhine lowland, Rheinhessen is an island of dryness and warmth. Summers are warm and winters mild, the annual temperature averages 50°F (10°C), and the temperature during the 180-day growing season, 63°F (17°C). Annual rainfall is about 20in (500mm), and although it may vary by 4in (100mm) either way, it is never high due to the mountain ranges in the west that hold back the clouds. The sunlight is intense and persistent, and the temperatures always warm. The landscape is defined by alternating forest-free limestone plateaus and wide valleys with hills moving like waves in an ocean.

The best soils for quality wines of distinctive character—the grands crus of Rheinhessen—are based on limestone of the Tertiary, or red sandstone, silt, and claystone or volcanic rock of the Oberrotliegend. But most of the soils are based on loess and very fertile. No wonder Bacchus and friends have to drink Müller-Thurgau first (16 percent), then Riesling (15 percent), and Silvaner (9 percent) for whites, Dornfelder (13 percent), Portugieser (6 percent), and Pinot Noir (5 percent) for reds. Some 69 percent of the area under vine is planted to white varieties, 31 percent to reds. And the positive image that Rheinhessen enjoyed from the Middle Ages onward was completely destroyed by Liebfrauenmilch. This export brand is one reason why Rheinhessen has become the largest wine region in Germany, though the famous original wine of the 18th and 19th centuries was grown in the 33.1-acre (13.4ha) *clos* in Worms called Liebfrauenstift Kirchenstück, which is classified to produce a Riesling Grosses Gewächs today.

Especially in Rheinhessen, many things that were initially successful failed. Another example is Nierstein, one of the finest origins for Riesling in Germany. The village and district of the same name were debased in 1971 with the inauguration of the *Grosslage* Niersteiner Gutes Domtal. Certainly, Nierstein itself, at the bottom of the famous Roter Hang ("Red Slope"), is included in the zone, but its total production represents no more than 2 percent of that of the *Grosslage*.

Last but not least, Rheinhessen pioneered new crossings such as Scheurebe, Faber, Bacchus, Morio-Muscat, Huxelrebe, Ortega, and Optima in the 1960s and '70s. But except for Müller-Thurgau (Rivaner) and Scheurebe (the latter a modern classic in Rheinhessen), they have been fading for years, whereas Dornfelder has still to reach its peak.

Rheinhessen has also become the world's largest Silvaner region. Producers have learned from the Franconians to be proud of the variety again and now produce some exceptional dry Silvaners, especially on limestone soils. Try Keller's Feuervogel, from old vines in the Morstein grand cru—but sit down first, or you might fall over.

Too many good things have happened in Rheinhessen during the past decade to dwell any longer on the bad old days. The most important developments have been brought about by a group of young producers called Message in a Bottle. This

Right: Nackenheim, at the northern end of the Rheinfront, whose Roter Hang vineyards follow the river south to Nierstein

association of kindred spirits was founded in 2002 by a new generation of winemakers, mostly from Wonnegau, who took over their family businesses, or at least the winemaking—not because somebody told them to, but because they wanted to. Moreover, they wanted to produce something special: fine Rheinhessen wine from traditional varieties.

"I believe that the potential to produce great wines in Rheinhessen is no less than in Burgundy or Champagne," says Oliver Spanier, who epitomizes the new self-confidence of its leading producers. "Yes, we can" has been the group's ethos ever since its foundation, and its 28 members have been demonstrating that producing wine in Rheinhessen can be fun. They present their wines at cool parties rather than at boring gala dinners, while the dynamism, spirit, and success of Message in a Bottle has inspired other young winemakers not only in Rheinhessen but throughout Germany.

Although the sad stagnation of the older generation lingers on, the focus now is much more on hip young stars, male and female; on a new generation of open-minded, well-trained, and well-connected producers who are striving for top-quality wines. Because they all recognized that it would be impossible to overcome the inertia of the region acting as lonesome cowboys, the internationally trained producers came together, exchanged experiences, developed new ideas, and shared the same vision. As a group of individuals, they wanted to rock sleepy Rheinhessen with attractive, characterful, drinkable, dry wines—and they really rocked it. (They rocked the aristocratic Rheingau as well, because for several years the Rieslings that people have been getting excited about have come from Rheinhessen rather than the Rheingau.) Founder members such as Klaus Peter Keller, Philipp Wittmann, Hans-Oliver Spanier, Carolin Kühling-Gillot, and Daniel Wagner are all stars today (and still part of the group), while others such as Christian and Jochen Dreissigacker,

Florian Fauth (Seehof), Johannes Geil-Bierschenk, Michael Gutzler, Max Pfannebecker, Johannes Thörle, Stefan Winter, and maybe some of the other 15 young producers are well on the way.

So, what happened to the former establishment, the so-called Rheinfront, with vineyards on the famous Roter Hang between Nierstein and Nackenheim? The leading estates of the 1990s—like Gunderloch (whose 2010s were the finest wines for several years), St. Antony, and Heyl zu Herrnsheim (the latter now a brand owned by the former)—are still returning to form after several years of fundamental change and less persuasive wines. Playing first fiddle here today is Weingut Kühling-Gillot, the Bodenheim estate owned by Carolin Spanier-Gillot and her winemaking husband Hans-Oliver Spanier.

The Nierstein district in the northeast of the region is the most famous of the three *Bereiche* in Rheinhessen, including villages such as Nierstein, Nackenheim, Bodenheim, and Oppenheim, which are all close to the Rhine. The finest wines are grown in the celebrated top sites of the Roter Hang, a steep east-, southeast-, and south-facing slope along the Rhine above Nackenheim and Nierstein. The vines—mostly Riesling—grow in red sediments of the Rotliegend (sandstone, silt, claystone), giving full-bodied yet very delicate and elegant wines of great finesse. They are defined by their silky texture, slightly herbal, almost-tropical fruit flavors, and subtle minerality. The best sites are Rothenberg in Nackenheim, and Pettenthal, Brudersberg, Hipping, Glöck, Ölberg, and Orbel in Nierstein. Most of the sites are classified for Grosses Gewächs production of Riesling by the VDP. In Oppenheim there is Sackträger and Kreuz (for Pinot Noir); and in Bodenheim, Burgweg (also for Pinot Noir).

The second district is Wonnegau, in the south of the region. With 1,888 acres (764ha) of vines, Westhofen, between the cities of Worms and Alzey, is one of the most important villages of the region.

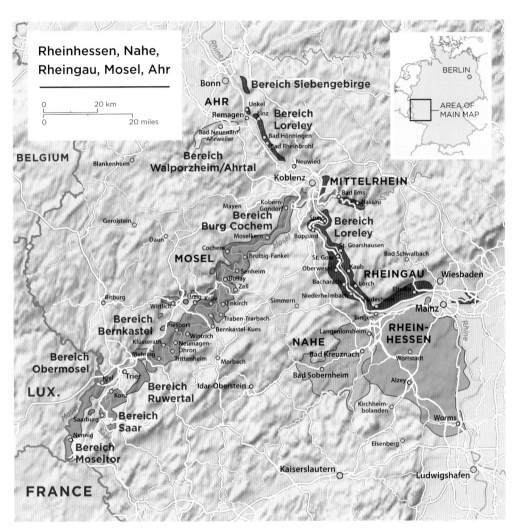

Rheinhessen, Nahe, Rheingau, Mosel, Ahr

In contrast to the "Red Slope" farther north, the vines here grow in calcareous loess, loam, and clay soils, which cover massive limestone rocks. The character of the deep soils is defined by the high proportion of clay (80 percent) and their excellent heat- and water-retention. Despite the high lime content, nutrient supply is good, though the stony subsoil is not easy to penetrate. Older vines whose roots have managed to get through have access to nutrients and water even in dry years. Riesling (in the stoniest soils) and Silvaner, as well as Pinot Blanc/Gris/Noir and Chardonnay, all perform very well here. The wines are always rich and firmly structured, yet they have great purity due to their cool and elegant minerality and the mix of fresh and salty fruit flavors. They can also have impressive length but benefit enormously from bottle age. The aging potential is tremendous, particularly in great vintages.

The best sites here are: Morstein (Riesling and Pinot Noir), Brunnenhäuschen, Kirchspiel, and Aulerde (all Riesling) in Westhofen; Hubacker (Riesling) and Bürgel (Pinot Noir) in Dalsheim; Frauenberg (Riesling and Pinot Noir) in Flörsheim; Zellerweg am Schwarzen Hergott (Riesling) in Mölsheim; and Kirchenstück (Riesling) in Hohen-Sülzen. Oliver Spanier and Daniel Wagner of Wagner-Stempel, the latter in Siefersheim, much farther west, where the vines grow in porphyry soils, have proved that forgotten or previously unrecognized terroirs can be of exceptional quality when they are interpreted properly. By contrast, Keller and Wittmann have perfected what their parents started more than 20 years earlier.

The great success of Wonnegau, especially since 2000, has pushed wine prices upward, at least for the best grands crus. Keller's mythical G-Max Riesling costs about €80 per bottle, and a Morstein Riesling from Wittmann or Keller is almost €40. Vineyard prices have also risen steeply. "I could not establish myself today in the way that I did," admits Spanier, who started his career in 1990, "because people no longer sell their vineyards—or only for crazy prices. Although they don't normally exploit the great potential of their vineyards, they won't give them to anybody else, because they have seen the prices people like Keller or Wittmann receive for their wines today."

The third Rheinhessen district, Bingen, is in the northwest. History has shown that it is possible to produce excellent wines here, too, especially in Scharlachberg, a grand cru based on quartzite that gives very pure, elegant, and vibrant Rieslings. Its full potential, however, has still to be realized.

A productive rivalry?

The crucial importance of Philipp Wittmann and Klaus-Peter Keller, the leading Riesling producers in Rheinhessen, merits some discussion of the relationship between them. They both produce wines that have been among Germany's finest for at least a few years. But not surprisingly, there has been much discussion among bloggers and wine journalists, merchants and sommeliers, and consumers as to whether Klaus-Peter Keller or Philipp Wittmann is the greatest producer of dry Riesling in Rheinhessen, if not all Germany.

This is a rather circular debate, of course. But it shows that the closer the two protagonists and their wines are—biographically, geographically, and qualitatively—the farther apart their wines taste, and the higher their supporters build the barricades. The debate is rarely framed in intellectual terms, not only in German wine circles, and tends to be negatively partisan. Ridiculous rumors circulate about the two producers, who advanced the Message in a Bottle group, as well as the Wonnegau district, together but have since found their own raisons d'être and very individual wine styles.

Keller and Wittmann are roughly of the same age, cultivate nearly the same grands crus, and have both vinified more than ten vintages. The enormous ambitions of these almost-neighboring producers have led them into a positive rivalry that has made their wines better and more distinctive with every year. Only history may tell which of them—if either—produces the better wines. While the wines are young, it is personal taste that may make us prefer the purity, elegance, and finesse of Wittmann, or the mineral core and race of the edgier Keller wines, which are no less pure but always need longer.

Is it really necessary, though, to decide whether Beethoven or Mozart was the better composer? Or whether apples or pears are the better fruit? Keller and Wittmann both produce thrilling Rieslings of great originality and expressive power. But because they are quite different personalities, their wine styles differ, too—and so much the better.

Whereas Wittmann is not only a brave wine producer but also the driving force of the VDP vineyard classification, being politically and socially active, Keller concentrates exclusively on his vines and the image of the family estate. "*Winzer* [vintner] is my profession but also my hobby, and the vineyard is the most important place I want to be," he says.

Indeed, Keller very rarely has either the inclination or the time to present his wines outside the winery, whereas Wittmann is always part of the show that represents not only Weingut Wittmann but the elite of Rheinhessen—a conventional but essential form of marketing. Without it, neither Rheinhessen nor perhaps even Keller or Wittmann themselves would have their present reputation.

Keller uses other channels to sell his wines and extend his reputation. You just have to browse the websites of certain opinion leaders and the relevant Internet forums to discover the spin doctors and virtual Keller fan clubs. There is a real club, too. Since there are already waiting lists for future wines, it is no easier to find a bottle of a Keller Grosses Gewächs than a ticket for Wagner's *Ring of the Nibelung* at the Bayreuth Festival. Additionally, with the G-Max Riesling, Keller produces a rare and expensive icon wine of superb quality—the golden calf of the Keller community. Wine freaks want to own it, if necessary in magnums, which can be purchased for absurd prices at the annual Bad Kreuznach auction. Wittmann does not produce such an icon wine, though he also produces special Riesling bottles for the auction, such as 150 Tage (2007).

Keller and Wittmann are both pioneers and style gods—and not only for colleagues in Rheinhessen. They lead a new generation of German wine producers, as Hans-Günther Schwarz did in the 1980s/90s or Rebholz in the 1990s/2000s. Wittmann and Keller have both made the desert flower, and they are both architects of Germany's Riesling future. There is no reason to downplay the historic importance of either of them.

Above: The future of dry German Riesling is largely in the hands of dynamic young producers like Keller and Wittmann

143

Weingut Keller

With his outstanding series of wines, especially the Riesling grands crus such as Morstein, Abtserde, and Hubacker, Klaus Peter Keller has become a guru to many young wine producers and wine freaks all over Europe since taking over the cellar in 2001 and the whole family estate in 2006. The young workers I met around the kitchen table during the 2011 harvest not only admire the wines Keller produces but also like his spirit and the way he shares his passion and knowledge about wine. After a day working in the vineyards, the whole team, including Klaus Peter and his wife Julia, comes together for dinner, drinking and discussing the finest wines—mostly Burgundy but also Rieslings from Alsace and other parts of Germany. "It's important to have an idea of what you want to produce. The finer the wines that you drink and get to know, the better you know how to produce them. It's a project for generations, not only for your own," says Klaus Peter.

He knows what he is talking about. His family came from Switzerland to Dalsheim in Wonnegau in 1789 and founded Weingut Keller. Klaus Peter is the ninth generation, and in Maximilian and Felix the tenth Keller generation is already part of the project. Dalsheimer Oberer Hubacker, which a Keller ancestor bought from a monastery, was the nucleus of the Keller estate and remains the most important site of the family today. Keller owns all 10 acres (4ha) of the original southeast-facing Hubacker (the site was extended to 56 acres [22.6ha] in 1971), which is dedicated 95 percent to Riesling. Many of the vines were planted in 1978 with massal selections from Oberemmel in the Saar Valley, homeland of Keller's late mother Hedwig. Generally, Keller is very keen on genetic diversity. He has planted or grafted many massal selections from the oldest vines of the Mosel and Saar but also from top estates in Alsace and, for his Pinots, in Burgundy.

Right: Klaus Peter and his son Maximilian, the ninth and tenth generations to have wielded pruners in the Keller vineyards

Currently, the Keller family cultivates 40 acres (16ha) of vines, 95 percent of which are located in Wonnegau and the rest on the Red Slope of Nierstein. About 75 percent of the total is dedicated to Riesling, 20 percent to Burgundian varieties (Pinot Blanc, Pinot Gris, and Pinot Noir) or Silvaner, and 5 percent to Rieslaner and Scheurebe. While a dry wine is produced from the latter, the former is used only for sweet wines. And although Keller's main focus is on dry wines, he is also one of the best, if smallest, sweet-wine producers in Germany, offering delicious Spätlesen, elegant and precise Auslesen, and highly noble BAs and TBAs. Some of Keller's wines fetch stratospheric prices at the annual auction in Bad Kreuznach.

Indeed, it's not easy to find a bottle of a Keller Grosses Gewächs, for the whole annual production is sold out between two weekends in May, when the Kellers open their doors and pour the latest wines en primeur. Those fine-wine merchants in Germany lucky enough to get some offer Keller wines by the bottle only—and only to their best clients. Thus, the Keller family and their long-term clients form an almost-closed community. And it becomes more closed the more newcomers knock on the door and ask only for the high-scoring grands crus or TBAs. There is no way to the Grosses Gewächs wines except via the already impressive basic or middle-range wines such as the Silvaner, Grauburgunder, or Riesling von der Fels. The latter is a dry blend of the younger parcels of all the grands crus, and it expresses Keller's main theme in a very distinctive way: Riesling on the rocks.

It is limestone that makes not only Hubacker a very special site, but also all the other most interesting vineyards in the hilly Wonnegau. Limestone also dominates the soils of the well-known Westhofen grands crus that Keller produces: Kirchspiel (7.5 acres [3ha]), Abtserde

Left: Harvest in the Westhofen grand cru Morstein, where handpicking is only the final act of a meticulous viticulture

(6.4 acres [2.6ha]), and Morstein (4.7 acres [1.9ha]), all Rieslings. Keller considers the soil much more crucial than the exposition of the vineyards for wine quality and style. The wines from the Westhofen crus and nearby Hubacker are always thrilling—as precise as a laser, as salty as oysters, and, at best, electrifying. By contrast, the Pettenthal Riesling GG, produced since the 2009 vintage, is rather delicate, elegant, and silky. It comes from an extremely steep 0.74-acre (0.3ha) parcel of the Nierstein grand cru and is grown on the famous red-sandstone soils of the Oberrotliegend, along the banks of the Rhine (Roter Hang). In 2011, Keller also started producing a Hipping Riesling GG, which comes from a 1.2-acre (0.5ha) parcel with a gradient of almost 80 percent. In both red-slope sites, the vines are more than 30 years old.

One of the most stunning things about Keller's wines is that they are enormously rich and complex but not high in alcohol, so they are very digestible. "A great wine has to reflect its origin in a precise yet effortless and relaxed way, so that it is always a pleasure to drink it," says Keller, who was trained at Geisenheim and served his apprenticeship at domaines Armand Rousseau and Hubert Lignier in Burgundy. It is obvious that such wines can only be created in the vineyard, not in the winery.

Keller strives for balance not only in his wines but in his vineyards, too. Each site and parcel is cultivated individually and with great respect to its varying needs, vintage to vintage. Because his final goal is loose bunches with small, ripe grapes, thick and healthy skins, intense flavors, good grip, and ripe yet vibrant acidity, Keller keeps his vines in a "positive stress" situation, which makes them more resistant to illness and rot. Thus, he boosted the planting density from 6,500 to 8,500 vines/ha, and the leaf canopy is lower than it was a few years ago. "We don't look for exorbitantly high sugar levels, since our wines should not have more than 12.5% ABV," Klaus Peter explains.

Much more crucial than sugar is intensity and precision of aroma and flavor, says Keller. So he does not pick when sugar levels are high enough, even if the weather is perfect. He believes that patience is one of the highest virtues when it comes to producing great wines. "Analytically, not that much changes in October," Keller says. "However, the flavor in the grapes improves a lot, because in the second half of the month the fruit enjoys ideal refrigerator conditions, with temperatures down to freezing during the night, while the days are still moderately warm. Thus, the berries develop fine phenolics and a ripe acidic structure."

Since the goal is to pick as late as possible, Keller prefers a slow and constant ripening process, which is less of a problem in cooler years if yields are kept low. "However, if we reduce the crop too early in warmer vintages, we would push a premature ripeness but also the danger of botrytis, since August and even the beginning of September can be very rainy." So in the warm and early 2011 vintage, Keller entered the harvest season with a higher crop than in 2010 and 2008. By contrast, he would not have picked fully ripe grapes in the late vintages of 2010 and 2008 if yields had been higher. While in 2010 and 2008, the last grapes were picked by November 20 and yields of the grands crus were kept at 30–35hl/ha, in 2011/2009, when the harvest was already finished by late October/early November, it was 45hl/ha. With climate change, which confronts German wine producers with much more extreme weather than years ago, "less is not always better," Keller insists.

His strategy is already sketched out between Christmas and New Year, as he anticipates every vintage in advance: "As we have learned over the past 15 years or so, even-numbered vintages, such as 2010, 2008 or 2002, are always cooler and harvested late. By contrast, odd-numbered vintages, such as 2011, 2009, 2007, 2005, or 2003, are warm and tend to an early ripeness."

The harvest team includes 20 workers plus the whole family, including the children. For the crus, there are five specialists plus Keller himself who are able to decide if the grape is fully ripe or should hang for another couple of days.

At the winery, no grape enters the presshouse before Klaus Peter's father, Klaus, has checked the quality. The 2011 vintage was his 46th harvest. Whether the grapes are destemmed or not, and whether there is maceration or not (and if so, for how long), depends on grape quality. There are no rules except this: "We don't want to produce monsters. We do what we consider best to extract the finest substances and to get an elegant and enjoyable fine wine." In some vintages, the must is fermented in stainless steel (mostly the warmer vintages); in other (cooler) vintages, in traditional wooden vats. After racking, the maturation is often in a different material, and it lasts until August for the crus. Most wines see both steel and wood.

As well as white wines, Keller also produces Spätburgunder—"more as a hobby," as he always says. Since his Burgundy days, he has good contacts and refers to Pinot Noir as Red Riesling. He produces two Spätburgunder Grosses Gewächs: the elegant, fruity, and silky Bürgel GG from a 1.5-acre (0.6ha) parcel planted with 40-year-old German Pinot Noir vines; and the fresh, pure, and straight Frauenberg GG from a 1.2-acre (0.5ha) parcel with younger selected vines from top Burgundy domaines. Both Pinots ferment spontaneously, in warmer vintages with stems, and in cooler years with fewer or without. The wines age for 20 months in French barriques (10–15 percent new), are never pumped, and are bottled without fining or filtration. Making Pinot Noir may have been "a hobby" for Keller, but since he grafted 70- to 75-year-old Silvaner vines in Morstein over to Pinot Noir from Jacques-Frédéric Mugnier's oldest vines in 2011, the hobby has become an ambitious one that we should all follow with interest.

FINEST WINES

Although there are excellent wines like the von der Fels, the Silvaner Feuervogel, the Riesling Spätlesen, and world-class noble sweet wines from Auslese to TBA (mainly from Riesling but also from Rieslaner and Scheurebe), the Riesling Grosse Gewächse from Wonnegau are the most regular of the finest wines, though quantities for all apart from the Hubacker GG are painfully small.

The **Kirchspiel GG** is grown on a very poor limestone soil on an east-facing slope. The acidity is always piquant, giving the slightly smoky, pure, elegant, almost weightless wine a playful raciness.

The **Morstein GG** comes from 50-year-old vines and is a real monolith, with a deep mineral soul that cares nothing for fruit, like the finest grands crus from Burgundy. While the expressive Morstein is made for thinking, as Jancis Robinson MW once said, the **Abtserde GG** is made for drinking. This amazingly fresh, pure, and thrilling wine is no less complex than the Morstein but seems less massive and more on the bright side of life. Almost 600 years ago, this was the favorite wine of the bishops of Worms—I guess because of the purity, vibrancy, and vivacity of the Abtserde, where the soil is as calcareous as in Chablis.

The **G-Max Riesling** is a mystery, in that Keller does not name its origin but says it's from very special old Riesling vines. Since it is dedicated to his great-grandfather Georg (who once blasted away the terraces of the Oberer Hubacker) and to Keller's eldest son Maximilian, it could be grown in Hubacker. Anyway, it's not worth worrying about, because the wine is rare (1,500 bottles) and expensive, as well as close to perfection.

Underlining that Hubacker is the family's most important vineyard, Keller poured me three vintages of the Grosses Gewächs in September 2011. In the Oberer Hubacker parcel, the massive yellow rocks are covered by clay layers of 24–32in (60–80cm), so there is always a good water supply—important in this dry area, with less than 24in (600mm) of annual rainfall. For the Hubacker GG, Keller picks only the grapes of vines that are older than 20 years, so it is always expressive: cool, pure, and precise, but it doesn't lack complexity, finesse, or elegance, and the interplay of acidity, salinity, and fruit is remarkably delicate and animating.

I remember Hubacker GG broader and fatter some years ago, and I was surprised how pure, delicate, light, and breezy it has become since 2008.

Hubacker Riesling GG

2010★ This is from one of the most beautiful harvests Klaus Peter can remember. Grapes were small, ripened very slowly, and were golden yellow when picked, with the highest extracts for more than 20 years, between November 12 and 15. The alcohol is 12.4% ABV, but the nose is concentrated and spicy, with beautiful aromas of ripe raisins. Dense, salty, and extremely mineral on the palate, this is like melting limestone—a very complex wine, with *Spiel*, fresh citrus flavors, and incredible length.

2009 "Perfect grapes, such as you might not see again very often in your lifetime," Keller's 84-year-old grandfather said when he saw the grapes arriving at the winery at the end of October. The wine still has leesy notes, yet is very dense and complex on the nose. Full-bodied, powerful, and extremely rich on the palate, with a creamy texture but also an appetizing acidity, freshness, and salinity. Still young and mighty but clearly of great potential.

2008★ This is from a rather cool and late-ripening vintage, in which the harvest did not finish until November 20 in the grands crus. Yields were as low as 30–35hl/ha. After vintages such as 2001, 2003, 2005, and 2007, when German vintners struggled to avoid overripeness, 2008 presented the opposite problem. "This is one reason why I love my work so much: you never know what will come next year," says Keller. "Nature is the mistress, and you have to adapt according to her caprices." In 2008, grapes were not destemmed and the maceration lasted 18–20 hours to reduce the high acidity. Very good concentration and precision. Dense, piquant, and straight on the palate; firmly structured, very mineral and vibrant, pure and salty, finishing with an animating grip. This is almost like electroshock therapy.

Weingut Keller

Area under vine: 40 acres (16ha); 75% Riesling; 20% Pinot Blanc, Pinot Gris, Pinot Noir, Silvaner; 5% Rieslaner, Scheurebe
Average production: 100,000–120,000 bottles
Best vineyards: *Dalsheim* Hubacker, Bürgel; *Westhofen* Morstein, Abtserde, Kirchspiel; *Nierstein* Pettenthal, Hipping
Bahnhofstrasse 1, 67592 Flörsheim-Dalsheim
www.keller-wein.de

Weingut Wittmann

The viticultural history of the Wittmann family dates back to 1663, but the first vintage was bottled only in 1921. Until the beginning of the 1990s, Weingut Wittmann was a mixed agriculture, but since then the family has concentrated exclusively on wine and has emerged as one of the finest Riesling producers in Germany.

The estate is located in the historical heart of Westhofen in Wonnegau, in hilly southern Rheinhessen. In the fertile glacial Rhine Valley, with its gentle slopes and almost Mediterranean climate, the Wittmann family cultivates 62 acres (25ha) of vines, growing in clay, marl, or loess soils covering the limestone rocks below. Two-thirds of the plants are Riesling, but there is also Silvaner, Scheurebe, Albalonga (for noble sweet wines only), Pinot Blanc, Pinot Gris, and Chardonnay for the whites, and Pinot Noir and St. Laurent for the rosé and the reds.

Since the 1990s, Weingut Wittmann has concentrated exclusively on wine and has emerged as one of the finest Riesling producers in Germany

Westhofen has an impressive range of crus, which lie side by side to the north and northeast of the village: Morstein, Brunnenhäuschen, Steingrube, Kirchspiel, and Aulerde. The grapes in Aulerde and Kirchspiel ripen seven to ten days earlier than those in Morstein and Brunnenhäuschen, which can both bear some of the finest Rieslings of Germany. All sites apart from Steingrube are classified for Grosse Lage production by the VDP, and Wittmann has parcels in all of them, plus Steingrube. The latter is never mentioned on a label but is the source of the remarkably Burgundian Weisser Burgunder S *trocken* and the Chardonnay S *trocken*, both grown on calcareous soils.

The vines have been cultivated organically (Naturland-certified) since 1990 and biodynamically (Demeter-certified) since 2004. Philipp Wittmann, who took over the cellar in 1998 and the estate in 2007, decided to go biodynamic mainly for quality reasons: "With the biodynamic approach, and fermentations with natural yeasts in large wooden barrels, we are striving for even more balance, authenticity, and tension in our wines," he explains.

Wittmann's raison d'être is to reflect the origin of his wines in the most authentic way possible. "I want to produce pure, straight, succulent, and deep wines that do not lack freshness, elegance, or finesse," he says. So he aims for ripe but not overripe, aromatically intense, healthy grapes that are not at all affected by botrytis.

In the vineyards, no herbicides, no fungicides, and no chemical fertilizers have been used for more than 20 years. With the biodynamic approach, Wittmann aims for natural balance in his vineyards, a slower ripening process, and physiologically ripe grapes with lower sugar levels but intense mineral flavors. Indeed, the bunches have become "looser, the berries smaller, and the skins thicker" since he has gone biodynamic, Wittmann reports. He adds that they reach full ripeness now with 90–96° Oechsle instead of 100°, which he prefers, since he does not want to produce wines with more than 12.5–13% ABV.

To fertilize the soil and enrich the humus content, every second row is covered with seeded herbs and legumes, while every other row is plowed over the summer. The planting density is 6,000 vines/ha, and the leaf canopy is kept quite short and open. Gentle leaf removal in the grape zone is performed shortly after flowering, but in August the eastern side of the grapes is completely deleafed. Depending on the vintage, Wittmann prefers halving bunches to green harvesting.

Right: The brilliant Philipp Wittmann, who converted his estate to biodynamics and is producing scintillating wines

Above: Although they may not be quite so old or ornate, Philipp Wittmann continues to ferment his top wines in large oak casks

In warm and early vintages such as 2011, he enters the harvest season with a higher crop, to be reduced through the first selective pickings.

For the Grosse Gewächse, Wittmann harvests only vines older than 20 years. Genetics play another important role regarding the wine quality. His father Günter Wittmann made selections from old vines, and Philipp continues the practice. He planted massal selections from Alsace and the Saar to increase the genetic diversity, which he believes is much better for the production of thrilling wines than clones from Geisenheim.

Harvest is done by hand, and always late for the grands crus. If the crop is healthy, skin contact can be quite long—up to 24 hours in vintages like 2010, or four hours in warmer vintages. After settling, the must ferments spontaneously, and fermentation is finished mostly before Christmas. While the Grosse Gewächse are at least 70 percent barrel-fermented (in 1,200-liter *Stückfass* and 2,400-liter *Doppelstück*), the more fruit-driven basic and village wines are fermented and aged in 50 percent stainless-steel tanks and 50 percent oak barrels of 1,200 to 5,400 liters. The Weissburgunder (Pinot Blanc) and Chardonnay are fermented and aged in 600-liter barrels and used barriques. Wittmann keeps the wines on their lees until bottling in April (for the basic wines) or June–August (for the GGs).

The wines, which are 95–98 percent dry, are marked by their purity, elegance, and finesse, as well as by their exciting complexity, immediacy, and animating length. Wittmann's basic line of varietal wines is very good, with a clear focus on brilliant fruit flavors, light body, and finesse. The Westhofen village wines—Riesling and Silvaner (which originates from Aulerde)—are delicious and the best buys. It is the Grosse Gewächse, however, that reflect the crème de la crème.

FINEST WINES

(Tasted in September 2011)

2010 Westhofener Riesling trocken ★ [V]

Sourced from the younger vines in Morstein (50%), Brunnenhäuschen, and Kirchspiel, this is amazingly fresh, subtle, and quite complex, with alluring fruit flavors. Very pure, elegant, and distinguished on the palate, delicate and spicy, the refined acidity giving way to a lingering salty finish. Delicious!

Aulerde Riesling GG

The south-facing Aulerde just north of Westhofen is the warmest of the crus. It is located in the lower part of the Westhofen basin, well protected, and rises gently from 300 to 400ft (90m–120m). The soil is deep clay, but there are no rocks, only gravelly and clay sand in the subsoil. Wittmann's Riesling vines are 50 years old and give a wine that is always ripe, rich, and round, with intense, almost-tropical fruit flavors. I find it lacks the thrilling purity and kicking spiciness of Kirchspiel and the complexity and distinctiveness of Morstein and Brunnenhäuschen. The 2010 is brilliant, deep, and spicy on the nose. It is well structured, thanks to a longer maceration, and the rich texture is lifted by the piquant minerality and long salty finish.

Kirchspiel Riesling GG

Kirchspiel is defined by limestone rocks that come to the surface in certain parcels of the upper parts of the site, where the stony marl topsoil is less deep. The east-facing site rises up to 500ft (150m) and is quite steep. Riesling performs brilliantly here and benefits from both morning sun and cool evenings and nights. It is always mineral, piquant, and racy, but also elegant and with *Spiel*—a real Riesling classic. The 2010 is quite intense in color, though the bouquet is very pure, displaying finest Riesling and limestone flavors that remind me of Puligny-Montrachet. The fruit is straight and dense and paired with a thrilling minerality that leads to a long and salty finish. Very good aging potential.

Brunnenhäuschen Riesling GG ★

This is a south-facing site rising from 720 to 780ft (220m–240m). The most interesting thing here is that the calcareous marl soil contains iron (terra rossa), which lends the wine richness, a thrilling minerality, and a powerful, complex finish. The 2010 is intense in both color and aroma. Rich, deep, and concentrated, this wine pairs ripe fruit flavors with spicy minerality, refined raciness, and filigreed yet persistent structure. Full and elegant, very pure, straight, and persistent—this is a great, emotional Riesling with the complexity of a Montrachet.

Morstein Riesling GG ★

The south-facing Morstein rise to 920ft (280m) though Wittmann's parcels are lower, at 600–720ft (180–220m). The limestone is covered by clay here, but the layers can be quite thin. Thus, the vines (mostly planted in 1982 and 1986) penetrate the rocks and give a wine that is impressively deep, complex, and long but that has great purity and multilayered finesse, too.

2010 ★ Very deep, dense, and distinctively mineral on the nose, displaying fully ripe fruit aromas. Very rich on the palate, almost viscous and less piquant and delicate than the Brunnenhäuschen on the attack. Needs some minutes, if not years, to develop its noble purity and refined acidity. Very powerful, complex, and intense; has a long way to go.

2009 ★ Probably the most exciting Wittmann Morstein so far. Very cool and precise on the nose (despite the warm vintage!). The palate is the playground of a delicate and elegant dancing cru that seems to consist of nothing but minerals and melting stones, so pure is it. The finesse and elegance are breathtaking.

2008 Discreet on the nose, yet fresh and refined. The fruit is quite mature, more dry and white than succulent and yellow. Very mineral, elegant, and full of finesse, though I find this bottle a little evolved.

2007 Clear on the nose: ripe and very ripe fruit flavors and hints of mint, which may be the first hint of maturity. Elegant on the palate, the firm minerality lending power, complexity, and length. Should age well, if less well than 2009 or 2010.

2005 A dry year. Discreet fruit aromas of Golden Delicious and herbs. The cool precision and mineral purity of this wine is thrilling. A creamy texture, and slightly bitter on the finish because of *bâtonnage*, but the wine is elegant, salty, and still young.

Weingut Wittmann

Area under vine: 62 acres (25ha); 65% Riesling
Average production: 190,000 bottles
Best vineyards: *Westhofen* Morstein, Brunnenhäuschen, Kirchspiel, Aulerde
Mainzer Strasse 19, 67593 Westhofen
Tel: +49 6244 905 036
www.wittmannweingut.com

Weingut Wagner-Stempel

aniel Wagner, born in 1971, cultivates a total of 44 acres (18ha) of vines—mostly Riesling but also Pinot Blanc, Pinot Gris, and Silvaner—to name only the most important varieties. The estate and vineyards are located in the village of Siefersheim, halfway between Bad Kreuznach (Nahe) and Alzey (Rheinhessen) in the so-called Rheinhessische Schweiz. The protected area in the hilly western part of the wine region was not known for fine wine until Wagner took over the family business in 1992. He has been a member of the VDP since 2004. Wagner's wines are the most arctic of the Rheinhessen. Although they share the ripe and intense yellow-fruit flavors of those from Wonnegau and the Red Slope, their cool, racy, mineral-spicy character resembles that of top Nahe wines.

The landscape around Siefersheim is very different from the rest of Rheinhessen, too. It is a very unproductive area because of the weathered rhyolite (porphyry with a high proportion of quartz) that forms the soils here. They are stony, acidic, and low in nutrients. The loamy topsoil is rather thin (less than 20in [50cm] in places), so the water-storage capacity is moderate, while the capacity to store heat is quite good. Vines (the older, the better—and especially Riesling) like these natural conditions, but even the oldest oak trees look puny rather than proud here. The climate is slightly cooler than in the rest of Rheinhessen, yet warmer than in the Nahe. Vines are cultivated at an altitude of 450–900ft (140–280m), and they ripen more slowly, with smaller grapes, than in the eastern parts of the region. Thus, yields are naturally low (or kept low with the younger vines), averaging between 20hl/ha in 2010 and 40hl/ha in 2008.

Wagner's organically cultivated vines are rather young, averaging only ten years because of many new plantings. But in his best sites—the cooler

Right: Daniel Wagner and his wife Cathrin, with one of the large old oak casks in which they produce stunning Rieslings

Heerkretz and the warmer Höllberg—there are several parcels with 25- to 40-year-old Riesling vines that do not need to be green harvested or have their yields restricted in any other way. So, the entire harvest is potentially part of the Riesling Grosses Gewächs produced from both sites.

With 6,000–7000 vines/ha, planting density is rather high, since Wagner prefers to keep his vines "on a diet," as he says. The canopy is kept quite low and open, the grape zone is deleafed in early June on the east side, then completely in August. Bunches that are too compact are halved in July.

Wagner aims for healthy, ripe, not overripe berries, with less than 100° Oechsle. He rarely picks before the end of October, and his most interesting site, Heerkretz, is not normally harvested until November. Acidity levels remain high, though, and the wines ferment dry. Only if possible are delicious *Prädikatsweine* (Spätlese or Auslese) produced.

Winemaking is very traditional. The hand-picked grapes are slightly crushed and kept on skins for 12–48 hours depending on the vintage and fruit conditions. The completely untreated must (no enzymes, no bentonite, no sulfur) ferments spontaneously in stainless steel or traditional oak for two weeks to three months, though Wagner prefers a short fermentation. The wines are kept on their lees until the end of May, when they are bottled unfined but Kieselgur-filtered.

Although Wagner's Silvaner and Pinot wines are very good, I prefer the late-ripening Rieslings that benefit most from the special natural conditions here, with a distinguished intensity, cool precision, and straight mineral character that is unique.

FINEST WINES

2010 Porphyr Riesling trocken [V]
Sourced from the younger vines in the Höllberg and Heerkretz crus, this *Gutswein* is one of the finest dry Rieslings in its price range in Germany. This 2010 shows fully ripe fruit aromas of yellow apples but is also cool, precise, and spicy on the nose. On the palate, it is full, elegant, and supple in texture, but the structure is very mineral and piquant, and the iron part of the soil seems to give it extra drive and grip. Very pure and thrilling on the finish.

Höllberg Riesling GG
The south-/southeast-facing Höllberg is not very steep but is very dry, sheltered, and warm. The weathered porphyry soil is quite stony and stores the heat very well, so this wine, fermented in traditional oak, is full and intense, but lacks neither mineral depth nor freshness. The 2010 is rich, succulent, and spicy, with a rather warm character compared to the Heerkretz.

Heerkretz Riesling GG
The Heerkretz is a south-/southwest-facing steep slope stretching over 2 miles (3.5km). It is much less homogeneous than Höllberg, and the grapes often struggle to reach ripeness. The soil is quite complex, with more red loam in the lower parts and more stones and glacial debris in the upper parcels. There are also belts with gravel, basalt, and shale limestone sediment in Heerkretz, which is mainly based on rhyolite rocks that often poke through to the surface. The grapes rarely ripen before November, and the character of the stainless-steel-fermented grand cru from 30-year-old vines is always intense and racy, very subtle in its bouquet, pure, and almost salty in taste, while the body is elegant and persistent.

2010 ★ This was picked through to November 8 and is probably the finest Heerkretz so far. Very cool and fresh on the nose, but with ripe and concentrated fruit aromas, too. Very salty and vibrant on the palate, if less pure, as a result of deacidification. The wine is still complete and harmonious.

2009 Brilliant on the nose, with ripe and succulent fruit aromas, but less overblown than the 2007, with subtle herbal scents, too. Rich and succulent but also firm, piquant, and racy, showing excellent depth, density, and length. Great potential and less sweet than previous vintages.

Weingut Wagner-Stempel
Area under vine: 45 acres (18ha)
Annual production: 150,000 bottles
Best vineyards: *Siefersheim* Heerkretz, Höllberg
Wöllsteiner Strasse 10, 55599 Siefersheim
Tel: +49 6703 960 330
www.wagner-stempel.de

Kühling-Gillot

Women have been in charge at Kühling-Gillot for generations. Carolin Spanier-Gillot took over the reins of the operation in 2002. She is an enologist and mother of two and has many other talents as well. She is responsible for the administration, selling, marketing, presentation, entertainment, and event management of Weingut Carolin Spanier-Gillot & HO Spanier. The company was founded after Carolin's marriage to Hans-Oliver Spanier in 2006. Since then, what were formerly two distinct wine estates have been transformed into two brands: Kühling-Gillot and BattenfeldSpanier. While the traditional Kühling-Gillot estate in Bodenheim has been renovated and transformed into a cool château cube with event and chill-out facilities, BattenfeldSpanier is still a working winery. It is Carolin's husband, known as HO, who cares for the 30 acres (12ha) of Kühling-Gillot vines, as well as for the 70 acres (28ha) of land owned by BattenfeldSpanier, and he is also responsible for the vinification, which takes place in Hohen-Sülzen.

On the Red Slope, Kühling-Gillot owns three of the very best sites. The wines have distinctive fruit aromas, elegance, and freshness, but also volume and a harmonious, silky texture

Regarding the final wines, however, all the important decisions and all the barrel tastings are shared by Carolin and HO, because he does not wish to be without her female intuition or taste. But hearing HO speaking about the differences between "his" and "her" wines, I discerned the following subtext. There are at least two quite different terroirs, which give birth to two very different types of wine: straight and striking mineral Rieslings for men from the limestone soils of Hohen-Sülzen and Zellertal (BattenfeldSpanier) on the one hand, and rather refined, elegant, and harmonious Rieslings for women from what is called Roter Hang on the other (Kühling-Gillot).

On the Red Slope, between the villages of Nackenheim and Nierstein, Kühling-Gillot owns three of the very best sites, which are almost completely planted with Riesling: the VDP Grosse Lagen Nierstein Ölberg, Nierstein Pettenthal, and Nackenheim Rothenberg. Further holdings are in Oppenheim (Kreuz) and Bodenheim (Burgweg), which are mainly planted with Pinot Noir and Pinot Blanc because of the marl and clay soils.

However, it is the red soil between Nackenheim and Nierstein that makes the Rieslings of the steep Red Slope unique. The soil was built up by calcareous sediments of clay, silt, and sandstone during the Rotliegend 280 million years ago and came back to the surface at the end of the Tertiary because of the Rhine rift and the formation of the steep slopes along the Rhine River. The soils of weathered rocks are shallow and do not have a good capacity to store water; nor do the roots penetrate the deeper rock easily. However, the dark red color, as well as the good aeration, cause rapid warming, and the carbonate-rich soils have enough nutrients and minerals (mostly iron), too.

Riesling performs best here and lends the wines distinctive fruit aromas, elegance, and freshness, but also volume and a harmonious, silky texture. They can have very good aging potential, especially in years with good water supply, but can taste slightly stressed or too evolved in dry years.

Viticulture, therefore, has to be adapted to the needs of each vintage, and HO Spanier reports that the vines are in better balance since they have been cultivated organically, with some biodynamic applications. In dry years, the rows between the vines are covered with straw, while green cover is kept rather short. Spanier never uses fertilizers, apart from a little compost if necessary. "If the soils and vines are balanced, so are the wines," he says.

Since Hans-Oliver has been making the Kühling-Gillot wines, they have become the leading brand from the Red Slope in terms of both quality and expression. The range of wines is well structured and is, says HO, "99 percent dry." When it comes to good varietal wines, whether white, red, or rosé, one is spoiled for choice, and there are two excellent premiers crus as well: Oppenheim Riesling and Nierstein Riesling. I do not know the Pinots very well, but the 2008 Spätburgunder Kreuz—deep, ripe, and fresh, with fine tannins and good length—matched perfectly the boar's liver that Carolin served me in fall 2011, after we had tasted the following wines.

FINEST WINES

Ölberg Riesling GG

This wine comes from most southerly location on the Red Slope and from the only site that faces due south. The gradient is more than 60 percent, so exposure to the sun is strong. As a result, the wine is always full-bodied, generous, and intense, but lacks neither elegance nor precision. The **2010** is refined and silky, but also complex, racy, and salty.

Rothenberg Riesling GG

The Rothenberg is located at the northern end of the Red Slope. Kühling-Gillot's parcel is at the top of the southeasterly slope and is only 1.2 acres (0.5ha), but it is the steepest one and enclosed by a stone wall like a Burgundian *clos*. The grapes benefit from the morning sun and the light that is reflected by the Rhine River. The soil is rather soft, so the roots go deep. According to Carolin, the vines were planted in 1933 and are ungrafted. The **2010** is rich, mild, and distinguished on the nose, displaying a delicate spiciness. Elegant and silky, this Riesling is characterized by its noble raciness, animating salinity, and nice grip. The finish is long, and the aging potential is very good.

Riesling Pettenthal GG

With a gradient of more than 70 percent and at altitudes up to 550ft (170m), Kühling-Gillot's east-

facing parcel in Niersteiner Pettenthal is probably the steepest vineyard in Rheinhessen. The topsoil is very poor, so the vines root deep in the rather soft rock of the Red Slope. Mechanical cultivation is impossible, so everything is done by hand. Carolin finds the grapes smell like diesel when they are picked, but fortunately there is no such aroma in the wine. Instead, it is characterized by the finest herbal aromas, lemon thyme and marjoram, and almost-tropical fruit flavors. The body is always full yet elegant and harmonious, and there is finesse even in warm and dry years, which, curiously, bring out the best in the greatest Pettenthal wines.

2010 Very refined on the nose. Precise and spicy fruit aromas, with floral and herbal notes. Very delicate and elegant, succulent yet brilliant, playful, and distinguished. Very good aging potential.

2009★ Deep, cool, and intense on the nose, with herbal aromas, hints of licorice, and ripe fruit flavors. Very rich and dense on the palate, yet countered by a vibrant acidity and piquant minerality. The wine never loses its precision, elegance, or finesse. A lush and lingering finish, but the soul remains northern.

2008 Brilliant on the nose, again with herbal aromas and maturing fruit flavors, so that the Pettenthal terroir starts to shine through. Salty and juicy on the palate, this is a delicate, cool, and racy Pettenthal, with a firm structure and good length, though it's more edgy than its successors.

2006 Picked surprisingly late, at beginning of November, whereas most German wines were harvested a month earlier this year because of massive rainfalls, warm temperatures, and the spread of botrytis. Pettenthal, however, stayed dry, and this wine is as clear and pure as ever on the nose, its fruit ripe and intense. On the palate, however, it is smoother than usual, lacking its characteristic cool and spicy minerality and delicate raciness. Very enjoyable with food, though.

Weingut Kühling-Gillot
Area under vine: 30 acres (12ha); 60% Riesling, plus Grauburgunder, Scheurebe, Spätburgunder
Average production: 80,000 bottles
Best vineyards: *Nierstein* Ölberg, Pettenthal; *Nackenheim* Rothenberg
Ölmühlstrasse 25, 55294 Bodenheim
Tel: +49 6135 2333
www.kuehling-gillot.de

Left: The multitalented Carolin Spanier-Gillot, latest in a long line of women to have run the family estate in Bodenheim

BattenfeldSpanier

Hans-Oliver Spanier, born in 1971 and known as HO, had 20 acres (8ha) of vines when he took over the family estate in 1990. "But it was all rubbish," he says today. After he tasted a 1990 Silvaner *trocken* from Heyl zu Herrnsheim, he knew what he wanted to produce: "Dry, top-quality wines that reflect their origin." Spanier was convinced that the potential of the southern Rheinhessen was far greater than its cheap-and-sweet image suggested: "You just have to have top sites for quality grapes such as Riesling, Silvaner, and Pinot Noir." Thus, he started to buy and exchange vineyards. "The better the vineyard, the easier it was to acquire it then, because good vineyards are always labor-intensive, and in the 1990s, many grape and wine producers preferred to earn their income expending as little time and effort as possible."

"Great authentic wines have to be cool and relaxed," says Spanier. With his 20th vintage, he has finally reached this goal. His grands crus, in particular, have never been better

After a couple of years Spanier owned some very good parcels in sites that were well known at the end of the 19th century but were then completely forgotten. Currently, he cultivates 70 acres (28ha) of vines in Hohen-Sülzen, Monsheim, and Mölsheim for BattenfeldSpanier and, since 2004, another 30 acres (12ha) in Oppenheim, Nackenheim, Nierstein, and Bodenheim for his wife Carolin Spanier-Gillot and the Kühling-Gillot brand. More than 60 percent of the BattenfeldSpanier vines are Riesling, but there is also Silvaner, Pinot Blanc, and Pinot Noir. The biodynamically cultivated vineyards are on limestone strips that can be found from Donnersberg across Zellertal to Westhofen and help elevate sites such as Am Schwarzen Herrgott, Frauenberg, Kirchenstück, Bürgel, Hubacker, and

Morstein to VDP Grosse Lage status. "Ground chalk—this is what gives our wines the X factor: depth and thrilling length," Spanier insists.

HO stresses that every vineyard is cultivated differently, depending on its needs. Yields are kept low, at 35–40hl/ha. After being slightly crushed, the grapes are kept on their skins for anything from eight hours up to three days, and at least the Grosse Gewächse ferment spontaneously in traditional wooden casks. The wines are kept on their lees until one day before being filtered and bottled.

"Great authentic wines have to be cool and relaxed," says Spanier. With his 20th vintage—2010—he has finally reached this goal. His grands crus, in particular, have never been better.

BattenfeldSpanier has a well-structured range of wines, all them vinified dry and made of botrytis-free grapes whenever possible. The characterful *Gutsweine* (Riesling, Weissburgunder, Silvaner, and Spätburgunder) are topped by complex village wines (Riesling from Mölsheim and Hohen-Sülzen, Weissburgunder and Silvaner from Hohen-Sülzen), which are outshone by four Grosse Gewächse: a *Stückfass*-fermented Kirchenstück Spätburgunder and the three Rieslings: Am Schwarzen Herrgott (Mölsheim), Frauenberg (Nieder-Flörsheim), and Kirchenstück (Hohen-Sülzen).

FINEST WINES

Zellerweg am Schwarzen Herrgott Riesling GG
From a south-facing site in the eastern part of Zellertal, bordering the Pfalz. The Riesling vines in Spanier's 3.7-acre (1.5ha) Grosses Gewächs parcel grow in a very poor soil of limestone rubble, and the grapes benefit from warm days and cool nights. The first vintage, **2010**, is deep, very mineral, and firmly structured, yet elegant and refined.

Kirchenstück Riesling GG
This is from a well-sheltered 7.5-acre (3ha) cru with deep calcareous marl soils. The vines average 35 years, and the wine is always rich, dense, and powerful; in **2010**, it is also straight, pure, mineral, and backed by racy acidity.

Above: Hans-Oliver Spanier, after 20 years achieving his ambition of producing "dry, top-quality wines that reflect their origin"

Frauenberg Riesling GG

In Frauenberg, Spanier owns 16 acres (6.5ha), but because the poorest limestone soils are in the highest part (up to 850ft [260m]), the Grosses Gewächs parcel is only 3.7 acres (1.5ha). The Frauenberg GG combines depth, raciness, and pronounced minerality with purity, elegance, and finesse, and I find it the finest of the grands crus.

2010★ This was harvested on November 4 and is cool, spicy, and elegant on the nose. It is less fruity than before, but its purity, transparency, and finesse are breathtaking. Very long and complex.

2009 This was also picked in early November. The color is deeper—almost golden—and the bouquet is rich, ripe, and herbal. Opulent and very intense on the palate, weighty and rather sweet, yet still a little bitter and greenish on the finish.

2008 This was harvested on November 16, with 88° Oechsle. Very elegant, racy, and refined, but with the first hints of maturity showing in the dried white-fruit flavors. Quite sweet but slightly drying on the finish.

2001★ Almost golden. Nice maturity; delicate herbal aromas. Graceful structure, with refined acidity, still vibrant and grippy, with a herbal reprise in the aftertaste.

Riesling CO

In great vintages like 2007, 2009, and 2010, there is a tiny production of the superb Riesling CO. It's made from selected vines of Schwarzer Herrgott and Frauenberg, whose grapes are picked last. Maceration lasts up to 56 hours, and the wine ferments spontaneously in a 600-liter wooden vat. It is released only three or four years after the harvest and is—like Keller's G-Max—quite expensive.

2010★ Very rich and complex, tightly woven, and finishing with astonishing long-lasting salinity.

2009 Even broader and seemingly sweeter, though the residual sugar is under 4g/l.

BattenfeldSpanier

Area under vine: 70 acres (28ha); 60% Riesling, plus Silvaner, Weissburgunder, Spätburgunder
Average production: 120,000 bottles
Best vineyards: *Mölsheim* Zellerweg am Schwarzen Herrgott (Riesling); *Nieder-Flörsheim* Frauenberg (Riesling); *Hohen-Sülzen* Kirchenstück (Riesling and Spätburgunder)
Bahnhofstrasse 33, 67591 Hohen-Sülzen
Tel: +49 6243 906 515
www.battenfeld-spanier.de

Rheingau

The Rheingau is not only a beautiful region but also, thanks to Riesling, one of the most prestigious small wine regions of the world. Riesling has been cultivated here since at least 1435; has contributed to numerous legendary wines, as well as stratospheric auction prices; and occupies 79 percent of the total 7,678 acres (3,107ha) under vine today. Riesling made the Rheingau famous and prosperous, as the many churches and castles show.

Riesling is grown in the best sites and benefits from excellent natural conditions. So, too, does Pinot Noir, the second most important variety, which was brought by Cistercian monks from Vougeot in 1107 and today occupies 940 acres, (380ha, 12.2 percent of the total). Chardonnay and Müller-Thurgau are also cultivated, but even more interesting are old rarities such as Silvaner (planted mainly in Lorch and Lorchhausen), Gelber Orleans and Weisser Hennish (both cultivated by Georg Breuer in tiny amounts), and Roter Riesling (reputedly the same as Savagnin), which a group of Rheingau growers (including Allendorf, Prinz, and Knyphausen) has been reestablishing.

On its long way from Switzerland to the North Sea, the Rhine flows mostly north through Germany. But between the rival cities of Wiesbaden (capital of the state of Hessen) and Mainz (capital of Rheinland-Pfalz), the river has to veer about 19 miles (30km) west, around the proud and mighty Taunus Mountains (*see map, p.141*). After Rüdesheim, it takes the chance to flow north again, carving through the more penetrable Rhenish Massif (Rheinisches Schiefergebirge) to create the picturesque Rhine Gorge (Oberes Mittelrheintal), a UNESCO World Heritage site. This stretches from Bingen/Rüdesheim up to Coblenz, and includes the Mittelrhein, with its racy Rieslings and spectacular grands crus such as Bacharacher Hahn or Bopparder Hamm.

The Rheingau, extending from Flörsheim-Wicker and Hochheim am Main in the east, to Lorch and Lorchhausen in the west, is on the right bank of the river, so most of the vineyards face south. Between the river and the Taunus Mountains (Rheingaugebirge), they are protected from cold wind and rain, and thus ideally suited to viticulture.

Although the Rheingau is one of the most homogenous German wine regions, it is still useful to divide it into three parts, since the Rieslings around Hocheim in the far east are very different from those of the central part between Walluf and Rüdesheim, which are different again from those of Assmannshausen upstream to Lorchhausen.

Hochheim stands slightly apart from what we might call the real Rheingau, since it is on the Main River rather than the Rhine. Shortly before the confluence of the two at Kostheim, about 4 miles (6km) west of Hochheim, the Main's right bank forms a south-facing and shadeless slope, with quite deep and warm soils. Sandy and loamy loess layers cover the clay or calcareous marl soils, mixed with gravel or limestone pebbles. The best wines from Hochheim are, therefore, rich and powerful but also silky and elegant. They are built on mineral foundations, which makes them pure, straight, and quite salty, as well as giving them great longevity.

In Walluf (still sedimentary loam soils but with a gravelly subsoil), the central and most famous part of the Rheingau starts, stringing together villages such as Eltville and Rauenthal, Erbach and Kiedrich, Hattenheim and Hallgarten, Oestrich and Winkel (including Schloss Vollrads), Geisenheim with Schloss Johannisberg, and Rüdesheim. It is here that the most renowned estates are found.

The farther the vineyards are from the river, the higher they are, the stonier their soils, and the more interesting the wines tend to taste. (Of course, there are exceptions, like Erbach Marcobrunn or Mittelheim St. Nikolaus, which are close to the river but among the best vineyards, the former already

Right: Schlossberg, one of many famous, steep Rheingau sites, whose wines have been among the most expensive in the world

classified in the Weinbau-Karte des Nassauischen Rheingau's in 1867.) Away from the Rhine, where loess, loam, or clay dominates, there are higher proportions of quartzite and slate from the Taunus Mountains, and the farther west, the purer the slate. The soils become lighter and stonier the steeper the sites are, and the farther west you go. We might say that Rüdesheimer Berg is the crowning glory of the central Rheingau. Vineyards like Berg Rottland (also classified by 1867), Berg Roseneck, and Berg Schlossberg are breathtakingly steep, the soils quite poor, mixing loess with quartzite and slate, with summer temperatures as high as 104°F (40°C).

After the Rhine has found its way north again, Assmannshausen (renowned for its Spätburgunder for more than 900 years), Lorch, and Lorchhausen form the third part of the Rheingau. Because the villages are part of the Rhenish Massif, soils are dominated by slate, which lends the Rieslings from Lorch in particular a discrete character. They are riper and less steely than a decade ago but are still characterized by their brilliant fruit flavors, racy acidity, and lingering salinity.

The better the soils drain, the easier it is to avoid botrytis (as in Rüdesheim, Assmannshausen, and Lorch, where botrytis is quite rare), but the harder it is to avoid drought stress during dry periods. For several years, Schloss Schönborn has irrigated vines in Rüdesheim Berg Schlossberg, to protect the plants from stress and prevent the slightly phenolic finish of the Erstes Gewächs, which has become more obvious in recent dry years. So far, Schönborn is the only top producer to irrigate.

Although the Rheingau lies at a latitude of 50 degrees north, the climate is almost Mediterranean, with an average of 1,603 hours of sunshine and 23in (582mm) of rain annually (1971–2000). This is mostly thanks to the moderating influence of the Rhine, which is up to half a mile (1km) wide near Oestrich, allowing even almonds, lemons, and figs to ripen. Summer sunshine helps the late-ripening Riesling reach perfect ripeness, even at moderate temperatures. But because the ripening process is slow, acidity levels remain high and flavors intense—a combination that helped make Rheingau Rieslings famous and among the most expensive wines worldwide in the 18th, 19th, and early 20th centuries.

Viticulture was practiced here long before that, though—as far back as Roman times—and there is documentary evidence that there were vineyards in Walluf by 770. Johannisberg is thought to have been planted by 850, if not earlier. In 1155, Archbishop Adalbert I of Mainz granted to the Cistercian Order what we know as Steinberg, now owned by Kloster Eberbach. By the 18th century, many of the vineyards belonged to the aristocracy, the Church, or farmers. Later, wealthy bourgeoisie also owned some top vineyards—among them Robert Weil, a former professor of German at the Sorbonne in Paris, who in 1875 began a new life in Kiedrich, where Gräfenberg was one of the nine Rheingau sites already classified in 1867.

Returning to the climate, it is remarkable that over the past decade, Riesling has tended to ripen between one and three weeks earlier than in the 1990s. In 2003 (an extremely hot and dry vintage), 2006 (when botrytis spread rapidly), and 2011 (early flowering and ripening), the harvest was finished by the beginning of October, whereas in cooler years such as 2008 and 2010, the best grapes were not picked before the middle of October.

"The weather is not reliable anymore," complains August Kesseler. "More often, the grapes have to ripen in a desert or are threatened by torrential rainfalls in August and September."

"Ripeness isn't a challenge, as it was for our ancestors, because average temperatures are higher than 20 years ago," says Wilhelm Weil from Weingut Robert Weil. "So it's much more crucial to harvest highly selectively, in an earlier, warmer, and shorter period today."

Above: The 50° north line of latitude runs through the Schloss Johannisberg vineyard, but the climate is moderated by the Rhine

Indeed, while in former times, harvest in the Rheingau took almost three months, today it's more like three weeks. Because the pre-harvest elimination of less good fruit has become quite normal, yields tend to be lower than previously, especially in vintages such as 2009 and 2010, when the loss was up to 40 percent.

To extend the hang time of the grapes and to preserve Riesling's idealistic image as being all about delicacy, elegance, finesse, and fragrance, some producers have started to invest in higher and cooler sites. In 2008, Weil cleverly started to offer his Kiedrich Berglagen Cru trio (Gräfenberg, Turmberg, and Klosterberg, the latter at more than 650ft [200m] in altitude), to stress the winery's competence, potential, and sustainability. Kühn (in Hallgarten Hendelberg, 800ft [250m]), Leitz (in Rüdesheim Berg Kaisersteinfels, 720ft [220m]), and Kesseler (in Lorch Schlossberg, up to 650ft [200m])

have also started successfully producing Riesling at higher and slightly cooler altitudes.

Space is limited, however. Most vineyards are quite close to the river, altitudes averaging only 260–500ft (80–150m). As Kühn has proven, though, it is possible to preserve ideal Riesling character in lower and warmer sites through particular viticultural techniques, such as high-density planting, greening-over, and canopy management, resulting in fully ripe grapes at less than 95° Oechsle.

Unlike 40 and more years ago, Rheingau Riesling is vinified dry rather than sweet, and classic Spätlese is produced in much smaller quantities. Nevertheless, Spätlese is considered part of the cultural heritage, and there are still delicious examples such as Schloss Schönborn's Pfaffenberger, Weil's Kiedrich Gräfenberg, Kesseler's Lorch Schlossberg Alte Reben, or the outstanding Schloss Johannisberger.

Above: The great Berg Schlossberg vineyard at the heart of Rheingau, where the high iron content of the rocky soil turns it red

The Rheingau rightly takes pride in its beauty, history, and the quality of its wines. Over the past 20 years, however, other German wine regions—such as Rheinhessen, the Pfalz, or the Nahe—have also learned to produce excellent Rieslings, and these are more in the vanguard of German Riesling today. Alas, many Rheingau producers (there were 853 in July 2010, with only 274 cultivating more than 25 acres [10ha] each) tend to ignore this, thinking that generic Rheingau Riesling still rules supreme.

Given the great potential of the region, the promise of Riesling and Pinot Noir, and the quality of wines from other German regions today,

I have found many Rheingau wines rather boring and uninspiring for many years. But as long as people, often from the wealthy Rhein-Main area, love to drink the rather sterile, soft, and sweetish Rheingau Rieslings, there might be no good reason for most producers to change either their half-hearted wine styles or their occasionally arrogant and narcissistic thinking, which is based to a great extent on former glory.

Anyway, the Rheingau is not a very dynamic region. Although the 1990s saw the demise of a number of well-regarded estates and changes of ownership, everything has been quite settled since, while newcomers and more imaginative winemaking techniques remain rare.

Johannes Josef Leitz in Rüdesheim is the best-known startup—but even his rapid rise began more than 25 years ago. Leitz's former cellar master, Eva Fricke, set up on her own in Lorch recently, while Peter Jakob Kühn, who changed his dry-wine style dramatically in 2002, has only recently managed to convince not only natural wine freaks but also ambitious fine-wine lovers. His expressive biodynamic wines are more highly regarded outside the Rheingau, where his top wines often seem to be too complex to pass the Erstes Gewächs tastings of the Rheingauer Weinbauverband.

The Erstes Gewächs may be another reason for the rather blind pride of many Rheingau producers and officials. Erstes Gewächs is the only legal classification of vineyards in Germany, and it is available only in the state of Hessen. Its message is clear: top-class wines grow on top-class soils. The classification, which was presented as a map in 2000, is based on a scientific study of the potential must weight of Riesling that was presented by the Rheingauer Weinbauverband one year earlier. It also factored in the impact of climate, topography, and soil on must weight, over a period of 29 years from 1961 to 1990. In the end, 79 of the total 118 *Einzellagen* were classified as potential Erstes Gewächs sites, representing about 2,720 acres (1,100ha), or roughly one-third of the total area under vine—much too much.

To qualify as Erstes Gewächs, the wine has to be made exclusively from either Riesling or Pinot Noir grapes that are cultivated in one of the classified parcels. The viticultural rules require a maximum of six buds per square meter, maximum yields of 50hl/ha, and handpicking. Must weights for Riesling have to be at least 85° Oechsle; for Pinot Noir, 90° Oechsle. The wines have to taste dry, though Riesling, which has to have at least 12.5% ABV, may contain 13g/l residual sugar,

and Pinot Noir, which has to have at least 13% ABV, 6g/l. Because the wines are bottled as QbA (*Qualitätswein bestimmter Anbaugebiete*), there are no restrictions on chaptalization or even the use of *Süssreserve*. Nor is there a stylistic definition. An independent tasting panel decides whether a wine is worthy to be labeled Erstes Gewächs.

But since the launch of Erstes Gewächs with the 1999 vintage, not only have too many mediocre wines qualified, there was also no stylistic unity. Some wines are dry, others are not; some reflect terroir, others do not; some gain complexity with bottle age, others should be drunk at once, because they probably won't survive more than two years.

Some famous and historic Rheingau producers are not profiled in this book. Estates like Domaine Assmannshausen and Kloster Eberbach (both Hessische Staatsweingüter), Schloss Reinhartshausen, Schloss Vollrads, Prinz von Hessen, and Freiherr Langwerth von Simmern (to name only the most prominent) still produce good wines today. But they are no longer benchmarks for Rheingau Riesling as they were in the 1890s, 1920s, '40s, '60s, or even '70s.

The wines most worth talking about nowadays, in my opinion, are much more exciting and are bottled by smaller family estates such as Kesseler in Assmannshausen (not only because some of his best wines are red), Leitz and Breuer in Rüdesheim, Kühn in Oestrich, Becker in Walluf, and Künstler in Hochheim. Robert Weil (mostly owned by Suntory) has also performed extremely well for more than ten years now, while Schloss Johannisberg and Schloss Schönborn still represent the old nobilities with some impressive wines.

Other ambitious family estates would have been included if there had been space: Graf von Kanitz and Eva Fricke (Lorch), Spreitzer and Querbach (both in Oestrich), Wegeler (Oestrich-Winkel), Johannes Eser's Johannishof (Johannisberg), Prinz (Hallgarten), and Flick (Flörsheim-Wicker). All of them are also well worth seeking out.

Weingut August Kesseler

August Kesseler cultivates a total of 52 acres (21ha) of vines in the best sites of Lorch (Schlossberg), Assmannshausen (Höllenberg, Frankenthal), and Rüdesheim (Berg Schlossberg, Berg Roseneck, Bischofsberg). Most of them are very steep and south- or southwest-facing. Some 55 percent of plantings are Riesling, 5 percent Silvaner, and 40 percent Pinot Noir. The latter has made Kesseler famous but has never been better than in the 2009 vintage, of which Kesseler bottled two memorable grands crus. "To maximize the enormous potential nature gave us in 2009, we selected as strictly as ever before for these Pinots," he says.

August Kesseler, born in 1958 and in charge of the family estate since 1977, may be an even bigger brand in the US, UK, Japan, and Scandinavia than in Germany, where the Rheingau is associated with nothing but Riesling. Thanks to the Cistercians of Kloster Eberbach, however, Pinot Noir has been cultivated here for 1,000 years, especially in Assmannshausen. Here, in the Höllenberg vineyard, with its gradient of 50–65 percent and its predominantly phyllite soils, the Domäne Assmannshausen of Hessische Staatsweingüter produced world-class Spätburgunder at least until the late 1940s. Today, it's August Kesseler who continues this great tradition.

Kesseler's Pinots are very deep, intense, ripe, and sweet, their texture round and velvety but also elegant and refined. For all their power and richness, though, they bear the cool breeze and transparency of the north, which makes them unique in Germany, if not the world.

Several arguments support this thesis. First, Kesseler's Pinot Noirs are Spätburgunder: in contrast to other top German producers, for new plantings, Kesseler prefers clones from Geisenheim to those from Dijon. "We want to keep

Right: August Kesseler, who more than tips his hat to his village's centuries-long reputation for Spätburgunder

169

our authentic Assmannshäuser style and do not want to imitate Burgundy," he says. The German clones (some from Weinsberg, most from Geisenheim), Kesseler argues, "have always been developed and improved, and they are adapted to our soils and our climate." He also likes the thinner skins of the German Spätburgunder, since he prefers a lighter, fresher, more refined and elegant style of Pinot.

Most of Kesseler's vines are extremely old. While the Spätburgunder in the Berg Schlossberg is 50 years old, the oldest Höllenberg vines are 90 years old. They are ungrafted, low-yielding, and the taste of the grapes is incomparable. In both grands crus, planting density is high, with 8,000 (Schlossberg) to 10,000 (Höllenberg) vines/ha. Newer plantings also average 9,000–10,000 vines/ha. To protect the plants from drought, Kesseler does not green-cover the rows between the vines.

Last but not least, the sites are very special. Assmannshausen Höllenberg is a steep, southwest-facing scarp with fast-draining and heat-storing phyllite soils and mixtures of weathered quartzite from the Taunus Mountains. Thus, the grapes come evenly to full ripeness and, due to the deep roots, are never stressed. Because Höllenberg is slightly cooler than the south-facing Rüdesheim Berg Schlossberg, and also because of the phyllite soil, the Spätburgunder from here is more refined and aristocratic than the enormously rich and fiery Rüdesheimer.

With a gradient of up to 70 percent, Berg Schlossberg is the steepest and hottest site in Rheingau. Kesseler is the only famous producer to cultivate Spätburgunder in this world-renowned Riesling *Lage*. His wine is big, rich, and ripe yet also very complex, surprisingly fresh, and elegant. "In the Rheingau, with its long ripening periods and late harvests, we attain fully ripe and fresh grapes, especially in Assmannshausen and Rüdesheim," Kesseler points out. In Berg Schlossberg, the

vines—whether Spätburgunder or Riesling—root deep in the fast-draining, heat-storing phyllite soils with sandy loess and loam admixtures and Taunus quartzite. "There is always a breeze from the northwest that cools a little and keeps the grapes healthy," says Kesseler. "Finally, the loam keeps the water and balances the heat quite well." Even so, to survive the "hell" of Berg Schlossberg, the vines have to root deep; and Kesseler believes that it is these old vines that make his Berg Schlossberg taste "so complex and marvelously mineral."

The Pinots are handpicked—and rarely before October. Selection is done in the vineyard, where Kesseler is very rigorous. Only the very best grapes are used. Moreover, in the Kesseler range, there are two Spätburgunders below the grands crus: Cuvée Max, a blend of declassified grapes from Höllenberg and Berg Schlossberg, which can be excellent; and the Rheingau Spätburgunder, which is a very good third wine made from declassified Max grapes and grapes of the Assmannshausen Frankenthal.

The grands crus are destemmed and, after a cold maceration of two to three days, fermented without the addition of cultured yeasts in open stainless-steel vats, after 5–7 percent of the must has been racked for an off-dry rosé called Saignée. There is no further extraction than reduced yields and the *saignée*, Kesseler says. After 20 days, the young red wine is racked into Burgundian barriques (30–40 percent new), where they age for 14–18 months before being bottled unfined but filtered.

In blind tastings, it's quite easy to pick out Kesseler's Spätburgunders, because they are appreciably sweeter than other top German Pinots, with residual-sugar levels of roughly 3g/l. On those occasions, I often dislike the wines more than I should, but I am always deeply impressed when I taste or drink them on their own. I also think that they will age for decades, like the stylistically similar old Spätburgunders from the Domäne Assmannshausen, whose 1945 and 1947 still tasted fantastic a few years ago.

"We add a *dosage* of noblest Spätburgunder BAs and TBAs to our Pinots, because this makes them rounder and more digestible and guarantees better and much longer bottle aging," Kesseler explains patiently.

He aims to express the sites and the special Rheingau climate in his top-quality wines, so Kesseler's focus is the vineyard, where he handpicks nothing but healthy and physiologically ripe grapes as late as possible. The manual, labor-intensive management of the vineyards is rigidly quality-oriented, whether pruning, debudding, crop-thinning, halving the Pinot bunches, green harvesting, or rigorous selective picking. Even so, Kesseler's top wines are not produced in every year. The Pinot grands crus were not made in 2000, 2006, 2008, 2010, or 2011, while the Erstes Gewächs Rieslings Berg Roseneck and Berg Schlossberg were not made in 2002, 2003, or 2006.

We should not forget, however, that Kesseler also produces delicious Rieslings in different styles—from dry, to noble sweet. In particular, his Rieslings from Lorch (5 miles [8km] north of Assmannshausen) are quite impressive today. Kesseler is convinced that, due to climate change, the cooler village, with its pure and well-draining slate soils, will be "the leading Rheingau spot in the near future."

FINEST WINES

2009 Assmannshausen Höllenberg Spätburgunder ★
Very dark color. Very deep and intense cassis, cherry, and blackberry aromas on the nose, yet extremely refined, fresh, and distinguished. Rich, supple, and sweet on the palate, but also cool and aromatic, with plenty of elegance and finesse, gracefully and silkily textured. Very long finish. Should age beautifully for at least 20 years. Unhappily, there are only 1,379 bottles.

2009 Rüdesheim Berg Schlossberg Spätburgunder ★
Very deep color. Burgundian Pinot aromas on the nose, with a touch of lime and smoked bacon—very deep and complex. Very rich and intense on the palate, concentrated, velvety, and voluptuous, balanced by its body, mineral backbone, delicate acidity, and fine tannins. Impressively complex and persistent, this world-class wine matches richness with finesse, power with grace, and it ripeness with freshness. Memorable but very rare (841 bottles).

Lorcher Schlossberg Riesling Spätlese Alte Reben
As for the excellent Erstes Gewächs Rieslings from Rüdesheim Berg Schlossberg and Roseneck, grapes from the 75-year-old vines in Lorcher Schlossberg are destemmed, macerated for one or two days, then fermented at about 64°F (18°C) in stainless-steel tanks, where they stay until June before being bottled. The **2009** shows ripe and complex Riesling aromas, seasoned by a spicy slate perfume. On the palate, it is elegant and racy, as well as deep, meaty, and firmly structured, while the finish is piquant and persistent. This delicious Spätlese (12.1g/l RS, 7.1g/l TA) should age at least ten years. The **2010** was quite young but already concentrated and very precise when I tasted it in September 2011, displaying ripe quince and spicy slate aromas on the nose. On the palate, the wine was round and succulent but also straight and tightly woven, balanced by a lingering salinity and its piquant acidity. This is a classic that will be at its best 15 years from the vintage. (13.2g/l RS, 9.1g/l TA.)

2010 Rüdesheim Berg Schlossberg Riesling Auslese Goldkapsel [V]
Very pure and dense on the nose, with spicy raisins. Succulent, sweet, and round, deep and complex, very mineral (salty) and spicy, driven by its vibrant and piquant acidity. A great life ahead.

Weingut August Kesseler
Area under vine: 52 acres (21ha);
55% Riesling, 40% Pinot Noir, 5% Silvaner
Best vineyards: *Lorch* Schlossberg;
Assmannshausen Höllenberg;
Rüdesheim Berg Schlossberg, Berg Roseneck
Average production: 110,000 bottles
Lorcher Strasse 16,
65385 Assmannshausen am Rhein
Tel: +49 6722 2513
www.august-kesseler.de

Weingut Peter Jakob Kühn

There are many castles in the Rheingau but considerably fewer fearless knights in shining armor. Peter Jakob Kühn, however, is one. Since the 2002 vintage, he has been one of the most divisive wine producers in Germany: a crackpot to some; a god to others. Although I would not call him God, his Rieslings from rather unsung sites in and around Oestrich electrify me like finest Montrachets from Anne-Claude Leflaive. In some senses, of course, the wines are incomparable: Rheingau Riesling from loam-covered quartzite soils here; Burgundian Chardonnay from calcareous soils there. Nevertheless, both wines are fascinating and stimulating—complex, pure, subtle, vibrant, full of tension, and, at best, transcendental.

There are many castles in the Rheingau but considerably fewer fearless knights in shining armor. Peter Jakob Kühn, however, is one. A crackpot to some; a god to others

Quite unusually for a Rheingau wine producer, Kühn—whose family estate was founded in 1703 and cultivates 50 acres (20ha) of vines today—bottles thrilling wines. In contrast, I would argue, most of his colleagues produce wines that have, for decades, served their local clients' wish for a soft drink called Riesling. Kühn's steel-fermented, fruit-driven wines had high scores and willing takers up to the 2001 vintage. It was Peter and his wife Angela who were not happy with what they produced.

"Our wines did not taste like the grapes we picked only months before and for which taste we invested so much time and work in the vineyards," Angela admits, before describing how those grapes tasted: "Ripe, intense, piquant—just beautiful."

"But then we lost all this in our rather one-dimensional wines," continues Peter, who wants his wines to express their natural beauty. "So we decided to remove all the agents we had for correction, fermentation, and fining, and we started to make wine without a safety net."

Initially, in 2002, Kühn might have been too ambitious, with extended maceration times and fermentations on the skins. While he won some new fans with these much more structured wines, many of his existing customers were shocked—the more so because the wines were bottled under crown cap. Kühn's Rieslings were removed from some of the best wine lists in Germany.

But Sir Peter, the Green Knight, continued the quest for what is still his holy grail: the purest, most natural expression of terroir. Although the family does not own world-famous sites such as Schloss Johannisberger or Rüdesheimer Berg Schlossberg, the Kühns do possess interesting parcels in Erstes Gewächs sites such as Mittelheim St. Nikolaus, Oestrich Doosberg, and Hallgarten Hendelberg. From Oestrich Lenchen there are some extraordinary sweet *Prädikat* wines—from Kabinett and Spätlese, right up to BA and TBA.

Having terroir is one thing; discovering and translating it, quite another. Kühn always went green in his vineyards, as long as the weather was fine. But after he abandoned all the agents in the cellar that had a negative effect on the wines' natural beauty, he also switched to biodynamic viticulture in 2004, and he has been Demeter-certified since 2009.

"Depth, complexity, harmony, and serenity in a wine require balance and diversity in the vineyard," Peter believes. His main focus is, therefore, the ecosystem of the vineyards and the vitality of the soils. He has planted up to 30 different herbs between every second row of vines, and 60 fruit and nut trees around his vines to enrich biodiversity. Beyond biodynamic standards, he switched to high-density planting, at 8,500–10,000 vines/ha, and trained the deleafed grape zone close to the ground

Right: Peter Jakob Kühn and his wife Angela, whose courage in striking out in a different direction is being amply rewarded

Above: The estate's sign adorned with vines and the Kühns'
holy grail: the purest, most natural expression of terroir

174

while keeping the leaf wall high but well aerated. In Doosberg and St. Nikolaus, the tips of the shoots are not cut but coiled, "so that everything—vines and grapes—achieves its intended purpose," Kühn says.

After a few years of experiments and trial and error, he now confesses himself quite happy with the results. The grapes ripen steadily and a little earlier, stay healthier, and reach good sugar levels—but not as high as ten years ago, he reports. He is, again, selling his wines easily and successfully, even to fellow producers who come and ask him for the recipe. "We have already come a long way," he says, "but we are not there yet."

Harvest is done by hand, and the grapes are selected in the vineyards. They are not destemmed but are kept on the skins for 8–24 hours, depending on the vintage. After pressing and settling, the lightly sulfured musts ferment spontaneously in stainless-steel tanks, fiberglass vats, or (for the grands crus including the Schlehdorn) in large wooden casks with a capacity of 600–2,400 liters. To stabilize them, all of the barrel-fermented Rieslings go through malolactic fermentation, which is especially necessary since these grands crus are neither fined nor filtered. In 2005 and 2009, Kühn also produced an Amphore Riesling, which fermented on its skins for eight to nine months in two carved Spanish 300-liter amphorae, where it also aged for almost two years.

Although Kühn—ably assisted by his Burgundy-trained son Peter Bernhard in the cellar and his wife Angela and daughters Sandra and Kathrin in administration—also produces remarkably good Spätburgunder and Sekt, it is the Riesling range that impresses most. Even the entry-level wine—the Jacobus Riesling *trocken*, which should be the cash cow—is quite complex. All of the wines are bottled under screwcap.

The Kühns have their own classification system: one grape on the label for a rather "simple" wine, like the Jacobus; two grapes for the excellent middle range (including the salty Quarzit, from younger Doosberg vines, and the powerful, mineral-rich Landgeflecht, from nearly 40-year-old vines in a special parcel of Doosberg with very deep clay soils); and three grapes for the grands crus. The latter sometimes have trouble passing the official Erstes Gewächs tastings of the Rheingauer Weinbauverband because they are deemed either "too dark" or "too idiosyncratic." But you should not wait until they are officially recognized as Erstes Gewächs and should, instead, like the Kühns themselves, put your trust in the grapes.

FINEST WINES

Oestrich Doosberg Riesling trocken

Doosberg is a 250-acre (101ha) site, but Kühn's top parcel is only 2.5 acres (1ha), south-/southwest-facing and at an altitude of 500ft (150m). The old vines (averaging 45 years) grow in loess-loam soils with almost no clay, but there are many quartzite seams in the subsoil that give Kühn's Doosberg a very pure and salty character. In comparison to the generous, rich, and silky St. Nikolaus, the Doosberg is rather aristocratic: cool, precise, and distinguished on the nose, with white rather than yellow fruits and subtle floral and herbal aromas. On the palate, this straight yet bright and elegant wine is backed by its thrilling minerality, racy acidity, and grippy structure. Flavors are, again, of white rather than yellow fruits and are lifted by floral and herbal aromas again on the finish. These were the common characteristics of the eight different vintages that Kühn poured me in November 2010. Best vintages: **2004★** (cooked fruits, light caramel), **2005★** (dried fruits, very spicy), **2006★** (highly aromatic and concentrated), **2008★** (very firm and complex, with great aging potential), **2009★** (rich and quite luscious).

St. Nikolaus Riesling trocken

In this rather flat 95-acre (38.3ha) site, Kühn has a leasehold of 7.5 acres (3ha), but only 2.5 acres (1ha) next to the Rhine is used for the "three grapes wine" and the Schlehdorn. The vines chosen for the St. Nikolaus cru are 60 years old and grow in deep alluvial and calcareous loess soils. Grapes ripen easily, especially since the Rhine is half a mile (1km) wide here, so temperatures stay quite high even at night. Kühn, however, does not want to bottle a heavy or opulent wine. He likes his Nikolaus rather bright and elegant, as well as mellow, so he picks the grapes at a moderate 90–92° Oechsle. The wine, though, is rich and complex, not only refined and vibrant. Best vintages so far: **2006★** (nice maturity, big and concentrated, very firm and striking), **2007★** (very deep and luscious, but nice grip, very salty and elegant), **2008★** (amazingly clear, pure, and distinguished on the nose, very delicate and balanced on the palate, with a lingering salinity), **2009★** (very aromatic, opulent, and dense, voluptuous but also vibrant and long).

Riesling trocken Schlehdorn

This is a deeply impressive and expensive barrel-fermented wine from the oldest Nikolaus parcel of 80-year-old vines. It is always very fine and precise on the nose, displaying a deep and spicy fruit intensity. On the palate, this monolithic Riesling-Montrachet has a sublime expression, is full and concentrated, very generous yet precise, beautifully balanced, and of gorgeous elegance. Serenity in liquid form. Kühn served me all vintages in September 2011. The first vintage was **2006**, which is dense and succulent, quite supple, and shows some botrytis. The **2007** is enormously rich and powerful on both nose and palate, displaying almost-tropical fruit favors. Very dense and succulent and striking; already quite mature. The **2008★** is deep and ripe yet cool, precise, and piquant on both nose and palate. Very complex and long but with finesse and grace. The **2009★** is big, ripe, and concentrated, yet more elegant and silken than the 2007 and better balanced. It flows with relaxed *grandezza* over the palate, while the finish is expressive and powerful. The **2010★** is crystal clear—a fascinating beam of Riesling, very pure, precise, and full of tension, finesse, and stimulating salinity. This is a monolith, matching depth and power with elegance and grace in a mind-blowing manner. Great aging potential.

Weingut Peter Jakob Kühn

Area under vine: 50 acres (20ha)
Average production: 120,000 bottles
Best vineyards: *Mittelheim* St. Nikolaus;
Oestrich Doosberg; *Hallgarten* Hendelberg
Mühlstrasse 70, 65375 Oestrich
Tel: +49 6723 2299
www.weingutpjkuehn.de

Weingut Künstler

T he origin of Weingut Künstler is in Southern
Moravia, in the Czech Republic. Founded
in 1648 in Untertannowitz, 50 miles (80km)
north of Vienna, it had to be rebuilt in 1965 in
Hochheim am Main by Franz Künstler, because the
German-speaking family was expelled, shortly after
World War II, from what had been its homeland
since the 12th century. In 1992, Franz's son Gunter
took over, and he has since become one of Germany's
most prominent Riesling producers.

Gunter and his wife Monika cultivate 91 acres
(37ha) of vines in the best sites in and around
Hochheim. Nearly 80 percent of the vineyards are
dedicated to Riesling, and more than 12 percent to
Pinot Noir. Some 76 percent of the family vineyards
are classified for Erstes Gewächs production, so
Künstler could produce no fewer than eight grands
crus. But he bottles only four every year: Kostheim
Weiss Erd Riesling, Hochheim Kirchenstück
Riesling, Hochheim Hölle Riesling, and Hochheim
Reichestal Spätburgunder. "We aim for world-class
quality, so only the very best wines are bottled as
Erstes Gewächs," Gunter explains. In outstanding
vintages such as 2008 or 2007, he also bottles,
under gold capsules, special selections of
Riesling from the oldest parcels of Kirchenstück
and Hölle (the latter being up to 50 years old).

More than 50 percent of the Künstler vines are
older than 20 years, with 14.6 percent older than
30 years, and 16.8 percent surpassing 40 years.
"You can't express *le goût de terroir* if the roots
don't go deep enough," Künstler points out.
So, after he had replanted the Weiss Erd with
Riesling between 1998 and 2001, he waited until
2009 before releasing the wine as Erstes Gewächs.

"If you have done your job in spring and
summer," Künstler insists, "then after pressing
there is nothing more to do, other than monitor
the birth of your wines." He, therefore, strives

Right: Gunter Künstler, whose scrupulous standards mean that
he offers only half as many Erstes Gewächs wines as he could

Gunter Künstler has become one of Germany's most prominent Riesling producers. His pure, deep, and powerful terroir-driven Rieslings are able to age gracefully for up to 20 years

Above: The cellar's ironwork may be elaborate, but Künstler's winemaking philosophy is to keep things as simple as possible

"In the 1990s, we were proud of our excellent sites. If yields were reduced, the grapes still didn't ripen before the middle of October, when temperatures were remarkably cool. Nowadays, the grapes can be ripe three or four weeks earlier, while it is still warm and can be quite humid. These conditions raise the risk of rot and make harvest much more expensive, since we pay our pickers not to harvest the grapes but to throw them away."

Gunter certainly needs to arrest ripeness in order to extend the hang time into October. At least in cool and rainy years, such as 2008 or 2010, golden falls have turned initially problematic vintages into great classics for those who pick late. "But we run much higher risks than we did a few years ago," he adds.

In the functional wine cellar here, modern and traditional techniques go hand in hand. After the Riesling grapes for the dry wines have been destemmed (whole-bunch pressing is performed for the noble sweet and sparkling wines), they are pressed. After settling (if necessary, centrifuging and must corrections are performed), the bright must is fermented in stainless steel or in traditional wooden casks. Künstler likes neither murky musts nor natural yeasts, believing that both may mask the purest expression of the terroir. He prefers a slow but continual fermentation, with the addition of selected yeasts from Epernay at temperatures of 63–68 °F (17–20 °C). The wines age on their fine lees until bottling. *Bâtonnage* is performed to round out the wines with higher acidity levels.

Künstler is well known for his pure, deep, and powerful terroir-driven Rieslings, which are able to age gracefully for up to 20 years. He is also a top producer of serious Spätburgunder. The Reichstal Spätburgunder Erstes Gewächs is a full-bodied, ripe, and intense Pinot of great elegance and finesse, grown on sandy loess-loam layers covering the deeper calcareous marl stones; it can improve with bottle aging of at least ten years.

for fully ripe and healthy grapes in every vintage, investing huge amounts of effort, money, and time in the vineyards. The rows are quite wide, not only because many were planted in the 1950s and '60s, but also because otherwise there would be a lack of ventilation. Because the deep loess-loam and marl soils store water well, in wet years every row is green-covered. Grape zones are partly deleafed shortly after flowering, then completely in August, when Pinot Noir bunches are halved. "Riesling, like Pinot Noir, has thin skins. But all that Riesling is about is in the skins, so I don't want the grapes to be affected by botrytis," Gunter explains.

However, with heavy rainfalls in August, when temperatures are still quite high, botrytis cannot always be avoided. The question is how to get rid of it. Strict selection has become more important recently all over Germany.

Harvests tend to start much earlier today than they did ten or 20 years ago, Gunter reports.

FINEST WINES

In September 2011, Gunter Künstler offered me two 2005–10 vertical tastings—one of the Kirchenstück, the other of the Hölle, both Erstes Gewächs Rieslings that are regularly among the Rheingau's finest. "The biggest difference between the two vineyards is 130ft [40m] in altitude," Künstler says. The Hölle site (120 acres [48.7ha], almost 86 percent classified as Erstes Gewächs) borders directly on the Main River, while the 37-acre (15.1ha) Kirchenstück (100 percent Erstes Gewächs) lies above. Both sites are south-facing and protected by the village of Hochheim. With a gradient of only 15 percent, though, they are not that steep. Both sites have been planted with vines since at least 1271–73 and belonged to the archbishopric of Mainz until 1803. The loess-loam soil of Kirchenstück is lighter than the rich calcareous marl soil of Hölle (literally, "steep slope" in Middle High German) and produces elegant and silken-textured Rieslings, whereas the latter yields a rich and powerful wine with great aging potential. With a wink, Künstler describes the Kirchenstück as "Hock-Lafite," whereas the monumental and persistent Hölle is named "Hock-Latour." Both wines are fermented and aged in traditional wooden casks with a capacity of 1,200–2,400 liters (*Stückfass* and *Doppelstück*). Here are my favorite wines of the tasting.

Hochheim Kirchenstück Riesling Erstes Gewächs

2010 This vintage turns out to be a real classic. Very aristocratic and piquant on the nose, with beautiful ripe and concentrated Riesling aromas. On the palate, it is silky, succulent, and intense, yet elegant, very precise, salty, and long—a great wine that should easily age 20 or more years. The **2009** is more opulent, broad, and rich on the nose, as on the tongue, but again piquant, salty, and well structured. The **2008** is very clear and dense, with the first hints of maturity on the serious nose. Elegant and perfectly balanced in the mouth—appetizing, luscious, and lingering. The **2007 (gold capsule)** ★ is fully ripe and mellow on the nose, with almost cooked, very intense aromas of peaches and apricots. But again, there is a pure, cool, and spicy depth as well, with sweet marjoram scents. On the palate, this great wine seems delicate rather than massive, but it is still beautifully succulent, dense, and piquant, elegant, and perfectly balanced, due to the refined acidity and the lingering minerality. Nice grip.

Hochheim Hölle Riesling Erstes Gewächs

2010 ★ **[V]** Very deep and distinguished on the nose, with ripe-fruit scents. Rich, round, and pure on the palate—a big and powerful wine that matches depth with precision, power with minerality, its full body with elegance, and succulence with vibrancy. This is an enduring monument that might easily have been released with a gold capsule as well. The **2009** is precise and pure, displaying ripe fruit aromas. Voluptuous, salty, and elegant on the palate, firmly structured but also kittenish and well balanced. The **2008** ★ is very fine on the nose but also intense, with piquant fruit aromas heralding another classic, which is as powerful and succulent, as elegant and persistent, as always, but also very distinguished and perfectly balanced. The **2008 (gold capsule)** ★ was completely closed but very promising. It is lighter than the regular Hölle but very fine and thrilling in its vibrancy and complexity. Body, fruit, acidity, and minerality are in perfect balance. The **2007 (gold capsule)** is ripe, dense, and complex on the nose. Despite the generous character of the vintage, this is neither fat nor broad on the palate, but full, round, and rich, very spicy, complex, and elegant.

1992 Hochheimer Reichestal Riesling Auslese trocken ★

One of the first efforts of the ambitious young Gunter Künstler turned out to be a great, almost ageless wine, with all the merits of a mature Rheingau Riesling. With only 12% ABV, boarding was completed, and still today nothing is missing. Mature, yet still concentrated and piquant on the nose, at almost 20 years of age this dry Auslese is intense, smooth, elegant, and persistent but, at the same time amazingly pure and light and extremely appetizing.

Weingut Künstler

Area under vine: 89 acres (36ha);
79.2% Riesling, 12.4% Pinot Noir
Average production: 200,000 bottles
Best vineyards: *Hochheim* Hölle, Reichestal,
Kirchenstück, Stielweg, Domdechaney;
Kostheim Weiss Erd (76% Erstes Gewächs sites)
Geheimrat-Humme-Platz 1a,
65239 Hocheim am Main
Tel: +49 614 683 860
www.weingut-kuenstler.de

Weingut Josef Leitz

This is the story of one of the most interesting Rheingau wine producer of the past 25 years: Johannes Josef Leitz. (I survived his bone-crushing handshake and was thus allowed to call him Josi, so I will proceed to do so here.) When he made his first vintage in 1985, he was only 21 years old. After the early death of his father in 1965, it was Josi's mother who looked after the vines for 20 years, initially with little Josi in her lap, and later with him on her back. "The vineyards were my sandbox," Josi says. When he started to realize his dream of making the finest terroir-driven Rieslings, the family estate owned less than 7.5 acres (3ha) of vines, and the cellar still had the equipment of the 1950s. It was Josi's grandfather, Josef Leitz, who, in the 1950s, rebuilt the winery, which had been completely demolished in World War II. From then on, nothing changed—until 1985.

For more than a decade now, Leitz has been recognized as a superstar abroad. But in Germany, wine aficionados have discovered the quality of his wines only recently

At that time, instead of investing in a more contemporary wine cellar, Josi took all the disposable family money to acquire more and better vineyards. He is now more convinced than ever that it is the unique origin of the vineyard, rather than the winemaking, that makes some wines great. Over the years, and especially since he took over the family estate in 1989, he happily bought and rented parcels in the very best sites of Rüdesheim. Since these vineyards were quite high and in the steepest sites—such as Berg Schlossberg, Berg Kaisersteinfels, or Berg Roseneck—it was much easier to get them then than now. Why? Because cultivating vines on gradients of up to

59 percent means no machines, just manpower: fitness, muscle, patience, passion, and vision. In short, 24,730 working hours per year.

Today, Josi Leitz cultivates 97.38 acres (39.41ha) of vines, most of them in Rüdesheim (72.55 acres [29.36ha]) and in Geisenheim (11.56 acres [4.68ha]), many of them planted in classified Erstes Gewächs sites and completely devoted to Riesling. Josi has restored abandoned vineyards, reconstructed ruined walls and terraces, and transformed Berg Kaisersteinfels, which was nearly scrubland only ten years ago, into one of the most interesting sites in the Rheingau. Leitz has been a superstar for a decade in Norway and Sweden (mostly for his dry wines), and for longer in the US (mostly for his off-dry wines). The UK and Japan are also important markets, and he exports roughly 90 percent of his production. In Germany, wine aficionados have discovered the quality of Leitz's wines only recently.

Leitz's thrilling late and super-ripe wines, mainly grown on slate and quartzite soils and bottled dry, are full and deep, yet always pure and firm, if not austere, in their structure. Even if it is impressive to drink them young (but decanted!), they become better and better over the years. While the early and easy-drinking (yet quite straight) export star Eins Zwei Dry Riesling is mainly sourced from Geisenheim's Erstes Gewächs site Rothenberg, the most interesting wines come from Rüdesheimer Berg. Josi's Magic Mountain— a barrel-fermented blend of preselected grapes and declassified tanks from the Rüdesheim crus— is a fine and quite complex wine through which to enter the magic world of the steep Berglagen that have been world-famous for hundreds of years.

Rüdesheimer Berg turns smoothly from a southerly to a westerly exposure, rising at a gradient of up to 59 percent from 340 to 900ft (105m–275m) in altitude. The vines grow in stony,

Right: The dynamic Johannes Josef Leitz, who has propelled his family estate into the top tier since taking over in 1985

Above: The wooden vats in which Leitz ferments his top wines, including those from Berg Schlossberg and Berg Kaisersteinfels

fast-draining soils and have to go deep to reach water and to survive the summer heat. "Vines have to suffer, otherwise the grapes don't get the intense flavors we are striving for," Josi believes.

His oldest vines are up to 80 years old, his best wines are from roughly 50-year-old vines, and the average age of all the vines is 35–40 years. Newer plantings are dense, with 8,000–9,000 vines/ha. Since 1996, Josi has manured his vineyards only twice, and he believes he was among the first vintners in the Rheingau who green-covered the rows between the vines. The latter step was crucial, though, to arrest the vigor of the plants and to deepen the roots, Josi reports. "And after we changed to the spur-pruned cordon system, we harvested much more concentrated grapes than before."

Last but not least, yields are remarkably low. After green harvest, only one bunch per shoot remains, while the canopy wall is quite high, as are the sugar levels of the late-harvested grapes. Their small and loose grapes are more golden than yellow, with some of them bronze when hand-picked. No other top Rheingau producer harvests as late as Leitz. But botrytis is neither accepted nor very common on the "magic mountain."

While the overripe grapes are whole-bunch pressed, the fully ripe and healthy ones are crushed and kept on their skins for up to 36 hours. After settling, the lighter, fruitier wines are fermented with cultured yeasts in stainless-steel tanks and bottled under screwcap. The rich and powerful Rieslings, though, ferment spontaneously in large wooden casks and are bottled under natural cork. All wines are vinified reductively and are kept on their lees until bottling. The broader, richer wines, however, have some microoxygenation. Residual sugar is welcome.

Because Josi does not accept the classification of the Erstes Gewächs sites, he does not bottle his wines as Erstes Gewächs. Until the 2010 vintage, his top range from the Rüdesheim crus were bottled as Alte Reben ("Old Vines"). But since this term is now so widely used, even for vines that are only 15 years old, he launched additional names for his Berg Kaisersteinfels (Terrassen), Berg Rottland (Hinterhaus), and Berg Schlossberg (Ehrenfels). In 2010, these wines were low-volume but mind-blowing special selections of the old vines. From the 2011 vintage onward, the new names will replace Alte Reben.

FINEST WINES

Berg Roseneck Riesling trocken Alte Reben
Grown on slate and quartzite debris with some loess-loam, this Riesling is relatively elegant and slender, displaying brilliant fruit and wet-stone aromas. On the palate, it has a pronounced minerality and is driven by racy acidity to a long life. The **2009** is succulent, round, and rich, while the **2010** is very clear, concentrated, and piquant, with a beautiful aroma of very ripe Riesling grapes.

Berg Rottland Riesling trocken Alte Reben/ Hinterhaus
The protected, south-facing Rottland starts climbing the mountain right behind the historic town of Rüdesheim. Vines grow in deeper loess-loam soils, with a high portion of decomposed gray slate. The wine is very rich and powerful, its fruit almost tropical. But its complexity, length, and salinity are equally exciting. The **2010 Hinterhaus★** (a unique selection of the most perfect grapes) is extremely rich, but also elegant and beautifully balanced by its refined acidity and lingering salinity.

Berg Schlossberg Riesling trocken Alte Reben
The king of Rüdesheim. Grown on pure quartzite and gray slate soils, with a high proportion of iron, this is one of the most noble and complex Rheingau Rieslings. Leitz's parcels are close to the ruined castle of Ehrenfels, west-facing and at a gradient of 58 percent. The **2009★** is round and spicy, with lemon and salt aromas on the nose. Complex, rich, and round on the palate, this powerful and persistent Riesling also has great elegance and finesse. The **2010★** is thrillingly cool, pure, and spicy on the nose, but velvety, highly complex, and very elegant in the mouth. The salty finish seems endless. The **2010 Ehrenfels★** is too rare and too good to expend many words on it. Yet its coolness, complexity, nobility, sublime concentration, succulence, and length make it unique. Perhaps the finest Berg Schlossberg of my life.

Berg Kaisersteinfels Riesling Alte Reben/Terrassen
The ancient vines (up to 70 years old) in this restored 3.7-acre (1.5ha) *Terrassenlage* (site with old terraces) above Berg Schlossberg, close to the forest, grow in very stony red-slate and quartzite soils. Because Leitz has learned that Rieslings from quartzite soils benefit from residual sugar, this elegant and refined wine has been off-dry since the 2004 vintage (with about 10g/l RS). Yields are naturally low, and the harvest is at least one week later than in Berg Roseneck. This love-me-or-leave-me Riesling is very expressive and drop-dead terroir-driven. The **2004★** has only 11.5% ABV but is still delicious today. The fruit is brilliant, mineral, and spicy, though with the first hints of maturity. On the palate, this is a dry, light, and delicate Riesling, piquant and sappy, very elegant and with nice aromas of dried apricots. The **2010 Terrassen★** is very dense, complex, mineral, and refined on the nose. Very pure and distinguished on the palate, yet beautifully textured and noble, with perfectly integrated acidity and lingering salinity on the finish. Probably the best Kaisersteinfels in history.

Weingut Josef Leitz
Area under vine: 97.4 acres (39.4ha); 100% Riesling
Average production: 400,000 bottles
Best vineyards: *Rüdesheim* Berg Roseneck, Berg Rottland, Berg Schlossberg, Berg Kaisersteinfels
Theodor-Heuss-Strasse 5, 65385 Rüdesheim am Rhein
Tel: +49 6722 48711
www.leitz-wein.de

Weingut Robert Weil

R obert Weil has been one of the icons of German wine culture for many years. Founded in 1875 by Dr. Robert Weil, a former professor of the Sorbonne university in Paris, the 200-acre (80ha) estate in Kiedrich is now directed by Wilhelm, the fourth generation of the Weil family. Although the beautiful estate has been owned mainly by Suntory since 1988, it has been managed by Wilhelm Weil, who has reestablished it as one of the leading German wine estates in terms of quality, size, and reputation.

Nothing but the finest Rieslings are produced. As more than 100 years ago, the wines are distinguished in terms of both their origin and their style, and offered in four different categories. The basic Rheingau Riesling *trocken* comes from Kiedrich Sandgrub and Wasseros. The Kiedricher Riesling *trocken* is from the grapes of younger Turmberg, Klosterberg, and Gräfenberg vines. Klosterberg and Turmberg are the two premiers crus, whereas Gräfenberg—already classified as *Weinlage 1 Klasse* in 1867—is the grand cru. All of the crus are made from vines between 15 and 60 years old, but so far only Gräfenberg is classified as Erstes Gewächs (or VDP Grosse Lage in future).

Prädikatsweine are also handcrafted in the crus. In Gräfenberg, all of the predicates have been produced every year since 1989: Spätlese, Auslese, Beerenauslese, Trockenbeerenauslese, and Eiswein. *Prädikatsweine* that are exceptionally concentrated and sweet are bottled with a gold capsule and auctioned at the annual Weinversteigerung in Kloster Eberbach, where Weil Rieslings can be purchased for stratospheric prices.

Turmberg (a 9.4-acre [3.8ha] monopole), Klosterberg (10 acres [4ha]), and Gräfenberg (25 acres [10ha], almost a monopole) lie side by side within 0.3 mile (500m) of each other, and in sight of the estate on the higher and cooler side

Right: Wilhelm Weil, under whom Robert Weil is again one of Germany's top estates in terms of quality, size, and reputation

Robert Weil has been one of the icons of German wine culture for many years. Nothing but the finest Rieslings are produced. And as more than 100 years ago, the wines are distinguished in terms of both their origin and their style

valley of the Rheintal. At altitudes of 590ft (180m; Gräfenberg), 650ft (200m; Turmberg), and 850ft (260m; Klosterberg), these south-/southwest-facing slopes are not really what you might consider mountains, though the gradient is up to 60 percent. They benefit from intense sunshine, as well as from cool night breezes streaming down from the Taunus Mountains to the Rhine.

"We are beneficiaries of climate change," Weil believes, stating. "In former times there were only two vintages every ten years when my grandfathers could produce the finest Rieslings from fully ripe grapes, whereas today physiological ripeness every year is a gift of nature."

For the highest predicates, the most experienced pickers go 15–17 times into the same vineyard, selecting grape by grape

Long hang time is crucial for the production of the finest Rieslings. Weil rarely starts to pick before the end of September and does not stop before November. (Only the 2003 and 2011 vintages were almost over by the beginning of October.)

The rocky, fast-draining soils, based mainly on phyllite, restrict the growth of the vines, yielding loose bunches of small grapes. Plantings with up to 6,000 vines/ha, hard pruning, green cover, canopy management, halved bunches, and green harvesting are all techniques to achieve the goal of long hang time and healthy, fully ripe grapes. In his top vineyards, Weil has maximum yields of 45–50hl/ha. Harvest is done by hand and is highly selective. For the highest predicates, the most experienced pickers go 15–17 times into the same vineyard, selecting grape by grape.

After a short maceration or whole-cluster pressing, the earlier-bottled estate wine and the Kiedricher, as well as the *Prädikatsweine*, are fermented with cultured yeasts at cooler temperatures in stainless-steel tanks. The late-harvested crus ferment spontaneously in traditional 1,200-liter *Stückfass* at higher temperatures, after the grapes have been macerated for several hours. Up to 20 percent is fermented on the skins and blended later. The wines are kept on their stirred lees for a longer period and bottled in July or August.

"Steel or wood is a question not of different quality levels but of different styles," Weil insists. "To produce fruity Rieslings with elegance and finesse, there is no better cask than stainless steel," he argues. "On the other hand, fully ripe grapes from old vines that should express their terroir more than the primary fruit, give a full-bodied wine with power and depth, which needs a wooden cask to underline its complexity and add longevity."

The very steep, southwest-facing Gräfenberg, with its phyllite and loess-loam soils, is the most complex and richest Riesling of the Berglagen trio. The vineyard was known by the 12th century, and late 19th-century Weil Gräfenberg Auslesen were among the most expensive wines in the world.

In September 2011, Weil lined up two verticals—one of the Erstes Gewächs, the other of the Gräfenberg Spätlese. "Erstes Gewächs and Spätlese is the real grand cru couple," Weil said. "Both wines are available in good quantities [30,00–40,000 bottles of the Erstes Gewächs; 8,000 bottles of the Spätlese], and you can easily drink a bottle of either on your own." The higher predicates, however, are meditation wines that you can only drink very slowly and in small quantities. Of course, Weil's Gräfenberg Auslesen, BAs, TBAs, and Eisweins are of world-class quality: rich and complex, yet precise, perfectly balanced, and very elegant. But I do not have much drinking experience of these wines, for two reasons: the high prices, and the extremely high concentration and sweetness. It's not my passion to lay down wines for my grandsons...

FINEST WINES

Kiedrich Gräfenberg Riesling Erstes Gewächs

The consistency of this grand cru over the years is impressive. As one of the finest Rheingau Rieslings year in, year out, it is always ripe, powerful, and complex, but also cool, elegant, and refined, and structured by its pronounced acidity and lingering saltiness. The **2001** is quite mature on the nose, creamy in texture, and slightly drying on the finish. The **2002**★ is deep, pure, straight, and vibrant—very salty on the lingering finish: great and still young. The **2003** is very rich and powerful but also firmly structured, salty, racy, and mineral. Due to summer drought, however, it's slightly drying on the finish. The **2004**★ is subtle on the nose, with herbal and schist aromas, whereas the palate is round and piquant, quite firmly structured, and a little bit more striking than usual. Still very young. The **2005** is already quite mature, very rich and creamy textured, but its soul is still vibrant and salty. Drink slowly and with food! The **2006** is less rich, powerful, and piquant than usual. With ripe and dense fruit aromas, it's creamy and elegant but ready to drink now. The **2007** did not show very well in the tasting. The nose was shy, the taste nutty, and the finish a little bit dry and bitter. The **2008**★ is a classic: cool, clear, and ruthless. The fruit is subtle yet concentrated, but the phyllite soil dominates both the nose and palate. This wine is pure and spicy, full of finesse and *Spiel*, very mineral and elegant indeed, but should not be drunk before 2015–20. The **2009** is generous again, very rich, round, and succulent, and still dominated by primary aromas. The **2010** is very pure, mineral, and racy, and it should develop, given enough time, into another classic.

Kiedricher Gräfenberg Riesling Spätlese

The Spätlese is made from fully ripe and slightly overripe but healthy grapes. The focus is on the fruit rather than on the terroir, but in the end the Gräfenberg personality still shines through, especially if you are lucky enough to be able to compare it with the Turmberg or Klosterberg Spätlesen. Both analytically and aesthetically, it is almost Auslese in style, because it's quite concentrated, rich, and sweet. However, Weil's goal is a Spätlese style that is "not too sweet but celebrates a kittenish balance between fruit, acidity, residual sugar, and minerality, so that you can easily drink a whole bottle all on your own."

The **2001** is luscious and very sweet on the palate, with a delicate salinity on the finish. The **2002** displays cool and smoky aromas, as well as a legal cannabis flavor. Very pure and piquant on the palate, still vibrant and exciting. The **2003** is voluptuous and refined, combining its vital sensuality with Gräfenberg's aristocracy. The **2004**★ has tropical fruit and gratifies the palate with a very succulent and concentrated texture, which is firmly structured by a marked acidity and salty minerality. The **2005** is nothing but voluptuous, thus everybody's darling. The **2006** is very supple and sweet yet lacks some swing. The **2007** shows ripe and spicy fruit aromas, tastes quite sweet, but is elegant and refined and pleases with a lingering, salty finish. The **2008**★ is an aristocrat: cool and pure on the nose, with fine aromas of slate and healthy raisins. Succulent on the palate, countered by a piquant acidity and lingering minerality—this is a perfect Spätlese. The tropical **2009**★ is enormously rich but also elegant, refined, and well structured. This wine has grace, as well as opulence, and should easily age 20–30 years. The **2010** is very pure and spicy on the nose, then precise, slender, and racy on the palate.

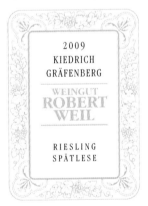

Weingut Robert Weil
Area under vine: 200 acres (80ha);
100% Riesling
Average production: 600,000 bottles
Best vineyards: *Kiedrich* Turmberg, Gräfenberg
Mühlberg 5, 65339 Kiedrich
Tel: +49 6123 2308
www.weingut-robert-weil.com

Weingut Georg Breuer

This estate in Rüdesheim attained its reputation in the 1990s, thanks to Bernhard Breuer and his Rieslings from Rüdesheim Berg Schlossberg and Rauenthal Nonnenberg. Breuer died suddenly in May 2004, when his daughter Theresa, born in 1984, was just finishing school. She studied at Geisenheim from 2004 to 2007, while also managing the estate with her uncle, Heinrich Breuer. Since 2011, she has run the estate alone but is still assisted by her father's right-hand man Hermann Schmoranz and, since 2004, the young Swedish cellar master Markus Lundén.

Theresa has 166 different parcels, adding up to 81.5 acres (33ha) of vines in Rüdesheim and Rauenthal. They include Riesling (80 percent), Pinot Noir (12), Pinots Gris and Blanc (7), and historic specialties Weisser Heunisch and Gelber Orleans (1). The finest vineyards are Rüdesheimer Berg Schlossberg, Berg Roseneck, and Berg Rottland, and the monopole Rauenthaler Nonnenberg. All sites are steep, south-facing, have pure slate and quartzite soils, and (apart from Nonnenberg) are classified as first growths. But as her father controversially did, Theresa refuses to release wines as Erstes Gewächs.

The well-structured wine range has also remained the same, with the four crus at the top; Terra Montosa as the second wine of the Rüdesheim crus; Rüdesheim Estate and Rauenthal Estate as village wines; and Sauvage as dry and Charme as off-dry Rheingau Rieslings. There is also an excellent barrel-fermented Grauer Burgunder, a vibrant Spätburgunder, and a complex vintage Sekt from Pinot Gris, Pinot Blanc, and Pinot Noir (with Riesling *dosage*). Theresa also picks fine Auslesen; in fact, the gold-capsuled ones are downgraded Beerenauslesen. BAs (2008) and TBAs (2005, 2007, 2009) are produced only in suitable vintages.

In the vineyard, Theresa eschews herbicides, and instead of synthetic fertilizers she uses organic manures. Yields are kept low, averaging 45hl/ha. Harvest starts with the Pinots, whereas Riesling is rarely picked before October. Picking is manual and selective. Botrytis is not accepted for dry wines, produced only from ripe and healthy grapes. The grapes are not destemmed but are lightly crushed and, depending on the year, kept on the skins for rather less than the maximum of six hours. After settling, the musts of the crus are fermented with cultured yeasts in traditional wooden *Stückfass* and *Doppelstückfass* casks from palatinate oak, while the less complex wines ferment in smaller stainless-steel tanks. Fermentation takes up to four months. The more easy-drinking wines are kept on their fine lees until April; the better wines, until the end of July. The Pinots ferment and age in (mostly used) barrels or large wooden casks.

Over the years, Theresa's wines have become better and finer. Much as I liked Bernhard Breuer's characterful, gripping, yet often austere and slightly phenolic wines, I find Theresa's range more brilliant, elegant, and pure, and fruitier and better balanced. "We have more men in the vineyards during the year than my father had, so our timing is better. We are more efficient, and we get better grapes," Theresa explains. Her earlier-picked Rieslings contain 1–1.5% less ABV and are light in color and body, brilliant on the nose, and racy (if not steely) on the palate, needing at least three years to open.

In 2010, Theresa completed a quartet of excellent yet quite different vintages. 2007 combines power and fullness with a cool and precise mineral soul, as well as a long and complex finish. 2008 is dense, powerful, and very mineral—a real Rheingau classic that needs a couple of years to show its true worth. 2009 is powerful and rich but also elegant and quite vibrant, and even the crus are opening up earlier than usual. 2010 was still too young when I tasted one year after the harvest. But I appreciated the concentration, purity, and steely acidity of the Rieslings.

Right: Theresa Breuer, who inherited her family estate in difficult circumstances but has more than upheld its reputation

Above: Barrels of different sizes are used to produce wines even finer than those released by Theresa Breuer's father, Bernhard

FINEST WINES

Rüdesheimer Berg Schlossberg Riesling trocken

The Berg Schlossberg Riesling, which is bottled with an annually changing artist label, is a real grand cru. No other wine has a comparable ripeness, depth, complexity, or length. Together with Leitz's Berg Schlossberg, Breuer's version is one of the outstanding Rieslings of the Rheingau (as long as the summer has not been too warm and dry). They both just need a couple of years of bottle age before they really start to show their impressive complexity, elegance, and finesse. Breuer's Berg Schlossberg comes from 25- to 30-year-old vines that grow in poor, weathered slate soils. Despite its depth and intensity, it is always full of elegance and finesse and has a racy salinity that makes you drink the bottle glass by glass.

2007★ This is very clear yet still restrained on the nose, displaying typical cool and herbal terroir aromas. On the palate, it is rich and powerful, multilayered, very salty, and vibrant, and the finish is excitingly complex and long.

1997★ Brilliant, elegant, and spicy on the nose, then very pure, racy, and vibrant on the palate, showing a succulent texture with a nice sweetness, perfect maturity, and balance. The long finish is again salty, piquant, and appetizing.

Rauenthaler Nonnenberg Riesling trocken

This comes from a southeast-facing, 14.3-acre (5.8ha) monopole, where the 40- to 60-year-old vines send their roots through a 5–10ft (1.5–3m) layer of loess-loam, deep into the phyllite soil. The Riesling from the 5-acre (2ha) heart of this top site comes from the oldest vines and is quite opulent and powerful, pairing its tropical fruit flavors with a racy yet appetizing acidity. Due to the higher acidity level, it always contains more residual sugar (7–9g/l) than the other crus. The best Nonnenberg wines are produced in warm and dry years, when the Rüdesheim crus struggle to cope with the drought. The **2007★**, which may be the best-ever Nonnenberg, shows brilliant and piquant Riesling aromas paired with scents of slate. On the palate, it is elegant, intense, and balanced by a refined acidity. The finish is long, complex, and succulent.

Weingut Georg Breuer

Area under vine: 81.5 acres (33ha);
80% Riesling, 12% Pinot Noir, 7% Pinot Gris,
1% Gelber Orleans and Weisser Heunisch
Average production: 240,000 bottles
Graben Strasse 8, 65385 Rüdesheim am Rhein
Tel: +49 6722 1027
www.georg-breuer.com

Schloss Johannisberg

After more than 900 years of viticulture and shifting ownerships, Schloss Johannisberg is certainly one of the most famous and traditional wine estates in Germany. Since 1720, Johannisberg—the steep slope below the yellow castle built by the prince bishop of Fulda in 1716— has been devoted exclusively to Riesling. It is, therefore, presumed to be the oldest Riesling estate in the world. As if that were not enough, the estate's managers have long claimed that the world's first Spätlese, from overripe and partly botrytized grapes, was picked here in 1770, and the first Eiswein in 1858.

I could easily fill many pages with the history of Schloss Johannisberg and the Metternichs who owned it from 1815 to 1992. But since everybody who might be more interested in this than in the wines already has many possible sources (including the estate's own informative website), I can skip forward to the present day.

Schloss Johannisberger—one of Germany's few vineyards without a village—faces south, with a gradient of up to 45 percent at altitudes of 360–590ft (112–180m). Some 52 acres (21ha) are classified as Erstes Gewächs. The 50th line of north latitude passes through the vines, which grow in quartzite soils covered by thick loess-loam layers that range from 28in (70cm) in the upper part, to 98in (250cm) in the lower part. The vines average 20 years of age, but the oldest are more than 60 years old.

Schloss Johannisberger wines, Fürst von Metternich once ordered, should be "fine, tasteful, and enjoyable." Christian Witte, managing director since July 2004, still agrees with that. Thus, the 85 acres (35ha) of vineyards are cultivated in an "environmentally friendly" way, yields are kept low, and the grapes are handpicked selectively in several passes—if possible, no earlier than the second half of October. During pressing and vinification, grapes and musts are handled with care. "The *Gesamtkunstwerk* [ideal artwork] wine

can only be produced according to nature," Witte says, borrowing a term from Richard Wagner.

The winemaking, however, is quite modern. After whole-cluster pressing, the musts are fermented with cultured yeasts in temperature-controlled stainless-steel tanks, as well as in large wooden casks up to 90 years old. The wines are kept on the fine lees until bottling.

Since 1820, Schloss Johannisberg has identified the different quality levels (or *Prädikate* today) by differently colored wax seals, then capsules, as follows: yellow for the dry or off-dry *Qualitätswein*; red for the Kabinett, offered dry, off-dry, and sweet; green for the sweet and supple Spätlese; silver for the full and elegant but not really exciting Erstes

Schloss Johannisberger wines are always full-bodied and elegant, matching their ripe fruit with piquant acidity and delicate minerality. The finest age very well

Gewächs; pink for the Auslese, marked by its noble sweetness and finest acidity; pink-gold for the honeyed yet elegant and graceful BA; gold for the gorgeous TBA (2009★); and finally, blue for the brilliant, concentrated, and piquant Eiswein (2008★). So far, so confusing...

To simplify a little: Schloss Johannisberger wines are always full-bodied and elegant, matching their ripe fruit with piquant acidity and delicate minerality. Whether dry, sweet, or noble sweet, they benefit from bottle age, and the finest age very well. This is amply demonstrated by the *bibliotheca subterranea* under the barrel cellar, built in 1721. Here are stored roughly 11,000 bottles, back to the 1748 vintage. Every couple of years, some of these rarities are sold at the wine auction at Kloster Eberbach, where they fetch high prices.

Since the 160-acre (65ha) GH von Mumm'sche Weingut has also belonged to Schloss Johannisberg since 1979, the firm Schloss Johannisberger Weingüterverwaltung (which is owned by Dr. Oetker) is the largest private wine producer in the Rheingau, cultivating 250 acres (100ha) of vines. Both estates, however, have their own vineyards, and the wines are still vinified separately.

FINEST WINES

Schloss Johannisberger Grünlack Riesling Spätlese
Whether Spätlese was actually invented at Schloss Johannisberg or elsewhere does not matter as much as its quality today, which is great and incomparable. The bouquet is very fine indeed, pairing ripeness, richness, and sexiness with freshness, nobility, and precision. The following trio, from a bigger lineup in August 2010, made me succumb totally.

2009★ This is enormously rich and sweet, but also brilliant, piquant, and succulent, balancing body, sweetness, minerality, and acidity in a perfect way. Drinking it now is great fun, but it is also a waste.

2005★ The bouquet matches ripe-fruit and honey aromas with a stony spiciness. The voluptuous richness on the palate is countered by the piquant acidity and lingering salinity. Drinking this elegant and playful Spätlese is really enjoyable now but still a waste of huge talent.

1964★ This wine was 46 years old when I drank it with Christian Witte in a Rheingau restaurant. The color was lucent green-yellow; the bouquet extravagant, with its caramel, dried chamomile, cooked quince, peach, and apple aromas; the texture luscious and mellow; the whole *Gesamtkunstwerk* just gorgeous—very succulent, intense, and long, yet light and frisky and with a mineral backbone. You can drink this one: it's old enough now.

Left: Managing director Christian Witte, overseeing wines worthy of Schloss Johannisberg's long and distinguished past

Weinbau-Domäne Schloss Johannisberg
Area under vine: 85 acres (35ha); 100% Riesling
Average production: 250,000 bottles
Best vineyard: Schloss Johannisberger (monopole)
65366 Geisenheim-Johannisberg
Tel: +49 672 270 090
www.schloss-johannisberg.de

Domänenweingut Schloss Schönborn

Domänenweingut Schloss Schönborn is another of the oldest and largest privately owned wine producers in Germany. Since 1349, and over 28 generations, it has been owned by the family of Graf von Schönborn, one of the most important noble dynasties in Germany. It is Paul Graf von Schönborn-Wiesentheid who represents the Hattenheim estate today, as well as the wine estates Graf von Schönborn in Hallburg (Volkach/Franken) and Casa Cadaval in Portugal. The family's wine treasury is one of the most spectacular in Germany, harboring the oldest bottled German wine, the 1735 Johannisberger. One bottle was auctioned in 1987 for 53,000 German marks, after it had been transferred to another bottle. The wine had "a golden-yellow color and a clear, light translucence with a light deposit. The fragrance was delicate and aromatic, reminiscent of Sherry. A full-bodied, well-matured wine with a dominant fruity note."

In September 2011, Peter Barth, chief operating officer of the Rheingau estate since 2001, harvested Schönborn's 662nd vintage. Since he has been responsible, Schloss Schönborn, whose wines were rather uninspiring in the 1980s and '90s, has reentered the elite of the region. Certainly, the potential of Schloss Schönborn is tremendous. Between Hochheim and Lorch, the estate owns 200 acres (80ha) of vineyard, but for quality reasons only 125 acres (50ha) are in production. Of the 38 sites—in nearly every Rheingau village—some 80 percent are classified as first growth.

Among the 30 wines that are produced every year, however (97 percent Riesling, 70 percent dry), only four Erstes Gewächs wines are released: Rüdesheim Berg Schlossberg, Hattenheim Pfaffenberg, Erbach Marcobrunn, and Hochheim Domdechaney. "We want to concentrate on the very best in this top category," explains Barth, who produces the grands crus only from the most renowned sites and from the oldest vines. Even the generic Riesling comes from prestigious vineyards.

The top Erstes Gewächs category is based on single-vineyard Kabinett *trocken* Rieslings. But there are also delicious sweet Spätlesen from top sites, such as the Pfaffenberger Spätlese: light-hearted (7.5–9% ABV, 80–90g/l RS, 8–9g/l TA), very precise and piquant, with beautiful elegance, finesse, and grace. Higher predicates, from Auslese to TBA, are also produced if possible. They are extraordinary but very rare, so the best are offered at the annual wine auction in Kloster Eberbach at the end of September. Mature Schönborn rarities can also be purchased here.

Schloss Schönborn is managed more like a family estate than a co-op. Although three-quarters of the vineyards could be machine-harvested, Schönborn employs 35 partners for several preselections and final harvest. Barth aims for concentration and intensity, so the fully ripe to slightly overripe yet healthy grapes are hand-picked as late as possible. Botrytis, however, is not tolerated at all for dry wines.

The grapes are slightly crushed and pressed without maceration. The cleared must ferments with added yeasts in stainless-steel tanks for four to six weeks at temperatures kept at 57–61°F (14–16°C). Some wines—such as Marcobrunn Erstes Gewächs—ferment and age in 2,400-liter wooden *Doppelstück*. All wines are kept on their fine lees until bottling. More generic wines are bottled in March; the Erstes Gewächs Rieslings, in May. Although they go on the market one year after harvest, the grands crus need another three or (better) five years to reveal their true worth, while the clear and fresh Kabinett wines taste fine one year after the harvest.

To taste the range of Rieslings made by Schloss Schönborn is to experience the whole complexity and diversity of Rheingau. In case you prefer to learn about this more realistically but on the highest level, you should taste the four grands crus.

Right: Peter Barth, who has returned Schloss Schönborn to the elite, with his wife and family amid traditional oak casks

FINEST WINES

Rüdesheim Berg Schlossberg Riesling Erstes Gewächs

Grown on dark phyllite in one of the steepest and hottest Rheingau sites, this is an extremely powerful and complex wine, with lingering salinity and great length. It appears, though, to have changed character since the Schönborn vines were irrigated—so a vintage like **2009** (with no rainfall in September) is big, intense, and powerful, and more like a Rheingau Smaragd than a Rüdesheim classic. On the other hand, like the **2010** (with 14.5% ABV after a rainy summer and golden fall), it is full and round, with no phenolic notes or other signs of stress. Another question is how the wines will age.

Hattenheim Pfaffenberg Riesling Erstes Gewächs

The gently south-facing Pfaffenberg, near the Rhine and next to the winery, is a 16-acre (6.5ha) Schönborn monopole. The deep, calcareous loess soil, with gravel, bears a fruity, rich, and smooth Riesling with elegant acidity. The **2010** is very clear and charming, thanks to the residual sugar, but also complex, enjoyably racy, and salty. In **2003** and **2007**, Barth additionally bottled a **Pfaffenberg Fass 161★** (Erstes Gewächs in 2003, Auslese *trocken* in 2007), which fermented spontaneously for more than one year in a *Doppelstück* (2,400-liter barrel). Pairing fullness, richness, and succulence with precision, minerality, and purity, both wines were gorgeous when I tasted them in September 2009.

Hochheim Domdechaney Riesling Erstes Gewächs

From deep marl soils in lower Rheingau, this is a slowly developing yet persistent wine of great depth, immense power, and complexity. The **2010** is very promising, showing noble ripe fruit and nutty flavors—a full yet elegant and succulent body, balanced by a delicate acidity and propelled by a complex minerality and great length.

Erbach Marcobrunn Riesling Erstes Gewächs

In this famous grand cru, Schloss Schönborn holds the largest part, with 5.7 acres (2.3ha). The vines are 60 years old and grow deep in the marl soils, which store water and heat very well. Since 2001, the Erstes Gewächs, fermented and aged in a 2,400-liter *Doppelstück*, has always been a great wine with enormous aging potential. Rich and powerful, this is a very complex and persistent Riesling with brilliant and piquant fruit aromas.

2010★ Still restrained, but firmly structured, very mineral and perfectly balanced. I would not touch it again until 2015 at the earliest.

2009 Very full-bodied, luscious, and succulent, with ripe peach and mango flavors. But thanks to the deep soil, the overall character remains cool and mineral, even in a dry and warm vintage like this.

2008★ Another cool year, so the Marcobrunn is very precise on the nose and crystal clear and elegant on the palate, though still closed and firm. The concentration is excellent, the acidity is very fine, and the finish is long and salty.

2007 This reflects both the cool summer and the Indian summer. It is well balanced, elegant, and already nice to drink, but the fresh and salty finish is exciting and promises further development.

2004★ Similar to 2008: subtle and precise on the nose, yet with ripe, almost-tropical fruit flavors. Perfectly balanced sweetness and brilliant acidity, concentrated fruit flavors, and minerality. This wine is absolutely thrilling, the salty finish amazing.

2003★ This impressively demonstrates that the combination of old vines and deep soil can manage desert weather and that the wine can age much better than expected. This is intense and opulent, but deep, cool, and precise as well. Very rich, round, and supple in the mouth, it celebrates the salty minerality and almost eternal vibrancy of the Marcobrunn easily in its stride.

Domänenweingut Schloss Schönborn
Area under vine: 125 acres (50ha);
97% Riesling, 70% dry
Average production: 350,000 bottles
Best vineyards: *Rüdesheim* Berg Schlossberg, *Erbach* Marcobrunn; *Hattenheim* Pfaffenberg; *Hochheim* Domdechaney
Hauptstrasse 53, 65347 Hattenheim
Tel: +49 672 391 810
www.schoenborn.de

Weingut JB Becker

Hans-Josef ("Hajo") Becker is one of the last great Rheingau individuals. His wines, mostly Riesling, are produced very traditionally but have been closed with Vino-lok glass stoppers since 2002. The Rieslings ferment in old wooden casks of 600–3,000 liters, are kept on lees as long as possible, and are bottled unfined as rich, mineral, firmly structured, really dry, quite austere wines, with remarkable aging potential. "My wines are rich and powerful, so they don't need residual sugar," Becker says. Normally, they contain about 5g/l RS, instead of the more normal 7–9g/l.

Becker has run the estate, founded by his grandfather Jean-Baptiste Becker in 1893, with his sister Maria since 1971. He cultivates not only his skillful mustache but opinions that are often at odds with those of his colleagues. He does not care, for example, about attractive primary fruit aromas: "We produce Riesling here. This is a serious grape variety that needs time in the cellar and in the bottle." For Becker, Riesling has to serve food, so it becomes really interesting only with maturity. The wine has to be fermented in wooden casks, "because otherwise you don't get the complexity of aroma that makes Riesling so special. Microoxygenation also gives better aging potential," he insists.

Becker cultivates 28.5 acres (11.5ha) of vines, 78 percent Riesling, in Walluf and Eltville, west of Wiesbaden. His top site is Wallufer Walkenberg, a southwest-facing 46-acre (18.5ha) *Einzellage* at 400–500ft (120–150m), with a gradient of 10–18 percent. Soils are quite deep here, with loess and loam over a gravelly subsoil. Becker's best wines come from vines up to 60 years old, though he holds only 3.7 acres (1.5ha): Riesling Kabinett *trocken*, Spätlese *trocken*, Spätlese *trocken* Alte Reben, and Auslese *trocken*. If possible, Becker produces noble sweet Rieslings, too. They are less sweet than others but higher in alcohol, for he loves to match them with food. His Walkenberg Spätburgunder is also excellent: barrique-free, elegant, pure, and silky.

FINEST WINES

Wallufer Walkenberg Spätlese trocken Alte Reben

I prefer the Walkenberg Riesling Spätlese *trocken* Alte Reben to the Auslese *trocken*, which can be rather too powerful and—regularly with 14.5% ABV—too alcoholic for my taste. By contrast, the old-vine Spätlese *trocken* is pure, firm, powerful, complex, and, with only 12–13% ABV, has an enjoyable body, as well as excellent aging potential, allowing it to develop over ten or more years.

As for the vinification: after the botrytis-free grapes have been destemmed and lightly crushed, they are kept on the skins for anything between 12 and 24 hours. After settling and fining, the must is fermented (spontaneously since 2007) in wooden casks of different sizes and kept on the lees until bottling in September of the following year.

2010 Clear, fresh, and ripe fruit aromas, mixing with nice mineral scents on the nose. Very salty on the palate, powerful and very complex, but neither too fat nor too weighty, thanks to the long lees contact in the barrel.

2009 With 8.2g/l TA, this Riesling has a proud acidity for the warm 2009 vintage. The residual sugar, however, is low (5.2g/l), so the wine is quite pure and straight, concentrated and firmly structured. Full and elegant Riesling flavors are paired with mineral flavors, and the finish is appetizingly salty.

2008 Clear and succulent on the palate, quite striking; very firm yet elegant, with pronounced acidity. Slightly drying and bitter still on the finish, but this will turn out to be a very enjoyable classic in a couple of years.

2002★ With 12% ABV and 9.9g/l residual sugar, this is a rather modern Rheingau classic. The bouquet is clear and piquant, displaying a fine aroma of cooked quince. On the palate, this pure and straightforward Riesling is tightly woven, very mineral, and long, with a lovely, lingering salinity on the finish.

Weingut JB Becker

Area under vine: 28.5 acres (11.5ha);
78% Riesling, 20% Müller-Thurgau, 2% Pinot Noir
Average production: 55,000 bottles
Best vineyard: *Walluf* Walkenberg
Rheinstrasse 5, 65396 Walluf
Tel: +49 612 374 890
No website

Nahe

The Nahe wine region was defined in 1971 but has a tradition of more than 2,000 years of viticulture. It is in the warm southwestern part of Germany, starting at Bingen, where the Nahe flows into the Rhine, and continues upstream to Monzingen and the less well-known village of Martinstein (*see map, p.141*). Defined by the natural park Soonwald-Nahe in the north, by the Nordpfälzer Bergland in the south, and by the Hunsrücker Hochwald in the west, it is largely protected by mountains of 1,640–2,625ft (500–800m) in altitude, open only to the hilly part of the Rheinhessen to the east. The topographic circumstances affect the climate (even, mild, dry), as well as the very special and highly diverse soil conditions and, last but not least, the typical character of the Nahe's wines.

The vines spread across 10,077 acres (4,078ha), along the Nahe River and its tributaries, mostly on gentle slopes but also on steep hillsides. There are 378 *Einzellagen* (single-vineyard sites), but only 258 are still cultivated, and the finest wines come from roughly 10 percent of these sites. Nearly all of these wines are Rieslings, and many rank among the world's finest white wines. Riesling (27 percent of total plantings) is followed by Müller-Thurgau (13 percent) and the red Dornfelder (11 percent), though neither of the latter produces great wines. Silvaner can be good, while Pinot Blanc and Pinot Noir can be very good, if not excellent, especially in the lower part of the area. In total, the Nahe is 75 percent white varieties and 25 percent red.

It's useful to divide the Nahe Valley into three parts: lower, middle, and upper. The lower Nahe starts in Bingen and ends in Bad Kreuznach and is influenced by the warm climate of Rheinhessen. The vegetative period starts earlier, and an average rainfall of just 20in (500mm) per year (the very wet 2010 was an exception) guarantees the best conditions for healthy grapes. Because soils are fine-grained and deep, with good water-storage capacity, vines do not suffer from drought. Pinot Blanc, Pinot Gris, Pinot Noir, and Riesling perform very well here; must weights are always high and acidity levels moderate, resulting in full-bodied, round wines balanced by soft acidity.

Farther upstream, and also in the northern and southern tributaries, the climate is more influenced by cooler air from the surrounding wooded mountain ranges. The area between the villages of Bad Münster am Stein and Schlossböckelheim therefore has a delayed vegetative period compared to the lower Nahe—up to eight days in summer and up to 12 days in fall. Thus, the grapes ripen later and under cooler conditions—the perfect stage for Riesling, which benefits from a longer maturation time, as well as from its naturally high acidity. The risk of late-season frost and botrytis is minimized because the vineyards are mostly on hillsides, and the initial shortfall in ripeness is rectified—a crucial factor for those fruity, racy, straightforward Rieslings with their rather slender bodies that are so highly regarded in the world of fine wine.

The upper part of the Nahe Valley goes from Schlossböckelheim up to the western sites of Martinstein.

The most fascinating feature in the Nahe is not the climate but rather the soil composition of its varied terroirs. As the junction between the Rheinisches Schiefergebirge (Rhenish Massif), the hilly Saar-Nahe-Becken (basin), and the Mainzer Becken, the Nahe Valley is the product of more than 400 million years of tumultuous geological activity. This has led to great geological plurality: experts believe there are more than 180 different types of soil, and these alternate even within the smallest parcels. Broadly speaking, vines are cultivated on schist, volcanic soils, or loess and clay. The real picture is much more complicated than that, however, as we will see in our exploration of some of the valley's finest wines over the next few pages.

Right: The decorative grape and vine motifs on an old house in Monzingen testify to the long tradition of Nahe viticulture

Weingut Dönnhoff

As a young man, Helmut Dönnhoff used to ask himself, "What did I do wrong in my life that I have to be here?" For the young Dönnhoff, everything about his environment seemed stacked against his ambitions. "There are so many places in the world where it is easier to grow wine than in the narrow and cool central part of the Nahe," he tells me on a sunny late-September day in 2010. "Vineyards are very steep and extremely poor and rocky, with less than 500mm [20in] of rain per year. We almost live in a kind of desert."

The feeling didn't last, however. In time, Dönnhoff came to feel he was blessed rather than cursed. "I discovered that exactly these conditions are the greatest premises for Riesling," he says. "Riesling loves suffering. It also benefits from our great differences between night and day temperatures. Although frost is an annual danger in May, late frost periods enable us to produce incredible icewines, since acidity levels always remain high and the fruit remains perfectly healthy. And Riesling loves difference. Its wines are so multifaceted here because the soils are so different, changing every 100 meters [330ft]. When I hear people talking about terroir, I always have to ask myself, 'Do they really only speak about terroir when they taste wines from the Old World versus wines from the New World, merely in an attempt to describe the difference?'"

Dönnhoff smiles and picks up a handful of stones of different shapes and colors from a patch of the Hermannshöhle Grosse Lage in Oberhausen. Grinding the stones with his fingers he takes a sniff and says, "Look—*this* is terroir. You taste the wine from here and then the wine from over there, and they taste different. And each of these wines tastes different from the wine from over there." He points to the Leistenberg vineyard in a tributary on the other side of the Nahe River,

Left: The highly dedicated, cerebral winemaker Helmut Dönnhoff is now working with his son Cornelius (*right*)

where he produces one of my favorite Kabinett wines. "Here, in the center and upper parts of the Nahe, we never speak about Riesling [Dönnhoff always pronounces it 'Rissling'], we just name the sites. We speak of Leistenberg, Hermannshöhle, Kupfergrube, Felsenberg, or Halenberg. They're all Riesling, but they are all so different."

Some 80 percent of Dönnhoff's 62 acres (25ha) of vineyards, plus another leased 12 acres (5ha), are planted with Riesling. Dönnhoff's Rieslings have long been celebrated in the world of fine wine. They are produced in a full range of styles—dry, off-dry, sweet, and noble sweet—with each wine taking on the character of the soil in which the grapes were grown. Decomposed slate soils yield crystalline, immediate wines full of elegance and finesse; volcanic soils (porphyry and melaphyre) produce very pure, spicy, mineral wines; more calcareous soils provide fruity yet complex and mostly dry wines. For committed enophiles, as well as professionals, these Rieslings are among the world's finest white wines. With around 50 percent of his production now exported, it's clear that, in almost 20 years, Dönnhoff has become a kind of German brand—a vinous Mercedes or Porsche—though his wines are still priced very reasonably.

Today, Dönnhoff owns vineyards in the villages of Schlossböckelheim, Oberhausen, Niederhausen, and Norheim. In total, eight of them are classified as VDP Grosse Lagen and qualified to produce Grosses Gewächs wines, but Dönnhoff produces only three GGs so far: Felsenberg GG (Türmchen), Hermannshöhle GG, and Dellchen GG. Because the soils are poor and very rocky, yields are naturally low (averaging around 50hl/ha), especially where vines are more than 65 years old. To force them even more, the planting density is quite high, amounting to 6,000 vines/ha. "I want them to suffer—not too much, but not too little," Dönnhoff says. Ultimately, what he is striving for is balance, in the vineyards and in the wines.

Even more important for Dönnhoff than site, must weight, and yields, however, is that every vineyard produces the wine to which it is best suited. For example, it is almost impossible to produce a grand cru or a higher *Prädikat* level such as Auslese or even Spätlese in Oberhäusener Leistenberg, which is a steep south-/southeast-facing slope with a soil of highly decomposed, almost clayey slate. The vineyard benefits from the morning sun but lies in the shadow in the afternoon and, located in a side valley of the Nahe, is cooler and more exposed to wind. Grapes reach physiological ripeness later and are rarely infected by botrytis, so they will neither reach must weights required for higher *Prädikat* levels nor become raisins for an Auslese. Leistenberg is in no way a mediocre vineyard, however. It is, rather, among the very best for the Kabinett style, which is (or should be) moderate in alcohol but with clear, precise fruit and pronounced acidity. "Riesling has to be like rock water or a mountain stream," Dönnhoff says. "It can be shy in the beginning, but it should have length and acidity that makes it dance across the palate."

Dönnhoff always picks very late, rarely before the middle of October ("first the potatoes, then the grapes") and continuing to the middle of November. Icewines, if possible, are mostly picked toward the end of December. For dry wines, a maximum of 5 percent of botrytis is tolerated. Many vineyards are picked at least three times; in vintages such as 2010, twice as often or more. Dönnhoff ferments and matures his sweet wines in stainless steel but also uses wooden casks for his top dry wines, especially in high-acid vintages.

We can look only at the most important of Dönnhoff's vineyards, all of them dedicated to "Rissling." In the Felsenberg grand cru, a steep, south-facing vineyard in Schlossböckelheim with extremely rocky soil based on decomposed porphyry, Dönnhoff produces two Rieslings: the full-bodied, mineral, slightly smoky Felsenberg;

and, from the central part of the vineyard, the Felsenberg GG Türmchen ("Little Tower") which is intense, complex, and powerful.

Grown in a south-facing *Lage* in Norheim, the Dellchen GG is rich, succulent, and voluptuous. The site is bordered by vertical volcanic rocks and completely terraced by dry-stone walls. The grapes benefit from a special mesoclimate, as well as from complex soil that mixes slate with decomposed volcanic stone. The steep and south-facing Hermannshöhle in Niederhausen is Dönnhoff's most famous vineyard and probably the best *Lage* in the Nahe Valley. The Riesling is grown on a black-gray-ish slate with limestone and porphyry, producing an aristocratic Grosses Gewächs and world-class *Prädikatsweine*.

Dönnhoff makes his dry wines with the same passion as his sweet wines, but his international reputation is mainly based on the noble sweets. A Spätlese with a mineral savoriness and luscious fruit emerges from the slate of Norheimer Kirschheck. From Oberhäuser Brücke—his exclusive site located at the riverbank on a thick layer of loess mixed with clay over gray slate—he harvests a brilliant icewine regularly and an exquisite Spätlese with racy acidity and tangy fruit.

FINEST WINES

(Tasted in August and September 2010)

2009 Felsenberg Türmchen GG ★
Very clear. Leafy and lime aromas. Pure, restrained but rich, voluptuous, silky, and elegant. Precise fruit flavors, perfectly balanced. Memorable length.

2009 Hermannshöhle GG ★
Clear, pure, subtle nose, with citrus and white peaches. Concentrated and succulent, very elegant, almost dancing, yet powerful and very persistent.

2009 Schlossböckelheimer Felsenberg Türmchen Spätlese [V]
Pure, earthy on the nose, a little nutty, smoky, almost flint stone. Intense, concentrated, very long, with mineral power; like melting stones. Impressive.

2009 Niederhäuser Hermannshöhle Spätlese ★ [V]
Smoky and fully ripe fruit aromas, almost raisins, yet fine, precise, and framed by herbaceous notes and an appetizing, piquant minerally touch. Rich and round on the palate, concentrated, with refined, elegant acidity enhanced by piquant schist aromas. Very long salty finish. Complex and full of tension.

2009 Norheimer Dellchen Spätlese (Auction) ★
An extremely clear and refined bouquet, yet still restrained. Concentrated texture, perfectly balanced by its noble acidity. Very salty, almost spicy on the finish, this is a super-complex and persistent Bauhaus Riesling: very austere and almost dry (for a Spätlese) in its purity.

2009 Niederhäuser Hermannshöhle TBA ★
Ripe tropical aromas mixed with honey, caramel, and whole wheat. Viscous yet piquant, racy, and crystalline on the palate; dried apricots, apricot confiture. Very elegant. Perfect TBA.

2009 Oberhäuser Brücke Eiswein
Crystalline definition of fruit on the nose, very pure, with fine concentration; grapefruit and toffee aromas. Very noble, concentrated, and complex on the palate, perfectly balanced by piquant, racy, yet ripe elegant acidity.

2008 Oberhäuser Brücke Eiswein ★
(Tasted in September 2009; 7% ABV, 260g/l RS, 12.5g/l TA, 180° Oechsle) The grapes for this wine were picked on December 30. Crystalline and spicy nose, with enchanting yellow-stone-fruit and herbal aromas. Utterly pure and piquant on the palate, firm and persistent, the sweet fruit perfectly balanced by pronounced but highly refined acidity; very deep and persistent—perfect icewine. Dönnhoff made another 2008 Brücke Eiswein, called **January**, since the grapes were picked in January 2009, with 200° Oechsle and a higher portion of botrytis. It was even richer than the December version but still perfectly balanced.

Weingut Dönnhoff
Area under vine: 75 acres (30ha); 100% white, 80% Riesling
Average production: 150,000 bottles
Bahnhofstrasse 11, 55585 Oberhausen/Nahe
Tel: +49 6755 263
www.dönnhoff.com

Weingut Emrich-Schönleber

Almost 200 years ago, Germany's most celebrated poet, Johann Wolfgang von Goethe, described the wines known as Monzinger as pleasant and easy to quaff but also capable of going to one's head without one's quite realizing it. What the wine aficionado felt in 1815 is still true today. Thanks to their saltiness and nervous acidity, the delicate wines of Monzingen in the upper Nahe Valley seem at first to float in the mouth, and it takes a while for their power, concentration, depth, and structure to dawn on the unsuspecting drinker. It also remains true today that even the most basic wines from the area can be quite complex, though "quaffable" is no longer really the best way to describe a Monzinger. These wines can, however, be adorable, especially if they are a Halenberg or Frühlingsplätzchen and come from a top producer such as Emrich-Schönleber.

The Emrich-Schönleber estate has been around for about 250 years, but it was only in the 1960s that the family decided to focus exclusively on wine, leaving other forms of agriculture behind. When Werner Schönleber took over the operation from his father in the 1970s, the family had no more than 7.5 acres (3ha) under vine. Little by little, Werner extended the vineyards, buying the best parcels in the top sites of Monzingen, Halenberg and Frühlingsplätzchen, concentrating mainly on Riesling. It is to the great credit of Werner and his son Frank that, over the past 40 years, they have maintained parcels in the steepest sites, despite the challenges involved in working them—sites that would, in all probability, have been abandoned if not for them. The family has also restored a number of top parcels that had been abandoned for decades, since they were suitable neither for mechanization nor for high yields.

"*Qualität kommt von Quälen* [quality comes from torture]," Werner Schönleber ruefully admits.

Right: The hardworking Werner and Frank Schönleber have played a vital role in returning the Nahe to its former glory

*"Quality comes from torture. The only chance
to recoup our effort and expense is to produce wines of
the highest possible quality."—Werner Schönleber*

"The only chance to recoup our effort and expense is to produce wines of the highest possible quality."

And this is exactly what he does. A member of the VDP since 1994, Emrich-Schönleber has been one of the very best wine producers in Germany for the past three decades. It was Werner Schönleber who put the names of Halenberg and Frühlingsplätzchen back on the map (the Prussian *Lagenkarte* from 1901 marked both sites as first class), and together with Helmut Dönnhoff and more recently Tim Fröhlich, he has transformed the formerly unknown Nahe Valley into one of the world's most highly regarded Riesling regions. In 2005, Frank Schönleber (born in 1979) assumed responsibility in the cellar, but his father still works in the vineyards and presents the wines around the world.

The vineyards, all of them in Monzingen, add up to 42 acres (17ha), with 85 percent Riesling. Most of the wines are fermented dry, but there are great *Prädikatsweine* as well: gorgeous Spätlesen, finest Auslesen, concentrated BAs, and memorable TBAs, though even these wines do not taste sweet, balanced as they are by the mineral backbone that gives all the Schönleber wines a spicy, almost salty character, as well as great complexity and length.

The vines are mostly grown on steep, south- and southwest-facing hillsides with rocky soils. Different kinds of slate dominate, though quartzite and quartz can also be found. The Halenberg grand cru is dominated by blue slate; the neighboring Frühlingsplätzchen grand cru, in contrast, is mainly red slate. Both sites have a very special, very warm mesoclimate, since they are protected from cool winds and benefit from the daily warm airflows from the Nahe Valley.

The warmest parcels of both sites, where the extremely poor soil leads to the lowest yields and the smallest berries with the most intense flavors, is where the Grosses Gewächs wines are produced: both Rieslings, both impressively complex, yet elegant and full of finesse. They need

about three to five years to open up and are beautiful to drink after five to ten years. Not that the other Rieslings from both sites aren't also of excellent, terroir-driven quality, whether they are made as classic *Prädikatsweine* or in dry styles, labeled as Monzinger Halenberg Riesling *trocken* and Monzinger Frühlingsplätzchen Riesling *trocken* (whereas the grands crus are simply known as Halenberg GG and Frühlingsplätzchen GG).

The Schönlebers work extremely hard in the vineyards throughout the year, generally harvesting quite late and always by hand—most of the Riesling is picked in the first couple of weeks of November; the Pinots, at the end of October. The grapes have to be fully ripe and healthy; up to 5 percent botrytis is tolerated but only if it's pure noble rot. The grapes are crushed but not destemmed, and skin contact before pressing lasts up to six hours. Both the basic wines and those with *Prädikat* are fermented (partly spontaneously) in stainless-steel tanks, with the grands crus in traditional wooden barrels because, Frank says, "We believe our wines achieve an even better balance and aging potential in wood." First racking and filtration take place at the end of February, then the wines spend another four to six weeks in tanks and barrels before bottling in April. The newly extended cellar—equipped with modernist stainless-steel tanks and more wooden barrels for the single-vineyard wines and the grands crus—lets the Schönlebers work with the highest-possible protection for grapes, musts, and wines.

The Emrich-Schönleber range comprises 18 wines each year, all of them delightful. Outstanding as the *Prädikatsweine* undoubtedly are, however, the eminently quaffable Spätlese from Halenberg is one of my favorites—a wine that never goes to my head but always lifts my spirits. Then, of course, there is the Halenberg Grosses Gewächs, a wine that, for many years, was unrivaled on the estate. But then came the A de L Riesling... Suffice it to say, this is an estate with an embarrassment of riches.

FINEST WINES

2008 Monzinger Halenberg Riesling Spätlese ★ [V]

This great wine is almost a political statement. It demonstrates that a real grand cru site can express itself not only in dry wines and Auslesen but also in Spätlesen, if they are made with skill and love for this classic German type of wine. Very clear and spicy, if not zesty, on the nose; pure, salty, and tightly woven on the palate. This excellent Spätlese is as mineral and elegant as Halenberg has to be. It's a real grand cru—and yes, it's quaffable.

Frühlingsplätzchen GG

Grown on red slate and in a vineyard that translates literally as "Spring's Little Place," this delicate Riesling from 25-year-old vines is never as dramatic as the Halenberg but is always subtle on the nose and palate and displays fine herbal, floral, and young peach aromas, together with fresh citrus notes. In the mouth, it's pure and direct, yet full of finesse and joy; well balanced, it finishes with an appetizing minerality.

2009 Richer and more luscious than earlier vintages. It seemed a bit too ambitious to me when I tasted it, much too young, in late summer 2010.

2008 ★ (12.5% ABV.) "We don't want more volume in our wines," says Werner Schönleber, who is perfectly happy with the 2008s. Very pure and fresh on the nose; citrus flavors, herbs. Full-bodied, yet also full of finesse, very precise and direct, always elegant. Great wine, with big potential.

2004 The first GG produced at this estate, which I tasted again in September 2010. Typically lingering without being overpowering. Caramel and delicious fruit aromas indicate the beginning of maturity, but the structure is still firm and the acidity fresh.

Halenberg GG

This Riesling from 20-year-old vines grown on blue slate shows more tropical fruit in its youth but is always very rich and complex, yet fine and elegant, backed up by beautiful acidity and an immense mineral, almost salty-tasting structure. No matter the vintage, the finish is consistently long.

2009 ★ (Tasted several times in fall 2010.) A monster: extremely rich and powerful, very concentrated, deep, and long. Ambitious, but nearly undrinkable now. Sweeter than usual (8g/l RS). Aging potential but not the classic pure Halenberg I prefer.

2008 ★ (12.5% ABV.) Very clear and deep on the nose, with herbal hints and citrus aromas but a chalky impression. Gorgeous and complex mouth feel, salty, very elegant and long.

2003 (Tasted September 2009.) A dry, hot, very atypical vintage. But almost six years after the harvest, it is still a Halenberg: very clear and fresh, with notes of dried fruits, citrus, herbs, and lavender. Big body, very rich and succulent, yet elegant and with a dusty-chalky texture; very long. Opening up now and should be even better from 2012.

2002 Monzinger Halenberg Auslese trocken ★

This, the precursor of the GG from the same site, was beautifully intense, deep, and still fresh (in color, as well as flavor) when I tasted it in September 2011. Herbal aromas. Very intense and complex on the palate, yet elegant and multilayered; a beautiful mineral texture, perfect balance, and very long salty finish. Memorable.

A de L Riesling

This Riesling is from a 2-acre (0.83ha) parcel called Auf der Lay ("On the Slate"), which is located on top of the Halenberg grand cru but is officially part of Frühlingsplätzchen. Vines were planted in the 1950s on soils of blue slate, but there is also quite a lot of gravel here. Schönleber purchased the parcel in 2006 and soon discovered the unique personality of the wine. The 400-liter annual production has been bottled in magnums (and larger sizes) since the 2008 vintage and then auctioned at the annual Weinversteigerung in Bad Kreuznach. The extremely small grapes yield a mind-blowingly concentrated and structured Riesling of pure minerality and amazing aging potential.

2009 ★ Extremely pure and deep, and initially it seems less grand and powerful than the two GGs. But in fact, it eventually emerges as even finer and more complex, though it still needs at least five years for the edges to be rounded off.

2008 ★ Fresh, amazingly precise and pure, elegant and linear, yet tightly woven and powerful. Only 12.5% ABV. At this early stage, I like it a little more than the 2009, but we'll see how things develop over the next couple of decades.

Weingut Emrich-Schönleber
Area under vine: 42 acres (17ha); 100% white, 85% Riesling, 60–65% dry wines
Average production: 120,000 bottles
Soonwaldstrasse 10a, 55569 Monzingen
Tel: +49 6751 27 33
www.emrich-schoenleber.com

Weingut Schäfer-Fröhlich

Born in 1974 and looking like a fan of British electro-pop band Depeche Mode from the 1980s, Tim Fröhlich is one of the German wine scene's younger superstars. His Rieslings from the upper Nahe Valley have a breathtaking purity, luminosity, grace, and finesse that combine with cool, precise fruit, minerality, and great complexity to place them among Germany's very best wines. The outstanding 2010s (which followed the equally outstanding 2009s and the great 2008s and 2007s) represent Fröhlich's 17th vintage and prove once again that, despite his young age, he is already a master of his guild and a genuine challenger to the long-established lords of the Nahe region: Helmut Dönnhoff and Werner Schönleber (Weingut Emrich-Schönleber).

Fröhlich's family began making wine in the village of Bockenau in 1800. In a sense, they had no choice: nothing but vines would grow on the steep and rocky slopes, with their slate and volcanic soils. When combined with the warm days and cool nights along the Hunsrück mountain range, however, those soils turned out to be a paradise for Riesling, and Tim Fröhlich's grandfather and, later, his parents earned praise for their Bockenau Rieslings. Today, the family owns vineyards in the best sites of Bockenau (Felseneck Grosse Lage and Stromberg), as well as in Monzingen (Halenberg and Frühlingsplätzchen, both Grosse Lagen) and Schlossböckelheim (Kupfergrube and Felsenberg, both Grosse Lagen). Some 85 percent of the vineyards are planted with Riesling, the rest with Pinot Blanc (10 percent), Pinot Gris (2 percent), and, for the family's own consumption only, Pinot Noir (3 percent). The average age of the vines is about 40 years; the oldest plants in the terraced parcels of the Stromberg site are more than 50 years old.

Tim Fröhlich's focus is on terroir-driven Rieslings. His pure, spicy, and elegant Bockenau

shows a distinguished character that derives from soils composed of blue slate and quartzite. His rich yet delicate Monzingen speaks of slate, quartzite, and gravel; the compact and spicy Schlossböckelheim of volcanic porphyry. The flinty Kupfergrube, the herbal Felsenberg, the powerful Halenberg, and the Frühlingsplätzchen, whose delicacy emerges with a few years of age, are likewise all uniquely expressive of their respective terroirs.

When it comes to winemaking, Tim believes that a terroir wine should be as pure as possible. He never adds cultured yeasts, and he neither adjusts the musts (in 2010 only, the *Gutsweine* and village wines were deacidified a little) nor fines the finished wines. He picks by hand, late: even the basic wines are rarely picked before November, while harvest of the Grosse Gewächse is generally left until the end of November. He is also highly selective, accepting only ripe and healthy grapes whose must weight is approximately 100–103° Oechsle.

In order to produce a perfect crop in such a cool region as the Nahe, the Fröhlichs have to work intensively in the vineyards from the beginning of the year. It's a formidable amount of work. In April or May, the Fröhlichs remove half the shoots, taking out every second shoot in order to have an open leaf wall. The canopy is up to 5ft (1.5m) high, and depending on the position of the sun, the grapes of the adjacent row will be shadowed in order to preserve cooler fruit flavors, with the grapes ripening close to the ground in order to benefit from the radiation from the rocky soils. When flowering has started, some leaves in the grape zone are plucked to provide more sunlight and aeration. In October, after the risk of sunburn has receded, the fruit zone is almost completely exposed. Tim never uses fertilizer, other than manure. In every second row, he plants a cover crop, either natural vegetation or a seed mixture that also protects younger parcels from erosion. In very warm years such as 2007 or 2009, straw shields every row from evaporation.

Left: The talented Tim Fröhlich, who has quickly established himself as one of Germany's most outstanding winemakers

There is great attention to detail in the winery, too, of course. The sorted grapes are not destemmed but crushed and—depending on the vintage, the character, and the style of the wine—are gently pressed after 6–24 hours of maceration. After settling, the unfiltered must ferments spontaneously in stainless-steel tanks at natural temperatures between 61° and 63°F (16–17°C) for a period of one to three months. Only the Pinots are fermented in barrels. The Grosses Gewächs wines stay on their gross lees until May; the sweet wines, until June or July; the basic wines, until the end of March. All of the wines are gently filtered only once and bottled without fining or stabilization.

There are five world-class Grosse Gewächse and a range of highly recommended *Prädikatsweine*, from Spätlese up to Trockenbeerenauslese and Eiswein—all of extraordinary quality. For me, however, it's the Rieslings from Bockenau that are most intimately associated with this estate. It was Tim Fröhlich who put Felseneck on the map, and I've no doubt at all that he will do the same for Stromberg in the near future.

FINEST WINES

(Tasted in September 2010)
2009 Felseneck GG ★
A brilliant nose, with ripe and concentrated fruit aromas and herbal as well as mineral scents. On the palate, this grand cru is straight, tight, and powerful, yet also pure and mind-blowingly elegant. Very salty on the aftertaste and with the exceptional length of a great wine.

2009 Felseneck Riesling Auslese ★
Aromatically, this is quite cool in style, with very fine fruit expression. Dancing on the palate, highly precise in its perfect fruit, salty taste, and terrific balance; incredibly delicate. There is also a terrific gold-capsule version of this *Prädikat*, which is made with 30 percent healthy berries. It is nothing but a perfect Auslese: sophisticated, mineral, and still very much a terroir wine.

2009 Felseneck Riesling Beerenauslese ★
Spicy and very clear; finely raisined. Concentrated and sweet on the palate, this fascinating, silky, and elegant BA is as light-footed as a fairy. Terrific—but it is again the gold capsule that is perfect, brilliantly combining elegance and finesse with concentration and richness in exquisite balance, while the pure, salty taste of Felseneck still shines through.

2009 Felseneck Riesling Eiswein
Picked on January 6, 2010, at 3.2°F (−16°C), the first drop took a day to emerge from the press due to the concentration of the 245° Oechsle must. An impressively focused, viscous, and spicy-sweet icewine concentrate.

2009 Felseneck TBA Goldkapsel ★
The botrytized raisins were collected one by one over a period of five weeks. The result: 50 liters of unforgettable TBA, with 450g/l of RS and 5.5% ABV, that will be auctioned in Bad Kreuznach one day. Purest aromas and flavors of passion fruit, orange, kumquat, and ginger, with perfect balance and elegance. Spicy, racy, never-ending.

Weingut Schäfer-Fröhlich
Area under vine: 50 acres (20ha)
Average production: 120,000 bottles
Schulstrasse 6, 55595 Bockenau
Tel: +49 6758 6521
www.weingut-schaefer-froehlich.de

Schlossgut Diel

T he story of Schlossgut Diel in Burg Layen in the lower Nahe Valley goes back more than 200 years, but it was Armin Diel who made the estate famous in the late 1980s. Today, the trained lawyer, wine official, and wine critic is backed up by his daughter Caroline Diel, who, since 2006, has been responsible for the 54 acres (22ha) of vineyards and the cellar (together with long-term cellar master Christoph Friedrich). Caroline studied viticulture and enology in Geisenheim and honed her skills at well-regarded peer estates such as Robert Weil, Ruinart, Romanée-Conti, and Pichon Longueville Comtesse de Lalande. With Caroline's knowledge, decisive nature, and superb taste, the wines of Schlossgut Diel have become even more brilliant, precise, and elegant, and their finesse is remarkable.

With Caroline Diel's knowledge, decisive nature, and superb taste, the wines have become even more brilliant, precise, and elegant, and their finesse is remarkable

Riesling (65 percent of the total) is king here, but Diel competes in numerous other disciplines, too. I find the estate's Pinot Blanc and Pinot Gris, though Burgundian in style, a little too generous in alcohol for my taste, but the Pinot Noir Cuvée Caroline is excellent, with the recent trio of vintages (2007–09) being very pure and refreshing, with particularly silky tannins. There are sparkling wines, too, and the Cuvée Mo Sekt—a barrel-fermented blend of Pinot Noir and Chardonnay (in 2004★) or Pinot Gris (in 2005), which is disgorged after almost five years—is impressively complex: creamy, nutty, yet fruity and refreshing.

The vineyards of Schlossgut Diel are in the valley of the Trollbach River. Although largely unknown, it is one of the driest and warmest regions in Germany. The average annual temperature is 49.5°F (9.7°C),

with summers that are warm but not hot (averaging 68°F [20°C] in July) and a low long-term average rainfall of 21in (534mm).

The three south-facing grands crus—Goldloch, Burgberg, and Pittermännchen—are in the village of Dorsheim, and all three were classified as *Lagen Erster Klasse* (first-class sites) in the historic Prussian *Lagenkarte* of 1901. The mostly steep slopes, partly with terraces, are well protected and can only be cultivated by hand or with the help of a cable winch.

Even adjacent plots of land can have quite different soil compositions, and the resulting wines are correspondingly individual. A thin layer of stony clay on rocky conglomerates dominates the Goldloch cru, in which Diel holds 12.8 acres (5.2ha). The Grosses Gewächs is rich and powerful, yet elegant, deep, and balanced by a piquant acidity. The same racy acidity and mineral freshness animates the delicious Riesling Spätlese.

The western extension of Goldloch is named Pittermännchen, and Diel cultivates a mere 2.5 acres (1ha) here. This site has a slightly different subsoil, with high portions of gray slate, quartzite, and gravel—a combination that provides a refined and elegant Riesling cru with racy acidity and a sophisticated structure. According to Armin Diel, the Rieslings with *Prädikat* produced here are much admired by Dr. Manfred Prüm of Joh Jos Prüm, and one can see why: in the 2008 vintage, both the Pittermännchen GG and the Pittermännchen Spätlese [V] were impressive, but the Pittermännchen Auslese Gold Capsule★ was really outstanding. Meanwhile, for the past couple of years, the Burgberg GG has emerged as the most complex dry Riesling from Schlossgut Diel.

The vineyards were in top condition when I toured them with Armin Diel in late September of the highly problematic and therefore labor-intensive year of 2010. Leaf walls were high and open, fruit shoots (six to eight per cane) stood bolt upright, and grapes were quite exposed due to

aeration and sunlight. "Botrytis does not fit our brilliant wine style. Therefore, we expose the whole grape zone in October," Caroline Diel explains. Botrytis is, of course, welcome for the production of the high-grade *Prädikatsweine*.

Winemaking is of a very high standard. Grapes are crushed but not destemmed, and skin contact before pressing lasts between three and 24 hours. After settling overnight, the musts are fermented at temperatures of 61–63°F (16–17°C) in stainless steel (basic wines and *Prädikatsweine*) or large traditional wooden barrels (the Grosses Gewächs wines). The crus start fermenting spontaneously but are inoculated if necessary in order to get them dry. The sweet wines are sulfured directly after fermentation has been stopped, but the dry Riesling crus remain on their lees until April or May before being racked. They are bottled in June, while the *Prädikate* are bottled in late winter, shortly before the basic wines, which are bottled in March or April.

FINEST WINES

Burgberg GG
Records of the Burgberg *Einzellage* date back as far as 1400, but Schlossgut Diel did not become a proprietor until the 1990s. With 4.4 acres (1.8ha), the Diel family owns exactly 50 percent today. Almost completely bordered by solid rocks, the steep hillside forms a kind of ancient amphitheater, so the vines (all Riesling) benefit from an extremely warm mesoclimate. The complex soil (clay, containing red slate and a high proportion of quartzite) creates a rich and concentrated Riesling with earthy and herbaceous flavors, a mineral texture, and an intense and enduring finish. In August 2010, Caroline and Armin Diel offered me a small vertical tasting of the past three vintages.
2007 Very rich and intense on the nose, with ripe, sappy fruit aromas. Very generous and succulent on the palate, yet pure and slightly salty. The supple, almost creamy texture is countered by subtle racy acidity and intense minerality on the long finish.

Left: Caroline Diel, whose education, experience, and good taste have helped take already high standards even higher

2008 Very clear on the nose, pure, with earthy aromas and fragrant fruit expression. Refined and elegant on the palate, very noble and pure, firmly structured, appetizing, with a pronounced minerality and finest fruit aromas returning on the finish. A classic.
2009 Clear and aromatic on the nose, still dominated by primary aromas. Succulent, refreshing, and piquant in the mouth; round and very elegant, with searing acidity and appetizing salinity. Long finish.

Dorsheimer Goldloch Riesling Spätlese [V]
The Goldloch Spätlese is always very fruity and almost baroque in style. Personally, I prefer a Pittermännchen *Prädikat*, because of its finesse and spice. That cru is very small, however, and availability is strictly limited, so the Goldloch is the best possible alternative.
1998 Made with 20–25 percent botrytized grapes, this wine has a spicy nose with delicate honey and caramel aromas. Although mature, it is still fresh, displaying distinctive fruit, smooth texture, and vibrant acidity. Very elegant and balanced.
2002★ Very clear, fresh, and herbaceous on the nose. Crystalline and elegant on the palate; precise fruit expression and subtle, racy acidity. Delicate.
2004 Cool and clear, somewhat creamy, slightly green. Quite powerful on the palate, which is well structured but also a bit dusty. Obviously not the best moment to taste this vintage, but there is potential.
2007★ Still young on the nose, with very intense fruit aromas. Succulent and voluptuous on the palate, but also piquant and salty, countered by a pronounced acidity.
2008★ A delicate nose, with fine aromas of honey and raisins: amazingly crystalline. Fairy-like, dancing on the palate; piquant and extremely appetizing, thanks to the crisp acidity.
2009★ Stone dust on the nose, very clear and cool, with restrained fruit. Concentrated and smooth, yet precise on the palate. Very juicy, but also refreshing and almost weightlessly delicate.

Schlossgut Diel
Area under vine: 54 acres (22ha); 65% Riesling; 35% Pinots Blanc, Gris, and Noir
Average production: 150,000 bottles
Burg Layen 16, 55452 Rümmelsheim
Tel: +49 672 196 950
www.diel.eu

Weingut Tesch

Martin Tesch is that rarest of individuals: a man who has proved it is possible for a German winemaker to be innovative, radical, *and* successful. At the end of the 1990s, Tesch, a microbiology graduate and all-around marketing talent, started his career as a vintner with a "chainsaw massacre" in his father's vineyards around the village of Langenlonsheim near Bad Kreuznach. "Too many varieties, too much wine," he said, as he set about implementing a strategy that he described as "concentration on the essentials," pulling out every non-Riesling vine in sight, with the exception of a few older parcels of Pinot Blanc and Pinot Noir. Those three varieties, particularly Riesling, were essential for the Literwein category that Tesch believed should form the basis of a much-reduced wine range—one that would replace the little-bit-of-everything chaos of a traditional family estate founded in 1723.

Martin Tesch is that rarest of individuals: a man who has proved it is possible for a German winemaker to be innovative, radical, and *successful*

The impact was swift and dramatic. In 2002, rather than offering 40 wines, Tesch released just 11, seven of them dry Rieslings. "I can't do anything but Riesling *trocken*," he said a few years before the then-nascent Riesling renaissance had blossomed into a full-blown fashion. Undoubtedly, Tesch was one of the pathfinders, with one wine in particular helping to define the zeitgeist: Riesling Unplugged. Sourced from several vineyards, this pure, lithe, lissom, and bone-dry Kabinett, with racy-to-crazy acidity, is presented in smart black bottles, is poured on every continent ("apart from the North and South Pole," says Tesch), and is one of the few wines that deserves that much over- and misused phrase "icon wine"—not just for Weingut Tesch but for modern German Riesling in general. First made in 2001, it has established itself in the kind of places where wine was traditionally scorned in favor of beer and other alcoholic drinks, such as quayside bars, clubs, rock festivals, football stadiums, and so on.

For all its radical packaging and mold-breaking popularity, however, Unplugged, like all Tesch's wines, is very traditional in both its style and the way it is made. This is not the kind of wine you'd call sexy; it's never super-ripe or full-bodied. Nor is it a rarity or the kind of drink you'd buy in a bar to impress somebody, à la prestige cuvée Champagne. It is simply very drinkable. As Tesch says, "Even people in Hong Kong drink it, and that's what it's made for. It's a drink, not a status symbol."

All of Tesch's wines—whether Riesling or not; whether grown on loess, loam, clay, limestone, or volcanic soils—are always dry, pure, straight, and an uncompromising reflection of their vintage. With alcohol levels of 11.5–12.5% ABV, they are moderate rather than rich and full-bodied, realistic rather than romantic. Tesch tries to avoid botrytis except in those years (such as 2006 or 2010) where it is unavoidable. Acidity levels are rather high but are balanced by extract and very rarely (such as in 2010) by residual sugar. The vines are rather old and cultivated close to organically, with low yields and a very selective manual harvest. Winemaking is quite unspectacular: the grapes are destemmed (in some but not all vintages) before being crushed and, after a few hours' maceration (the riper the grapes, the shorter the time), gently pressed. After the must has settled, it is fermented with its own cultured yeasts in steel tanks, at natural temperatures of 59–66°F (15–19°C). After four to six weeks, the wine is racked for the first time (but still unsulfured). After another six to eight weeks on its fine lees, it is racked or not for the second time, fined (with bentonite), filtered and bottled. Since the 2002 vintage, all the wines are closed with Stelvin+.

Above: The visionary Martin Tesch, who manages to be both radical and traditional, even with his mold-breaking Unplugged wines

FINEST WINES

Riesling Unplugged

This wine is a brand. It is the quintessence, as well as the cash cow, of Weingut Tesch, though Martin Tesch did not divulge how much he bottles annually. It should be a multiple of the 3,000 bottles from the first vintage, 2001. According to Tesch, Unplugged is a "naked" wine that has not been adorned or refined by adding enzymes, aromatic varieties such as Scheurebe or Traminer, or even icewine. Indeed, it's pure Riesling *trocken*: Either you love (and drink) it, or you leave it. Residual sugar is very low (1.5–2.5g/l), and acidity is typically about 7.5g/l. A vertical tasting of the first ten vintages in July 2011 showed that this Riesling is best after 4–5 years. The very best vintages—like **2004** (extremely dry but still balanced; a classic), **2007** (very elegant and balanced), **2008** (very pure), and **2009** (richer than 2008)—can age up to 7 or 8 years as well.

Riesling Remigiusberg

This is the finest and most complex Riesling of the five single vineyards. Grown on decomposed volcanic soils, this incomparable wine shows a very distinguished spicy nose with delicate herbal notes and a very fine fruit expression. On the palate, it's filigreed and almost soft, yet sophisticated, elegant, and persistent. This highly expressive but also subtle Riesling tastes best after 5 or 6 years, but can also age 10 years or more. Best vintages: **1999**, **2001**, **2004**, **2007**, **2008**, **2009**.

Weingut Tesch

Area under vine: 37 acres (15ha) plus
12 acres (5ha) that are rented
Average production: 150,000 bottles
Naheweinstrasse 99, 55450 Langenlonsheim
Tel: +49 670 493 040
www.weingut-tesch.de

Mosel

Welcome to the region with the oldest but, nonetheless, the most lively, light-footed, filigreed, aromatic, delicate, and charming palate-dancers in the world! If you have no idea about German wine at all, the Mosel, Saar, and Ruwer wines are the ones that you should taste first. It's mostly Riesling—and if not, you can mostly forget it—and it's mostly grown on steep and steeper rocky hillsides along a mystical green river and its small tributaries. These snake through a picturesque valley that was finally formed through volcanic eruptions about 15 million years ago, although the foundation for the characteristic colored Devonian slate soils came into being long before that, about 411 million years ago.

The region's "modern" history started with 30,000 thirsty Romans crossing the Alps and heading north roughly 2,000 years ago. Since no wine was imported to the region that would eventually become Germany, the clever Romans started to cultivate the untouched wilderness near Trier, wresting terraces from the precipitous rocks where they face to the south and planting vines on them. What they harvested and fermented—reportedly light and fresh—slaked their thirst so wonderfully that viticulture has continued without interruption to the present day. (The way they trained the vines, on single poles with heart-shaped arcs, and the way they crushed the grapes are still in use today—in the vineyards, as well as in the museums worth visiting.) The Romans, whose empire was falling into ruins, eventually returned to Rome, though their descendants still appreciate Mosel Riesling today. Indeed, is there any wine lover anywhere who does not love the alluring lightness and finesse of a classic Mosel Riesling? What the Romans failed to do through force of arms, Mosel Riesling did with charm: it conquered the world.

Right: The village of Bernkastel at a bend in the Mosel River, and the famous Doctor vineyard on the steep slopes above

Viniculture along the Mosel extends from France up to Coblenz, where it joins the majestic Rhine (*see map, p.141*). The whole Mosel region (formerly more correctly called Mosel-Saar-Ruwer) has 21,921 acres (8,871ha) under vine, of which more than half are on the steep slopes for which the area is famous. Some 91 percent of the crop is white varieties, and 9 percent is red. Riesling dominates, with 60 percent. The Elbling (6.2 percent) is more interesting than the Müller-Thurgau (13.6 percent) for at least two reasons: the Romans loved the former variety for its discreet charm and lightness, and it is still the star of the Upper Mosel.

With vineyards following almost every twist and turn of the river for all of its 155 miles (250km), the Mosel is Europe's largest Riesling region. Until recently, only on slopes that hardly ever saw the sun or that were too steep did viticulture pause. But over the past 20 years, a large area has gone fallow, and the pace has recently picked up, leading to *cris du coeur* from growers and observers. Although a few idealistic and masochistic young producers—such as Daniel Vollenweider in Traben-Trabach—are rescuing steep old vineyards that would have been lost otherwise, consumers must be prepared to pay prices high enough to recoup the cost of Mosel steep-slope viticulture or else it will not survive.

A slope of 115 percent is not steep enough to deter the most daring growers, as Winninger Uhlen on the terraced Lower Mosel dizzily demonstrates. Since the 1950s, the flat valley floor has also been planted with vines, though fruits other than wine grapes would fare better here. Because the mountain ranges of the Hunsrück (to the south) and the Eifel (to the north) always threaten cold surges, most of the vineyards are protected by woods at the top of the slopes. The river valleys with the steepest slopes give the best protection. Although temperatures are quite cool, the vines benefit from the gradient, as well as from the stony soils and terraces, which store the heat of the day and radiate it at night.

Climate plays a crucial role for the delicate style of Mosel wines. The region is in the moderate climate zone at the northern border of viticulture in Europe. With winds from the south and the west, the climate is Atlantic and characterized by cool summers and relatively mild winters. Annual weather patterns vary, so the individual years can be distinctly different regarding sunshine hours and precipitation, which is clearly reflected in the wines. Annual average temperatures range from 48.4°F (9.1°C) in the Upper Mosel, to 50.9°F (10.5°C) in Coblenz. This is quite a difference, but almost nothing compared to the difference in rainfall: 31.5in (800mm) in Trier, and 26.4in (670mm) in Coblenz. On the Saar, though, annual precipitation averages 35.4in (900mm). If the slopes here were not so steep and the slate soils not so fast-draining, viticulture would be impossible. But in good years, you can find what are probably the world's finest Rieslings here, among Kanzem (taste an Altenberg), Wiltingen (Scharzhofberger), and Serrig (Schloss Saarsteiner).

In the Mosel, Saar, and Ruwer valleys, fog is frequent in fall and winter, and frost is an ever-present risk in fall and early spring due to cold air masses streaming down the hillsides. On the other hand, viticulture on the edge creates the possibility of something really spectacular like Eiswein (especially on the Saar), BA, or TBA, which are among the world's finest sweet wines.

The intensity of sunlight is a crucial factor in a northern viticultural area like the Mosel. Intensity varies with exposure and gradient, so the steep slopes snaking along the rivers contribute to the differences from one vineyard site to the next. *Einzellagen* are extremely important for the character of a Mosel wine, and the smaller a site is, the more individual the wine can be. The famous Bernkasteler Doctor comprises little more than 7.5 acres (3ha), and its Rieslings are unmistakable and unique. It might sound strange that several top producers—such as Clemens Busch, Reinhard Löwenstein (both Mosel), and Peter Lauer (Saar)—subdivide their crus into several small parcels, some less than 1.2 acres (0.5ha), according to the mesoclimate and the particular type of soil (or the color of the slate). But when you taste these wines, you fully understand why they do it, even if in marketing terms it is nonsense. On the other hand, how many *Mona Lisa* paintings exist? One. So several hundred bottles of a liquid masterpiece is much more, and they are available for far less than the price of a painting from a world-famous artist.

While we're on the subject of price, a Mosel wine, even a single-vineyard Spätlese, can be extremely cheap. Do not touch it, knowing that it probably comes from the former orchards on the valley floor. When it comes to Mosel wine, please be willing to pay for it. Go to YouTube, key in "Mosel vineyard," "Loosen jamiegoode," or "Winninger Uhlen," and you will easily understand what top producer Nik Weis told me: "The Mosel is a region that cannot be successful in the long term with cheap wines. We've only two options: either invest in our labor-intensive viticulture and produce such great wines that wine lovers the world over are willing to pay for it, or let goats graze on the hills." I don't want to see that scenario, and neither will you once a top-notch Ockfener Bockstein Kabinett or Wehlener Sonnenuhr Spätlese passes your lips.

Soils also define the character of a wine. In the Mosel, it is predominantly well-weathered Devonian slate, rich in minerals (like potassium or magnesium) and organic components (nitrogen, phosphorus) that nourish the plants and give the wines an intense mineral-like character—so much "more than just fruit." Very often the topsoil is extremely thin due to the steepness of the slope, so the vine roots penetrate the schistous rock. In Mosel, there are still many ungrafted vines of 60 to more than 100 years old, since phylloxera never

Above: Devonian slate, as on the house of one of the Mosel's top producers, JJ Prüm, is among the region's defining features

conquered the slate soils. These are black, blue, gray, green, brown, or red, and each color signals a slightly different character of the soil and the wine.

The long ripening period combines with the countless different terroirs to create optimal conditions for Riesling, so other varieties, white or red, are much less important here. This does not mean Mosel wine is all the same. On the contrary, the styles and tastes of Mosel Riesling are manifold. From filigree and dry, to rich sweet wines from botrytized grapes and even Eiswein, everything is possible. To find your own favorite here can turn into a true passion as you discover that there are so many different styles. And then the very different vintages mean that even the finest wines vary widely from year to year—in terms of style rather than quality. Even a Scharzhofberger can be full and rich one year and lean and sophisticated the next. Both are fascinating, and both are an integral part of wine culture here. Taste these wines again when mature, when they are 20, 30, or 40 years old, and you will bless that difference as well. "Riesling is Riesling is nonsense," we say in Germany, and this is nowhere more true than in Mosel. You just have to try it.

Weingut Markus Molitor

"nbelievable!" "It's sheer lunacy!" "He is completely mad." "Brilliant!" Whenever I leave the annual release tasting of Markus Molitor in the Wehlener Klostergarten, I hear visitors competing to describe the indescribable. It's hard enough to find words for the dozens of individual—really individual—wines from the latest vintage that Molitor shows each year. But he also shows another dozen older Riesling Auslese wines dating back to the 1988 vintage. Whereas most of the former are just (I use the term loosely) promising indications of handcrafted wines of near-perfect quality, the latter remain amazingly fresh and far from being fully developed. Molitor would love to show still earlier vintages, but he took over the family business only in 1984.

Molitor was just 20 years old at the time, but he was full of ambition and vision. "My goal from the very beginning was to bring back the former glory of the Mosel and to produce highly distinctive wines that clearly reflect their individual vineyard identities, the different selections, and the vintage character over a wide span of years," he says.

Molitor started with 10 acres (4ha) of vines; now he owns 100 acres (40ha)—one of the largest family-run wine estates in the Mosel. He owns vineyards in 18 sites between Brauneberg and Traben-Trabach, predominantly located in the best and steepest sites of the Middle Mosel: Brauneberger Klostergarten, Bernkasteler Lay, Graacher Himmelreich and Domprobst, Wehlener Sonnenuhr and its continuation Zeltingener Sonnenuhr, Ürziger Würzgarten, and Erdener Treppchen. Since 2012, he has also rented parcels in two top Saar sites: Ockfener Bockstein and Saarburger Rausch.

Due to the high diversity of sites, slate types, and microclimates, as well as the production of several predicates in dry (white capsule), off-dry (green), and sweet (gold), the wines of Markus Molitor

Left: The uncompromising Markus Molitor amid his precious vines, a high proportion of which are very old and ungrafted

represent every variation of Mosel wine. Each year he selects and bottles at least 50 different wines; in vintages with a lot of botrytis, even more. In 2010, ten TBAs were selected in Zeltinger Sonnenuhr alone, plus several TBAs from other sites. It might seem like madness for one producer to offer 50 or 60 wines each year, but once you taste them, you realize that each one is stamped with Molitor's imprimatur and that every single one was worth bottling—all the more so when you consider that there are several thousand bottles of each apart from the highest predicates.

The exceptional quality of Molitor's vast portfolio rests on a number of factors. First of these is the quality of his vine material: Molitor has a very high proportion of ungrafted vines, up to 100 years old, as well as massal selections drawn from these old vines. Then there is his famously uncompromising devotion to quality in the vineyard and cellar, which includes organic farming, a lot of manual work, rigorous selections, and traditional winemaking without using enzymes, additives, fining agents, or industrial yeasts. He rejects anything that might compromise the authenticity, complexity, or longevity of the wine. After being macerated for up to two days, depending on the style and vintage, a large proportion of the basket-pressed Rieslings are fermented and aged (the best for one year or more) in traditional oak barrels of 1,000–3,000 liters.

Molitor employs an astonishing 50 experienced vineyard workers to carry out canopy management during the summer and for the two months of harvest. That might seem excessive, but not a single grape goes into the basket press without being sorted at least twice or being accepted by the rigorous chief himself. Indeed, when it comes to grape selection, Molitor is fanatical. For dry wines, even grapes with the slightest touch of botrytis are separated from the healthy ones already in the vineyard, so they cannot infect the healthy ones. Since he aims for rich and physiologically ripe grapes, Markus and his team keep yields low at 10–55hl/ha, according to the vintage, parcel, and planting density. Picking, especially for the dry Spätlese and Auslese wines, is very late to ensure higher extracts, riper and less aggressive acidity levels, and phenolic ripeness, to give structure to the wines. Each parcel is picked several times, and the different ripeness levels are carefully separated.

For example, a sweet Spätlese is picked significantly earlier than a Spätlese *trocken* to ensure higher acidity to balance the residual sugar. The *trocken*, by contrast, needs more ripeness, intensity, and structure and is therefore picked about three weeks later and from the oldest vines.

To produce a classic Auslese at Molitor, a grape should ideally have 50 percent raisins for creamy texture and 50 percent healthy berries for balancing freshness. According to the pre-1971 wine law, he produces three kinds of Auslese: * means fine Auslese, ** finest Auslese, and *** very finest Auslese. These stars correspond not with sugar levels (the more the better) but with the levels of finesse (the finer the better). A three-star Auslese, especially a *trocken* one, is very rare because it requires perfect physiological ripeness in combination with 100 percent healthy grapes. Sweet and off-dry three-star Auslese wines are regularly produced, however, since botrytis is acceptable for both styles.

Producing BAs and, especially, TBAs at Molitor is like manufacturing a Rolls-Royce. A group of the most experienced pickers goes ahead of the others to pick raisin by raisin out of the clusters. These raisins are sorted again up to three times on a table in the cellar. The high-end TBAs are among the finest wines in the world and, since they are auctioned, also some of the most expensive.

With so many top-class wines (predominantly at remarkably attractive prices) and clients who are prepared to follow him wherever he may lead, Molitor is not duty-bound to produce certain wines each year, as is the case with more mainstream brands (including many Grosse Gewächse); the vintage alone decides which wines will be produced. Over more than 20 years, Molitor has built up a catalog that lists at least four vintages, but if you're looking for something special, he is always willing to help. When the new vintage is presented in the fall, only 40 percent of the previous vintage has sold out. Many top wines enter the market only after a couple of years, and the finest are held back for auction, where Molitor plays in the same quality and price league as Egon Müller-Scharzhof and JJ Prüm.

Molitor's wines are extraordinary: deep, rich and well structured, but not lacking freshness, grace, or the ability to inspire. A word of advice, however: by all means buy the newest vintages, but always appreciate the mature ones.

FINEST WINES

2007 Graacher Himmelreich *** Pinot Noir ★
Surprising as it may seem, there is a tradition for Pinot Noir even in the Mosel, and this example from the middle part of the extremely steep slope in Graach is one of the finest in Germany. Molitor planted his first Pinots in 1988, and a few years later, he added massal selections from Chambolle and Chambertin. Fine fruit flavors, red cassis, whole wheat (no botrytis!), sweet and harmonious, extremely subtle. Ripe, intense, and full on the palate, quite jammy, but with enormous depth, concentration, and power. The texture is silky and very elegant, as is the acidity; the finish is smoky and the ripe tannins still a little biting on the finish, providing structure for this very potent grand cru.

2009 Zeltinger Sonnenuhr Kabinett Fuder 6 [V]
One of the most impressive wines in Germany for its complexity, lightness, freshness, and drinkability. This is a dry Kabinett with 11.5% ABV but sourced from the oldest, ungrafted vines in higher altitudes, so sugar levels are moderate. Ripe and intense fruit, with spicy slate aromas. On the palate, ripe apricots, peaches, precise, fresh acidity; salty-slaty taste.

2001 Zeltinger Sonnenuhr Auslese *** trocken ★
This is Riesling dressed as Bâtard-Montrachet though its soul is clearly Zeltingen Sonnenuhr. Most of the vineyards here are 80+ years old; several parcels are terraced. The soil is very stony and poor, dominated by blue Devonian slate. Yields are ridiculously low (10–20hl/ha), leading to impressive Rieslings that match complexity and ripeness with amazing elegance and finesse. The 2001 was dry; newer vintages have about 5g more residual sugar, which should bring even more aging potential. Brilliant concentration and depth, with delicate aromas due to the small oak barrels used for fermentation and aging. (Toasting is much reduced in the equivalent wines today.) Very clear, fresh, pure. Powerful and super-dense on the palate: ripe peaches; breathtaking length, with vibrant, salty minerality. Still a baby, yet a giant one. Awesome.

1993 Zeltinger Sonnenuhr Auslese *** ★
Golden color, with green reflections. Concentrated flavors of perfectly ripe fruits, absolutely clear and noble, with aromas of honey, raisins, apricots, quinces. Concentrated and piquant on the palate, firmly structured and sweet only at the beginning, but very soon marked by its piercing minerality and thrilling complexity, which leads to an impressively lingering salinity. Vital and appetizing. Brilliant.

1998 Zeltinger Sonnenuhr Auslese ** (auction) ★
Although Molitor believes this wine should be even better to get three stars, I cannot think of anything missing here. To me, this golden-yellow wine is a perfect Auslese from one of the legendary Eiswein vintages of the Mosel. The raisins were singly picked after the frost, which intensified both aroma and acidity. Very pure and elegant, with finest raisin and apricot tart aromas on the nose. Elysian finesse and subtlety on the palate. Extremely fine, elegant acidity and salty minerality balance this light, noble, yet intense, persistent wine in a gorgeous way. Finishes with delicate caramel flavors.

2009 Brauneberger Mandelgraben Eiswein
Yellow-green. Stone and tropical aromas (pineapple, peach). Precise, crystalline palate, noble texture, with honey flavors, kumquat, and bitter oranges—but the slate is always present. Piquant. Great wine.

Weingut Markus Molitor
Area under vine: 100 acres (40ha)
Annual production: 200,000–300,000 bottles
Haus Klosterberg, 54470 Bernkastel-Wehlen
Tel: +49 6532 954 000
www.markusmolitor.com

Weingut Egon Müller-Scharzhof

W hen I first visited the Scharzhof ten years or so ago, I had the peculiar feeling that everything had been staged somehow—that it was not quite real. Over the years, however, I've come to understand that there's nothing fake here: this is "real life," all right; it's just that real life here is rather different from what it is elsewhere.

Scharzhof lies outside the village of Wiltingen. Driving toward Oberemmel, you pass the steep, world-famous Scharzhofberg on your left. There, set back from the street at the foot of the hill like a stage decoration, stands the proud, pale yellow baroque manor house. A tug on a rope sounds an ancient bell, and a couple of minutes later (should you have an appointment) the door opens to a friendly welcome from Egon Müller IV. He guides you to the oval marble table by the window at the entrance (which feels more like a threatening exit once you've finally managed to get yourself inside these holy halls), and there you find the complete Scharzhofberger range of the latest vintage—nothing but Riesling, of course—lined up in a circle, bottle by bottle, and each with a small INAO tasting glass beside it. It is you now who is on stage. Egon Müller, meanwhile, retreats into the shady recesses of the hall where he takes on the role of the muted, bored spectator. You begin to taste the exciting, fascinating range arrayed before you, starting with the lovely Scharzhof estate Riesling, moving through several elfin-like Kabinette, delicious Spätlesen, and sophisticated Auslesen, before ending with highly noble rarities such as TBA or Eiswein that have been fermented for the most part in carboys due to the tiny quantities. Tasting these wines generally takes me at least an hour as I grope for the right words to describe wines that seem beyond all description. These aristocratic wines are so subtle,

Right: Egon Müller with one of his 40 harvesters, putting healthy grapes in one bucket and botrytized grapes in another

Egon Müller-Scharzhof is widely regarded as Germany's finest Riesling estate. These aristocratic wines are subtle, light, transparent, sophisticated, and filigreed and, at the same time, unbelievably intense

light, transparent, sophisticated, and filigreed, and at the same time so unbelievably intense, concentrated, and arresting, that nobody speaks— and very few spit—during the tasting, and there are two very good reasons why.

First, Egon Müller-Scharzhof is widely regarded as Germany's finest Riesling estate for quality and style. Purchased from the République Française in 1797 by Egon Müller's great-great-grandfather Jean-Jacques Koch, the Scharzhof is now driven by the fourth generation, the 1959-vintage Egon Müller IV. He has been in charge since 1991 and, unlike his ancestors, has had the fortune of not seeing a bad vintage for the best part of a quarter of a century. Looking back to the years before 1988—years that now feel like a different era—he says, "In the past, we had problems getting our grapes fully ripe. With climate change, we are having fewer problems in reaching sufficient sugar levels, so that now we can concentrate on the ripeness of flavors and acidity." He does this also for Le Gallais in Kanzem, the small second estate of the family, with its famous monopole Braune Kupp in Wiltingen, whose Rieslings are also crafted in the Scharzhof.

The second reason for behaving more like Dionysus than Apollo is that Müller's Rieslings from Scharzhofberg are both rare and expensive. The family owns 40 acres (16ha) in total and 21 acres (8.3ha) in the famous grand cru. Most of the vines here are old, and about 7.5 acres (3ha) are ungrafted. Planting density in the Scharzhofberg averages between 6,000 and 10,000 vines/ha.

Müller bottles a range of Prädikat wines, but the diverse Kabinette, Spätlesen, and Auslesen differ in style rather than in quality. Because they come from different parcels and casks (1,000-liter *Fuders*) there are varied shades in taste, and Müller gives all his wines a corresponding *Fuder* number. Scharzhof's finest, most focused and sophisticated Rieslings are exclusively sold as Goldkapseln (gold capsules) at the annual wine auction in Trier, where Müller's Scharzhofbergers regularly achieve the highest prices. Unfortunately, even a non-Goldkapsel Auslese costs nearly €200 per bottle.

The 69-acre (28ha) Scharzhofberg itself is probably Germany's most highly regarded vineyard, although the reasons offered for why that should be so are somewhat banal. "Hoeing, hoeing, hoeing," was Egon Müller III's explanation to a group of young Geisenheim students some years ago. But "terroir," as Egon Müller IV explains it today, doesn't get us so much further. "It's a combination of factors; there is something special about the hill," he says, smiling like the Sphinx.

The Scharzhofberg hill has a steep, south-facing slope of pure slate in one of Germany's coolest wine-growing spots. It does not see the Saar River, for it is located in a side valley that is cooler than famous riverside sites such as Altenberg (Kanzem) or Gottesfuss (Wiltingen). The stony soils of the Scharzhofberg drain well and warm up quickly. Here, Riesling ripens slowly and late, taking up all the minerals, aromas, and flavors that the soil and the sun and the cool nights have to offer. When there is botrytis ("we can't avoid it"), the grapes gain a concentration that can be spellbinding in the Auslese, BA, and TBA wines.

A late harvest is crucial for Müller, who, at the end of October or even into November, goes into the vineyard with about 40 pickers. They pick healthy grapes in one basket and botrytis grapes in another. "That makes about 1,000 liters of regular wine and 50 liters of botrytis wine a day," he explains.

All of the wines (except TBA) are fermented and matured in traditional *Fuders*. Fermentation starts at about 50°F (10°C) and seldom stops before January. Bottling is quite early (March) to avoid oxidation and to conserve delicacy and finesse.

"Our wines taste good one to three years after bottling, then they close down for about ten years before reemerging as real classics," explains Müller. Once at that stage, they keep their legendary style for many years. The Kabinette and Spätlesen always taste drier then, making them perfect with food. "If someone prefers to drink Riesling as young wine, it is not necessary to buy a Scharzhof. These develop their value only with time," he advises.

The classic expression of Scharzhofberger is Auslese—the wine for which Müller is always striving. "They are difficult to match with any dishes except cheese when young. Give them 40 or 50 years, though, and there will be almost no dish that does not benefit from a mature Auslese. You can even match it with wild boar. You definitely don't ask for Burgundy then." Fine. I'll be 85 or 95. You?

FINEST WINES

Since the finest wines here are auctioned, the rare BAs, TBAs, and Eisweine are beyond the reach of most of us. Kabinett and Spätlese should be stored for at least 10–15 years and 20 years respectively. A beautiful and affordable representative of the unrivaled finesse and transparency of Scharzhof is the **Scharzhof Riesling #1**, worth every penny as young wine but still delicious, if not even more impressive, after a decade.

Scharzhofberger Kabinett
For finesse, sophistication, and precision, Egon Müller's Scharzhofberger Kabinett is unmatched by any wine in the world, especially when it is botrytis-free. The subtlety of aroma and taste is unique, and it always amazes me that just a hint of flavor can be so satisfyingly full and persistent. Especially in cooler vintages such as **2004★**, the wine is light as an elf and glimmers like a mirage, its structure delicately engraved like the veins of a fresh green Riesling leaf. In riper vintages, the Kabinett is a study in harmonious opposition, as the auctioned **2009 (#16)★** impressively demonstrates: juicy fullness, controlled power, and good length, paired with lightness, purity, and finesse—sublime. It's hard to put a figure on when best to drink a Scharzhofberger Kabinett. I love its ageless period, which is normally 12–20 years after harvest, but I have tasted 30-year-old wines—like the delicious 1976 veteran, which was mature but retained its freshness, intensity, and length. For Müller, there is no better wine with Asian cuisine than Kabinett.

Scharzhofberger Auslese
Here are some highlights from the past six decades. The luscious, dense, highly elegant and piquant **2009 (#10)★** would have been noble and balanced enough to be gold-capsuled, but the **#21★** was even finer and was thus dressed in gold and auctioned for €570. It is a cool and aristocratic Scharzhofberger, with a concentrated and viscous texture and a highly noble honey-sweetness that is counterpointed by a piquant and mineral raciness that gives an almost salty and astonishingly dry finish with impressive length. **1971 (#16)★** is an almost transcendental wine experience today, combining the complexity and finesse of a perfectly mature wine with the concentration and freshness of a young one. Very well balanced; still playful and persistent. The sweetness is fading away gradually now, but this is still an extraordinary wine right at its very peak. **1959 (#73)★** is still fresh after all those years and drinking superbly now. Intense bouquet, with beautiful fruit and smoky notes of slate and pepper, green tea, dried apricots, and lime. Luscious palate, dense and spicy, with some bitter botrytis notes that are more obvious as the residual sugar fades away. Elegant finish of chamomile and green tea.

2003 Scharzhofberger Trockenbeerenauslese (auction)★
At less than 6% alcohol, this is a legendary TBA. Clear orange in color, hinting at its astonishing concentration. Terrific, extremely intense nose, with otherworldly fruit purity of dried apricots, mango, honey, wax, and flowers. This is the quintessence of a Scharzhof TBA. Dense, thick, and sweet like honey, but the purest fruit expression, cut in a magical way by brilliant, ripe acidity. There is actually finesse in this unforgettable, immortal wine.

1996 Scharzhofberger Eiswein # 2
Beautifully concentrated and precise on the nose: dried oranges and apricots, with hints of honey and caramel. Opulent sweetness and noble concentration on the palate; again, very clear and exact and cut by racy, electrifying acidity.

Weingut Egon Müller-Scharzhof
Area under vine: 40 acres (16ha)
Annual production: 80,000 bottles
Best site: Scharzhofberger
54459 Wiltingen
www.scharzhof.de

Reichsgraf von Kesselstatt

With a history of more than 660 years, Reichsgraf von Kesselstatt is one of the most traditional wine estates in the Mosel and owns important parcels in the best sites of the Mosel, Saar, and Ruwer valleys. No other Mosel estate has a comparable portfolio of grands crus. If you want to discover the Mosel-Saar-Ruwer region in just one day, Schloss Marienlay in Morscheid/Ruwer is the place to go.

You won't be greeted by a member of the Reichsgraf family, but there can be few more welcoming people than current owners Annegret Reh-Gartner and her husband Gerhard Gartner. It was Reh-Gartner's father, Günther Reh, who bought the estate in 1978. A decade later, in 1989, Reh-Gartner was *Gault Millau*'s Winemaker of the Year. Although she is light-years away from retiring, Reh-Gartner already deserves a lifetime achievement award. In almost 30 years of managing one of the most important wine estates in the Mosel region, she has never stopped developing sustainable innovations and marketing strategies.

One of her most important decisions was to reduce the many different vineyards down to a total of 89 acres (36ha), of which 30 acres (12ha) are located in the steepest slopes and classified Erste Lage (soon Grosse Lage). The most renowned sites include: in the Mosel, Josephshöfer (a Graach monopole), Bernkasteler Doctor (0.15 acre [0.06ha] yielding an impressive Grosses Gewächs bottled in magnums), Brauneberger Juffer Sonnenuhr (terrific GG 2010), Piesporter Goldtröpfchen (excellent GG 2010), and Wehlener Sonnenuhr; in the Saar, Scharzhofberger, Wiltinger Gottesfuss, and Wiltinger Braunfels; and in the Ruwer, Kaseler Nies'chen.

Reh-Gartner makes wines in a classic Mosel style: light and filigreed but intense and complex. That does not necessarily mean off-dry or naturally sweet, however. Due to climate change,

Right: The dynamic Annegret Reh-Gartner, who presides over an unparalleled range of Mosel grand cru vineyards

With a history of more than 660 years, Reichsgraf von Kesselstatt is one of the most traditional wine estates in the Mosel region. No other Mosel estate has a comparable portfolio of grand cru sites

she argues, it is possible to produce top-quality dry wines, too. Consequently, Kesselstatt is one of the forerunners regarding the production of Mosel Grosses Gewächs, of which seven of the 2010 vintage were bottled. These wines are dry but not very high in alcohol (11.5–12.5% ABV. "We try not to worry about sugar levels and must weights anymore, though this is much easier to say than to do. It is much more important to keep the elegance and minerality in our wines and to express the individuality of each site."

This philosophy is applied first in the vineyards, which are run by viticulturist Christian Steinmetz. Most of the vines are trained in wire frames today, and yields are kept under 50hl/ha for the Grosses Gewächs but at 60–65hl/ha for the light Kabinett style. These wines also come from grand cru sites but are not labeled as Erste or Grosse Lage, since this term is permitted so far only for higher predicates.

Wolfgang Mertes has been the cellar master here since 2005. He has fully accepted the shift toward dry Riesling (still not self-evident in the Mosel), as well as the terroir and marketing idea that gives each site and quality level its own profile. The Estate Riesling RK, the village, and the Grosse Gewächse have to be fermented dry. The latter are never chaptalized (though it is permitted). Some 50 percent of the Josephshöfer GG is fermented and aged in traditional oak (2,400-liter), the Nies'chen and the Scharzhofberger with a proportion of up to 30 percent. The rest, including the predicate wines, is fermented in stainless steel. The GGs are kept on the lees until August; the other wines, until May.

Kabinett wines are always off-dry yet not too sweet, with 8–11% ABV and residual-sugar levels of 20–40g/l, depending on the site. With 60–80g/l RS and about 8% ABV, the botrytis-free Spätlesen are also drier today than a few years ago but could be even drier for my taste. The higher predicates are free to express themselves as world-class Auslesen, BAs, and TBAs.

FINEST WINES

(Tasted in January 2012)
Josephshöfer
According to Reh-Gartner, this site in Graach was first mentioned 1,400 years ago and has belonged to RvK since 1858. The grand cru parcel is 9.4 acres (3.8ha) entirely on the steep slope that rises up to 590ft (180m), with an inclination of 60%. The deep soil of weathered Devonian slate gives very rich, mineral, powerful, ageworthy wines.

2010 GG Refined fruit intensity on the nose. Full, supple, noble texture; this is a rich grand cru of great finesse and elegance: silky, fresh, and balanced, with lingering salinity.

1999 Auslese (gold capsule Jubilee Edition)★ Intense yellow. Noble, rich, and ripe, yet not mature on the nose—a great expression of the terroir, displaying some herbal flavors. Thrilling palate, vibrant, pure, and complex; very elegant, extremely salty, and long. This is an impressive expression of the Josephshöfer terroir—can any other type of wine compete with this noble beauty? Although it is a great pleasure to drink it now, it will hold for another two or three decades.

2002 Kaseler Nies'chen Spätlese★
Grown in the Ruwer Valley on a rocky blue-slate soil, this is, besides the aristocratic Scharzhofberger, the most mineral wine RvK produces. Fresh color. Brilliant, elegant, and distinctive on the nose, sweet herbal and mineral aromas. Very clear and almost dry on the palate, propelled by its vibrant, yet refined acidity and lingering salinity. Very well structured and juvenile, this is a light-hearted, swinging wine, with very good length. Excellent.

2009 Scharzhofberger GG
This vintage demonstrates that the mythic site, in which RvK holds 16 acres (6.5ha), can also produce great dry Rieslings. Brilliant on the nose, noble and aristocratic. Very elegant and tightly woven on the palate. Refined acidity. Multilayered fruit flavors. Well balanced and salty. Delicious.

Reichsgraff von Kesselstatt
Area under vine: 89 acres (36ha)
Average production: 180,000–220,000 bottles
Schloss Marienlay, D-54317 Morscheid
Tel: +49 6500 91690
www.kesselstatt.com

Weingut Dr. Loosen

Six grand cru sites, just one grape variety—Riesling, what else?—and two styles: dry quality wines and sweet quality wines with *Prädikat*. Unusually for a German, Ernst Loosen likes to keep things simple, apart from the wine itself, of course. As one of the best-known wine producers in the Mosel and a worldwide traveling ambassador for German quality wine, he cultivates spectacular steep, rocky, and partly terraced vineyards in Erden (Prälat, Treppchen), Ürzig (Würzgarten), Wehlen (Sonnenuhr), Graach (Himmelreich), and Bernkastel (Lay). Most of the vines are ungrafted, rooted in weathered slate soils of different colors for 60 to more than 100 years. The vineyards are worked virtually organically, and yields are kept low. The sites were already classified Erste Lage in 1868 and today bear Grosses Gewächs wines, as well as *Prädikatsweine* of excellent quality.

Loosen says he likes to produce "intense and concentrated wines" that are "delicious to drink and proudly proclaim their origin." The origin he is so proud of is the picturesque area between Bernkastel and Erden, where, in just a few miles, one cru has followed the next since the time of the Romans, who managed to conquer and to cultivate the rocky slopes with vines. Although the sites are very close together, they are extremely different, especially their soils.

The area is best known for sweet Prädikat wines, and Loosen's exports are almost exclusively focused on his delicious Kabinett, Spätlese, and Auslese wines; just 2 percent of his exported Dr. Loosen wines are dry. Nevertheless, with more than ten years of experience with dry Rieslings in his JL Wolf estate in Wachenheim/Pfalz, since the 2008 vintage, Loosen has been putting a lot of his energy into upgrading his dry Mosel wine, investing in new 1,000- and 3000-liter barrels and keeping the Grosses Gewächs wines on the lees for one year.

"Dry wines reflect the different terroirs much more clearly than sweet wines because there is

Above: Weingut Dr. Loosen, Ernst Loosen's headquarters, though he spends much of his time traveling the world

neither primary fruit nor sweetness dominating the true character," Loosen believes. He also says he finds it "extremely challenging" to produce a great dry white wine with a maximum of 12.5% ABV. "The Mosel is uniquely able to produce classic wines with low alcohol but intense flavors and a thrilling minerality," he says, adding that to realize this "unique potential" is also "our duty."

For this reason, Loosen dedicated himself to rescuing the classic Kabinett style, which he describes as "distinct" to the Mosel. "A Kabinett has to be a clear, light, fresh, mineral, and exciting wine that gracefully dances over the palate."

According to Loosen, producing an authentic Kabinett today is much more labor-intensive and expensive than producing a higher predicate such as Auslese or even Beerenauslese. "We have to select very carefully to get the right grapes, which should have 100 percent healthy berries with must weights not more than 81–82° Oechsle and crisp acidity," Loosen says. "It's crazy—in the past, we selected grapes to get higher must weights, whereas today, due to climate change, we select for Kabinett."

"Dry wines reflect the different terroirs much more clearly than sweet wines because there is neither primary fruit nor sweetness dominating the true character"—Ernst Loosen

Loosen believes a wine's drinkability is its most important asset, and he thinks that a hang time of not much more than 100 days between flowering and harvest is still the right span. "The grapes are ripe and also often botrytized then, so there is no reason to wait," he says.

FINEST WINES

Erdener Treppchen

Long ago, stone steps were built into this vineyard's steep hillside to help workers reach the vines. The iron-infused, red-colored slate soil produces firm and mineral-structured wines that are among the most demanding in the Middle Mosel. They benefit greatly from a few years in bottle to develop their potential, even the Kabinett.

2010 Riesling Kabinett [V] I thought the era of light-hearted wines like this had passed long ago. This Kabinett is absolutely delicious: floral and springlike on the nose, earthy, with a touch of Condrieu—why not? Sappy and round, very fruity, and quite intense on the palate, perfectly balanced and animating in the salty finish, this is a light, mineral, and cheerful Kabi near to perfection.

Left: The playful, dog-loving Ernst Loosen, who is doing his utmost to preserve the classic style of Mosel Kabinett

Erdener Prälat

This is a completely south-facing cru of 3.7 acres (1.5ha) with weathered red slate soils and an inclination of 55–65%. The vineyard's exposure, in combination with the warming effect of the river and the massive heat-retaining cliffs that surround it, ensures exceptional ripeness in every vintage. The wines produced here are noble, rich, and concentrated, but also multifaceted.

2009 Riesling Alte Reben GG Complex and dense nose; deep, intense (rather tropical) fruit, with floral and refined earthy aromas—just great. Full, round, and complex on the palate, very long, piquant, and salty; powerful yet refined and with impressive expression. Creamy textured and with a clever balance of alcohol (13% ABV), residual sugar, and mineral acidity. Wait until 2016 to drink.

2009 Riesling Auslese (Long Gold Capsule) ★ Noble fruit intensity. Generous, full, and concentrated palate, sappy and creamy but also fresh and piquant, and with a lingering salinity that keeps you drinking this extraordinary, and expensive, Auslese that would be best stored for a couple of decades.

Wehlener Sonnenuhr

One of Germany's most famous and finest vineyards, thanks to the elegant and sophisticated Rieslings produced here. The Sonnenuhr is a precipitously steep and rocky, south-exposed vineyard with virtually no topsoil but purest blue slate, which gives purity and delicate acidity to the wine to balance the ripe and juicy yet refined fruit. Loosen describes a typical Sonnenuhr wine as "an aristocratic and charming palate-dancer." Due to *Flurbereinigung*, his formerly 186 different parcels came down (happily) to 10 in 2011.

2010 Riesling Spätlese ★ The nose is predestined for a long and famous career; clear, with bright fruit flavors and the steam of raindrops evaporating on warm (blue or gray) slate tiles in summer. This is the kind of wine you drink when you are thirsty but that makes you more thirsty the more you drink. Pure, mineral, and spicy, this is a signature Riesling of the Mosel with just 7.5% ABV. Drink now and forever.

Weingut Dr. Loosen

Area under vine: 40 acres (16ha) or 54 acres (22ha)
Average production: 190,000 bottles
St Johannishof 1, 54470 Bernkastel
Tel: +49 6531 3426
www.drloosen.de

Weingut Joh Jos Prüm

To drink a Riesling from Joh Jos Prüm is to enjoy a springtime of the heart and mind. These distinctively floral wines from top sites in Bernkastel, Graach, Wehlen, and Zeltingen have a unique combination of lightness, finesse, elegance, and (most of all) energy that has set the stylistic template for delicately sweet and piquant Mosel wines for nearly a century. No matter what kind of mood you are in, the world always seems a better place with a glass of Prüm in hand; these are gracious, charming, wines that go straight to the heart, leaving you only with the desire to finish the bottle quickly, resolving to finish a second bottle more slowly and reflectively. Consequently, my notes on the numerous wines I've tried from this world-famous estate are best described as "brief."

In other words, the wines of JJ Prüm transform professional, dispassionate critics into hedonistic epicures, and I suspect that this is the intention. When you are invited to share your thoughts with the family in the estate close to the Mosel in Wehlen, you find that you are drinking, rather than tasting: each bottle, which is always served without any indication of its age, must be finished before another is opened. And if you ask the friendly Dr. Manfred Prüm about his philosophy, you will most likely see him smiling mildly, a twinkle in his eye, as he raises his glass as if to say, "To give pleasure."

The Joh Jos [Johann Josef] Prüm estate came into being in 1911, the result of a division of the long-established original estate (SA Prüm today), and over three generations it has developed its X factor: a unique combination of purity, delicacy, charm, and eternal vitality. Since 2003, owner Dr. Manfred Prüm, who took control in 1969, has been working with his daughter, Dr. Katharina Prüm, the fourth generation. The wine style remains unchanged.

Although the family portfolio includes numerous vineyards, the Graacher Himmelreich (21 acres [8.5ha]) and, particularly, the Wehlener Sonnenuhr (18.5 acres [7.5ha]) are the most

important when it comes to both quantity and quality or style. Whereas the Himmelreich yields very clear, filigreed, and dancing Rieslings, the illustrious Wehlener Sonnenuhr produces the most sensual, elegant, complex, and iconic wines, which are widely associated with the estate. The well-weathered blue-gray slate soils of the steep and particularly rugged south/southwest site are deeply penetrated by the roots of mainly ungrafted vines that are still trained and bound on poles. Viticulture is almost organic and aims for healthy, well-balanced vines. Yields are kept "neither too high nor too low,"

Above: Dr. Manfred Prüm and his daughter Dr. Katharina Prüm, whose family estate has long produced legendary wines

says Katharina, who prefers a long ripening period to intensify the aromas of the berries. Harvest is always late and starts with the picking of the beloved Kabinett, which is always light and crisp.

Generally, Katharina emphasizes the different predicates, which she defines not as quality levels but different wine styles. All the wines have a perfect level of residual sugar; they are all fresh, vivid, and low in alcohol, retaining an affinity with food even as standard Auslese. The gold-capsuled (abbreviated to GK) finest Auslese or the choice long gold cap (LGK) Auslese are richer and more concentrated, delicious with dessert or cheese. It is these wines on which the estate built its great reputation, and they still fetch extremely high prices at the annual auction in Trier. BA and TBA are produced only when they will be completely convincing; and, while the prices are too steep for all but the richest collector, one can always commit their taste to memory at the pre-auction tastings.

In the past, the wines of JJ Prüm could be closed and quite off-putting when young, and it was not always easy even for professionals to appreciate their full potential. This was mainly due to the reductive vinification in combination with spontaneous fermentation (rather than the result of an excessive addition of sulfur dioxide, as was often misleadingly maintained). However, the series of extraordinarily warm and ripe vintages of the last decade resulted in richer, more succulent wines that are more immediately accessible.

That said, Prüm wines are still not designed for drinking young. Their incredible longevity means they are able not only to hold their freshness and drinkability but to pass through numerous stages of maturation. These are characterized by the reduction in sweetness and fruit intensity and the increase in mineral spiciness and an increasingly dry taste. Even a Kabinett is best consumed five years after harvest, though it is still delicious after 20 years. Spätlesen can easily age 30 years, whereas gold-capsuled Auslesen are most stunning after 30–40 years when served, for example, with venison. BAs and TBAs can age for more than 50 years and develop an inimitable combination of richness and fullness with finesse and vibrancy.

"Our wines benefit from being decanted no matter if one likes to enjoy a younger or a mature wine," says Katharina. "Fifteen minutes, three to four hours, or even one day, depending on the wine and the vintage, can improve the wine significantly. The main thing, though, is to keep the carafe cool."

FINEST WINES

(Tasted in January 2012 and September 2010)
2007 Wehlener Sonnenuhr Riesling Kabinett ★
White-yellow color. Delicate bouquet of perfectly ripe Riesling grapes, still fresh and subtle and with hints of slate. The attack is racy yet very refined. Generous and delicate fruit of sublime ripeness; full, though the wine is filigreed and piquant, with an animating salinity. It is light and moderately sweet, with pure grape flavors and a delicious, harmonious, and sensual taste of great finesse.

2004 Wehlener Sonnenuhr Spätlese
From a cooler, often-underrated vintage. Bright white gold. Very precise, fresh, and elegant on the nose, showing delicate fruit, flavored by subtle slaty and herbal aromas. Racy attack on the palate; light, clear, and cheerful; thrillingly mineral. The moderate sweetness gives this rather firm, piquant, and salty wine a charming fruitiness and juiciness. Very elegant and pure, quite direct, with good grip and length. Still on its way.

2009 Wehlener Sonnenuhr Spätlese (auction) ★
Clear and very refined bouquet, with floral flavors. Firm, yet slender and racy structured sensual fullness. Elegant. Delicate fruit finesse.

1995 Wehlener Sonnenuhr Riesling Auslese
Golden yellow. Juicy, delicate, and vibrant on the palate, with a slaty, piquant minerality and a medium sweetness, this is a cheerful, light-footed, grippy and animating Auslese, with persistent salinity and good fruit intensity. Benefits a lot from being decanted for several hours.

2009 Wehlener Sonnenuhr Riesling Auslese (auction) ★
Finest fruit aromas, with a noble slate flavor—very precise. Brilliant palate; delicate sweetness completely dissolved by the salty minerality and delicate raciness. Perfectly balanced and elegant, a typical JJ Prüm Sonnenuhr of the highest level—a noble drug.

2003 Wehlener Sonnenuhr Riesling Auslese GK ★
Chamomile and mint aromas. Very rich, sweet, and elegant, this elixir flows over the palate like a calm river over its bed and will do so for decades.

1994 Wehlener Sonnenuhr Riesling Beerenauslese (auction) ★
Grand, highly noble BA of inexplicable delicacy and finesse. Extremely clear and precise on nose and palate; amazingly cheerful.

Weingut Joh Jos Prüm
Area under vine: 50 acres (20ha)
Annual production: 180,000 bottles
Best sites: *Wehlen* Sonnenuhr;
Graach Himmelreich
Uferallee 19, 54470 Bernkastel-Wehlen
Tel: +49 6531 3091
www.jjpruem.com

Weingut Van Volxem

Light, fragrant, harmonious, salubrious,"—Roman Niewodniczanski never tires of emphasizing the characteristics that have always made Saar wines unique. "We have the tradition and the responsibility to produce some of the world's finest Rieslings—and these should not be dry," Niewodniczanski says.

A great-grandson of the founder of the German Bitburger brewery, Niewodniczanski is a fiery wine enthusiast. While his brother Jan became manufacturing director of the brewery, Roman's vision was to revive the kind of Saar Rieslings that had been so appreciated a century ago, fetching higher prices than Bordeaux first growths. "Those wines were neither dry nor sweet but something in between, although they tasted rather

Roman's vision was to revive the kind of Saar Rieslings that had been so appreciated a century ago, fetching higher prices than Bordeaux first growths

dry," Niewodniczanski says. "Their fascinating character was defined by origin and vintage rather than analytical data. The pronounced acidity and minerality of Saar Rieslings needs some residual sugar to get the balance right and to give quaffable reflections of our unique terroirs."

To understand which sites were considered great in the Saar's illustrious past, Niewodniczanski consulted a 19th-century Prussian tax map. It highlighted the best vineyards, many of which had been forgotten in the 20th century. After the Niewodniczanski family bought and restored Weingut Van Volxem in 2000, Roman started to "collect" once-famous sites, all of them on steep slate slopes, restoring the vineyards with great passion and at considerable expense, before finally realizing his vision of Saar grands crus.

In just a decade, he extended the area under vine to 104 acres (42ha), including renowned grands crus such as Altenberg in Kanzem; Scharzhofberger, Volz, and Gottesfuss in Wiltingen; and Goldberg in Wawern. The latter is a 35-acre (14ha) cru that Niewodniczanski bought in its entirety from several different producers. He left just 7.5 acres (3ha) of old Riesling vines untouched, but the rest was pulled out completely, since it was planted with what he calls (in characteristically blunt fashion) "shit grapes" such as Dornfelder, Müller-Thurgau, and Kerner. "The site was used as an unregulated rubbish tip, too, so we had to get all the trash out. Then bulldozers reorganized the site, including the exposition of some parcels, and we brought innumerable truckloads of compost in to prepare the soil for new plantations." Many of the parcels in the other sites are really old, some with ungrafted pre-phylloxera vines up to 130 years old, Niewodniczanski says. Even the 150,000 bottles of the delicious estate Riesling Saar is from vines that are at least 30 years old, whereas Alte Reben means 50 years old and more.

Up to 45 workers care for the vines, which are cultivated organically. Because he makes all his wines in a very traditional way and without any additives, Niewodniczanski aims for healthy yet fully ripe berries of golden-yellow color and, for the crus, with a maximum must weight of 100 Oechsle. Therefore, he has replanted not clones but massal selections of the oldest vines in the Saar and Mosel valleys. The large part of the natural low-yielding vines has loose-fitting bunches with berries as small as peas. Harvest is always very late (October/November) and rigorously selective.

At the winery, the grapes are inspected again on sorting tables. When I last visited the estate, I saw a dozen workers selecting grapes, breaking out single grapes and sorting grape by grape for the predicates. After some hours of maceration, the juice is pressed either in a pneumatic press or in a giant high-tech basket press and, after settlement, fermented with indigenous yeasts in stainless steel or 120–2,400-liter barrels made from oak trees in the family's 12,350-acre (5,000ha) forest in the Eifel. No additives are used, since Niewodniczanski's goal is to produce authentic Saar wines. Fermentation can last several months, and even then the wines are kept on the lees until Niewodniczanski and his brilliant cellar master Dominik Völk decide to rack. The barrel-fermented grands crus are generally sold out even before they've been bottled (unfined). The estate wines sell out soon after release.

Although Van Volxem's Rieslings taste completely different from the wines of, say, Egon Müller, they are of extremely high quality. The bouquet recalls ripe and yellow fruits such as peach, apricot, passion fruit, and papaya in a wine that is mostly about slate and the specific character of the different sites. *Prädikatsweine* are rare but beautiful: delicate, piquant, salty, and of great intensity. The grands crus are full, ripe, intense, and creamy when young, yet also pure, piquant, and mineral. They taste much less sweet than you might expect but, with 10–12% ABV and sugar levels at 9–14g/l, less dry than you might think. If you're lucky enough to get your hands on some crus from this estate, you should store them for at least five or six years to allow them to assume ever-higher levels of typicity, complexity, and drinking pleasure.

FINEST WINES

2010 Altenberg Alte Reben ★
Dense and complex on the nose, yet also clear and with earthy-floral aromas. Full and supple on the palate but firmly structured and complex. Vibrant and elegant. The piquant raciness and thrilling minerality mean it tastes drier than it really is; it will be a delicious table wine one day.

2010 Gottesfuss Alte Reben ★
From vines planted in 1880. Very concentrated on the nose: pure Riesling, fully ripe yet precise, floral and spicy. Succulent and intense on the palate; dense, piquant, and firm, but also fine, elegant, and very long due to its amazing salty finish.

2010 Goldberg
Subtle yet intense; spicy, ripe golden Riesling grapes dressed in yeasty veils. Full and succulent on the palate, quite powerful and sweet; well structured, piquant, and racy, with good length.

2004 Scharzhofberger P
(tasted in June 2010) This is from the Pergentsknopp parcel. Clear, ripe, and deep on the nose, showing earthy, floral, and herbal slate aromas in combination with fruity scents of oranges and cooked peaches. Noble and perfectly balanced on the creamy-textured palate, but there is also subtlety, finesse, and elegance, as well as a lingering salinity in the finish. Very complex and just beginning to show its full potential.

Weingut Van Volxem
Area under vine: 104 acres (42ha)
Average production: 220,000 bottles
Dehenstrasse 2
54459 Wiltingen
Tel: +49 650 116 510
www.vanvolxem.de

Weingut Clemens Busch

Light-footed as a gazelle, Clemens Busch jumps between his stone terraces. He wants to show me the terroir between the closely planted vines on poles, which is the source of his inspiration and the foundation of his family's life: the Pündericher Marienburg—at its heart, one of the most privileged vineyards on the Mosel.

Here you will find 25 acres (10ha) of the total of 32 acres (13ha) of vineyards farmed by Clemens, his wife Rita, and their son Florian. The site, based on gray slate, includes almost the entire hillside across the river of Pünderich and since 1971, curiously enough, also the flat area around the village on the right bank of the Mosel, where there is no slate at all. The original Marienburg faces south/southeast and rises to 50–70 percent at its steepest. It is very rocky, divided into numerous parcels, and mostly terraced.

To cultivate these vineyards demands a lot from the growers. The construction of the very small terraces alone must have cost blood, sweat, and tears, while machines, which would alleviate at least some of the effort, cannot be used in the Marienburg. Economically speaking, cultivation here is apt, at best, to manage meager profitability—and the Busch family makes things even more costly by insisting on farming biodynamically.

In eco-viticulture, the vines need far more attention from the grower than in conventional production, particularly on the Mosel, where the climatic situation is far less stable than in the Rhine Valley. In average vintages, Clemens Busch climbs through his vineyards every seven to ten days (significantly more in wet years) to spray biological agents, especially herbal tea, against fungal disease.

"Sometimes, we ask ourselves whether it makes sense to work as painstakingly as we do," Clemens says. But he believes that going organic is "the only possible way to our style and our idea of high quality [...]. Only then can the wine be authentic and true to the individual origin and the natural grape flavor."

Clemens's idea of authenticity is reflected in the fact that he has divided the Marienburg into various terroirs, just as it used to be before 1971, when the site consisted of several small *Einzellagen*. "The individual designations were absolutely justified," says Clemens, who has discovered over the years that the wines from different parts of today's Marienburg taste very different. "Not only the different types of slate—gray, red, blue—play a major role, but also the specific microclimates that are influenced by fissures, vineyard walls, different degrees of inclination of the slope, and exposure."

To highlight these differences in Marienburg, of which 12 acres (5ha) are classified Grosse Lage by the VDP, each parcel is picked, fermented, and bottled separately, and the appropriate wines are labeled under the name of old parcel designations.

- Fahrlay: Dominated by blue slate, this site delivers concentrated, mineral, and spicy Rieslings.
- Falkenlay: The sheltered fillet of Marienburg, where the vines root in deep gray slate soils, leads to rich dry or medium-dry Rieslings, with refined minerality and finest Auslesen and higher.
- Raffes: Spectacular selection from the oldest, terraced section of the Falkenlay, which provides a particularly firm, dense, and complex wine.
- Rothenpfad: A 2.7-acre (1.1ha) parcel that was replanted a couple of years ago but also has a good number of very old vines. The red shale soils give particularly spicy and delicate GG, as well as the lighter estate wine Riesling vom roten Schiefer.
- Marienburg: The original area of the Marienburg Erste Lage (it will be renamed Grosse Lage very soon) is dominated by gray slate and gives powerful and very complex Rieslings such as the GG, which is sourced from the oldest vines, or its second wine, Riesling vom grauen Schiefer.

The personable family produces mainly Riesling with the main focus on expressive, full-bodied, dry or medium-dry grands crus harvested as late as mid-November and characterized by their

Above: Clemens Busch, his wife Rita, and their son Florian, whose organic methods help them express their complex terroirs

depth, density, concentration, and complex (merciless) minerality. Sweet and noble sweet *Prädikatsweine*—from Kabinett to TBA—are also produced. The Auslesen and higher predicates, however, are absolutely world-class, especially the highly noble, focused, yet subtle selections from the different mini-crus. Naturally, they are very rare and rather expensive, especially the lovely, intense, and incredibly refined gold-capsuled wines. All the wines are fermented spontaneously over several months, most of them in traditional *Fuder* of 1,000 liters. They are bottled without fining and released in the September after the harvest.

FINEST WINES

Marienburg Felsterrasse
One of the estate's most fascinating wines, and one of the finest dry to medium-dry Rieslings in Germany. Rare. Sourced from a small, wild, yet terraced parcel, with very old vines (at least 75 years old, most of them ungrafted) that send their roots into bright gray slate soils rich in iron but much less decomposed than in other parts of Marienburg. It's hard enough to visit, let alone cultivate. The Riesling is always deep and concentrated but also intensely mineral, very elegant, and, in a great vintage like 2010★, cheerful, too. Beautifully balanced due to a charming touch of unfermented sugar, this wine is great to drink now but will get much more complex with bottle age. The 2009★ is rich and succulent but very pure, precise, and salty—a melting rock, if you will, but much more subtle and complex.

Marienburg Raffes
This highly complex Riesling needs several years to develop its full potential and time (at least a day or so) in the decanter when young. Extremely rare and relatively expensive. The 2010★ is fresh and zesty on the nose, with herbal aromas. Clear, succulent, and elegant on the palate, but also very piquant, dense, and firmly structured. It is drier and edgier than the Felsterrasse and more powerful, although analytically there is less alcohol in the Raffes (13.5%, instead of 14% ABV). Great wine, with enormous aging potential. The 2008★ is significantly cooler, greener, and spicier on the nose than the 2009. But the wine is dense and complex, the slaty raciness very delicate, and the salinity no less intense than in the 2009. An elegant and refined wine, with an impressively lingering minerality. Great.

Weingut Clemens Busch
Area under vine: 32 acres (13ha)
Annual production: 80,000 bottles
Best site: *Pünderich* Marienburg
Kirchstrasse 37, 56862 Pünderich
Tel: +49 654 222 180
www.clemens-busch.de

Weingut Forstmeister Geltz-Zilliken

On 27 acres (11ha), Hans-Joachim Zilliken, known as Hanno, produces a varied range of characteristic Saar Rieslings. With the exception of one wine—Ockfener Bockstein—they are all from the top-class Saarburger Rausch vineyard and belong to German wine's highest class. After the *Gutsweine* and the Saarburger village wines—which are all produced as dry, medium-dry, and sweet—comes the Rausch Grosses Gewächs and its off-dry twin Diabas, and then the estate's pinnacle: Zilliken's sweet and noble-sweet *Prädikatsweine*, which are incomparable, especially the Spätlese and the Auslese.

"Our goal is to produce Rieslings with the highest level of finesse and lightness," says Geisenheim-trained Dorothee Zilliken, who joined her father in 2007. And this they achieve; although the fruit and sweetness of the Zilliken wines is extremely concentrated, they seem to be almost weightless, always finishing invitingly fresh.

To me, Zilliken's wines are surrounded by an aura of mystery that defines them very clearly. Part of the explanation can be found in the Rausch. The steep and well-protected south-/southwest-facing site, in a tributary of the Saar due north of the village of Saarburg, where Zilliken holds 25 acres (10ha), is mainly characterized by its unique soil: fine-petaled, well-weathered gray Devonian slate and a significant portion of green-colored volcanics known as Diabas. Hanno and Dorothee believe it is the latter that makes it different from all other Saar wines. "The Diabas lends the Rausch wines a particular elegance, finesse, precision, and marked acidity," Dorothee says.

Indeed, the acidity is strikingly nervous but articulated delicately and gives the Zilliken wines an unmistakable piquancy. But there is something else—a unique zest, something ethereal, a cool flavor of a dark and humid forest. Psychology always has a role to play in wine tasting, and I've sometimes wondered if I've detected this special wooden tone just because of the estate's name (*Forstmeister* literally means forester). But ten years ago, when Hanno took me three stories below ground to his cellar, I recognized the volatile flavors at once. I understood at that moment that it wasn't only the Rausch and its meticulous cultivation that shapes the Rieslings of Hanno Zilliken. This cool and damp cellar (always 50°F [10°C], always 100 percent humidity)—with its almost mystical ambience, its numerous dark German *Fuder* barrels, in which the wines are fermented (mostly spontaneously) and aged, and its rows of bottles containing older vintages—also plays a part in defining the style.

Although the lush yet precise, refined, and elegant Zilliken wines are extremely attractive when young, I prefer the succulent sweet Spätlese when it is ten or 15 years old, or the even finer, more concentrated and sophisticated Auslese when it is 15–20 years old. "With aging," explains Hanno, "sweetness becomes less intense, whereas the smoky notes become more prominent and the mineral intensity increases. Sweetness and acidity melt together into a homogeneous whole then, while new elements start to break through. In the end, the wine tastes almost dry. As long as body and extract balance the developed aromas, sweetness, and acidity, it stays alive" (*Tong* 9).

When I taste mature vintages from the early 1990s or before, I find something that has been missing in more recent vintages, which tend to be richer, rounder, and more pleasing when young. This might change with bottle age, but in my view, the consolidation and reallocation of Rausch from 1999 to 2008 has not been without consequence for the wines. The Zillikens had to replant about 17 acres (7ha)—the other 7.5 acres (3ha) are still planted with 50- to 100-year-old vines. They also started to train their vines onto wires instead of poles. Combined with climate change, this may have led to a slight shift in style: richer and more tropical but less cool, fresh, silky, zesty, and ethereal.

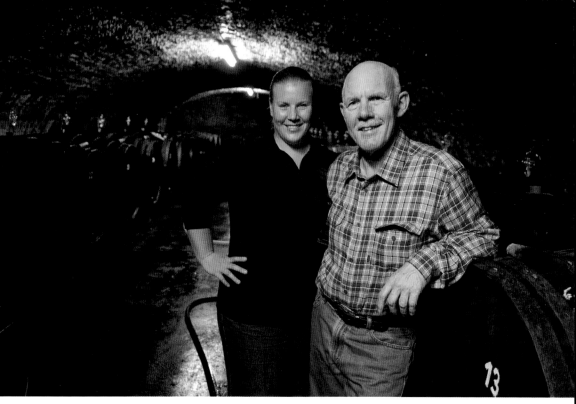

Above: Hans-Joachim Zilliken and his daughter Dorothee, who produce brilliant, racy wines from one of the Saar's top sites

FINEST WINES

(Tasted in February 2012)
Zilliken's Rieslings are always brilliant and marked by a racy yet filigreed acidity and lingering salinity that guarantees extraordinary longevity and an increasingly full-flavored, multilayered taste.

2010 Saarburger Rausch Spätlese ★
Bright color. This is an alluringly lush Auslese presented as Spätlese. Very clear, zesty, and cool on the nose, precise aromas of lovely raisins and tropical fruits such as pineapple. Super-clear and dense on the palate, driven by a brilliant, racy acidity and lingering salty structure. Monolithic and rich, yet still light and inviting and very well balanced, this is an addictive experience.

1997 Saarburger Rausch Spätlese ★
Greenish gleaming white gold. After decanting, a beautifully mature Riesling, with fully ripe Riesling aromas and the typical ethereal aromas of the Zilliken cellar, with a touch of caramel. Mellow and sweet on the palate but drier than the 2010 today. Very delicate and filigreed, with spicy and grippy tannins and a refined yet still racy and piquant acidity, which is completely dissolved by the noble fruit flesh. Seductively spicy. Perfect food wine.

2010 Saarburger Rausch Auslese
Dense, intense, and topical on the nose; noble. Very succulent and mineral, with a concentrated fruit texture. A thrilling Auslese.

2010 Saarburger Rausch Auslese GK ★
Very clear, pure, piquant, and filigreed on the nose. Dancing on the tongue, showing lovely finesse and elegance. Silky texture despite its enormous concentration and sweetness. Piquant and lingering salty finish. Extremely appetizing. Grand.

2003 Saarburger Rausch Trockenbeerenauslese (auction) ★
A fine and noble TBA, with fresh tropical-fruit aromas on the nose. Very sweet, rich, and elegant, with a viscous texture, yet cheerful and piquant at the same time. Great potential still to develop for many decades. Unforgettable.

Weingut Forstmeister Geltz-Zilliken
Area under vine: 27 acres (11ha)
Annual production: 60,000–70,000 bottles
Best site: *Saarburg* Rausch
Hecking Strasse 20, 54439 Saarburg
Tel: +49 6581 2456
www.zilliken-vdp.de

Weingut Fritz Haag

Wilhelm Haag was once asked for his views on what characterizes great Riesling. His whimsical but vivid response says much about the man and his wines: a Riesling, he said, is great "when you want to take a bath in it." Haag is the man who, over a period of almost 50 years, made Weingut Fritz Haag one of the world's outstanding Riesling producers. His charming wines from the grands crus Juffer and Juffer Sonnenuhr in Brauneberg were of an inimitable clarity, delicacy, fragility, elegance, and eternal youth. Although Haag retired officially in 2005, passing responsibilty to his younger son Oliver (his elder son Thomas runs the Schloss Lieser estate in the neighboring village) he is, thankfully, still part of the family estate. But his presence has not hindered Oliver, who has gone about the task of following a living legend undaunted and with great passion, clear thinking, and admirable sensitivity to the changing needs of the global market, of climate change, and of his own discoveries and preferences.

With the change from Wilhelm to Oliver, the wines of Fritz Haag have shifted in much the same way as Viennese classical music developed from Haydn and Mozart to Beethoven and Schubert. Still part of the same family, they have become more contemporary: riper, fuller, meatier, rounder, more intense, powerful, and complex. Whereas Wilhelm believed dry Rieslings from Brauneberg were a "mission impossible" ten years ago, he says (perhaps with slight exaggeration) that 60–70 percent of the estate's production is dry today. This is due to a combination of factors, such as climate change, modern viticulture with canopy management, longer hang-time, and better selection, with a larger harvest team picking each parcel two or three times. Nearly all vines are trained on to wires today, so that they can be accessed by both labor and machinery and the crop can be harvested easily. Even more crucial, though, Oliver says, is the improvement in the balance between leaf and fruit.

The estate bottles a complete range of wines— from generic estate Rieslings, to the Grosses Gewächs and through all *Prädikate*. Gold-capsuled high-octane wines fetch the highest prices at the annual auction in Trier and are among the most beautiful, mystical wines on earth.

You don't have to spend a fortune here, though. The unique combination of ripeness, flavor, and purity is also found in the Kabinett and Spätlese wines when sourced from the classified crus Juffer (where the family holds 16 acres [6.5ha]) and Juffer Sonnenuhr (7.5 acres [3ha]). The latter's 26-acre (10.5ha) area is located in the rocky center of the 78-acre (31.5ha) Juffer and runs up the hillside with a breathtaking gradient of up to 80 percent. The deep, well-weathered or shallow, stony slate soils and the concave depression create a special microclimate that leads to ripe, full-flavored, and mineral-structured wines. The adjacent Juffer vineyard has slightly heavier soils, so the wines are a little bit less refined, filigreed, and multifaceted than the Sonnenuhr but still of excellent quality.

FINEST WINES

Brauneberger Kabinett [V]

This is one of my favorite Fritz Haag wines, and the glass is always finished before I've even started thinking about it. The ripe grapes are sourced from both crus (Juffer and Juffer Sonnenuhr), but the fermentation is stopped before the sugar is completely transformed into alcohol, leading to a light, fresh, delicate, medium-dry wine, with piquant slate and intense fruit and a dancing raciness.

Brauneberg Juffer Sonnenuhr GG

The dry Grosses Gewächs can be quite rich, dense, and powerful; the 2010 needs a couple of years to show that it is, indeed, not a wine from the Pfalz. The 2009★, however, is bright, floral, and fine-boned, displaying fine yet intense Riesling flavors combined with a transparent texture and fascinating purity. Very persistent and with great potential for aging.

Above: Wilhelm Haag and his younger son Oliver, who is taking the wines of this famous family estate in a drier direction

Brauneberg Juffer Sonnenuhr Spätlese

Always ripe, succulent, and intense, this is a sensual, erotic wine based on slate, piquant spiciness, and raciness. It is so filigreed, deep, and alluring that you can hardly stop drinking it. Oliver poured me some riper vintages in January 2012: the **2004** is lean, sleek, and filigreed, with subtle fruit flavors and a delicate mineral acidity. Slight caramel notes announce the adolescence, whereas sweetness and the pronounced acidity still proclaim eternal juvenility. The **2003** is enormously juicy and still will be in 20–30 years, whereas **1999★** has now reached a prefect drinking age: very clear and floral-slaty on the nose and revitalizing on the palate, this wine is less sweet than its modern successors, but the elegant raciness and piquant minerality make it extremely delicate and delicious to drink now and in 20 years.

Brauneberg Juffer Sonnenuhr Auslese

The lunacy continues with a wine style based on fully ripe Riesling grapes and combining intense and concentrated fresh fruit flavors with lightness and delicacy. Is this really alcohol? The white-capsuled Auslese wines taste dangerously delicious when young but benefit from bottle age over 30 or 40 years. When the bottle has a gold capsule, you have a delicious result of the art of selection and fine winemaking. The hand-selected noble sweet top-quality wines are rich and intense, but the fruit is also fresh and remarkably refined, thanks to the slaty flavors and the low alcohol. If the gold capsule is long, it covers the finest and most concentrated Auslese possible. It is very rare and highly expensive but well worth the extravagance. I remember two wines I tasted in September 2010. The **2009 gold cap** was very subtle and fine, matching tropical-fruit flavors and intensity with a cool and slaty piquancy. The **2009 long gold cap★** was exceptionally noble, extremely elegant and perfectly balanced, characterized by the finest raisin aromas and flavors. An eternal wine.

Weingut Fritz Haag

Area under vine: 40.5 acres (16.5ha)
Annual production: 125,000 bottles
Best sites: *Brauneberg* Juffer, Juffer Sonnenuhr
Dusemonder Strasse 44
54472 Brauneberg
Tel: +49 6534 1347
www.weingut-fritz.haag.de

Weingut Heymann-Löwenstein

Heymann-Löwenstein is one of the most controversial wine estates in Germany. There is no argument about the excellent quality of the Rieslings produced in the Lower Mosel called "Terrassenmosel"; it is the rich and rather medium-dry style that wine freaks discuss. And it's not just the wines: Reinhard Löwenstein himself divides opinion. He expresses the terroir idea with a theoretical, multidisciplinary rigor unique in Germany. Not only has he written an ingenious and profound book on the subject (*Terroir*), he is also famously severe about it, being unwilling to dumb down complex cultural issues such as terroir or authentic wine. Correspondingly, most of his wines—rich, concentrated, complex, and demanding—are not designed for mass consumption, but they are never less than thrilling for those who take their time to attune to them intellectually and emotionally. Indeed, Löwenstein's Auslesen and higher predicates are world-class.

In and around Winningen, Löwenstein and his wife Cornelia cultivate 37 acres (15ha) of Riesling in some of the steepest and most spectacular sites of the Mosel. With inclinations of up to 115 percent, the innumerable small terraces appear to have been placed in layers on top of each other, which is why they are known as "hanging gardens."

Winninger Uhlen is perhaps the most complex site and gives the most fascinating wines. Stretching 1 mile (1.65km) in length, the 35-acre (14ha) site, in which Löwenstein holds 13.5 acres (5.5ha), defines a giant amphitheater exposed from southwest to southeast. The vines are well protected from cool fall winds by the forest at the top of the hillside. The mighty vineyard walls (13 miles [21km] in total) in combination with the stony topsoil not only help prevent erosion but store and reflect the heat of the sun, leading to very high soil and plant temperatures. Thus, physiological ripeness of the grapes is always guaranteed, due to the early budding and long ripening period. The resulting wines are always extremely ripe, very rich, and powerful but rarely dry. The 23.6in (600mm) of annual rainfall is "a good compromise between the needs of the vines and our goal to produce expressive terroir wines," says Löwenstein. As a wine grower—one who aims for deep roots so the vines subsist on the slate soils rather than added dung or irrigation—he regards himself as an integral component of his understanding of terroir.

Löwenstein is engrossed by the 400 million-year-old sea bed and its numerous sediments that, after they had become the Rhenish Massif, defined the ground on which he wants to make his wines sing. The microclimatic situation does not vary within Uhlen, but the sediments are extremely diverse, forming a total of seven different layers of slate. Löwenstein has divided the original site into three parts according to the slate formation. Thus, he produces three different Uhlen crus: Roth-Lay, Laubach, and Blaufüsser Lay. If you add the Röttgen, Stolzenberg, and Kirchberg, you have a grand cru sextet where each wine plays the same instrument—Riesling—but sounds entirely different.

All the wines are made from golden-yellow grapes with intense flavors and are crafted almost the same way. Must weight is often more than 100° Oechsle; in 2010, it was up to 120°. Yields are kept low (since 50 percent of the vines are ungrafted, there is not much crop anyway), and the grapes are handpicked (mostly in six weeks in October and November), lightly crushed, and macerated for 12–20 hours. Then the must is slowly pressed, filtered, and fermented spontaneously, mostly in large wooden *Fuder* casks (2,000–3,000 liters), normally until the following spring. In recent years, the wines (other than the nobly sweet among them) have undergone malolactic fermentation, though in the high-acid 2010 they would not, and in the end, Löwenstein was delighted with their delicious difference. The young wine is kept on lees at least until July, whereas the Roth-Lay usually needs more

Above: Reinhard Löwenstein and his wife Cornelia, who produce challenging, thrilling wines from some of the Mosel's best sites

than a year to ferment. All wines are bottled unfined and marketed about a year after harvest, except for the Roth-Lay, which is sold two years after harvest.

Roth-Lay is particularly suited to producing botrytis grapes, which makes it a perfect terroir for noble sweet *Prädikatsweine*. Like the medium-dry or medium grand vin—which is also made with a high proportion of botrytis grapes but is still characterized by its thrilling minerality—the Auslese is not only sweet but shows a distinctive, aristocratic salinity, as well as remarkable finesse and elegance. This is also explained by the very warm microclimate in the lower terraces close to the river, which can shrivel the overripe healthy berries to raisins without botrytis. Indeed, the finest *Prädikate*, such as the gold-capsuled Auslesen or the TBA, are often picked at the beginning of the harvest in October.

FINEST WINES

If you just want to get a sensual idea about the wines from the terraced part of the Lower Mosel, the **Schieferterrasen** and the **vom blauen Schiefer [V]** are ideal. Both are floral, pure, piquant, relatively light, and inviting. If you are looking for a racy, sophisticated terroir wine that is great fun to drink due to its erotic fruitiness, the funky **Röttgen** is the one and only. If you prefer to engage with wine on an intellectual and spiritual level, the **Uhlen** trio should be your choice. The cold, pure, aristocratic, and highly complex **Roth-Lay** is from reddish, gray, and dark slate soils rich in hematites and quartzite. The zesty **2004★** is a very elegant, persistent, and expressively mineral wine that retains finesse—very promising. The **2010 Auslese gold cap★** mixes a lovely, pure, precise, and refined raisin aroma with cool and clear slate flavors; very subtle on the rich and sweet palate, yet balanced, almost filigreed and elegant—a delicious elixir full of finesse. The rather round yet compact, deep, and salty **Laubach** is from gray slate soils that are abnormally rich in calcium and lend the wine a full, silky body and a smoky-nutty aroma. The **2009 Auslese long gold cap★** displays purest botrytis aromas on the concentrated yet elegant and highly noble nose. The viscous texture amalgamates raisins, divine sweetness, and piquant acidity; perfect balance and elegance—grand. The **Blaufüsser Lay** from silt and clay blue-gray slate soils has a cool and piquant Riesling character that is marked by its salty and crystalline acidity and edgy minerality.

Weingut Heymann-Löwenstein
Area under vine: 37 acres (15ha)
Annual production: 100,000 bottles
Best sites: *Winningen* Uhlen; Röttgen
Bahnhof Strasse 10
Tel: +49 2606 1919
www.heymann-loewenstein.de

Weingut Schloss Lieser / Thomas Haag

Thomas Haag, son of Wilhelm Haag (Weingut Fritz Haag), is a quiet, humble, and likable man. As a wine grower, however, he is a star. Over the past 20 years, he has reestablished Schloss Lieser, step by step, as one of the finest Riesling producers in the Mosel. He started as operations manager in 1992, when the estate (founded in 1904) was in rather a bad way. Five years later, he and his wife Ute bought it, and Weingut Schloss Lieser again became the source of some of the most delicate and gracefully chiseled Rieslings.

Currently, 32 acres (13ha) of Riesling are cultivated in steep and very steep sites. While the parcels in Graacher Himmelreich and Lieser Schlossberg provide the grapes for the estate wines, the three grands crus—Niederberg Helden in Lieser, and Juffer and Juffer Sonnenuhr in Brauneberg—give dry Grosses Gewächs wines, as well as sweet and noble sweet wines with *Prädikat*.

Thomas bottles extremely clear, precise, lean, and elegant wines of great finesse and with an almost fragile structure. At the same time, they give impressive expressions of their origins

Whatever the quality level, Thomas bottles extremely clear, precise, lean, and elegant wines of great finesse and with an almost fragile structure. At the same time, they give impressive expressions of their origins and taste as accurate as Thomas is when shaping his thoughts and vineyards. The quality of his 2010s was through the roof, as it was in 2009, 2008, 2007, 2006...

Nearly all the vines are trained onto wires, which makes them easier and more efficient to manage, including a hard and early pruning, one of the ways in which yields are kept low. The grapes for each wine are picked at exactly the right time, then processed very gently. After they are slightly crushed and pressed, the settled musts for the off-dry wines ferment spontaneously, while the juice for the dry wines is inoculated. Fermentation takes place in stainless-steel tanks, since Thomas believes that steel preserves the acidity slightly better. "This is important to balance the higher Oechsle levels we get today and to keep the wines alive," he says. Alive? He certainly succeeds in that objective: his wines are always balanced and bright, full of electricity, energy, and tension.

While Wilhelm Haag at Fritz Haag did not have a great passion for dry Mosel Rieslings for many years ("Impossible!" he said to me in early 2004), his two sons have nevertheless shifted toward dry wines. At Schloss Lieser, 30–35 percent of the production is *trocken*, mainly to meet demand in Germany. The exported *feinherb* (medium) estate Kabinett accounts for 20 percent, and the rest is *feinfruchtig* (sweet) or *edelsüss* (noble sweet).

FINEST WINES

Lieser Niederberg Helden

Located next to the village of Lieser and the Mosel, this south-facing 62-acre (25ha) vineyard amphitheater, up to 80% steep, is characterized by its well-weathered blue slate soils, which provide a good water reservoir and yield deep, dense, and rather succulent Rieslings of grace and elegance. The Grosses Gewächs needs more time to open up than the Juffer Sonnenuhr, but the high-octane sweet wines are always impressive right from the beginning. Because the *Flurbereinigung* was finished by the end of the 1960s here, the vines are older than in Brauneberg, where consolidation took place 20 years later.

2010 Auslese (long gold cap) Clear, dense, and reductive on the nose. Transparent, small-boned, light, and dancing on the palate, almost weightless in its beautiful balance. Very elegant, refined, and animating.

1995 Auslese (gold cap) This delicate and graceful Auslese is a signature wine for the Schloss Lieser style. A very clear and refined nose, with subtle herbal aromas. Feathery and almost fragile on the palate, very elegant and balanced, yet also succulent and complex, with a delicate salinity.

2006 Beerenauslese A subtle spiciness on the nose, in combination with finest raisins. Honey-sweet yet delicate and elegant on the palate, nobly textured but with a fresh orange tang. Sleek and beautifully balanced.

Brauneberger Juffer & Juffer Sonnenuhr
Divided from the Niederberg Helden only by the small village of Lieser, the Juffer comprises almost 80 acres (32ha) and encloses the Juffer Sonnenuhr with 26 acres (10.5ha) in the center. The exposition, inclination, and soils are the same as in the Niederberg Helden, but the wines are nevertheless slightly different. The Juffer Sonnenuhr in particular, with its lighter soils, is inimitably subtle, refined, filigreed, and multifaceted.

2009 Brauneberger Juffer Kabinett [V]
This shows a terrific subtle spiciness on the nose. On the palate, it is elegant, salty, velvety, and quite complex—a superb Kabinett. The **2010** is light, delicately sweet and sappy, but enormously racy and piquant as well, and the finish celebrates a lingering minerality.

2009 Brauneberger Juffer Sonnenuhr Spätlese (auction)★ This is a signature wine not only for the Thomas Haag style but for the Spätlese predicate as a whole: exemplary elegance and refinement. It is clear and cool on the nose, then intense, vigorous, piquant, salty, spicy, and very long on the palate. In short, delicious, perfectly balanced, and very erotic.

2009 Brauneberger Juffer Sonnenuhr Auslese (long gold cap)★ This very noble, highly elegant and potent wine raises even more question marks than it does exclamation points. How can a highly concentrated Auslese be at once so clear, clean, cool, elegant, pure, earthy, slaty, and spicy—in short, so incredibly and inexpressibly beautiful?

Right: Thomas Haag, who left his family estate to recreate Schloss Leiser as a prime source of Mosel Riesling

Weingut Schloss Lieser / Thomas Haag
Area under vine: 32 acres (13ha)
Annual production: 100,000 bottles
Best sites: *Brauneberg* Juffer, Juffer Sonnenuhr; *Lieser* Niederberg Helden
Am Markt 1
54470 Lieser
Tel: +49 6531 6431
www.weingut-schloss-lieser.de

Weingut Sankt Urbans-Hof

Nicolaus Weis, the grandfather of Sankt Urbans-Hof's current owner Nik Weis, built this estate on a little hill near the village of Leiwen in 1947. Nik's father Hermann, one of Germany's most important grape breeders, then took up the reins, expanding the estate by purchasing additional top-quality vineyards on the Saar. Compared to many other top Mosel estates, then, the history of Sankt Urbans-Hof is relatively short. But its reputation could hardly be higher.

On 81.5 acres (33ha) of vines in the Middle Mosel and on the Saar, the family produces a wide range of remarkably light and filigreed Rieslings of exceptional elegance, finesse, and piquancy. These are classic Mosel Rieslings that dance over the palate like hard-rocking elves—imagine, if you can, Richard Wagner's *Ride of the Valkyries* played by a chamber orchestra, and you are almost there. The wines compel you to drink glass after glass, but thanks to the low alcohol and fair prices, they leave you neither drunk nor poor—unless you fall in love with an auctioned Auslese, BA, or TBA.

Nik's Rieslings can be reductive and show the maverick aromas of spontaneous fermentation when young. In this respect, they are not dissimilar to the delicious Kabinett, Spätlese, or Auslese wines of Joh Jos Prüm, though they are even more sophisticated, piquant, and spicy. Indeed, their style might be described as being halfway between the purity, transparency, and finesse of Scharzhof and the alluring charm and drinkability of Prüm. But however you describe it, the Nik Weis style, which he has been creating since taking over in 1997, is particular: always exciting and surely unrivaled.

The vineyards lay the foundation for the high-quality wines produced here; the cellar (run by Rudolf Hoffmann) merely puts the finishing touches to the viticultural work (guided by Hermann Jostock), bringing to life Nik's vision: "To express the unique character of a vineyard's origin in the taste of its wines due to a special combination of soil, microclimate, variety, tending, and human knowledge."

The family's holdings now include six *Einzellagen*. Of these, three are in the Saar: Wiltinger Schlangengraben, Schodener Saarfeilser Marienberg, and the VDP Grosse Lage Bockstein in Ockfen (a full 25 miles [40km] from Leiwen). The other three are in the Mosel: Mehringer Blattenberg and the Grosse Lagen Laurentiuslay in Leiwen and the world-famous Goldtröpfchen in Piesport. The genetic material for Riesling in these sites is very old. "This is why we replace our vines only when they die," explains Nik. "In some of our sites, ungrafted vines are over 80 years of age."

In the cellar, Nik and his team are minimalists. To preserve the individual vineyard character, modern technology including enzymes, synthetic fining agents, and other such chemicals are rejected in favor of traditional craftsmanship and natural methods. The cool cellar provides the best conditions for slow fermentations and the development of freshness, fruitiness, and aromatic flavors. Traditional 1,000-liter Mosel *Fuder* are used alongside stainless-steel tanks.

The range of wine styles runs the usual gamut from Qualitätswein to Kabinett and Auslese, with BA and TBA when the necessary proportion and purity of botrytis are reached. Except for some dry and medium-dry wines produced mainly for the German market, nearly all the other wines are sweet or noble sweet *Prädikatsweine*. "A special wine has a special character," explains Nik. "The delicately sweet fruitiness of a Mosel wine is as typical as bubbles in Champagne."

He is, therefore, content that his most important markets are overseas or in European markets that do not share the obstinate fixation on dry styles of Nik's compatriots, most of whom have still not fully understood, in Nik's words, that "the trio of residual sugar, crisp acidity, and minerality create a harmoniously juicy, fruity sensation."

Above: Nik Weis, who is realizing his vision of terroir-driven wines in Rieslings of exceptional elegance, finesse, and piquancy

FINEST WINES

Ockfener Bockstein

Although it has a southwest exposure and 50% slope, this site is in a side valley of the Saar and is influenced by cool winds coming down from the Hunsrück, so it produces aromatic grapes with fresh and floral aromas rather than high sugar levels—perfect for crisp Kabinett wines and characterful Spätlesen. The gravelly gray slate soils lend the wines a certain smokiness.

2010 Kabinett [V] This shows fresh lime and grapefruit aromas with a dense core. Piquant, crisp, and fruity on the palate; round, light, refined, and perfectly balanced. Pink grapefruit on the finish. Cheerful, appetizing, and promising.

2009 Spätlese ★ This displays floral aromas. Piquant, light, almost weightless, and cheerful on the juicy, salty, and perfectly balanced palate. Good length, extremely inviting. Absolutely delicious.

Leiwener Laurentiuslay

A very sunny site exposed south and southwest. Decomposed dark slate soils absorb the excessive heat during the day and release it during the cool of night. Good water-storage capacity. Grapes ripen early and contain higher sugar levels for more opulent, full-bodied wines.

2010 Spätlese A floral and mineral nose. Juicy and creamy in texture; quite intense, dense, and almost *trocken*, due to its piquancy and lingering minerality. Good length and potential.

2010 Auslese Subtle, yet concentrated and promising on the nose: pineapple, lime, and herbs. Succulent, concentrated, piquant palate, racy and salty, with a lingering minerality and fruitiness. Delicious. Very precise, well balanced, and long.

Piesporter Goldtröpfchen

Nik's ancient parcels host ungrafted vines that are probably at least 80 years old. The decomposed slate soil has a high water-storage capacity and the large slate cliffs absorb the heat of the sun and give it back at night. All the wines grown here have a natural sweetness, with passion-fruit and grapefruit aromas, and can stay fresh for more than 30 years.

2009 Auslese ★ Very refined and delicate on the nose, with floral and slaty aromas. Very filigreed, elegant, and beautifully balanced on the palate, this is a hymn to finesse and lightness; long, complex.

2010 Beerenauslese ★ Very noble, concentrated, and balanced on the nose—finest Riesling raisins. Very dense, yet delicate and precise on the palate. Refined acidity. Appetizing, filigreed, and long.

> **Weingut Sankt Urbans-Hof**
> Area under vine: 81.5 acres (33ha)
> Annual production: 250,000 bottles
> Best sites: *Leiwen* Laurentiuslay; *Piesport*
> Goldtröpfchen; *Ockfen* Bockstein
> Urbanus Strasse 16, 54340 Leiwen
> Tel: +49 650 793 770
> www.urbans-hof.com

Weingut Reinhold Haart

Karl-Theo Haart from Piesport is a quiet enthusiast. The first time you meet him, he seems reluctant to say anything much about his wines, sites, and thoughts. If you can avoid clichés and hackneyed phrases, however, his eyes and heart soon light up, and he begins to talk. Theo then seems even younger than his son Johannes—just happy to exchange his thoughts with somebody who shares his passion for naturally sweet Rieslings. When the ice is broken, he pours one great wine after another, and it is your turn to lie: enough!

It's not that Haart is an overlooked genius by any means. He has been running the traditional 18.5-acre (7.5ha) family estate with distinction since 1971, and he is widely accepted as one of the very best Riesling producers in Germany. But his wines have a personality that is much wilder and more expressive than his own nature (his marvelous beard aside). Indeed, even Haart's Kabinette are spicy-mineral,

Haart is widely accepted as one of the very best Riesling producers in Germany. But his wines have a personality that is much wilder and more expressive than his own nature

yeasty, and very complex; the Grosses Gewächs, where there is no sugar to hide behind, even more so. I personally like Haart's unpolished style, and it is amazing how extraordinarily fresh the wines are even ten, 15, or more years after bottling, especially when they are Piesporter Goldtröpfchen.

Although the family owns parcels in other top sites, such as Domherr or Ohligsberg, the 160-acre (65ha) Goldtröpfchen is the Hausberg of the Haarts, where the viticultural tradition has been documented since 1337; no wonder the family estate is one of the oldest private wine estates in Mosel. The bright-yellow-painted house is located on the left bank at the Ausoniusufer, just a few yards from

the Mosel. The famous Goldtröpfchen grand cru rises steeply behind the house. Goodness knows how much blood, sweat, and tears have flowed from vintners like Theo Haart to irrigate the vines here, which root in deep, weathered slate soils. Haart holds 10 acres (4ha) in the center of the site, which is exposed to the south, while slopes in the west and east protect from cold winds but never from sunlight—there is no shadow until sunset.

This leads to rich, succulent, and intense wines packed with ripe yellow and golden fruits, salty minerals, exotic spices, and vibrant acidity that structures even the higher predicates and holds the complex whole in a taut balance. The natural sweetness is never sticky but amplifies the luscious fruit and lends the wines an extraordinary longevity. Curiously, these wines taste drier than they really are after a couple of years. The dry wines, particularly the promising GG, need four or five years to start the journey toward their as-yet-unknown destination.

FINEST WINES

2010 Piesporter Goldtröpfchen Kabinett [V] ★
Yellow-golden color. Light, delicate structure, playful in nature. Lavish abundance of brilliant fruit with refined raciness and piquant spices. The Spätlese is even more lush and persistent, but can a Kabinett be more succulent, sensual, or beautiful without losing its light-hearted soul?

2009 Piesporter Goldtröpfchen Auslese
Perfectly balanced, almost levitating, graceful, noble; earthy-slaty flavors and striking salinity.

1994 Piesporter Goldtröpfchen Auslese (auction wine) ★
Dried-apple nose. Noble maturity, very delicate and elegant, subtle finesse, persistent. Delicious.

Weingut Reinhold Haart
Area under vine: 18.5 acres (7.5ha)
Annual production: 45,000 bottles
Ausoniusufer 18, 54498 Piesport
Tel: +49 6507 2015
www.haart.de

Weingut Peter Lauer

T his small traditional Saar wine producer in Ayl bottles some of the finest, most classic Rieslings in Germany: pure, precise, piquant, racy, mineral, and chiseled, but also ripe, concentrated, compact, and complex. Against the clichéd expectations for this area, and due to the particular terroirs of Devonian slate, they taste predominantly dry, though most of the wines are analytically medium-dry with 10–20g of residual sugar per liter. With moderate alcohol levels of 10–12.5%, they are enormously intense, expressive, and delicate, proving that terroir wines require neither higher alcohol levels nor legally dry analytical data. "Nature does not care about our strange wine law, and thus we do not force our wines to conform to state-defined flavors," says Florian Lauer, responsible for production since 2005.

In six different sites, each of them with a gradient of up to 90 percent, Lauer organically cultivates 20 acres (8ha) of Riesling. Since 1971, the former single-vineyard designations such as Scheidterberg, Rauberg, Schonfels, or Sonnenberg have been part of the famous but widely extended *Einzellage* Ayler Kupp (slate), whereas the small and homogeneous Saarfeilser (gravel) belongs to three demarcations: Ayl, Schoden, and Wiltingen. For Lauer, though, a large site such as Ayler Kupp has many different terroirs rather than a single, defining terroir character. Soil composition, exposition, altitude, inclination, and microclimate of the vineyards, in combination with the age of the vines and the harvest dates, all make crucial contributions to the individual character of the wines. Celebrating to the fullest Riesling's ability to reflect its origin, each of the better parcels (from 0.6 to 1.2 acres [0.25–0.5ha] in size) is picked and fermented separately, which leads to a bewildering number of different casks and wines (though fewer since Florian took over). Vinification is traditional.

Lauer's goal is to produce elegant and authentic Saar "wines for advanced Riesling lovers," and they are certainly not known for their easy charm. They are immediately thrilling, but you need to have patience with their purity and firm structure; they benefit a great deal from being decanted for several hours and from not being served too cool. The wines I describe below—just a small excerpt of what fascinates me here—were even more impressive five days after opening and at a serving temperature of 59–61 F (15–16°C), which is another reason why they would be my desert-island wines.

FINEST WINES

2010 Ayler Kupp Unterstenbersch Fass 12

This dense, mineral, and thrilling medium-bodied wine comes from the lowest part of the south-facing Ayler Kupp (Unterstenberg) and benefits from the well-weathered slate soils, which give it its striking character and complexity. A serious and mineral nose, with the aromatic Riesling flavors still kept under a thin yeast layer. Pure, dry, firm, grippy, and steely on the palate, yet very elegant and precise, with a ripe and intense fruit core. It develops an impressive and thrilling mineral and fruit-intense length, with an animating and persistent salty finish. Floral aromas on the aftertaste. Dry Saar Riesling at its best!

2010 Scheidt Beerenauslese ★

Although sourced from a lesser, flatter southeast-to east-facing site with lighter slate soils, this BA (one of a sensational six in 2010) is beautiful in its finesse, elegance, and balance. A marvelous nose of great nobility, intensity, and precision (raisins). Viscous and lush on the palate, but also pure, precise, and piquant in its racy minerality. Full of finesse, joy, and piquancy, ending with an animating salinity and clear, sweet, and intense fruit flavors of nectarines and peaches. A superb BA.

Weingut Peter Lauer
Area under vine: 20 acres (8ha)
Annual production: 35,000–75,000 bottles
(2010 and 2011 figures respectively)
Best sites: *Ayl* Kupp; Saarfeilser
Trierer Strasse 49, 54441 Ayl
Tel: +49 6581 3031
www.lauer-ayl.de

Maximin Grünhaus / C von Schubert

The venerable Maximin Grünhaus estate is at the bottom of a long, steep, south-facing slope on the left bank of the River Ruwer. It is managed by Dr. Carl von Schubert, whose family has owned the Schlosskellerei for five generations. The history of Maximin Grünhaus dates back even further, to at least 966, when vineyards were given to the Benedictine monastery of St. Maximin in Trier, which managed the estate until the late 18th century.

The Rieslings of Maximin Grünhaus—since the late-19th century labeled with the prominent *Jugendstil* (Art Nouveau) label—were always praised for their inimitable clarity, fragility, and finesse. Due to climate change and modern viticulture, however, the wines have become richer recently. More dry

The Rieslings of Maximin Grünhaus were always praised for their inimitable clarity, fragility, and finesse. The wines have become richer recently

Rieslings are produced these days, and the predicate wines have become sweeter. The Kabinett is picked with a must weight of 90° Oechsle and has 45–55g of residual sugar per liter to keep the alcohol level at 8 or 8.5% ABV. Twenty years ago, a wine like this would have been an Auslese, while the Auslese of today is concentrated and sweet, like a former BA. And Spätlese? With 70g/l of unfermented sugar, it is very intense and sweet, and you had better wait 20 years unless you want to serve it with dessert.

For more than 1,000 years, three contiguous monopoles have been cultivated here: Abtsberg, Herrenberg, and Bruderberg. The latter is the smallest and least favored vineyard, and it used to provide wine for the lay brothers. Herrenberg was reserved for the monks while wines from the Abtsberg were exclusively served at the table of the abbot. This was a very clear classification, and

it is still valid today through all the styles. Among the dry wines, the medium-dry or medium Superior is impressive, while among the *Prädikatsweine*, the Kabinett and Spätlese reflect the Grünhäuser terroir in the most delightful way.

FINEST WINES

Maximin-Grünhäuser Herrenberg
This 47-acre (19ha) southeast-facing "premier cru" is less steep and warm than the Abtsberg but benefits from deeper soils, with better water-storage capacity. The vines grow in reddish Devonian slate, which contributes to more full-bodied, supple, and fruity wines that are accessible soon after bottling. The **2006 Superior** is a sleek, elegant, and complex wine, deeply expressive and spicy, and a delicious partner with food due to its lingering mineral structure. The **2010 Spätlese** will need 15–20 years to reach its peak, although it is very attractive young. The nose mixes tropical-fruit aromas with floral and earthy aromas, while the palate is light, round, mellow, and tickled by the refined and salty raciness.

Maximin-Grünhäuser Abtsberg
Covering 35 acres (14ha), the grand cru inclines 40–70% and turns from southeast to southwest. The vines grow in blue Devonian slate and give extraordinarily fine and elegant Rieslings, which are delicately structured and marked by their racy acidity and distinctive slaty spiciness. The appetizing **2010 Kabinett** is delicately herbal and intense on the nose, while the palate is full, dense, succulent, and deep, and the body is light, racy, and mineral. The **2010 Spätlese★** is a great Abtsberg. Aloof, pure, cool, and aristocratic on the slaty nose, it is dense, piquant, precise, and salty. The sweetness is completely integrated, making Abtsberg intellectual rather than sensual. The **2010 Auslese #37★** is world-class: very discreet yet aristocratic on the nose, and beautifully precise, elegant, and piquant on the persistent palate.

C von Schubert'sche Gutsverwaltung Grünhaus
Area under vine: 75 acres (30ha)
Annual production: 180,000 bottles
Hauptstrasse 1, 54318 Mertesdorf
Tel: +49 651 5111
www.vonschubert.com

Weingut Willi Schaefer

Cult producer Willi Schaefer, whose family has practiced viniculture in Graach since 1121, cultivates no more than 10 acres (4ha) of vines, and his annual production of 35,000 bottles sells out quickly. Schaefer, who took over the family estate from his father in 1971 and has been assisted by his son Christoph since 2002, produces some of the Mosel's most fascinating wines. These are wines unmatched in their brightness, precision, and focus, combining ripe and generous fruit with purity, lightness, and finesse.

How can one account for such wines, which have a clarity that comes close to perfection? Schaefer's reply is rather more straightforward than his wines: "We make them as gently as possible and treat the grapes, the musts, and the wines with respect."

Many winemakers say the same thing, but few adhere to the principles as rigorously as Schaefer does. He treats all of his wines in exactly the same way—in the vineyards, as well as in the winery. The only discernible variations in taste are due to the different origins and the different wine styles, which require different selections. So, if you like Mozart and prefer a more fruity, charming, and accessible style, drink a Graacher Himmelreich. If you appreciate Beethoven or more slaty-mineral and linear wines to store and to drink later, the Graacher Domprobst is your choice. Both wines originate in Devonian blue slate soils, but their compositions vary. Whereas the Himmelreich has a lighter texture, the Domprobst is rockier.

A question of style rather than character arises at Schaefer: do you prefer Kabinett, which is always lighter (though not necessarily in alcohol) and less concentrated than a Spätlese; or do you prefer Spätlese, which is less intense than an Auslese; and so on. If you prefer a Grosses Gewächs, look elsewhere or understand that to err is human, even at Schaefer.

The Schaefers work meticulously in the vineyards and pay enormous attention to even the smallest details. "Since we aim for healthy and well-balanced fruit, we have to have healthy and balanced vines first," Willi says. The vines, incidentally, are quite old, at up to 60 years of age, and 60–70 percent of them are ungrafted. Thus, yields are rather low—but not too low, since otherwise the characteristic Schaefer finesse and lightness would be lost.

The most important tools the Schaefers possess are their tongues. They even taste water, which is filled into the old barrels for some days before harvest, to see if any bad flavors are lurking. At harvest, grapes are continuously tasted to help assess the optimum picking time; during the gentle whole-bunch pressing, the juice is tasted to decide when to stop pressing. Later, father and son repeatedly taste each 1,000-liter *Fuder* to decide when to stop the natural fermentation, and after racking on to the fine lees, the wines are tasted once again to discern the right moment to finish the *élevage*.

The results are sapid antidepressants and stunning reflections of the Graacher terroirs (of which, by the way, I prefer the Beethoven site).

FINEST WINES

2007 Graacher Domprobst Riesling Spätlese (auction)
A fresh, spicy, and cool nose. Elegant and racy on the palate; perfectly balanced, graceful, and pure.

2007 Graacher Domprobst Riesling Auslese (auction)
Piquant on the nose, cool and spicy, and still dominated by the rocky slate rather than fruit. An erotic palate: full, elegant and sensual, but countered by the racy acidity. Persistent and addictive. Dangerous.

Weingut Willi Schaefer
Area under vine: 10 acres (4ha)
Annual production: 35,000 bottles
Best sites: *Graach* Domprobst, Himmelreich
Hauptstrasse 130, 54470 Graach
Tel: +49 6531 8041
No website

Weingut Selbach-Oster

Although the wine is always excellent and the history dates back more than 350 years, the estate of Johannes Selbach in Zeltingen is less well known in Germany than in the United States or Canada, where Selbach-Oster has been a top German name for many years.

The family estate cultivates 50 acres (20ha) of Riesling in some of the best sites of the Mittelmosel, such as Zeltinger Himmelreich and Schlossberg, Zeltinger and Wehlener Sonnenuhr, Graacher Domprobst and Himmelreich, and Bernkastel Badstube. More than 50 percent of the plantings are old ungrafted vines, yielding small grapes with concentrated fruit flavors.

Selbach aims for a typical modern Mosel style, which reflects the minerality of the rocky Devonian slate soils, as well as the elegance and finesse of the Riesling fruit in clear, crisp, elegant, low-alcohol, yet full-flavored handcrafted wines.

"Our philosophy of winemaking is hands-on in the vineyards and hands-off in the cellar," Selbach says. Grapes are normally handpicked in two or three passes and processed gently. The musts ferment mainly in traditional old oak barrels but also in stainless-steel tanks, although eventually the wines are mostly blends from both.

In 2007, two thrilling new wines saw the light of day. Their underlying idea is quite unusual for German viniculture: the Schmitt and Rotlay plots of Zeltinger Schlossberg and Sonnenuhr respectively, both with old ungrafted vines, are picked like a French grand cru—rather late (mid- or late November) but only once. This means healthy, just-ripe, ripe, overripe, and botrytized grapes, with must weights of 90–120° Oechsle are picked and processed together, to express nothing but the vineyard and vintage. Both wines are rare but well worth seeking out. (I have still to try the third in the series, Anrecht from Zeltinger Himmelreich.) Nor should you miss the elegant and persistent Zeltinger Sonnenuhr Spätlese *trocken*, or the piquant and mouthwatering Zeltinger Sonnenuhr Kabinett (2010★), both of which have a distinctive mineral and spicy character.

FINEST WINES

Zeltinger Schlossberg Schmitt

The Schmitt plot is located in the Zeltingen Schlossberg, which gives more succulent and fruit-intense wines compared with the more spicy and aristocratic wines of the Sonnenuhr. The **2009 Spätlese trocken** was made from the same grapes as the sweet counterpart, but because the barrel fermented completely dry and tasted great as it was, Selbach kept it alone. Ripe yet subtle nose. Rich, succulent, and expressive on the palate; very salty, racy, and lingering. This is a complex wine whose best time is still to come. The other part is called **2009 Riesling Schmitt★** and is dense, sweet, and piquant like an Auslese, with the fruit exploding on the palate, leaving a piquant and racy-mineral taste with a lingering salinity. If you are lucky enough to have some, you should keep it for at least 15–20 years. The **2008 Riesling Schmitt** is very delicate, refined, and transparent and less tropical. Spicy rather than fruity on the nose, it is remarkably subtle and mineral on the tongue, combining fullness with elegance, *Spiel*, and a clear and piquant salty finish.

Zeltinger Sonnenuhr Rotlay

Rotlay is Selbach-Oster's best parcel. The soil is pure and shallow blue slate, so rather dry, giving cool and distinctive wines of great expression. The **2009★** is very elegant and filigreed, sweet, salty, sappy, quite charming but well balanced, and blessed with great potential. The **2008★** shows a cool and slaty-flowery nose, while the palate is racy, succulent, and quite sweet, yet clear, piquant, and well balanced. Very mineral and preordained for great development in bottle.

Weingut Selbach-Oster
Area under vine: 52 acres (21ha)
Annual production: 130,000 bottles
Best sites: *Zeltingen* Sonnenuhr, Schlossberg; *Wehlen* Sonnenuhr; *Graach* Domprobst
Uferallee 23, 54492 Zeltingen
Tel: +49 6532 2081
www.selbach-oster.de

Weingut Vollenweider

I n a way, it's all Egon Müller's fault," explains Swiss Daniel Vollenweider. It was a 1990 Scharzhofberger Auslese that wowed him so much that he felt he had to produce Riesling as well. He left his job as a surveying technician, studied viticulture and winemaking, and finally founded his own estate in Traben-Trabach, with little more than his overwhelming passion. He bought and restored a six-story building and some parcels in the Wolfer Goldgrube, his first vintage being 2000. Initially, he focused on classic *Prädikatsweine* and quickly became successful in export markets, but he remained unknown in Germany for many years. Now he is one of the quiet superstars of the German wine scene and has to allocate his wines.

Vollenweider now cultivates 11 acres (4.5ha) of Riesling vines, mostly ungrafted and very old. The main part (8.5 acres [3.5ha]) is in the Wolfer Goldgrube, a south-/southwest-facing, very steep and labor-intensive site that was never *flurbereinigt.* "Viticulture in very steep sites is an integral part of the cultural heritage of the Mosel Valley," says Daniel, who dedicates himself to the classic Mosel wine style: aromatic, clear, fresh, and lean. Thus, he prefers the traditional single pole to training on wires, because the high-density plantings cause more shadow and slower ripening. Vollenweider also learned that deleafing changes the traditional style too much, giving richer, riper, fruitier wines. He aims for physiologically ripe grapes that are fermented spontaneously in stainless-steel tanks and give brilliant, well-structured, sweet and noble sweet wines, as well as profound dry wines.

Vollenweider had a well-structured range of estate, village, and single-vineyard wines. The quality wines without predicate taste dry, while the whole-cluster Kabinett and Spätlese wines are sweet, clear, elegant, piquant, and botrytis-free. The Auslese (including the amazingly rich and intense gold capsule) is a vineyard selection of botrytized grapes, while the rare BA and TBA are made from carefully cellar-selected single raisins. It is hard to single out only a few wines, and I have to focus on the latest heart-stopping wines here.

FINEST WINES

Wolfer Goldgrube

This is one of the most convincing dry Mosel wines, especially in 2010. I cannot remember a Mosel Riesling that was analytically drier than this, which fermented down to 3g/l RS but lacks nothing, least of all acidity (10g/l). Whereas many producers buffered the high acidity levels with higher residual-sugar levels this vintage, Vollenweider's Riesling was left to nature's will and skill and emerged as an amazingly salty and firmly structured wine of great purity and mineral expression.

The 2010 Beerenauslese ★ is an incredible liquid monument of the highest art of selection. Its brilliance, balance, delicacy, elegance, and finesse are almost Scharzhof-like. I have rarely tasted a BA that was as filigreed and precise as this, which, despite its 300g/l RS seems weightless due to the refined acidity and salty finish.

Schimbock

This wine, sourced from a secluded, terraced, west-facing plot of Traben Würzgarten just a few yards from the Mosel River is a fascinating provocation because there is nothing gentle or Mozart-like here; rather, Lou Reed meets Metallica in Traben-Trabach. To get a traditional Riesling with considerable phenolic rub, which is able to stand up to many kinds of food, the must of the botrytis-free berries is kept on the skins for 24–26 hours before being basket-pressed and fermented in stainless-steel tanks. The 2008 ★ is medium-dry and shows a clear, elegant, ripe fruit with herbal and floral aromas, as well as a characteristic note of hay. On the palate, this expressive and complex wine is succulent, piquant, and elegant, and it is marked on the finish by its lingering salinity.

Weingut Vollenweider
Area under vine: 11 acres (4.5ha)
Annual production: 25,000–30,000 bottles
Best site: *Wolf* Goldgrube
Wolfer Weg 53, 56841 Traben-Trabach
Tel: +49 6541 81 44 33
www.weingut-vollenweider.de

Weingut von Othegraven

Weingut von Othegraven in Kanzem/Saar was founded in 1805 by Maximilian von Othegraven and has been owned by seven successive generations of the same family. Over three decades, Dr. Heidi Kegel restored it to the top flight, and it is now in the hands of her grand-nephew, German TV quiz and chat show host Günther Jauch, and his wife, Thea. Jauch, who lives in Berlin, is not a trained winemaker, and his conversation tends to focus on German politics and economics. Over the years, however, he developed a passion for wine and, in Andreas Barth, he employs the best possible cellar master. Indeed, Barth—who also runs his own small Weingut Lubentiushof in Niederfell in the Lower Mosel, and has been working at von Othegraven since 2004—has been responsible for making this beautiful estate at the bottom of the Altenberg grand cru one of the best in the Saar.

Barth makes a very pure, spicy, somewhat wild style of wine. He ferments (partly in oak, partly in stainless steel) with natural yeasts and gives each wine the time it needs to finish. "The longer the fermentation or the lees contact, the more complex the wine. There is no reason to tear the process apart unless it is not finished," Barth says.

Von Othegraven has 38.5 acres (15.5ha) of vines in the Saar district, including two of the best sites: Kanzem Altenberg and Ockfen Bockstein, both classified Erste Lage (soon Grosse Lage). Nothing but Riesling is cultivated and the wine range is divided into dry wines (vO, Max, Altenberg GG, and Bockstein GG) and classic *Prädikatsweine* (from Kabinett to TBA). Under Jauch, the proportion of dry Rieslings has continued to increase, rising to around 75 percent of production, due to strong demand for this style in Germany. The *trocken* wines are impressive, particularly the crus. "Grosses Gewächs to me means saying goodbye to the variety," says Barth: "A cru is an interpretation of the vineyard rather than of the variety."

All the same, and for many years now, the subtle Kabinett, sensual Spätlese, and focused Auslese from the Altenberg have been among my very favorite German Rieslings.

FINEST WINES

Kanzem Altenberg
This is an exceptional cru of 46.2 acres (18.7ha) on the right bank of the Saar River. It rises north of the village of Kanzem from 476 to 653ft (145m–260m) above sea level, with an inclination of 50–85% and a south/southeasterly exposure. It has greenish and gray slate and also, at the bottom, weathered soil of the Rotliegendes—very stony and poor. The vines have an average age of 60 years, while even the youngest parcel is 25 years old. The wines are true reflections of the Altenberg terroir: very pure, mineral, and salty. They need some years to show their full potential.

2009 GG
Fully ripe and concentrated fruit flavors, paired with a cool mineral soul. Full-bodied, rich, and elegant; creamy due to long lees contact and 40% aging in traditional oak. Mineral and spicy.

2009 Kabinett
Very clear and spicy on the nose. Light and dancing, graceful and seductive. Appetizing salinity, too.

2010 Spätlese Alte Reben★ [V]
Finest fruit and spice flavors, dense and noble. Delicate and piquant, beautifully succulent and precise. Grapefruit flavors and pure slate. Terrific.

2009 Auslese Alte Reben★ [V]
Extremely fine and precise raisin aromas. Refined acidity on the attack; noble fruit, with perfect botrytis; piquant slate flavors, very delicate and elegant; beautifully balanced. Gorgeous.

Weingut von Othegraven
Area under vine: 38.5 acres (15.5ha)
Annual production: 100,000 bottles
Best sites: *Kanzem* Altenberg; *Ockfen* Bockstein
Weinstrasse 1
54441 Kanzem
Tel: +49 6501 150 042
www.von-othegraven.de

Weingut Geheimrat J Wegeler

This family-owned wine estate was originally located in Oestrich in the Rheingau and is well known for the excellent Geheimrat J Riesling, but for more than 100 years it has also cultivated vineyards in the Mosel. When the Deinhard firm, owned at the time by Julius Wegeler, bought 3 acres (1.2ha) of the Bernkasteler Doctor for the then-irrational sum of 100 Gold Marks per square meter in 1900, it made the entire Doctor the most valuable vineyard site in Germany. After this acquisition of one of the most famous vineyard sites in Germany, the estate and the cellar were built in Kues in 1901–02. Today, Wegeler comprises 35 acres (14ha) of vines planted exclusively with Riesling in some of the top sites of the Mosel, such as Bernkasteler Badstube, Graacher Himmelreich, and Wehlener Sonnenuhr. Since most of the wines are served in top German restaurants, more than 60 percent of them are dry. However, the classic *Prädikate* from the Bernkasteler Doctor are unrivaled and, in vintages such as 2010, of world-class quality.

FINEST WINES

Bernkasteler Doctor

The very steep 8-acre (3.26ha) Doctor vineyard, in which Wegeler is the largest shareholder, rises from 410–656ft (125m to 200m) over the roofs of Bernkastel and is the town's proud landmark. Exposed to the south and southwest, with a gradient up to 65%, the weathered Devonian slate soils host ungrafted Riesling vines up to 80 years old and provide some of the finest and most distinctive wines in Germany, especially when sweet or noble sweet. For the past couple of years, Wegeler has been the top producer of Doctor wines. Crafted in stainless steel by Norbert Breit, these are always rich but very elegant and well balanced, and they need one to two decades to develop their great potential. The delicious **2001 Kabinett** has smoky, shaded lemon fruit on the nose. Light yet intense and elegant on the palate, this full and fruity wine is currently between youth and adolescence—a beautiful wine, perhaps the last flowering of a dying myth.

The **2010 Spätlese** ★ is rich, lush, full, sweet, and intense—an erotic, elegant wine, with a fascinating interplay of rich sweetness, racy acidity, and piquant minerality. This is the finest Doctor Spätlese since the incredible 1937 from Dr. Thanisch. The electrifying **2010 Auslese** ★ is very clear, precise, and concentrated on the nose, showing finest raisin and smoky aromas. Dense and bitingly piquant on the palate, where the enormous sweetness and concentration starts to dance with thrilling raciness, precise minerality, and lingering salinity. Highly elegant; great potential. I would (if only I could) store it 50 years. A terrific wine—the finest Auslese I know since the extremely rich, opulent, yet elegant and beautifully balanced **1959** ★ from Thanisch, which is prefect to enjoy now.

The **2010 Beerenauslese** ★ is brilliant and spicy on the nose, with aromas of honey and kumquat. Highly elegant, refined, and filigreed on the palate, despite the enormous concentration and sweetness. Laser-clear raisin flavors and transparent texture; the sweetness is completely absorbed by the racy acidity and lingering minerality. Close to perfection.

The **2010 Trockenbeerenauslese** ★ is perfection itself. Bottled with 22.1g/l TA and 360g/l RS, it is analytically a near relative of the legendary Wwe Dr. Thanisch 1921 TBA, the first TBA in Mosel history. Apricot colored; very viscous. Super-concentrated and intense fruit aromas on the nose (kumquats, oranges); very spicy and still Doctor-like in its cool and aristocratic smokiness. Brilliant and electrifyingly piquant and racy on the palate, this is a highly concentrated, viscous TBA, with a mineral soul and a grippy structure. Too great for many more words. Made for future generations. (Back to the mahogany-colored Thanisch 1921 TBA, which I was lucky enough to taste in September 2010. Very clear in its noble, mature, malty-spicy aromas. Wonderfully elegant and herb-caramelly on the palate; dense, yet almost dry, and still with a firm and persistent mineral structure. Expressive and unforgettable—all the more so since it was the last bottle of the Doctorberg cellar.)

Weingüter Geheimrat J Wegeler
Area under vine: 35 acres (14ha)
Annual production: 110,000 bottles
Best sites: *Bernkastel* Doctor; *Wehlen* Sonnenuhr
Martertal 2
54470 Bernkastel-Kues
Tel: +49 6531 2493
www.wegeler.com

Ahr

The Ahr Valley, named after a tributary of the Rhine, is Germany's fourth-smallest wine region. It is about 30 miles (50km) south of Cologne and 30 miles north of Coblenz, with 1,381 acres (559ha) of vines (*see map, p.141*). Although the valley is more northerly than the Mosel (only Sachsen and Saale-Unstrut are farther north), it is a red-wine region, with some of the most impressive, and expensive, German Pinot Noirs. Besides Assmannshausen Höllenberg in the Rheingau and some parcels in the Mosel, the Ahr is the only wine region in Germany to grow Pinot on slate. It is not clear whether the Romans brought the variety, but its history here stretches back to the late 9th century.

Pinot Noir holds 61.7 percent of the area under vine (850 acres [345ha]) today and has clearly lifted the image of the region over the past 20 years to one of the finest for Pinot Noir outside Burgundy. While until a few decades ago the pale red Ahr wines were called Ahr-Bleichert and were, at best, a local occurrence, their origin is recognized as a red-wine paradise today. In 2008, Meyer-Näkel's 2005 Pfarrwingert Spätburgunder GG won the International Pinot Noir Trophy at the *Decanter World Wine Awards*.

Between Walporzheim in the west and Altenahr in the east, the vines are cultivated on very steep slopes rising from 650 to 975ft (200m–300m) above sea level, exposed south and southwest. Many parts have been terraced for centuries. Since the vines grow in poor, stony soils of weathered slate, graywacke, and volcanic rock, the grapes benefit from the warmth that is stored during the day and radiated during the night. This storage-heater effect is amplified by the dark stone walls, which are up to 10ft (3m) high. In summer, ground temperatures can reach 158°F (70°C), says Gerhard Stodden of Weingut Jean Stodden, and workers have to take a siesta. West from Walporzheim, down to Heppingen, the valley is much wider and less steep. Vineyards are at 325–650ft (100–200m) above sea level, and the slate

soils are covered with loess and loam, giving even fruitier, smoother wines.

The Ahr has an almost Mediterranean climate—even winters are mild. Sunshine hours average almost 1,500 per year, and the average temperature is 49°F (9.5°C). Due to its sheltered location between the Eifel and Ardennes highlands, precipitation is only 24in (615mm) per year, so botrytis is very rare, especially where the soils drain well. This, along with the long vegetative period of 120–130 days, is another reason for the dominant role of red wine, particularly Pinot Noir.

The proportion of red varieties is 85.2 percent today, while the whites occupy 14.8 percent. The latter are dominated by Riesling, with almost 8 percent of the total area, but the wines are of no great importance outside the region itself. Among the reds, the once-popular Blauer Portugieser (94 acres [38ha]), the most important variety after Pinot Noir, will soon be displaced by Frühburgunder (Pinot Madeleine, 91 acres [37ha]), an early-ripening mutation of Pinot Noir that gives dark and intensely fruity wines. The indigenous grape has been cultivated with growing enthusiasm recently, though it is even more fickle than Pinot Noir. Frühburgunder has already qualified for Grosses Gewächs production for several years.

Although the grapes ripen two or three weeks earlier now than 30 years ago, and must weights in the best parcels reach 105° Oechsle, Werner Näkel has no anxieties about climate change or the future of Ahr Pinot Noir: "Our colleagues in Burgundy already pick their first Pinots at the end of August in some years. As long as they do not think of other grape varieties, I don't either."

From the 1950s until the mid-1970s, Ahr producers tended to cultivate almost as many acres with white varieties as with red. Only in the later 1970s did red wines—which used to be not only pale, since maceration was minimal, but also off-dry or sweet—come back into vogue, though

Above: The dauntingly steep and terraced Ahr vineyards help explain the price, as well as the quality, of the region's top wines

not always with the best clones. Mariafelder and Ritter clones were dominant, but the latter in particular can give good results today because the vines are 40 years old now. Werner Näkel, who was probably the most innovative, successful, and influential producer, started to plant Pinot clones from Burgundy in the mid-1990s and was the first to use barriques in the mid-1980s, resulting in a more international style of Pinot Noir.

Today, there is at least a sextet of top producers, all of whom could have made it into this book had space permitted: Nelles in Heimersheim, JJ Adeneuer in Ahrweiler (whose Walporzheimer Gärkammer Spätburgunder GG can be world-class), Kreuzberg and Meyer-Näkel in Dernau, Jean Stodden in Rech, and Deutzerhof in Mayschoss.

But I have decided to profile the pioneering Meyer-Näkel and its antipode, Jean Stodden. Gerhard and Alexander Stodden produce less charming but equally thrilling and ageworthy Pinot Noirs and Pinot Madelaines.

Ahr Pinots are generally quite expensive, for three main reasons: small production (the region cannot be extended); high demand (especially in the well-heeled region of Cologne/Bonn); and the extremely labor-intensive cultivation on the steep slopes, where everything has to be done by hand. "If you don't get a high price for your wine, you have to give up, because otherwise you're the one who pays," say Werner Näkel. Even wines from co-ops are expensive. But when you taste those from the Mayschoss co-op, you realize that they are worth it.

Weingut Meyer-Näkel

It was his biggest advantage, says Werner Näkel—who became one of Germany's most important Pinot Noir producers in the 1990s—that he had no formal education in viticulture or winemaking. He studied sports, mathematics, and information technology in Bonn, to become a teacher, and drank dry Rieslings from Alsace instead of sweet Pinot Noirs from the Ahr. But in 1980, he changed tack. Although his father was already bottling dry red wines, Werner was more inspired by Burgundy. Among many other producers there, he met Henri Jayer, whose personality and wines gave him a kiss as transforming as that bestowed on the Frog Prince. A decade on, Werner Näkel had become the Ahr Jayer. His Spätburgunder grands crus were among the best and most expensive German red wines.

By the 1990s, Werner Näkel had become the Ahr Jayer. His Spätburgunder grands crus were among the best and most expensive German red wines

Since 2005, his daughters Meike and Dörte, who both studied viticulture and enology at Geisenheim, have increasingly taken responsibility for wine production, while Werner cares for the vines or his other projects: Quinta da Carvalhosa in the Douro (Portugal) and his joint venture with Neil Ellis in Stellenbosch (South Africa). Since then, the wines have become even fresher, finer, and purer, and an even greater pleasure to drink, even young. The first vintage of the new, less opulent and oaky style was 2006. When I tasted the three crus five years later, they were still vibrant and evolving.

The estate cultivates 42 acres (17ha) of vines today, of which 80 percent are Pinot Noir and 10 percent Frühburgunder. "Riesling, Pinot Blanc, and Dornfelder are used for wines that have a market within a radius of 30km [18 miles]," Werner explains.

The Pinots are planted in top sites, of which three are classified as Grosses Gewächs. All the wines are cold-macerated and fermented for three weeks in 3,500-liter wooden vats, then aged in medium-toast barriques from Taransaud and François Frères. The proportion of new barriques ranges from 50 to 100 percent for the crus, but none is used for the basic wines. Of these, the Blauschiefer is a typical Ahr Spätburgunder: very fresh, cherry-fruity, and delicate, with a perfume of blue slate. It is great fun to drink young, though an excellent vintage such as 2009 can age for ten years. The Spätburgunder S is a B selection of the grands crus (mostly Sonnenberg), though it is a very delicate and filigreed Pinot of great finesse. The three powerful Spätburgunder GGs are exceptional, but even they are topped by the SR, a very rare and expensive special selection from seedless Pinot grapes, sold at the annual auction in Bad Kreuznach. In Pfarrwingert, Frühburgunder is also cultivated and marketed as Grosses Gewächs.

FINEST WINES

2009 Spätburgunder S
This excellent "premier cru" is a blend of the B parcels of all the three grands crus (mostly Sonnenberg) and is just beautiful. Very refined, floral, and slightly smoky, this is a Pinot of perfect fruit ripeness and an alluring intensity. Round, velvety, and elegant on the palate, this is a mouthful of wine with violet and slate aromas, cherries, hints of licorice, and a nice salinity on the finish. Quite long. A gentle, alluring, and seductive wine that you probably won't want to miss after your first meeting.

2009 Pfarrwingert GG
Näkel holds six parcels in this grand cru, adding up to 3.7 acres (1.5ha). The south-facing slope is 60 percent steep, and the 40-year-old vines (no French clones) grow in slate and graywacke soils with a little bit of loess and loam. Very delicate and floral on the slaty nose, with perfect fruit ripeness of red cherries and sloes and a hint of cassis; fresh and noble. Dense, fresh, and juicy on the palate, beautifully pure, filigreed, and silky, the slate coming through perfectly and lending finesse, transparency, and vitality.

Above: Ahr pioneer Werner Näkel, who, along with daughters Meike (*left*) and Dörte (*right*), continues to produce superb wines

2009 Kräuterberg GG★

This is from very old slate terraces, slate soils, and often no more than 25 vines per terrace. The walls are up to 10ft (3m) high and, in combination with the slaty soil, create a very warm microclimate. Näkel owns 1.7 acres (0.7ha) here, of which 50 percent are French clones from the mid-1990s, and the rest 40-year-old Ritter clones. Deep and intense on the nose, yet well balanced and distinctive. Ripe dark fruit, herbal, oriental spice, and smoke aromas. Refined and silky on the palate, with red cherries. The acidity is vigorous, and due to the firm tannins, the wine is slightly more astringent and wild than the Pfarrwingert, but with great aging potential. The 1997, 1999, and 2006 all taste great today.

2009 Sonnenberg GG

The warmest site, with a lot of loess covering the slate. Näkel holds 3 acres (1.2ha) on this 30 percent slope. Deep, complex, meaty, and smoky on the nose, quite discreet by comparison with the other crus. Cassis and floral aromas, as well as the smell of pure slate. On the palate, rich, round, concentrated, and of great substance. Pure fruit flavors, mellow, silky, and persistent, with a luxurious sweetness, though the wine loses none of its elegance or finesse.

Weingut Meyer-Näkel

Area under vine: 42 acres (17ha)
Average production: 100,000–120,000 bottles
Best vineyards: *Dernau* Pfarrwingert; *Walporzheim* Kräuterberg; *Bad Neuenahr* Sonnenberg
Freidensstrasse 15, 53507 Dernau
Tel: +49 2643 1628
www.meyer-naekel.de

Weingut Jean Stodden

When Gerhard Stodden started to produce wine in 1973, he was still a student of economics and did not know much about wine. But he questioned almost everything to do with viticulture and winemaking. His family has grown vines since 1578, and it was Gerhard's grandfather, Alois Stodden, who began to handcraft and bottle Spätburgunder for himself in 1900. Gerhard was one of the first Ahr producers to ferment Spätburgunder until it was completely dry. He also introduced malolactic fermentation and green harvest, which was condemned as a "sin" by his mother at the time. His red wines were quite austere, though: resolute and marked by their power and firm tannic structure.

Alexander Stodden prefers not to produce wines of easy charm and superficial suavity. Instead, he goes for persistence and longevity, producing some of the region's finest wines

Since 2001, Gerhard's son Alexander has played an active part in the business, and the first vintage in which both Stoddens combined forces has resulted in some of the finest wines I have tasted from this tiny region: their 2001 Spätburgunder and Frühburgunder, from Herrenberg, a VDP Grosse Lage. Both wines have developed beautifully over the decade and are still very elegant and youthful, if also perfect to drink now.

Rotweingut Stodden is in Rech and has 16 acres (6.5ha) of vines in the villages of Rech, Dernau, and Mayschoss, as well as in Ahrweiler and Bad Neuenahr. Some 90 percent of the vines are in Steillagen, mostly Pinot Noir (88 percent) and Frühburgunder (7 percent), plus a little Riesling (5 percent) for Sekt.

Alexander's goal is to produce rich and concentrated wines of great freshness and finesse.

Thus, he prefers old vines; the oldest at Stodden are about 80 years old and ungrafted, while the average age is 35 years. New plantings are at 7,000 vines/ha to force the roots deep into the soil. Yields are kept low: at 50hl/ha even for the entry-level wines and only 30–35hl/ha for the Grosse Gewächse. The crop is reduced by winter pruning, then by thinning in early summer and, if necessary, by green harvesting.

Handpicking is late but on the basis of taste rather than sugar level. "Pinot is like bananas," Alexander explains. "The green ones do not taste of anything. The brown, overripe ones are too sweet and sticky. Only yellow bananas taste ripe and fruity." The problem with Pinot grapes, though, is that color is not much of a guide. "That's why we taste them. When they are ripe but still have good acidity, we pick." For the drinkability and longevity of the wine, it's better to harvest grapes with 92–97° Oechsle rather than with 100°, Alexander believes. If necessary, he chaptalizes, but finds 14% ABV too high for Pinot Noir, even if it cannot be avoided in certain years. Asked whether he fears climate change, Alexander replied, "If the climate is warming, we rather profit from that. All we need to do is adapt our schedules. So today, we do not leaf-pluck in August but during flowering instead, to bring on *coulure*."

Since Alexander has been making the wines (including cold maceration and a more oxidative vinification), they have become less astringent, though he still prefers not to produce wines of easy charm and superficial suavity. Instead, he goes for persistence and longevity. "I am not a winemaker who polishes the wines for earlier drinkability," he readily admits. "I am, rather, a wine watcher. After fermentation and once the wine is in barrel, I do nothing but taste from time to time."

Before he does nothing, he bleeds off up to 20 percent of the must (*saignée*), to give the final wine more color and structure. All the red wines are aged in wood, the basic wines in 1,000-liter barrels, the better wines in French barriques, all new for the grands crus, which age for up to 18 months and are bottled unfined and unfiltered.

The family holds parcels in three Grosse Lagen. Herrenberg in Rech is a steep, partly terraced south-facing site with a gradient of 60 percent. It is predominantly planted with Pinot Noir, which grows in weathered slate. The oldest vines were planted in the first third of the past century and are ungrafted. They yield no more than 25hl/ha, and in top vintages their grapes are selected for the Alte Reben Spätburgunder, a very rich, weighty, concentrated but also subtle, elegant, and expensive wine. The Grosses Gewächs is from 20- to 50-year-old vines and is pure, powerful, dense, and mineral.

Ahrweiler Rosenthal has deeper, less stony, yet multifaceted soils, with graywacke, loam, loess, and slate. The vines were mass-selected from the oldest Herrenberg vines and planted in 1993. The Grosses Gewächs is very pure, refined, fresh, and firm.

Neuenahr Sonnenberg is on the lower part of the river, where the valley is wider and the slopes less steep. There is almost no slate here but a lot of sandy loess and loam. Selected from 30-year-old vines, this is Stodden's most charming wine. It is full-bodied, rich, juicy, fruity, elegant, and fresh.

The Mayschosser Mönchberg, from a steep, terraced, almost-Mediterranean site, is a powerful wine sold at the annual auction in Bad Kreuznach.

FINEST WINES

Recher Herrenberg Frühburgunder
Frühburgunder ripens two or three weeks earlier than Pinot Noir, and the challenge is to keep the freshness while getting intense fruit flavors. Stodden prefers to pick this variety with 90–92° Oechsle and to chaptalize up to 13.2% ABV.

2009★ Pure and direct on the nose, with cherry, slate, and lime aromas. Pure, fresh, and vibrant, but also elegant and refined. Piquant finish. Great wine.
2007 Brilliant and fresh on the nose; very fine Pinot aromas, with floral and slate scents. Full, silky, and very elegant on the palate; vibrant and with a delicate touch of sweetness. Harmonious finish.

2001★ Brilliant on the nose: a very clear, dense, and fresh bouquet, with precise aromas of ripe wild cherries, as well as peas. Very pure and vital, still youthful, silky, and elegant. Cherry aromas again, and the acidity is as fresh as in 2009. Fascinating.

Herrenberg Spätburgunder GG
2009★ Very distinctive, pure, and elegant on the nose, showing delicate herbal and slate aromas, as well as beautiful fruit ripeness. Intense and concentrated on the palate, but not too upfront. Silky, but structured by firm and still slightly floury tannins and a refined acidity. Still youthful but very promising.
2008 Aromas of balsam, graphite, and slate, alongside fresh red- and just-ripe blackberries. Silky and fresh, with a fascinating refined acidity structuring the intense fruit flavors. The tannins are smooth and completely integrated. Delicate and alluring wine.
2001★ Still labeled "Auslese trocken ***," this was the forerunner of the Grosses Gewächs. Very noble on the nose, intense and sweet but refined, displaying complex aromas of flesh, slate, graphite, limes, lemon grass, and balsam. On the palate, this is a perfect marriage of slate and Pinot: silky and intense, powerful and persistent, with a delicate sweetness and appetizing astringency. At ten years old, it is only now entering its drinking window.

Weingut Jean Stodden
Area under vine: 16 acres (6.5ha)
Average production: 45,000 bottles
Best vineyards: *Rech* Herrenberg; *Ahrweiler* Rosenthal; *Mayschoss* Mönchberg
Rotweinstrasse 7–9, 53506 Rech
Tel: +49 2643 3001
www.stodden.de

Glossary

Abfüllung bottling

Alleinbesitz monopole; a vineyard owned by a single producer

Alte Reben old vines

Amtliche Prüfungsnummer or **AP-Nummer** This is a 10–12-digit number indicating that the wine has passed Germany's official test for faults and typicity. Wines are often referred to by the penultimate group of digits in the string—for example, "AP #12"—since that is the number under which the grower has chosen to submit his or her wine for approval. The final pair of digits shows the year in which approval was requested and granted.

Anbaugebiet defined production area or region; in Germany, there are currently 13 quality wine regions and 26 *Landwein* areas

Anreicherung chaptalization; the addition of sugar or grape concentrate to the must to raise alcohol levels. Forbidden for *Prädikatsweine*

Auslese literally "picked out"; legally, the predicate above Kabinett and Spätlese. Auslese (which can be dry or sweet) is made from fully ripe bunches from which unripe or bad grapes have been removed (see p.23).

BA informal abbreviation for Beerenauslese

Beerenauslese Literally "picking-out of berries"; legally, the predicate above Auslese. Made from overripe or botrytized grapes

Bereich district; an aggregation of sites in numerous neighboring villages within a wine region. In theory, wines of a single *Bereich* should share a taste profile. Forty-one *Bereiche* are legally defined.

Bocksbeutel literally "goat's scrotum" or "bookbag"; the wine bottle traditionally used for wines from Franken and parts of Baden

Botrytis cinerea noble rot

Doppelstück 2,400-liter cask

edelsüss nobly sweet

Einzellage(n) legally registered "single-vineyard" site(s)

Eiswein icewine; made from grapes of minimum BA must weight, frozen on the vine and pressed frozen (see p.24)

Erben heirs

Erste Lage(n) first-class site(s); a vineyard classification used by members of the VDP. Up to and including the 2011 vintage, all Grosses Gewächs wines, as well as the off-dry Erste Lage wines with or without predicate from the Mosel, came from Erste Lage sites. In 2012, the VDP renamed the best vineyards Grosse Lage (not to be confused with *Grosslage*), and Erste Lage now refers to sites classified one level below (see p.25).

Erstes Gewächs (Erste Gewächse) first growth(s); a quality designation used solely in the Rheingau since 1999 for wines meeting the following criteria: they must be made from Riesling or Pinot Noir grown in classified sites; maximum yields of 50hl/ha; hand-picking; at least 12% ABV for Riesling or 13% ABV for Pinot Noir; must taste dry, with a maximum of 6g/l RS (Pinot Noir) or 13g/l RS (Riesling) respectively

Erzeugerabfüllung estate bottling; a designation for *Qualitätswein* or *Landwein* made entirely from grapes grown, processed, and bottled by the producer (*Erzeuger*) or a grower cooperative. Any *Süssreserve* must also have been produced from the grower's own grapes.

Feinherb Literally "fine" or "subtle" and "dry"; a legally permitted but undefined (and untranslatable) term for wines ranging from virtually dry (but not legally *trocken*) to slightly sweet. Many growers employ *feinherb* as an alternative to the legally defined but intuitively vague (and among consumers unpopular) *halbtrocken*.

Flurbereinigung vineyard reorganization to improve access and consolidate different holdings within a site, typically involving heavy earth-moving equipment (see p.32)

Fuder an approximately 1,000-liter cask mainly used in the Mosel

GG initials referring (inter alia on labels) to Grosses Gewächs

Goldkapsel gold capsule or foil on the bottle, denoting a wine considered better or finer by the producer; usually a *Prädikatswein* and very often an auction wine made in a very small lot. The very finest wines are often bottled (and auctioned) as *lange Goldkapsel* (long gold capsule). The initials "GK" are often used in this respect—for example, "GK Auslese."

Grosse Lage(n) new VDP designation for classified vineyard(s) of top quality (formerly called Erste Lage)

Grosser Ring growers' association in the Mosel (identical to the Mosel VDP)

Grosses Gewächs (Grosse Gewächse) great growth(s), abbreviated on the wine label as GG; not an official designation but used by most VDP members since 2001 for their top dry wines from top single-vineyard sites classified as Erste Lage (or, since 2012, Grosse Lage). Certain further standards are applied—for example, the wines have to be made exclusively from Riesling, Silvaner (only in Franken), Pinot Gris, Chardonnay, Pinot Noir, Frühburgunder (only in the Ahr), or Lemberger (only in Württemberg); the grapes have to be hand-picked; and yields may not exceed 50hl/ha. The designation Grosses Gewächs will probably replace that of Erstes Gewächs in the Rheingau, at least among Rheingau VDP members.

Grosslage a collective vineyard designation, embracing a number of single-vineyard sites. A *Grosslage* (such as Piesporter Michelsberg) can easily be mistaken for a superior single-vineyard site by consumers but is rarely used today, even though some *Grosslage* wines can be pretty good—Randersackerer Ewig Leben, for example.

Gutsabfüllung designation for wines from producers who have grown and processed the grapes. Besides the qualification needed for *Erzeugerabfüllung*, a *Gutsabfüllung* can only be bottled by an operation (1) with fiscal accounting, (2) whose winemaker has successfully passed an examination in enology, and (3) that has cultivated the vines whose grapes are processed for the *Gutsabfüllung* since at least January 1 of the vintage year.

Gutswein(e) estate wine(s); wine made from grapes that were processed on the estate where the final wine was also bottled. Often the entry-level wine of an estate—for example, Gutsriesling. See also *Weingut*

Halbstück oval 600-liter cask

halbtrocken designation for a wine whose residual sugar content is higher than is allowed for legally *trocken* wines but not higher than 18g/l (see p.20)

Handlese manual harvest. Occasionally, the terms *handgelesen* or *handverlesen*— "hand-harvested" or "hand-sorted"—will even find their way on to labels, albeit without official authorization.

Kabinett The lowest must-weight predicate of German wine law. Although one may expect a wine with lower alcohol content, no upper limit to finished alcohol is stipulated but rather only—as with all German *Prädikate*—a minimum must weight. Created as a category by the 1971 wine law, its name alludes to (and was intended to trade on the luster of) "Cabinet", a term borrowed from the English and used for two centuries (including on labels) to refer to wines an estate owner deemed to be of especially high quality. With the coining of "Kabinett", it became illegal to label a wine as "Cabinet."

Landwein wine with a protected geographical designation. The classificatory rung of German wine law between *Deutscher Wein* (the lowest) and *Qualitätswein bA* or *Prädikatswein*. Currently, 26 German *Landwein* areas are defined.

Lese harvest

mineral, minerality (*mineralisch, Mineralität*) Although there is no commonly agreed definition of these widely used terms, in this book they refer to an appetizing salty or stony taste that invites another sip.

Monopollage a monopole or single vineyard owned by a single producer

Mostgewicht must weight; sugar content of grapes at harvest

naturrein, Naturwein until 1971, a designation for wines that had not been chaptalized

Oechsle scale for measuring grape sugars based on the density of grape juice

Ortswein(e) village wine(s); a designation often used by VDP members who have classified their origin in a four-tier model: *Gutswein*, *Ortswein*, Erste Lage,

Grosse Lage. *Ortsweine* are made from grapes grown in a single village. Unlike Burgundy, no village sites are defined in Germany, so *Ortsweine* are sourced from one or several *Einzellagen* of a village.

Prädikat predicate; used to classify the higher type of *Qualitätswein*, which is a *Prädikatswein* (formerly *Qualitätswein mit Prädikat*, QmP). There are six predicates in German wine law, based on minimum must weights: Kabinett, Spätlese, Auslese, Beerenauslese, Eiswein, Trockenbeerenauslese.

QbA abbreviation universally used to refer to a *Qualitätswein* that is not entitled to a *Prädikat*

QmP abbreviation sometimes used for *Qualitätswein mit Prädikat*

Qualitätswein, Qualitätswein bestimmer Anbaugebiete (QbA) wine from a defined region, indicated on the label, officially certified as meeting minimum requirements in terms of quality

R informal but frequently used abbreviation for "reserve," a term that cannot legally be used for German wines

Restsüsse or *Restzucker* residual sugar (RS)

Rotling a wine of pale to bright red color that is produced from a blend of white and red grape varieties or musts

Schiefer slate

Schloss castle or château

Selektive Lese selective harvest/picking

Spätlese Literally "late harvest"; legally, the second predicate after Kabinett. Made from fully ripe grapes that were usually picked late (see p.23)

Spiel literally "play"; often used to describe the delicate interplay of acidity and sweetness, but also minerality and/or alcohol

Steillage or **Steillagenwein** valid designation for a wine that is produced exclusively from grapes grown in a vineyard with an inclination of at least 30%

Stück or **Stückfass** oval 1,200-liter cask

Süssreserve unfermented or part-fermented grape must

TBA informal abbreviation for Trockenbeerenauslese

trocken indication for dry wine; a wine with a maximum of 9g of residual sugar per liter (see p.20)

Trockenbeerenauslese or **TBA** Literally "picking-out of dried berries"; the most noble predicate wine, made from botrytized or overripe, shriveled grapes that look like raisins (see p.24)

VDP Verband Deutscher Prädikatsweingüter or Association of Prädikatswein Producers. Established in 1910 as Verband der Naturweinversteigerer but renamed VDP in 1972, it presently incorporates nearly 200 estates, most of them among the finest wine producers in Germany.

Versteigerung auction

Vorlese a harvest in advance of the main harvest, mostly for lower quality levels or to eliminate rotten or defective bunches (in which case, also referred to as a case of "negative Auslese")

but sometimes also for higher-*Prädikat* wines

Weingut literally "wine estate." The indication may be used only for an estate producing *Qualitätswein* or *Landwein*.

Weissherbst pale pink *Qualitätswein* or *Prädikatswein* made from the immediate pressing of a single red grape variety; for a better color, the addition of a small portion of red wine is allowed. In contrast to rosé wine, no color is prescribed, so a *Weissherbst* can also be white.

Winzer vintner, wine grower

wurzelecht ungrafted (vines)

Bibliography

Hans Peter Alhaus, *Kleines Wörterbuch der Weinsprache* (Munich; 2006)

Stefan Andres, *Die Grossen Weine Deutschlands* (Frankfurt, Berlin, Vienna; 1972)

Friedrich von Bassermann-Jordan, *Geschichte des Weinbaus*, 2 vols; reprint of the 2nd edition, 1921–22 (Landau; 1991)

Wolfgang Behringer, *Kulturgeschichte des Klimas: Von der Eiszeit bis zur Globalen Erwärmung* (Munich; 2007)

David Bird, *Understanding Wine Technology: The Science of Wine Explained* (New Edition, San Francisco; 2005)

Owen Bird, *Rheingold: The German Wine Renaissance* (Bury St Edmunds; 2005)

Dieter Braatz, Ulrich Sautter, Ingo Swoboda, *Weinatlas Deutschland* (Munich; 2007)

Michael Broadbent, *Grosse Weine* (Munich; 2004) (English title: *Vintage Wine*)

Stephen Brook, *The Wines of Germany* (London; 2003)

Daniel Deckers (editor), *Zur Lage des Deutschen Weins: Spitzenlagen und Spitzenweine* (Stuttgart; 2003)

Daniel Deckers, "Zurück in die Zukunft: Eine Kurze Geschichte des Trierer Vereins von Weingutsbesitzern der Mosel, Saar und Ruwer," in *1908–2008: 100 Jahre Grosser Ring Mosel-Saar-Ruwer*, edited by VDP Die Prädikatsweingüter Grosser Ring Moser-Saar-Ruwer (Trier; undated)

Daniel Deckers, *Im Zeichen des Traubenadlers: Eine Geschichte des deutschen Weins* (Mainz; 2010)

Daniel Deckers, "Von Hoher Hulturhistorischer Bedeutung: Die Älteste Weinlagen-Klassifizierung der Welt im Rheingau Entdeckt," in *Fine – das Weinmagazin* 12 (2011), pp.46–48

Deutscher Wein, Statistik 2011/2012 (Deutsches Weininstitut, Mainz; 2011)

Deutscher Weinatlas: Anbaugebiete, Bereiche, Lagen, Rebsorten, Qualitäten, (Deutsches Weininstitut, Mainz; 1993, 1997, 1999)

Horst Dippel, "Hundert Jahre Deutsches Weinrecht: Zur Geschichte eines Sonderwegs," in *Zeitschrift für Neuere Rechtsgeschichte* (1998)

Christina Fischer & Ingo Swoboda, *Riesling: Die Ganze Vielfalt der Edelsten Rebe der Welt*, (München; 2007)

Ulrich Fischer, "Making Sense of Riesling and Terroir," in *Tong* 9 (2011), pp.29–36

Rüdiger Glaser, *Klimageschichte Mitteleuropas: 1000 Jahre Wetter, Klima, Katastrophen* (Darmstadt; 2001)

Fritz Goldschmidt, *Deutschlands Weinbauorte und Weinbergslagen* (Mainz; 1910)

Jamie Goode & Sam Harrop, *Authentic Wine: Toward Natural and Sustainable Winemaking* (Berkeley, Los Angeles, London; 2011)

Gute Gründe für Rheinhessenwein: Steine. Böden. Terroir, edited by Rheinhessenwein eV and Landesamt für Geologie und Bergbau Rheinland-Pfalz (Alzey-Mainz; undated)

Thom Held, *Berührt vom Ort die Welt Erobern* (Zurich; 2006)

Reinhard Heymannn-Löwenstein, *Terroir: Weinkultur und Weingenuss in einer Globalen Welt* (Stuttgart; 2007)

Ronald S Jackson, *Wine Science: Principles and Applications* (3rd edition, Burlington, London, San Diego; 2008)

Hugh Johnson, *Der Grosse Johnson: Die Enzyklopädie der Weine, Weinbaugebiete und Weinerzeuger der Welt* (5th edition, Munich; 2004) (*Hugh Johnson's Wine Companion*, 5th edition; 2003)

Hugh Johnson, *Weingeschichte: Von Dionysos bis Rothschild*, (Munich; 2005) (*The Story of Wine*, "new illustrated edition"; 2004)

Hugh Johnson & Stuart Pigott, *Atlas der Deutschen Weine: Lagen, Produzenten, Weinstrassen* (Bern, Stuttgart; 1987)

Hugh Johnson & Jancis Robinson, *Der Weinatlas* (6th edition, Munich; 2007) (*The World Atlas of Wine*, 6th edition; 2007)

Klaus Peter Keller, "My Love for Dry Riesling," in *Tong* 9 (2011), pp.42–44

Reinhard Löwenstein, "Von Öchsle zum Terroir," in *Frankfurter Allgemeine Zeitung*, October 7, 2003

Caro Maurer, "Erste Lage in Germany: A Classification in Course of Development," unpublished dissertation, Institute of Masters of Wine (London; 2011)

Hermann Mengler et al, *Das Buch vom Jungen Alten Silvaner* (Würzburg; 2009)

Frank Patalong, "Klimawandel Lässt Deutsche Weinberge Erröten," in Spiegel Online; 2011

Stuart Pigott, *Die Grossen Deutschen Riesling Weine* (2nd edition, Düsseldorf, Vienna, New York, Moscow; 1995)

Stuart Pigott, "Deutschland und Österreich," in *1900–2000: Das Jahrhundert des Weines, Die Weine des Jahrhunderts*, edited by Stephen Brook (Bern; 2000), pp.128–137 (*A Century of Wine*)

Stuart Pigott, *Die Grossen Weissweine Deutschlands* (Munich, Bern; 2001)

Stuart Pigott, *Weinwunder Deutschland* (Wiesbaden, 2010)

Stuart Pigott (editor), Ursula Heinzelmann, Chandra Kurt, Manfred Lüer & Stephan Reinhardt, *Wein Spricht Deutsch: Weine, Winzer, Weinlandschaften* (Frankfurt; 2007)

Helmut Prössler, *Bernkasteler Doctor: Der "Kurfürstliche" Weinberg* (Koblenz; 1990)

Alexia Putze, *Die Weinklassifikation des Verbandes Deutscher Prädikats- und Qualitätsweingüter eV (VDP) – Pro & Contra*, Diplomarbeit Fachhochschule Wiesbaden Standort Geisenheim, Fachbereich Weinbau und Oenologie, Studiengang Weinbau (Geisenheim; 2010)

Josef H Reichholf, *Eine Kurze Naturgeschichte des Letzten Jahrtausends* (5th edition, Frankfurt; 2007)

Stephan Reinhardt, "Generation Riesling: Der Riesling Wird Modern," in *Welt am Sonntag*, August 8, 2004

Stephan Reinhardt, "King Riesling's Queen: Silvaner," in *The World of Fine Wine* 19 (2008), pp.172–75

Jancis Robinson, *Oxford Companion to Wine*, 3rd edition, www.jancisrobinson.com

David Schildknecht, "Riesling's Global Triumph: A Phyrrhic Victory?" lecture at the International Riesling Symposium, Schloss Reinhartshausen (Rheingau), November 11–12, 2010

David Schildknecht, "VDP, GG, EL, etc" in *The World of Fine Wine* 31 (2011), pp.34–35 and pp.204–9

Hans Reiner Schulz, "The Future of German Riesling", in *Tong* 9 (2011), pp.37–40

Stephen Skelton, *Viticulture: An Introduction to Commerical Grape Growing for Wine Production* (London; 2009)

Manfred Stock, "Warum Bleibt es beim Wein so Schön? Klimawandel und Wein", in *Der Verschwundene Hering und das Geheimnis des Regenmachens: Umweltforschung in der Leibniz-Gemeinschaft*, edited by Wissenschafts-gemeinschaft Gottfried Wilhelm Leibniz, Bonn, 2003, pp.37–39

Manfred Stock et al, "Weinbau und Klima: Eine Beziehung Wechselseitiger Variabilität," in *Terra Nostra* (Berlin; 2003), pp.422–26

Manfred Stock et al, *Perspektiven der Klimaänderung bis 2050 für den Weinbau in Deutschland (Klima 2050)*, Potsdam Institute for Climate Impact Research (PIK-Report 106/2007)

Terra Palatina: Von den Grund-Lagen des Pfälzer Weins, edited by Detlev Janik/Pfalzwein eV (Annweiler; undated)

Terroir an Mosel, Saar und Ruwer: Klima, Winzer, Boden, edited by Mosel-Saar-Ruwer Wein eV et al (Trier; 2006)

Terroir in Baden: Wurzel Badischer Weinvielfalt, edited by Badischer Wein GmbH (Karlsruhe; undated)

Terry Theise, *Reading Between the Wines* (Berkeley, Los Angeles, London; 2010)

Gerhard Troost, *Die Technologie des Weines* (2nd edition, Stuttgart; 1955)

Hanno & Dorothee Zilliken, "The Magic of Sweetness," in *Tong* 9 (2011), pp.17–21

Zur Lage der Region, Beiträge zur Lagenklassifikation in Deutschland Mittelhaardt/Pfalz, edited by Beate M Hoffmann, Gisela Wintering (Grünstadt; 1998)

Index

Author's Acknowledgments

It was a positive shock when, one day in late December 2010, my phone rang and I learned that I had been chosen to write the book on Germany in the Finest Wines series, which had started so successfully two years earlier. This has been a great honor, and I want to thank everybody in the Finest Wines team, starting with publisher Sara Morley, who would still be a brilliant manager if she gave me half her organizational talent. A very special thanks, though, goes to the editors, Neil Beckett and David Williams, and the subeditor, David Tombesi-Walton: there could have been no better editorial team. Neil, my nocturnal correspondent, is also a great motivator, psychologist, and hot-toddy expert.

Another expert is Jon Wyand, the much-awarded photographer. I was not allowed to see his photographs until I had almost completed the book: I suspect that Jon and Neil were afraid that I might rather discuss the photographs than finish the text. So, the only thing I knew was Jon's reputation and talent and what the producers featured in the book told me about him. They said he was the least complicated photographer they had ever met. He rarely needed more than one hour at each estate—exactly the opposite of what Côte d'Or producers told Bill Nanson after Jon had been to shoot for *The Finest Wines of Burgundy*! In any event, the German producers became fans of Jon, and a few days before Christmas (when my book should have been finished but wasn't), I discovered one of the reasons why. Jon had sent each producer his selection of portraits as a Christmas present. These were the most fascinating pictures I had ever seen of any of them. Jon really captured the essence of the individuals and saw into their souls. Insights that often took me several years to acquire, Jon seized in less than an hour. I had never seen German wine producers looking more relaxed or more themselves in front of a camera. I have no idea how Jon did it, but it must have been a combination of experience, expertise, and genius. As a result of his efforts, I was inspired to finish the book in a good mood (not that easy in the long and dark northern German winters, which have thrown me badly from my bicycle twice). Seeing the final result, I am proud to have worked with you, Jon: thank you.

On Jon's behalf, I want to thank Stefanie Kress from the VDP, who graciously organized all his appointments, even though several producers presented in this book are not VDP members.

I also have to thank David Schildknecht for his meticulous and extremely helpful comments on this book. David is a walking library, but he is also full of passion regarding the wines of Germany. Moreover, he is indebted to nothing but his own clear, independent, and occasionally unpopular thoughts, which can provide invaluable alternative perspectives.

Sadly, I could profile here only 70 of the many excellent German wine producers, so I apologize to all those I would have loved to include but for whom I couldn't find space.

Finally, I want to say sorry to my two little boys—Ben, 8, and Mats, 3—who missed their dad for a period of nine months. Although I was with them at the breakfast table whenever possible, I was so completely absorbed by my thoughts and deadlines that I often finished breakfast in ten minutes flat and parted by saying, "See you tomorrow, guys…" You will both be much older when you read these lines, and the book will surely be out of print. But you should know that it is dedicated to you little lion and whale conservationists.

And, of course, to you, Kirsten.

Eltville, Rheingau, March 29, 2012